OECD/G20 Base Erosion and Profit Shifting Project

Neutralising the Effects of Hybrid Mismatch Arrangements, Action 2 - 2015 Final Report

OECD

BETTER POLICIES FOR BETTER LIVES

Please cite this publication as:
OECD (2015), *Neutralising the Effects of Hybrid Mismatch Arrangements, Action 2 - 2015 Final Report*, OECD/G20 Base Erosion and Profit Shifting Project, OECD Publishing, Paris.
http://dx.doi.org/10.1787/9789264241138-en

ISBN 978-92-64-24108-4 (print)
ISBN 978-92-64-24113-8 (PDF)

Series: OECD/G20 Base Erosion and Profit Shifting Project
ISSN 2313-2604 (print)
ISSN 2313-2612 (online)

Photo credits: Cover © ninog – Fotolia.com

Corrigenda to OECD publications may be found on line at: *www.oecd.org/about/publishing/corrigenda.htm*.

Foreword

International tax issues have never been as high on the political agenda as they are today. The integration of national economies and markets has increased substantially in recent years, putting a strain on the international tax rules, which were designed more than a century ago. Weaknesses in the current rules create opportunities for base erosion and profit shifting (BEPS), requiring bold moves by policy makers to restore confidence in the system and ensure that profits are taxed where economic activities take place and value is created.

Following the release of the report *Addressing Base Erosion and Profit Shifting* in February 2013, OECD and G20 countries adopted a 15-point Action Plan to address BEPS in September 2013. The Action Plan identified 15 actions along three key pillars: introducing coherence in the domestic rules that affect cross-border activities, reinforcing substance requirements in the existing international standards, and improving transparency as well as certainty.

Since then, all G20 and OECD countries have worked on an equal footing and the European Commission also provided its views throughout the BEPS project. Developing countries have been engaged extensively via a number of different mechanisms, including direct participation in the Committee on Fiscal Affairs. In addition, regional tax organisations such as the African Tax Administration Forum, the *Centre de rencontre des administrations fiscales* and the *Centro Interamericano de Administraciones Tributarias*, joined international organisations such as the International Monetary Fund, the World Bank and the United Nations, in contributing to the work. Stakeholders have been consulted at length: in total, the BEPS project received more than 1 400 submissions from industry, advisers, NGOs and academics. Fourteen public consultations were held, streamed live on line, as were webcasts where the OECD Secretariat periodically updated the public and answered questions.

After two years of work, the 15 actions have now been completed. All the different outputs, including those delivered in an interim form in 2014, have been consolidated into a comprehensive package. The BEPS package of measures represents the first substantial renovation of the international tax rules in almost a century. Once the new measures become applicable, it is expected that profits will be reported where the economic activities that generate them are carried out and where value is created. BEPS planning strategies that rely on outdated rules or on poorly co-ordinated domestic measures will be rendered ineffective.

Implementation therefore becomes key at this stage. The BEPS package is designed to be implemented via changes in domestic law and practices, and via treaty provisions, with negotiations for a multilateral instrument under way and expected to be finalised in 2016. OECD and G20 countries have also agreed to continue to work together to ensure a consistent and co-ordinated implementation of the BEPS recommendations. Globalisation requires that global solutions and a global dialogue be established which go beyond OECD and G20 countries. To further this objective, in 2016 OECD and G20 countries will conceive an inclusive framework for monitoring, with all interested countries participating on an equal footing.

A better understanding of how the BEPS recommendations are implemented in practice could reduce misunderstandings and disputes between governments. Greater focus on implementation and tax administration should therefore be mutually beneficial to governments and business. Proposed improvements to data and analysis will help support ongoing evaluation of the quantitative impact of BEPS, as well as evaluating the impact of the countermeasures developed under the BEPS Project.

Table of contents

Table

Abbreviations and acronyms

BEPS	Base Erosion and Profit Shifting
CFA	Committee on Fiscal Affairs
CFC	Controlled Foreign Company
CIV	Collective Investment Vehicle
CRS	Common Reporting Standard (Standard for Automatic Exchange of Financial Account Information in Tax Matters)
DD	Double deduction
D/NI	Deduction / no inclusion
FIF	Foreign Investment Fund
FTA	Forum on Tax Administration
GAAP	Generally Accepted Accounting Practice
IFRS	International Financial Reporting Standards
JITSIC	Joint International Tax Shelter Information and Collaboration
OECD	Organisation for Economic Co-operation and Development
PE	Permanent Establishment
REIT	Real Estate Investment Trust
TRACE	Treaty Relief and Compliance Enhancement
WP1	Working Party No.1 on Tax Conventions and Related Questions
WP11	Working Party No.11 on Aggressive Tax Planning

Executive summary

Hybrid mismatch arrangements exploit differences in the tax treatment of an entity or instrument under the laws of two or more tax jurisdictions to achieve double non-taxation, including long-term deferral. These types of arrangements are widespread and result in a substantial erosion of the taxable bases of the countries concerned. They have an overall negative impact on competition, efficiency, transparency and fairness.

With a view to increasing the coherence of corporate income taxation at the international level, the OECD/G20 BEPS Project called for recommendations regarding the design of domestic rules and the development of model treaty provisions that would neutralise the tax effects of hybrid mismatch arrangements. This report sets out those recommendations: Part I contains recommendations for changes to domestic law and Part II sets out recommended changes to the OECD Model Tax Convention. Once translated into domestic and treaty law, these recommendations will neutralise hybrid mismatches, by putting an end to multiple deductions for a single expense, deductions without corresponding taxation or the generation of multiple foreign tax credits for one amount of foreign tax paid. By neutralising the mismatch in tax outcomes, the rules will prevent these arrangements from being used as a tool for BEPS without adversely impacting cross-border trade and investment.

This report supersedes the interim report *Neutralising the Effect of Hybrid Mismatch Arrangements* (OECD, 2014) that was released as part of the first set of BEPS deliverables in September 2014. Compared to that report, the recommendations in Part I have been supplemented with further guidance and practical examples to explain the operation of the rules in further detail. Further work has also been undertaken on asset transfer transactions (such as stock-lending and repo transactions), imported hybrid mismatches, and the treatment of a payment that is included as income under a controlled foreign company (CFC) regime. The consensus achieved on these issues is reflected in the report. As indicated in the September 2014 report, countries remain free in their policy choices as to whether the hybrid mismatch rules should be applied to mismatches that arise under intra-group hybrid regulatory capital. Where one country chooses not to apply the rules to neutralise a hybrid mismatch in respect of a particular hybrid regulatory capital instrument, this does not affect another country's policy choice of whether to apply the rules in respect of the particular instrument.

Part I

Part I of the report sets out recommendations for rules to address mismatches in tax outcomes where they arise in respect of payments made under a hybrid financial instrument or payments made to or by a hybrid entity. It also recommends rules to address indirect mismatches that arise when the effects of a hybrid mismatch arrangement are imported into a third jurisdiction. The recommendations take the form of linking rules that align the tax treatment of an instrument or entity with the tax treatment in the counterparty jurisdiction but otherwise do not disturb the commercial outcomes. The rules apply automatically and there is a rule order in the form of a primary rule and a secondary or defensive rule. This prevents more than one country applying the rule to the same arrangement and also avoids double taxation.

The recommended primary rule is that countries deny the taxpayer's deduction for a payment to the extent that it is not included in the taxable income of the recipient in the counterparty jurisdiction or it is also deductible in the counterparty jurisdiction. If the primary rule is not applied, then the counterparty jurisdiction can generally apply a defensive rule, requiring the deductible payment to be included in income or denying the duplicate deduction depending on the nature of the mismatch.

The report recognises the importance of co-ordination in the implementation and application of the hybrid mismatch rules to ensure that the rules are effective and to minimise compliance and administration costs for taxpayers and tax administrations. To this end, it sets out a common set of design principles and defined terms intended to ensure consistency in the application of the rules.

Part II

Part II addresses the part of Action 2 aimed at ensuring that hybrid instruments and entities, as well as dual resident entities, are not used to obtain unduly the benefits of tax treaties and that tax treaties do not prevent the application of the changes to domestic law recommended in Part I.

Part II first examines the issue of dual resident entities, i.e. entities that are residents of two States for tax purposes. It notes that the work on Action 6 will address some of the BEPS concerns related to the issue of dual resident entities by providing that cases of dual residence under a tax treaty would be solved on a case-by-case basis rather than on the basis of the current rule based on the place of effective management of entities. This change, however, will not address all BEPS concerns related to dual resident entities, domestic law changes being needed to address other avoidance strategies involving dual residence.

Part II also deals with the application of tax treaties to hybrid entities, i.e. entities that are not treated as taxpayers by either or both States that have entered into a tax treaty (such as partnerships in many countries). The report proposes to include in the *OECD Model Tax Convention* (OECD, 2010) a new provision and detailed Commentary that will ensure that benefits of tax treaties are granted in appropriate cases to the income of these entities but also that these benefits are not granted where neither State treats, under its domestic law, the income of such an entity as the income of one of its residents.

Finally, Part II addresses potential treaty issues that could arise from the recommendations in Part I. It first examines treaty issues related to rules that would result in the denial of a deduction or would require the inclusion of a payment in ordinary income and concludes that tax treaties would generally not prevent the application of these rules. It then examines the impact of the recommendations of Part I with respect to tax treaty rules related to the elimination of double taxation and notes that problems could arise in the case of bilateral tax treaties that provide for the application of the exemption method with respect to dividends received from foreign companies. The report describes possible treaty changes that would address these problems. The last issue dealt with in Part II is the possible impact of tax treaty rules concerning non-discrimination on the recommendations of Part I; the report concludes that, as long as the domestic rules that will be drafted to implement these recommendations are properly worded, there should be no conflict with these non-discrimination provisions.

Part I

Recommendations for domestic law

Introduction to Part I

Background

1. The role played by hybrid mismatch arrangements in aggressive tax planning has been discussed in a number of OECD reports. For example, an OECD report on *Addressing Tax Risks Involving Bank Losses* (OECD, 2010) highlighted their use in the context of international banking and recommended that revenue bodies "bring to the attention of their government tax policy officials those situations which may potentially raise policy issues, and, in particular, those where the same tax loss is relieved in more than one country as a result of differences in tax treatment between jurisdictions, in order to determine whether steps should be taken to eliminate that arbitrage/mismatch opportunity." Similarly the OECD report on *Corporate Loss Utilisation through Aggressive Tax Planning* (OECD, 2011) recommended countries "consider introducing restrictions on the multiple use of the same loss to the extent they are concerned with these results."

2. As a result of concerns raised by a number of OECD member countries, the OECD undertook a review with interested member countries to identify examples of tax planning schemes involving hybrid mismatch arrangements and to assess the effectiveness of response strategies adopted by those countries. That review culminated in a report on *Hybrid Mismatch Arrangements: Tax Policy and Compliance Issues* (Hybrids Report, OECD, 2012). The Hybrids Report concludes that the collective tax base of countries is put at risk through the operation of hybrid mismatch arrangements even though it is often difficult to determine unequivocally which individual country has lost tax revenue under the arrangement. Apart from impacting on tax revenues, the Hybrids Report also concluded that hybrid mismatch arrangements have a negative impact on competition, efficiency, transparency and fairness. The Hybrids Report set out a number of policy options to address such hybrid mismatch arrangements and concluded that domestic law rules which link the tax treatment of an entity, instrument or transfer to the tax treatment in another country had significant potential as a tool to address hybrid mismatch arrangements. Although such "linking rules" make the application of domestic law more complicated, the Hybrids Report noted that such rules are not a novelty as, in principle, foreign tax credit rules, subject to tax clauses and controlled foreign company (CFC) rules often do exactly that.

Action 2 of the BEPS Action Plan

3. Action 2 calls for the development of "model treaty provisions and recommendations regarding the design of domestic rules to neutralise the effects of hybrid instruments and entities." The Action Item states that this may include:

(a) Changes to the OECD Model Tax Convention to ensure that hybrid instruments and entities (as well as dual resident entities) are not used to obtain the benefits of treaties unduly;

(b) Domestic law provisions that prevent exemption or non-recognition for payments that are deductible by the payer;

(c) Domestic law provisions that deny a deduction for a payment that is not includible in income by the recipient (and is not subject to taxation under CFC or similar rules);

(d) Domestic law provisions that deny a deduction for a payment that is also deductible in another jurisdiction; and

(e) Where necessary, guidance on co-ordination or tie-breaker rules if more than one country seeks to apply such rules to a transaction or structure.

Part I recommendations

4. Part I of this report sets out the recommendations for the design of the domestic law rules called for under Action 2. It recommends specific improvements to domestic law, designed to achieve a better alignment between those laws and their intended tax policy outcomes (specific recommendations) and the introduction of linking rules that neutralise the mismatch in tax outcomes under a hybrid mismatch arrangement without disturbing any of the other tax, commercial or regulatory consequences (hybrid mismatch rules).

5. In terms of specific changes to domestic law, Chapters 2 and 5 of this report recommend improvements to domestic law rules that:

(a) Deny a dividend exemption, or equivalent relief from economic double taxation, in respect of deductible payments made under financial instruments.

(b) Introduce measures to prevent hybrid transfers being used to duplicate credits for taxes withheld at source.

(c) Alter the effect of CFC and other offshore investment regimes to bring the income of hybrid entities within the charge to taxation under the laws of the investor jurisdiction.

(d) Encourage countries to adopt appropriate information reporting and filing requirements in respect of tax transparent entities established within their jurisdiction.

(e) Restrict the tax transparency of reverse hybrids that are members of a control group.

6. In addition to these specific recommendations, Part I also sets out recommendations for hybrid mismatch rules that adjust the tax outcomes under a hybrid mismatch arrangement in one jurisdiction in order to align them with the tax outcomes in the other jurisdiction. These recommendations target payments under a hybrid mismatch arrangement that give rise to one of the three following outcomes:

(a) *Payments that give rise to a deduction / no inclusion outcome* (D/NI outcome), i.e. payments that are deductible under the rules of the payer jurisdiction and are not included in the ordinary income of the payee.

(b) *Payments that give rise to a double deduction outcome* (DD outcome), i.e. payments that give rise to two deductions in respect of the same payment.

(c) *Payments that give rise to an indirect D/NI outcome*, i.e. payments that are deductible under the rules of the payer jurisdiction and that are set-off by the payee against a deduction under a hybrid mismatch arrangement.

D/NI outcomes

7. Both payments made under hybrid financial instruments and payments made by and to hybrid entities can give rise to D/NI outcomes. In respect of such hybrid mismatch arrangements this report recommends that the response should be to deny the deduction in the payer jurisdiction. In the event the payer jurisdiction does not neutralise the mismatch, this report recommends a defensive rule that would require the payment to be included as ordinary income in the payee jurisdiction. Specific recommendations and recommendations for hybrid mismatch rules that are designed to address D/NI outcomes are set out in Chapters 1 to 5.

DD outcomes

8. As well as producing D/NI outcomes, payments made by hybrid entities can, in certain circumstances, also give rise to DD outcomes. In respect of such payments this report recommends that the primary response should be to deny the duplicate deduction in the parent jurisdiction. A defensive rule, that would require the deduction to be denied in the payer jurisdiction, would only apply in the event the parent jurisdiction did not adopt the primary response. Specific recommendations and recommendations for hybrid mismatch rules designed to address DD outcomes are set out in Chapters 6 and 7.

Indirect D/NI outcomes

9. Once taxpayers have entered into a hybrid mismatch arrangement between two jurisdictions without effective hybrid mismatch rules, it is a relatively simple matter for the effect of that mismatch to be shifted into a third jurisdiction (through the use of an ordinary loan, for example). Therefore, in order to protect the integrity of the recommendations, this report further recommends that a payer jurisdiction deny a deduction for a payment where the payee sets the income from that payment off against expenditure under a separate hybrid mismatch arrangement. Recommendations for the design and application of an imported mismatch rule neutralising such indirect D/NI outcomes are set out in Chapter 8.

Mismatch

10. The extent of a mismatch is determined by comparing the tax treatment of the payment under the laws of each jurisdiction where the mismatch arises. A D/NI mismatch generally occurs when a payment or part of a payment that is treated as deductible under the laws of one jurisdiction is not included in ordinary income by any other jurisdiction. A DD mismatch arises to the extent that all or part of the payment that is deductible under the laws of another jurisdiction is set-off against non-dual inclusion income.

11. The hybrid mismatch rules focus on payments and whether the nature of that payment gives rise to a deduction for the payer and ordinary income for the payee. Rules that entitle taxpayers to a unilateral tax deduction for invested equity without requiring the taxpayer to make a payment, such as regimes that grant deemed interest deductions

for equity capital, are economically closer to a tax exemption or similar taxpayer specific concessions and do not produce a mismatch in tax outcomes in the sense contemplated by Action 2. Such rules, and rules having similar effect, will, however, be considered separately in the context of the implementation of these recommendations.

12. The hybrid mismatch rules are not generally intended to pick-up mismatches that are attributable to differences in the value ascribed to a payment. For example, gains and losses from foreign currency fluctuations on a loan can be said to give rise to mismatches in tax outcomes but these mismatches are attributable to differences in the measurement of the value of payment (rather than its character) and can generally be ignored for the purposes of the hybrid mismatch rules.

Hybrid element

13. While cross-border mismatches arise in other contexts (such as the payment of deductible interest to a tax exempt entity), the only types of mismatches targeted by this report are those that rely on a hybrid element to produce such outcomes. Some arrangements exploit differences between the transparency or opacity of an entity for tax purposes (hybrid entities) and others involve the use of hybrid instruments, which generally involve a conflict in the characterisation of the instrument (and hence the tax treatment of the payments made under it). Hybrid instruments and entities can also be embedded in a wider arrangement or group structure to produce indirect D/NI outcomes.

14. In most cases the causal connection between the hybrid element and the mismatch will be obvious. There are some challenges, however, in identifying the hybrid element in the context of hybrid financial instruments. Because of the wide variety of financial instruments and the different ways jurisdictions tax them, it has proven impossible, in practice, for this report to comprehensively identify and accurately define all those situations where cross-border conflicts in the characterisation of a payment under a financing instrument may lead to a mismatch in tax treatment. Rather than targeting these technical differences, the focus of this report is on aligning the treatment of cross-border payments under a financial instrument so that amounts that are treated as a financing expense by the issuer's jurisdiction are treated as ordinary income in the holder's jurisdiction. Accordingly this report recommends that a financial instrument should be treated as hybrid where a payment under the instrument gives rise to a mismatch in tax outcomes and the mismatch can be attributed to the terms of the instrument.

Rule order

15. In order to avoid the risk of double taxation, Action 2 also calls for "guidance on the co-ordination or tie-breaker rules where more than one country seeks to apply such rules to a transaction or structure." For this reason the rules recommended in this report are organised in a hierarchy so that a jurisdiction does not need to apply the hybrid mismatch rule where there is another rule operating in the counterparty jurisdiction that is sufficient to neutralise the mismatch. The report recommends that every jurisdiction introduce all the recommended rules so that the effects of hybrid mismatch arrangements are neutralised even if the counterparty jurisdiction does not have effective hybrid mismatch rules.

Scope

16. Overly broad hybrid mismatch rules may be difficult to apply and administer. Accordingly, each hybrid mismatch rule has its own defined scope, which is designed to

achieve an overall balance between a rule that is comprehensive, targeted and administrable.

17. Table 1.1 provides a general overview of the hybrid mismatch rules recommended in this report.

Table 1.1 General Overview of the Recommendations

Mismatch	Arrangement	Specific recommendations on improvements to domestic law	Recommended hybrid mismatch rule		
			Response	Defensive rule	Scope
D/NI	Hybrid financial instrument	No dividend exemption for deductible payments Proportionate limitation of withholding tax credits	Deny payer deduction	Include as ordinary income	Related parties and structured arrangements
	Disregarded payment made by a hybrid		Deny payer deduction	Include as ordinary income	Control group and structured arrangements
	Payment made to a reverse hybrid	Improvements to offshore investment regime Restricting tax transparency of intermediate entities where non-resident investors treat the entity as opaque	Deny payer deduction	-	Control group and structured arrangements
DD	Deductible payment made by a hybrid		Deny parent deduction	Deny payer deduction	No limitation on response, defensive rule applies to control group and structured arrangements
	Deductible payment made by dual resident		Deny resident deduction	-	No limitation on response
Indirect D/NI	Imported mismatch arrangements		Deny payer deduction	-	Members of control group and structured arrangements

Bibliography

OECD (2013), *Action Plan on Base Erosion and Profit Shifting*, OECD Publishing, Paris, http://dx.doi.org/10.1787/9789264202719-en.

OECD (2012), *Hybrid Mismatch Arrangements: Tax Policy and Compliance Issues*, OECD Publishing, Paris, www.oecd.org/tax/exchange-of-tax-information/HYBRIDS_ENG_Final_October2012.pdf.

OECD (2011), *Corporate Loss Utilisation through Aggressive Tax Planning*, OECD Publishing, Paris. http://dx.doi.org/10.1787/9789264119222-en.

OECD (2010), *Addressing Tax Risks Involving Bank Losses*, OECD Publishing, Paris, http://dx.doi.org/10.1787/9789264088689-en.

Chapter 1

Hybrid Financial Instrument Rule

Recommendation 1

1. Neutralise the mismatch to the extent the payment gives rise to a D/NI outcome

The following rule should apply to a payment under a financial instrument that results in a hybrid mismatch and to a substitute payment under an arrangement to transfer a financial instrument:

(a) The payer jurisdiction will deny a deduction for such payment to the extent it gives rise to a D/NI outcome.

(b) If the payer jurisdiction does not neutralise the mismatch then the payee jurisdiction will require such payment to be included in ordinary income to the extent the payment gives rise to a D/NI outcome.

(c) Differences in the timing of the recognition of payments will not be treated as giving rise to a D/NI outcome for a payment made under a financial instrument, provided the taxpayer can establish to the satisfaction of a tax authority that the payment will be included as ordinary income within a reasonable period of time.

2. Definition of financial instrument and substitute payment

For the purposes of this rule:

(a) A financial instrument means any arrangement that is taxed under the rules for taxing debt, equity or derivatives under the laws of both the payee and payer jurisdictions and includes a hybrid transfer.

(b) A hybrid transfer includes any arrangement to transfer a financial instrument entered into by a taxpayer with another person where:

(i) the taxpayer is the owner of the transferred asset and the rights of the counterparty in respect of that asset are treated as obligations of the taxpayer; and

(ii) under the laws of the counterparty jurisdiction, the counterparty is the owner of the transferred asset and the rights of the taxpayer in respect of that asset are treated as obligations of the counterparty.

Ownership of an asset for these purposes includes any rules that result in the taxpayer being taxed as the owner of the corresponding cash-flows from the asset.

(c) A jurisdiction should treat any arrangement where one person provides money to another in consideration for a financing or equity return as a financial instrument to the extent of such financing or equity return.

(d) Any payment under an arrangement that is not treated as a financial instrument under the laws of the counterparty jurisdiction shall be treated as giving rise to a mismatch only to the extent the payment constitutes a financing or equity return.

Recommendation 1 (*continued*)

(e) A substitute payment is any payment, made under an arrangement to transfer a financial instrument, to the extent it includes, or is payment of an amount representing, a financing or equity return on the underlying financial instrument where the payment or return would:

(i) not have been included in ordinary income of the payer;

(ii) have been included in ordinary income of the payee; or

(iii) have given rise to hybrid mismatch;

if it had been made directly under the financial instrument.

3. Rule only applies to a payment under a financial instrument that results in a hybrid mismatch

A payment under a financial instrument results in a hybrid mismatch where the mismatch can be attributed to the terms of the instrument. A payment cannot be attributed to the terms of the instrument where the mismatch is solely attributable to the status of the taxpayer or the circumstances in which the instrument is held.

4. Scope of the rule

This rule only applies to a payment made to a related person or where the payment is made under a structured arrangement and the taxpayer is party to that structured arrangement.

5. Exceptions to the rule

The primary response in Recommendation 1.1(a) should not apply to a payment by an investment vehicle that is subject to special regulation and tax treatment under the laws of the establishment jurisdiction in circumstances where:

(a) The tax policy of the establishment jurisdiction is to preserve the deduction for the payment under the financial instrument to ensure that:

(i) the taxpayer is subject to no or minimal taxation on its investment income; and

(ii) that holders of financial instruments issued by the taxpayer are subject to tax on that payment as ordinary income on a current basis.

(b) The regulatory and tax framework in the establishment jurisdiction has the effect that the financial instruments issued by the investment vehicle will result in all or substantially all of the taxpayer's investment income being paid and distributed to the holders of those financial instruments within a reasonable period of time after that income was derived or received by the taxpayer.

(c) The tax policy of the establishment jurisdiction is that the full amount of the payment is:

(i) included in the ordinary income of any person that is a payee in the establishment jurisdiction; and

(ii) not excluded from the ordinary income of any person that is a payee under the laws of the payee jurisdiction under a treaty between the establishment jurisdiction and the payee jurisdiction.

(d) The payment is not made under a structured arrangement.

The defensive rule in Recommendation 1.1(b) will continue to apply to any payment made by such an investment vehicle.

Overview

18. The policy behind Recommendation 1 is to prevent a taxpayer from entering into structured arrangements or arrangements with a related party that exploit differences in the tax treatment of a financial instrument to produce a D/NI outcome. The rule aligns the tax treatment of payments under a financial instrument by adjusting the amount of deductions allowed under the laws of the payer jurisdiction, or the amount of income to be included in the payee jurisdiction, as appropriate, in order to eliminate the mismatch in tax outcomes. Recommendation 1 applies to three different types of financing arrangement:

(a) Arrangements that are treated as debt, equity or derivative contracts under local law ("financial instruments").

(b) Arrangements involving the transfer of financial instruments where differences in the tax treatment of that arrangement result in the same financial instrument being treated as held by more than one taxpayer ("hybrid transfers").

(c) Arrangements involving the transfer of financial instruments where a payment is made in substitution for the financing or equity return on the transferred asset and differences between the tax treatment of that payment and the underlying return on the instrument have the net-effect of undermining the integrity of the hybrid financial instrument rule ("substitute payments").

Arrangements treated as financial instruments under local law

19. Recommendation 1 is primarily targeted at arrangements that are taxed as debt, equity or derivative contracts (i.e. financial instruments) under the laws of the payer and payee jurisdictions. While the Recommendation encourages jurisdictions to extend their existing rules for taxing financial instruments to cover any arrangement to the extent it produces an equity or financing return, it is recognised that the final determination of the type of arrangements falling within the definition of a financial instrument (and therefore potentially subject to adjustment under the hybrid financial instrument rule) must ultimately be left to each jurisdiction.

20. Although Recommendation 1 is described as applying to "hybrid financial instruments", it does not specify the particular features of a financial instrument that make it "hybrid". The wide variety of financial instruments and the different ways they can be characterised and treated for tax purposes make it impossible to comprehensively and accurately identify all the situations where a payment under the instrument can give rise to a hybrid mismatch. Rather the hybrid financial instrument rule focuses on whether the payment is expected to give rise to a mismatch in tax outcomes and whether that mismatch is attributable to differences in the way the instrument is taxed under the laws of the payer and payee jurisdictions.

21. If the conditions for the application of the hybrid financial instrument rule are satisfied then the response recommended in the report is to align the tax treatment of the payments made under the arrangement so that the payer is not entitled to claim a deduction for the financing or equity return paid under the arrangement unless the payment is treated as ordinary income of the payee. The mechanics and rule order for the adjustments are set out in Recommendation 1.1. The primary recommendation is for the payer jurisdiction to deny a deduction to the extent the payment gives rise to a D/NI outcome. If the payer jurisdiction does not apply the recommended response, then the

defensive rule calls on the payee jurisdiction to treat the deductible payment as ordinary income under a financial instrument.

22. The primary and defensive rules are limited to adjusting the tax consequences that flow from the difference in the tax treatment of the instrument and should not generally affect the underlying character of the payment (e.g. whether it is treated as interest or a dividend) or the quantification or tax treatment of a taxpayer's overall gain or loss on the acquisition or disposal of an asset acquired under a financial instrument.

Hybrid transfers

23. A hybrid transfer is any arrangement to transfer a financial instrument where, as a consequence of the economics of the transaction and the way it is structured, the laws of two jurisdictions take opposing views on who is the owner of the underlying return on the transferred asset. Payments under a hybrid transfer generally give rise to a D/NI outcome where one party to the transfer claims a deduction for the underlying financial or equity return on the transferred asset that is paid (or treated as paid) to the counterparty under the terms of the hybrid transfer, while the counterparty treats that same payment as a direct return on the underlying financial instrument itself (and therefore excluded or exempt from taxation). Recommendation 1 deems this type of asset transfer to be financial instrument so that the D/NI outcome arising under such an arrangement falls within the scope of the hybrid financial instrument rule, regardless of how the hybrid transfer is characterised under local law.

24. Because hybrid transfers are treated as a type of financial instrument, the same rules will apply for testing whether the mismatch in tax outcomes is a hybrid mismatch. A D/NI outcome under a hybrid transfer will only be subject to adjustment under the hybrid financial instrument rule where the mismatch can be attributed to differences in the tax treatment of the arrangement under the laws of the payer and payee jurisdictions and any adjustment required to be made under that rule will be limited to the tax consequences that flow from that difference in the tax treatment.

Substitute payments

25. The final category of arrangements that are brought within the scope of Recommendation 1 are transfers of financial instruments where the transferee receives a payment in substitution for the financing or equity return on the transferred asset (a substitute payment) and differences between the tax treatment of substitute payment and the underlying return on the instrument have the potential to undermine the integrity of the hybrid financial instrument rule. A substitute payment that gives rise to a D/NI outcome will be subject to adjustment under the hybrid financial instrument rule where the underlying financing or equity return on the transferred asset would otherwise have been taxable in the hands of the transferor or is treated as exempt or excluded from income in the hands of the transferee or where the transfer has the effect of taking financial instrument outside of the scope of the hybrid financial instrument rule.

26. Unlike the other rules in Recommendation 1, which only apply where and to the extent the mismatch is attributable to the terms of the instrument, the substitute payment rules apply to any type of D/NI outcome regardless of how it arises.

Recommendation 1.1 - Neutralise the mismatch to the extent the payment gives rise to a D/NI outcome

27. The hybrid financial instrument rule applies to substitute payments and payments under a financial instrument to the extent those payments give rise to a D/NI outcome.

Payment

28. The definition of "payment" is set out in further detail in Recommendation 12. A payment is any transfer of value and includes an amount that is *capable of being paid* such as a future or contingent obligation to make a payment. As illustrated in **Example 1.13**, the definition of payment includes the accrual of a future payment obligation even when that accrued amount does not correspond to any increase in the payment obligation during that period. The definition specifically excludes, however, payments that are only deemed to be made for tax purposes and that do not involve the creation of any new economic rights between the parties. Thus, as illustrated in **Example 1.14**, the hybrid financial instrument rule does not apply to an adjustment resulting from a deemed interest charge. Such adjustments are made purely for tax purposes and do not correspond to any present or future transfer of value.

D/NI outcome

29. A payment gives rise to a D/NI outcome to the extent it is deductible under the laws of the payer jurisdiction and not included in income under the laws of any jurisdiction where the payment is treated as being received (the payee jurisdiction). The hybrid financial instrument rule only looks to the expected tax treatment of the arrangement, based on the terms of the instrument and the character of the payments made under it, to determine whether the payment gives rise to a mismatch.

Deductible

30. A payment will be treated as "deductible" if, after a proper consideration of the character of the payment and its tax treatment under the laws of the payer jurisdiction, the payer is entitled to take the payment into account as a deduction in calculating its taxable income. A payment under a financial instrument will be treated as deductible to the extent that payment is treated as a separate deductible item under local law. Deductible payments made under a financial instrument will generally include interest, as well as: issue discount and redemption premiums; facilities and lending fees and payments under a derivative contract to the extent they are treated as separate items of deductible expenditure.

31. The concept of "deductible" also extends to payments that trigger other types of "equivalent tax relief". The meaning of this term is illustrated in **Example 1.11** where a dividend payment gives rise to a tax credit that can be set-off against a tax liability of the payer or refunded to the shareholder. While such credits are usually provided as a means of relieving economic double taxation on distributed income, in that example, the dividend that triggers the credit is not subject to a second layer of tax under the laws of the payer jurisdiction. The credit is therefore economically equivalent to a deduction in that, in the absence of any tax at the shareholder level, it will have the effect of reducing the amount of income under the arrangement that will be subject to the tax at the full rate in the payer jurisdiction.

Included in ordinary income

32. Ordinary income refers to those categories of income that are subject to tax at the taxpayer's full marginal rate and that do not benefit from any exemption, exclusion, credit or other tax relief applicable to particular types of payments (such as indirect credits for underlying tax on the income of the payer). A payment will be treated as included in ordinary income to the extent that, after a proper determination of the character and treatment of the payment under the laws of the payee jurisdiction, the payment is required to be incorporated as ordinary income into a calculation of the payee's taxable income. A payment of ordinary income under a financial instrument will generally include interest, dividends and other investment returns that are subject to tax at the payee's full marginal rate. Income is considered subject to tax at the taxpayer's full marginal rate, however, notwithstanding that the tax on the inclusion is reduced by a credit or other equivalent tax relief granted by the payee jurisdiction for withholding tax or other taxes imposed by the source jurisdiction on the payment itself.

D/NI outcomes in respect of payments under a financial instrument

33. Because the hybrid financial instrument rule looks only to the expected tax treatment of the payment under the laws of the counterparty jurisdiction, rather than its actual tax treatment in the hands of the counterparty, it is not necessary for the taxpayer or tax administration to know the counterparty's tax status or how that payment was actually treated for tax purposes in order to determine whether the payment has given rise to a mismatch. The application of this principle is illustrated in **Example 1.26** where a trader acquires shares under an asset transfer agreement. That example notes that, the trader's deduction for the acquisition cost of the shares will not be a product of the terms of the instrument and the character of the payments made under it but rather of the particular status of the payer. Therefore the fact that transfer agreement may constitute a hybrid transfer (so that the consideration paid for the shares is treated as payment under a financial instrument), will not result in the payment being treated as giving rise to a D/NI outcome in a hybrid financial instrument. The same principle is illustrated in **Example 1.29** where a share trader is entitled to interest in respect of the unpaid purchase price under a share sale agreement. The interest component of the purchase price is treated as giving rise to a separate deductible expense under the laws of the purchaser's jurisdiction while the share trader treats the entire amount payable under the share sale agreement as consideration for the sale of the shares. In this case the payment is treated as giving rise to a mismatch in tax outcomes, even though the payment is, in fact, included by the share trader in ordinary income as proceeds from the disposal of a trading asset.

D/NI outcomes in respect of substitute payments

34. The substitute payment rules apply to any actual mismatch in tax outcomes, regardless of the circumstances in which the deduction arises, including any amount taken into account in calculating the gain or loss on disposal of a trading asset. The application of the substitute payment rule is illustrated in **Example 1.34** where a trader acquires shares under a hybrid transfer. Although, in that case, the deduction claimed by the trader for the payment of the manufactured dividend is not attributable to the terms of the instrument (and therefore does not give rise to hybrid mismatch under a financial instrument), the example notes that the payment may still be a substitute payment that is subject to adjustment under the hybrid financial instrument rule.

Interaction between Recommendation 1.1(a) and Recommendation 2.1

35. The determination of whether a D/NI outcome has arisen requires a proper assessment of the legal character of the instrument and tax treatment of the payment in each jurisdiction. A payment under a hybrid financial instrument will not be treated as giving rise to a D/NI outcome if the mismatch will be neutralised in the counterparty jurisdiction by a specific rule designed to align the tax treatment of the payment with tax policy outcomes applicable to an instrument of that nature. Specific rules of this nature will include any rules in the payee jurisdiction, consistent with Recommendation 2.1, that limit the availability of a dividend exemption or equivalent tax relief to payments that are not deductible for tax purposes. This principle is illustrated in **Example 1.1** where a taxpayer borrows money under an interest bearing loan from a related taxpayer in another jurisdiction. The borrower is allowed a deduction for the interest paid on the loan while the holder treats the payment as a dividend. A proper consideration of the character of the payment and its tax treatment in both jurisdictions will take into account rules in the payee jurisdiction designed to limit double taxation relief on dividend payments made out of after-tax profits. Accordingly, if the payee jurisdiction does not extend its dividend exemption to a payment that is deductible under the laws of the payer jurisdiction, then no mismatch will arise for the purposes of the hybrid financial instrument rule. Similar outcomes are identified in **Example 1.2**, **Example 1.3** and **Example 1.4**.

Inclusion under a CFC regime

36. The hybrid financial instrument rule is only intended to operate where the payment gives rise to a mismatch in tax outcomes and is not intended to give rise to economic double taxation. In certain cases, a payment under a hybrid financial instrument that gives rise to a D/NI outcome, as between the payer and payee jurisdictions, may be included in income under a CFC regime. A country aiming to avoid economic double taxation in these cases should consider how to address the mismatch in tax outcomes under the hybrid financial instrument rule in light of the fact that the payment has been included in ordinary income by the shareholder under a CFC regime and determine whether the CFC inclusion is to be considered as included in ordinary income for the purposes of determining whether there is a D/NI outcome under the hybrid financial instrument rule.

37. Where a country takes into account a CFC inclusion in the parent jurisdiction, a taxpayer seeking to rely on that inclusion in order to avoid an adjustment under the hybrid financial instrument rule should only be able to do so in circumstances where it can satisfy the tax administration that the payment has been fully included under the laws of the relevant jurisdiction and is subject to tax at the full rate. This will include demonstrating that:

(a) The payment would ordinarily be required to be brought into account under the CFC rules in the parent jurisdiction.

(b) The CFC regime actually requires the payment to be attributed to the shareholder (i.e. the payment does not qualify for an active income exception).

(c) The quantification and timing rules of the CFC regime have actually brought that payment into account as ordinary income on the shareholder's return.

38. In addition, payments that are treated as exempt from the hybrid financial instrument rule on the grounds of a CFC inclusion should be eligible for such exemption only to the extent that the payment:

(a) Has not been treated as reduced or offset by any deduction or other relief other than in respect of expenditure incurred by the parent under the laws of the parent jurisdiction.

(b) Does not carry an entitlement to any credit or other relief.

(c) Does not give rise to an imported mismatch.

39. The application of this principle is illustrated in **Example 1.24** where a company makes an intra-group payment under a hybrid financial instrument. In that example, the CFC regime in the parent jurisdiction that treats certain items of passive income (e.g. rents, royalties and interest) derived by controlled foreign entities as "CFC income" attributable to shareholders in proportion to their shareholding in the CFC. In that example the taxpayer is not able to treat an item of CFC income as included in ordinary income under the laws of the jurisdiction of the parent to the extent that income was treated as reduced by expenditure incurred by the payee or to the extent that payment was sheltered by any credit or other relief in the parent jurisdiction. The example also notes that the taxpayer would further need to satisfy the tax administration that the payment has not been set-off against a hybrid deduction under an imported mismatch arrangement.

40. The rules that determine the type, amount and timing of attributed income under a CFC regime can make the determination of whether an amount has been included in ordinary income under a CFC regime difficult and fact intensive. Accordingly, when introducing the hybrid financial instrument rule into local law, countries may wish to balance the need to avoid double taxation outcomes and the burden of making such a determination in setting any materiality thresholds that a taxpayer must meet before a taxpayer can treat a CFC inclusion as reducing the amount of adjustment required under the rule.

Application of the rule in the case of exemption, reduced rate or credit

41. A deductible payment will be treated as giving rise to a mismatch whenever the payee jurisdiction subjects the payment to taxation at a rate that is less than the full marginal rate imposed on ordinary income, regardless of the form in which such tax relief is provided. The particular mechanism for securing tax relief in the payee jurisdiction, whether by exclusion or through exemption, rate reduction, credit or any other method, should not generally impact on the final outcome under the hybrid financial instrument rule.

42. Certain countries tax different types of income at different rates. For example, business or employment income may be taxed at a different rate from investment income. These differences should be taken into account in determining whether the payment has been subject to tax at the taxpayer's full marginal rate. In the context of the hybrid financial instrument rule, the payee's *full marginal rate* is the tax the payee would expect to pay on ordinary income derived under a financial instrument, so that a mismatch will not arise, for the purposes of the hybrid financial instrument rule, simply because the payee jurisdiction taxes income from financial instruments at a lower rate than other types of income. This is illustrated in **Example 1.3** where an interest payment is subject to tax at a reduced rate of taxation under the laws of the payee jurisdiction. **Example 1.3** notes that if the reduced tax rate is no less than the rate that applies to any other payment of ordinary income under a financial instrument (such as ordinary interest on a loan) then no mismatch will arise for the purposes of the hybrid financial instrument rule.

Partial exemption or reduced rate

43. In those cases where the payee jurisdiction only provides taxpayers with a partial exemption or reduced rate on a payment under a hybrid financial instrument, the amount of the deduction that is denied should generally be no more than is necessary to eliminate the mismatch in tax outcomes between the payer and payee jurisdictions and a deduction should continue to be allowed to the extent the payment is subject to tax in the payee jurisdiction at the full rate. The application of this principle is illustrated in **Example 1.2**, where the payee jurisdiction provides a partial tax exemption for a payment of interest under a subordinated loan, and in **Example 1.3**, where the payment under the hybrid financial instrument is subject to tax in the payee jurisdiction at 10% of the normal corporate rate.

44. Cases of partial tax relief usually arise in the context of debt/equity hybrids where the payee jurisdiction treats the payment as a dividend and provides for a credit, reduced rate or partial exemption which does not fully relieve the shareholder from tax on that dividend. In most cases, these types of payments will be covered by Recommendation 2.1, which deals with the granting of tax relief for deductible dividends, so that, in practice, the number of actual cases where the payer jurisdiction will be called upon to deny the deduction in respect of a payment that is subject to partial relief may, in fact, be limited.

45. In the cases of partial dividend relief, the limitation on tax relief in the payee jurisdiction may be intended to re-capture the benefit of a reduced rate or deferred taxation at the corporate level or to offset the benefit of other shareholder tax reliefs (such deductibility of interest expenses). In these cases, a full denial of the deduction will be more effective at preserving the intended tax policy outcomes in the payee jurisdiction and achieve a better equality of outcomes with payments under an ordinary equity instrument. This approach would need to be applied on a jurisdiction by jurisdiction basis, taking into account the tax policy outcomes in the counterparty jurisdiction, and may be unnecessary if the payee jurisdiction introduces comprehensive rules restricting taxation relief for deductible dividends in line with Recommendation 2.1.

Calculating the amount of the adjustment in the case of an underlying foreign tax credit

46. Unless the payee jurisdiction has adopted Recommendation 2.1 and denies the benefit of an underlying foreign tax credit for a deductible dividend, the primary response under the hybrid financial instrument rule will be to deny a deduction for such a payment to the extent it is sheltered from tax in the payee jurisdiction.

47. Unlike other methods of relieving double taxation, which either exempt the income in the payee jurisdiction or subject it to tax at a reduced rate, foreign tax credits are sensitive to changes in the calculation of the payer's taxable income and differences in tax rates between jurisdictions. The interaction between the hybrid financial instrument rule (which ensures a payment is not deductible to the extent it is sheltered from tax by an underlying foreign tax credit) and the foreign tax credit (which provides the shareholder with a credit for underlying taxes paid by the company) can also result in a circular calculation where the denial of a deduction in the payee jurisdiction under the hybrid financial instrument rule (due to the fact that payment is not included in ordinary income) increases the amount of tax payable in that jurisdiction, which, in turn, has the effect of increasing the foreign tax credit available in the payee jurisdiction and reducing the amount of the payment that is treated as included in ordinary income.

48. In practice the complexity of foreign tax credit calculations (including the potential for circularity) can make it difficult for taxpayers to calculate the required adjustment under the hybrid financial instrument rule. Accordingly, when determining the amount of the adjustment a taxpayer is required to make in respect of a payment that carries an entitlement to a foreign tax credit, countries should strike a balance between rules that are clear and easy to apply and that avoid the risk of double taxation. **Example 1.4** sets out an illustration of the type of adjustment that can be made under a hybrid financial instrument rule to a payment that is subject to an underlying foreign tax credit. In that case the payer country denies the deduction only to the extent the credit is sufficient to shelter the payment from taxation. In that example the potential for circularity can be avoided if the payee jurisdiction does not allow the crediting of any increased foreign taxes that arise due to the application of the hybrid financial instrument rule or if the incremental tax increase does not, in practice, have a material impact on the amount of the underlying foreign tax credit attributable to the payment.

Nature and extent of the adjustment required

49. The underlying principle of the hybrid financial instrument rule is to align the tax treatment of payments under a financial instrument so that a taxpayer cannot claim a deduction for a financing expense unless that payment is required to be included in ordinary income in the payee jurisdiction. The primary and secondary rules achieve this outcome by adjusting the amount of deductions allowed under the laws of the payer jurisdiction, or the amount of income to be included in the payee jurisdiction, as appropriate, in order to ensure that the aggregate tax treatment of the arrangement is the same regardless of the form of instrument used or whether the adjustment is made in the payee or payer jurisdictions. The adjustment should be no more than is necessary to neutralise the instrument's hybrid effect and should result in an outcome that is proportionate and that does not lead to double taxation.

No impact on other tax consequences

50. The adjustment in respect of a payment under a hybrid financial instrument does not affect the character of the payment made under it. Although the effect of the primary rule is to deny the payer a deduction, in order to bring the tax treatment of the payment in line with the tax treatment in the payee jurisdiction, the rule does not require a change to the character of the instrument or the payment made under the instrument for tax purposes. This is illustrated in **Example 1.1** where the hybrid financial instrument rule denies the payer a deduction for the interest payment made under a debt/equity hybrid but does not require the payer jurisdiction to treat the payment as a dividend for tax purposes.

Only adjust tax consequences that are attributable to the terms of the instrument

51. The adjustment to the tax consequences of a payment under a hybrid financial instrument should be confined to those that are attributable to the tax treatment of the instrument itself. The adjustment is not intended to impact on tax outcomes that are solely attributable to the status of the taxpayer or the context in which the instrument is held. **Example 1.5** and **Example 1.8** both describe cases where an adjustment under the defensive rule in the payee jurisdiction will not impact on the tax position of the taxpayer because that taxpayer is either not subject to tax on ordinary income or because it derives that income through an exempt branch. Although the payee may not be subject to any additional tax liability as a consequence of an adjustment under the secondary rule, the

primary rule can still apply to deny the deduction in the payer jurisdiction if the payment would be expected to give rise to a mismatch in tax outcomes.

52. This principle can further be illustrated by contrasting the outcomes described in **Example 1.27** and **Example 1.28**. In both these examples, the arrangement between the parties is an asset sale agreement that provides for the payment of the purchase price to be deferred for one year and for the purchase price to incorporate an adjustment equal to twelve months of interest on the unpaid purchase price. The purchaser's jurisdiction treats the interest portion of the purchase price as giving rise to a separate deductible payment for tax purposes while, under the laws of the seller's jurisdiction, the entire purchase price (including the interest component) is treated as consideration for the transfer of the asset. As described in **Example 1.27**, the asset sale agreement is treated as giving rise to a deductible financing expense for the purchaser and the purchaser's jurisdiction should therefore deny a deduction for that payment under the hybrid financial instrument rule. In **Example 1.28**, however, the purchaser acquires the asset as part of its activities as a trader and is able to include the purchase price as expenditure when calculating any taxable gain/loss on the asset. **Example 1.28** concludes that the hybrid financial instrument rule should not affect the ability of the trader to take the full amount payable under the asset transfer agreement into account when calculating the gain or loss on disposal of the asset. Taxpayers that buy and sell securities in the ordinary course of a business of dealing or trading in securities (such as securities dealers, banks and brokers) will treat the net profit or loss on each trade as included in taxable income, or deductible for tax purposes, as the case may be, regardless of the exact way in which the return on the transaction is accounted for or the manner in which the transaction is analysed for tax purposes. In **Example 1.34** a financial instrument is acquired by a trader under a hybrid transfer. Although the payment of the manufactured dividend under the share loan is deemed to be a payment under a financial instrument, the hybrid financial instrument rule will only operate to deny a deduction that is attributable to the terms of the instrument itself and will not prevent a trader from taking the expenditure incurred under the hybrid transfer into account in calculating the trader's overall (taxable) gain or loss on the asset.

Mismatch that is solely attributable to differences in the valuation of a payment

53. In order for a D/NI outcome to arise, there must be a difference in the way a payment is measured and characterised under the laws of the payer and payee jurisdictions. Differences in tax outcomes that are solely attributable to differences in the value ascribed to a payment (including through the application of transfer pricing) do not fall within the scope of the hybrid mismatch rule. If the amount of the payment is characterised and calculated in the same way under the laws of both jurisdictions, then differences in the value attributed to that amount under the laws of the payer and payee jurisdictions will not give rise to a D/NI outcome. In certain cases, however, particularly in the case of more complex financial instruments that incorporate both financing and equity returns, the way a payment is measured and characterised under local law may depend on the value attributed to each of its components and this difference in characterisation may give rise to a mismatch.

54. A mismatch does not arise simply because of differences resulting from converting foreign exchange into local or functional currency. This principle is illustrated in **Example 1.17**, where a fall in the value of the local currency results in foreign currency payments under a loan becoming more expensive in local currency terms. Under local law, the payer is entitled to a deduction for this increased cost. This deduction, however, is not reflected by a corresponding inclusion in the payee jurisdiction. The

difference in tax treatment does not give rise to a D/NI outcome, however, as the proportion of the interest and principal payable under the loan is the same under the laws of both jurisdictions. This principle is also illustrated in **Example 1.15**. That example considers the tax treatment of an equity premium that a noteholder receives on the maturity of a convertible note. The equity premium will not be treated as giving rise to a D/NI outcome simply because the payer and payee jurisdictions treat the shares received on conversion as having a different value for tax purposes. **Example 1.16** considers a situation where both the issuer and the holder treat a convertible note as being issued at a discount representing its equity value. The higher valuation given to the equity value of the note in the issuer's jurisdiction results in the issuer recognising a larger accrued discount, which results in greater portion of the payments being treated as deductible in the issuer's jurisdiction. The example concludes that, in this case, the way in which the component elements of the note are valued has a direct impact on the way a payment is measured and characterised for tax purposes and, accordingly, the difference in tax outcomes should be treated as giving rise to a mismatch in tax outcomes.

Timing differences

55. The hybrid financial instrument rule does not generally apply to differences in the timing of the recognition of payments under a financial instrument. The hybrid financial instrument rule should apply, however, where the taxpayer is not able to show that the mismatch in tax outcomes is merely one of timing. Recommendation 1.1(c) therefore clarifies that a payment will not be treated as giving rise to a D/NI outcome provided the tax administration can be satisfied that the payment under the instrument is expected to be included in income within a reasonable period of time.

Application of Recommendation 1.1(c)

56. A payment should not be treated as giving rise to a mismatch if it will be required to be included by the payee in ordinary income in an accounting period that commences within 12 months of the end of the payer's accounting period. If the payment does not meet the requirements of this safe harbour, the payer should still be entitled to a deduction for the payment if it can establish, to the satisfaction of the tax administration, that the payee can be expected to include the payment in ordinary income within a reasonable period of time.

Expected to be included in income

57. A payment can expected to be included in ordinary income where there was a reasonable expectation at the time the instrument was issued that the payment would be made and that such payment would be included in ordinary income by the payee at the time it was paid. If the terms of the instrument and other facts and circumstances indicate that the parties placed little commercial significance on whether payment would be made, or if the terms of the instrument are structured in such a way that such payment, when it is made, will not be treated as giving rise to ordinary income in the hands of the payee, then the payment cannot be said to be reasonably expected to be included in income.

Reasonable period of time

58. The determination of whether this payment will be made within a *reasonable period of time* should be based on the time period that might be expected to be agreed between unrelated parties acting at arm's length. This determination should take into

account such factors as the terms of the instrument, the circumstances in which it is held and the commercial objectives of the parties, taking into account the nature of the accrual and any contingencies or other commercial factors affecting payment. For example, a secured loan that is used to finance infrastructure investment may be expected to have longer payment terms than an unsecured loan that is used to fund working capital.

59. The application of these principles is illustrated in **Example 1.22** in respect of a subordinated loan where the interest is treated as deductible by the payer in the year it accrues but is only treated as income by the payee when it is actually paid. In that example, the lender is a minority shareholder in the borrower and there is a dividend blocker on the shares that prevents the borrower from making any distributions to its majority shareholder while there is accrued but unpaid interest on the loan. This type of contractual term incentivises the payer to make regular interest payments on the loan in order that it can continue to pay dividends to its majority shareholder and, accordingly, it can be concluded that the interest payments can be expected to be made within a reasonable period of time even in circumstances where the term of the loan is indefinite and interest payments are at the discretion of the borrower.

60. This outcome can be contrasted with the lending arrangement described in **Example 1.21** where the period over which interest accrues leads the tax administration to conclude that the parties have placed little commercial significance on whether payments under the loan will be made. Alternatively, in that example, interest may accrue over a shorter term but the lender has the power to waive its interest entitlement at any time before it is actually paid without adverse tax consequences. That example concludes that the taxpayer will be unable to establish, at the time the interest accrues, that the payment can reasonably be expected to be included in income within a reasonable period of time.

Recommendation 1.2 - Definition of financial instrument and substitute payment

61. Recommendation 1.2 defines when an arrangement should be treated as a financial instrument and when a payment should be treated as a substitute payment.

Definition of "financial instrument" to be determined under local law

62. The underlying policy of Recommendation 1 is to align the tax treatment of the payments made under a financing or equity instrument so that amounts that are not fully taxed in the payee jurisdiction are not treated as a deductible expense in the payer jurisdiction. Accordingly, Recommendation 1.2(c) encourages jurisdictions to treat any arrangement that produces a financing or equity return as a financial instrument and to tax those arrangements under the domestic rules for taxing debt, equity or derivatives.

63. The definitions of "equity return" and "financing return" set out in Recommendation 12.1 provide further detail on the types of payments that should be brought within the hybrid financial instrument rule under domestic implementing legislation. These terms are intended to be in line with those used in international and generally recognised accounting standards and to capture any instrument issued by a person that provides the holder with a return based on the time-value of money or enterprise risk.

64. The hybrid financial instrument rule should not, however, apply to: arrangements for the supply of services such as lease or licensing agreements; arrangements for the

assumption of non-financial risk (such as insurance) or to asset transfers that do not incorporate the payment of an equity or financing return.

65. Notwithstanding that countries should make reasonable endeavours to adopt similar definitions of financial instrument; there will continue to be cases where it is difficult to determine whether a contract should be treated as a financial instrument or some other type of agreement, such as sales contract or a contract for the assumption of risk. While Recommendation 1.2(c) encourages jurisdictions to ensure that the hybrid financial instrument rules apply to any arrangement to the extent it produces a financing or equity return, the rules are not intended to standardise the categories of financial instrument or to harmonise their tax treatment and, where the dividing line is unclear and the payment representing the financing or equity return is actually embedded into another transaction with a different character, it should be left to the laws of each country to determine whether and to what extent the payment is made under a financial instrument. Therefore, on the facts of any particular case, the question of whether an arrangement is a financial instrument (and therefore potentially subject to adjustment under the hybrid financial instrument rule) should be answered by reference to the domestic tax treatment of that arrangement.

Application of financial instrument definition to assets transfers

66. An arrangement that is treated as an asset transfer under local law will not generally be treated as a financial instrument under Recommendation 1, although, if such an arrangement is a hybrid transfer or incorporates a substitute payment, it may still be brought within the scope of the rule (see below). The application of the hybrid financial instrument rule to an ordinary asset transfer agreement is illustrated in **Example 1.26** where the purchase price paid by a trading entity to acquire shares gives rise to a D/NI outcome due to the fact that the trader is entitled to treat the purchase price as deductible, while the vendor does not include the payment in ordinary income. Although the payment gives rise to a D/NI outcome, the asset transfer agreement described in **Example 1.26** does not provide for an equity or financing return and therefore is outside both the language and intended scope of Recommendation 1.

67. **Example 1.27** provides an illustration of the type of transaction that could be treated as a financial instrument in one jurisdiction and an asset transfer in another. In this case the purchase price for the transfer of an asset includes an interest component which is intended to compensate the payee for the deferral in payment. The buyer treats the interest portion of the purchase price as giving rise to a separate deductible expense for tax purposes while the vendor treats the entire amount (including the interest component) as consideration for the transfer of the asset. In this case the example concludes that the payment is not subject to adjustment under the hybrid financial instrument rule in the jurisdiction of the vendor because the arrangement does not fall within the rules for taxing debt, equity or financial derivatives under local law. From the vendor's perspective, the transaction is indistinguishable from the transaction in **Example 1.26**. A further illustration is provided in **Example 1.30** where an agreement for the sale and purchase of shares in an operating subsidiary contains an earn-out arrangement that provides the vendor with a return based on enterprise risk. While some jurisdictions may treat this payment as deductible, other jurisdictions would treat this type of earn-out clause simply as a mechanic for calculating the purchase price for the sale of an asset and would not treat payments made under such a clause as an equity return under a financial instrument. It is therefore left to local law to determine whether the equity return is to be

characterised as a return under a financial instrument and brought within the scope of the hybrid financial instrument rule.

Application of the rule in cases where the counterparty does not treat the arrangement as a financial instrument

68. Taxpayers that enter into an arrangement that falls within the scope of the hybrid financial instrument rule should continue to apply the rule even when the counterparty does not treat the arrangement as a financial instrument and/or the counterparty jurisdiction has not implemented the report's recommendations. In such cases, however, the amount of the adjustment under the rule will be restricted to the amount of equity or financing return under the instrument. This principle is illustrated in **Example 1.25** where the lender provides finance to a related company under a finance lease. Although the lease is, in substance, a financing arrangement, the leasee treats the arrangement as an ordinary operating lease and the payments under the lease as deductible rental payments. The lessor is resident in a jurisdiction that has implemented the hybrid mismatch rules and, consistent with Recommendation 1.2, the lessor is required to treat the arrangement as a loan and the rental payments as periodic payments of interest and principal on that loan. The hybrid financial instrument rule is, however, only intended to capture mismatches that arise in respect of the equity or financing return and, accordingly, Recommendation 1.2(d) restricts the adjustment under the hybrid financial instrument rule to the extent of the financing return under the instrument.

Certain payments made to acquire a financial instrument treated as made under that financial instrument

69. A payment will be treated as made *under a financial instrument* if the payment is either required by the instrument or is in consideration for a release from a requirement under the instrument. The release from a requirement under a financial instrument does not, however, constitute a payment for the purposes of the hybrid financial iinstruemnt rule. This principle is illustrated in **Example 1.18** and **Example 1.20**. In **Example 1.18** a holder receives a one-off payment in consideration for agreeing to a change in the terms of a loan. The example concludes that the payment should be treated as a payment made under the instrument, as it is a payment in consideration for the release from an obligation under that instrument. In **Example 1.20** a parent company forgives a loan owed by one of its subsidiaries and claims a deduction for the unpaid principal and interest. Although the release of the debt does not trigger ordinary income for the subsidiary, the resulting D/NI outcome is not caught by the hybrid financial instrument rule because the release of rights under a financial instrument is not a payment under that financial instrument.

70. A payment made by a person in consideration for the transfer of an existing financial instrument is a payment for the disposal of the instrument rather than a payment made under it (although the payment to acquire that share or bond may include a substitute payment or be made under another separate financial instrument). This principle is illustrated in **Example 1.36** in respect of the transfer of a bond that carries the right to accrued but unpaid interest. The purchaser pays a premium for the bond that reflects this accrued interest component. The premium is deductible under the laws of the purchaser's jurisdiction and treated as giving rise to an exempt gain under the laws of the seller's jurisdiction. Although this payment gives rise to a mismatch in tax treatment the payment will not be treated as a "payment under a financial instrument" unless the

contract to acquire the bond is otherwise treated as a financial instrument under Recommendation 1.

71. A payment made to acquire an instrument should, however, be treated as a payment made under that instrument if the acquisition discharges, in whole or part, obligations owed under the instrument or neutralises the economic and tax consequences for the issuer. This is illustrated in **Example 1.19** where an issuer of a bond pays a premium to buy back a bond from the holder. While the cost of acquiring the bond from the holder is consideration for the transfer of the bond and not a payment required by the terms of the bond itself, the payment secures a release from the issuer's obligations under the instrument and will therefore be treated as a payment made under that financial instrument.

Hybrid transfers

72. The report recommends that jurisdictions treat certain transfers of financial instruments (*hybrid transfers*) as financial instruments within the scope of the hybrid financial instrument rule even when that jurisdiction would ordinarily treat payments made under that arrangement as made under an asset transfer agreement. A hybrid transfer is any arrangement to transfer a financial instrument where, as a consequence of the economics of the transaction and the way it is structured, the laws of two jurisdictions take opposing views on whether the transferor and transferee have ownership of the underlying asset. Ownership, in this context, means the owner of the payment flows on the underlying asset as opposed to legal ownership of the asset itself.

73. While a hybrid transfer can arise in the context of an ordinary sale and purchase agreement where there is a conflict in the determination of the timing of the asset transfer (see **Example 1.37**), the hybrid transfer rules are particularly targeted at sale and re-purchase (repo) and securities lending transactions where the rights and obligations of the parties are structured in such a way that the transferor remains exposed to the financing or equity return on the financial instrument transferred under the arrangement.

74. In the case of repo transaction that gives rise to a hybrid transfer, the transferor is taxed on the arrangement in accordance with its substance, so that the underlying transfer is ignored for tax purposes and the payments under the hybrid transfer are treated as payments under a financial instrument, while the transferee generally respects the legal arrangements entered into by the parties and treats the hybrid transfer as an asset sale. An illustration of a repo transaction that is treated as a hybrid transfer is set out in **Example 1.31**. In that example the parties enter into a collateralised loan that is structured as a repo over shares. The transferor's jurisdiction taxes the arrangement in accordance with its substance (treating the purchase price for the shares as a loan and the transferred shares as collateral for that loan) while the repo is taxed in the transferee's jurisdiction in accordance with its form (the sale and re-purchase of an asset). Both taxpayers therefore treat themselves as the owner of the subject matter of the repo (the transferred shares) and the arrangement therefore falls into the definition a hybrid transfer.

75. Examples of securities lending transactions that give rise to a hybrid transfer are set out in **Example 1.32**, **Example 1.33** and **Example 1.34** and also in **Example 2.2**. In these cases the transferee (the borrower under the arrangement) agrees to return the transferred securities (or their equivalent) plus any dividends or interest received on those securities during the term of the loan. The transferor's jurisdiction taxes the arrangement in accordance with its substance, disregarding the transfer and treating the transferor as if it continued to hold the underlying securities, while the transferee's jurisdiction treats the

transfer in accordance with its form and taxes the arrangement as the purchase and sale of securities.

76. Hybrid transfer's generally give rise to a D/NI outcome because one jurisdiction treats the equity or financing return on the transferred instrument as a deductible expense under that hybrid transfer, while the other jurisdiction treats that same amount as a return on the underlying asset (and, accordingly, as excluded or exempt from taxation or eligible for some other type of tax relief). Therefore, when applying the secondary rule, the payee may be required to make an adjustment to the tax treatment of the payment on the underlying instrument even though this payment is not treated by the payee jurisdiction as a payment under the hybrid transfer itself. Thus, in **Example 1.31** the transferee is required to apply the secondary rule to include a dividend payment on the transferred share in ordinary income despite the fact that, under local law, this payment would be regarded as a payment on the underlying shares and not a payment under the repo itself. In **Example 1.32** the transferee under a share-lending transaction makes a deductible payment of a manufactured dividend. Although the recipient of the manufactured dividend treats that dividend as having been paid on the underlying shares, the payment is treated as giving rise to a D/NI outcome under a hybrid financial instrument because of the deduction claimed by the counterparty to the share loan.

77. Hybrid transfers are treated as a type of hybrid financial instrument because they are, in substance, financial instruments rather than asset transfers and they give rise to a difference in tax treatment that allows them to be used as part of a structured arrangement to engineer a cross-border mismatch. As with other types of financial instrument, the hybrid transfer rules do not take into account whether the funds obtained under the transfer have been invested in assets that generate a taxable or exempt return. The adjustment that the transferor is required to make in respect of payment under a repo or stock loan will therefore not be affected by whether the transferor is taxable on the financing or equity return on the transferred asset. For example, the outcomes described in **Example 1.31** and **Example 1.33** are not affected by whether the transferor under the repo or the share lending arrangement, is taxable on the dividend it receives on the shares.

78. As hybrid transfers are a type of financial instrument, an adjustment is only required under the rule if the mismatch in outcomes can be attributed to the tax treatment of the hybrid transfer under the laws of the payer and payee jurisdictions. An adjustment to the tax treatment of payments under a hybrid transfer will not affect the ability of a trading entity to claim a genuine trading loss in respect of the disposal of an asset. This principle is explained further in **Example 1.34** and **Example 1.37**.

Substitute payments

79. The other category of asset transfers that are subject to adjustment under Recommendation 1 are transfers of financial instruments where the payment of a financing or equity return under that asset transfer gives rise to a D/NI outcome that has the effect of undermining the integrity of the hybrid financial instrument rules. The transfer will have this effect where:

(a) the transferor secures a better tax outcome on the payment under the asset transfer than it would have obtained if it had held onto the underlying instrument;

(b) the transferee treats the payment under the asset transfer as deductible while the return on the underlying instrument will be treated as exempt or excluded from income; or

(c) the transfer has the effect of taking instrument outside of the scope of the hybrid financial instrument rule.

80. The substitute payments rule neutralises any D/NI outcome in respect of the payment of a financing or equity return under asset transfer agreement when the transfer of the underlying financial instrument would give rise to one of the above outcomes. Under this rule a taxpayer that buys a financial instrument for a consideration that includes a financing or equity return, will be denied a deduction for the payment if: that return would have been included in ordinary income of the payee; would not have been included in ordinary income of the payer or would have given rise to hybrid mismatch if it had been made directly under the financial instrument.

81. The substitute payment rules apply to any type of D/NI outcome (regardless of whether such outcome is attributable to the terms of the instrument, the tax status of the parties or the context in which the asset is held). The rule is, however, confined to payments that give rise to a financing or equity return in respect of the underlying instrument. It would not ordinarily apply, for example, to a payment made to settle a claim for a breach of warranty under an asset sale agreement.

82. **Example 1.30**, **Example 1.35**, and **Example 1.36** explain the application of the hybrid financial instrument rule to substitute payments. In **Example 1.30** the hybrid financial instrument rule is applied to a purchase price adjustment under a share sale agreement where differences between the tax treatment of dividends and sale consideration in the payee/transferor jurisdiction allow the payee/transferor to substitute what would otherwise have been a taxable dividend for a non-taxable exchange gain. **Example 1.35** illustrates how the substitute payment definition prevents a payer/transferee manufacturing a deduction for a payment under an asset transfer agreement when the transferee has no economic loss. **Example 1.36** describes a situation where the transfer of a financial instrument takes the instrument outside the scope of the hybrid financial instrument rule. In that example the substitute payment definition will apply to adjust the tax consequences for the parties to the transfer to neutralise any mismatch in tax outcomes.

Recommendation 1.3 - Rule only applies to a payment under a financial instrument that results in a hybrid mismatch

83. Section 1.3 sets out the general rule for determining when a mismatch under a financial instrument is a hybrid mismatch.

Identifying the mismatch

84. A mismatch will arise in respect of a payment made under a financial instrument to the extent that the payment is deductible under the laws of one jurisdiction (the payer jurisdiction) and not included in ordinary income by a taxpayer under the laws of any other jurisdiction where the payment is treated as being received (the payee jurisdiction).

85. The identification of a mismatch as a hybrid mismatch under a financial instrument is primarily a legal question that requires an analysis of the general rules for determining the character, amount and timing of payments under a financial instrument in the payer and payee jurisdictions. In general it will not be necessary for the taxpayer or tax administration to know precisely how the payments under a financial instrument have actually been taken into account in the calculation of the counterparty's taxable income in order to apply the rule. It is expected that taxpayers will know their own tax position in

respect of a payment so that, in practice, a mismatch will be identified by comparing the actual tax treatment of an instrument in the taxpayer jurisdiction with its expected tax treatment in the counterparty jurisdiction.

86. In order to determine whether a payment has given rise to a mismatch, it is necessary to know the identity of the counterparty and the tax rules applying in the counterparty jurisdiction. In most cases the counterparty will be the person with the obligation (or right) to make (or receive) the payment and the counterparty jurisdiction will be the jurisdiction where that person is tax resident. In certain cases, however, where the counterparty is transparent or has a taxable presence in more than one jurisdiction, it may be necessary to look to the laws of more than one jurisdiction to determine whether the payment will give rise to a mismatch.

Deduction in any jurisdiction sufficient to trigger the application of the rule

87. A payment that is treated as paid under the laws of more than one jurisdiction only needs to be deductible under the laws of one jurisdiction in order to trigger a potential D/NI outcome. This principle is illustrated in **Example 1.23** where a hybrid entity borrows money from a related person in the same jurisdiction under an instrument that is treated as equity under local law. The hybrid entity is treated as making a non-deductible/exempt dividend payment for local law purposes but the payment under the instrument is treated as deductible under the laws of the parent jurisdiction. The arrangement therefore gives rise to a D/NI outcome even though, as between the direct payer and payee, there is no mismatch in tax treatment.

88. In those cases where the payer is transparent, the burden will be on the taxpayer claiming the benefit of the exemption or relief from taxation to establish, to the satisfaction of its own tax administration, that the payment has not given rise to a deduction under the laws of another jurisdiction.

Inclusion in any jurisdiction sufficient to discharge application of the rule

89. If the payment is brought into account as ordinary income in at least one jurisdiction, then there will be no mismatch for the rule to apply to. This principle is illustrated in **Example 1.8** which involves the payment of interest to a branch of a company that is resident in another jurisdiction. In this case it is necessary to also look to the laws of both the residence and the branch jurisdiction to definitively establish whether a mismatch has arisen.

90. It will be the taxpayer who has the burden of establishing, to the reasonable satisfaction of the tax administration, how the tax treatment of the payment in the other payee jurisdiction impacts on the amount of the adjustment required under the rule. The initial burden of proof may be discharged by the taxpayer demonstrating that the payment has actually been recorded as ordinary income on the tax return in the other jurisdiction.

Mismatch attributable to the terms of the instrument

91. The hybrid financing instrument rule only applies where the mismatch in tax treatment is attributable to the terms of the instrument rather than the status of the taxpayer or the context in which the instrument is held.

92. Differences in tax treatment that arise from applying different accounting policies to the same instrument will be treated as attributable to the terms of the instrument if the differences in accounting outcomes are based on the terms of the instrument itself. This is

illustrated in **Example 1.21** in respect of a payment under a bond that carries a contingent entitlement to interest. The loan is treated as debt under the laws of both the payee and payer jurisdictions. However, due to differences in the way the interest is accounted for tax purposes by the two countries, the interest is treated as deductible by the payer in the year it accrues but is only treated as income by the payee when (and if) such interest is actually paid. In this case the difference in accounting treatment gives rise to a hybrid mismatch unless the taxpayer can establish, to the satisfaction of the tax authority, that the payment will be included in income under the law of payee jurisdiction within a reasonable period of time.

93. It is not uncommon for the tax treatment of an instrument to depend on such factors as whether the issuer and holder are related or on the period an instrument has been held. Such factors directly affect the relationship between the holder and issuer and should be treated as part of the terms of the instrument. In **Example 1.1** the hybrid financial instrument rule is applied to a dividend payment, even though the exemption only applies where the payee has held more than 10% of the shares in the payer for at least one year prior to the payment date. **Example 1.13** provides an illustration of this principle in respect of a payer where the conditions for deductibility turn, in part, on whether the payment is made intra-group. The fact that the borrower and lender are members of the same group is an element of the relationship between the parties and should therefore be included within the terms of the loan instrument for the purposes of determining the application of the hybrid financial instrument rule notwithstanding that there may be no requirement for the loan to be held intra-group.

94. The *terms of the instrument* should also include any element directly affecting the relationship between the payer and the payee and the circumstances in which an instrument was issued or held if those circumstances are economically and commercially relevant to the relationship between the parties and affect the tax treatment of the instrument. This is illustrated in **Example 1.12** where all the shareholders subscribe for debt in proportion to their shareholding in the issuer. Under the laws of the holder's jurisdiction, debt that is issued in proportion to equity is re-characterised as a share and payments on such debt are treated as exempt dividends. The resulting difference in characterisation between the jurisdiction of the issuer and the holder gives rise to a mismatch in tax outcomes. The fact that the shareholder subscribes for debt in proportion to its shareholding is commercially significant to the relationship between the parties so that a mismatch in tax outcomes which is dependent on such facts should be treated as attributable to the terms of the instrument.

Mismatch that is solely attributable to the status of the taxpayer or the context in which the instrument is held

95. The test under Recommendation 1.3 for whether a payment under a financial instrument has given rise to a *hybrid* mismatch focuses on the ordinary or expected tax treatment of the instrument. A mismatch that is solely attributable to the status of the taxpayer or the context in which the financial instrument is held will not be a hybrid mismatch. One way of testing for whether a mismatch is attributable to the terms of the instrument is to pose a counterfactual test that asks whether the terms of the instrument were sufficient to bring about the mismatch in tax outcomes. This can be done by contrasting the parties' actual tax treatment with what it would have been if the instrument had been held directly and both the payer and payee were ordinary taxpayers that computed their income and expenditure in accordance with the ordinary rules applicable to taxpayers of the same type. If the same mismatch would have arisen had the

instrument been directly entered into by a taxpayer of ordinary status, then the mismatch will be attributable to the terms of the instrument itself rather than the status of the taxpayer or the context in which the instrument is held.

Tax status of the counterparty

96. The hybrid financial instrument rule does not apply to mismatches that are solely attributable to the status of the taxpayer. Where, however, the mismatch can also be attributed to the tax treatment of the instrument (i.e. the mismatch would have arisen even in respect of payment between taxpayers of ordinary status) the hybrid financial instrument rule will continue to apply although the adjustment may not, in practice have any impact on the tax position of the parties to the arrangement. An example illustrating the application of this principle is set out in **Example 1.5** where a deductible interest payment is made to a sovereign wealth fund that is a tax exempt entity under the laws of its own jurisdiction. The rule will not apply if the tax exempt status of the fund is the only reason for the D/NI outcome. If the hybrid financial instrument rule would ordinarily apply to such an instrument, however, then it will continue to apply and may result in a denial of a deduction for an amount paid under the arrangement.

Circumstances in which the instrument is held

97. The hybrid financial instrument rule does not apply to mismatches that are solely attributable to the circumstances under which an instrument is held. This principle is illustrated in **Example 1.8** where the payee holds the instrument through a foreign branch. The fact that the loan is held through a foreign branch is not a term of the instrument or part of the relationship between the parties. Therefore, if the mismatch arises solely due to the operation of the branch exemption in the residence country then the mismatch will not be a hybrid mismatch. The principle is also illustrated in **Example 1.9** where a taxpayer holds a bond issued by a company through a tax exempt savings account. In that case any mismatch in tax outcomes is not attributable to the terms of the instrument but the conditions under which the instrument is held.

Payments to a taxpayer in a pure territorial regime

98. A mismatch in tax treatment that arises in respect of a cross-border payment made to a taxpayer in a pure territorial tax regime (i.e. a jurisdiction that excludes or exempts all foreign source income) will not be caught by the hybrid financial instrument rule because the mismatch in tax outcomes will be attributable to the nature of the payer (i.e. to the fact that the payer is a non-resident making payments of foreign source income) rather than the terms of the instrument itself. This principle is illustrated in **Example 1.7** where the payee jurisdiction does not tax income from foreign sources. In the example, a related non-resident payer makes a payment of deductible interest that is treated as foreign source income. The resulting mismatch is not attributable to the terms of the instrument but to the fact that the payee is exempt on all foreign source income. The mismatch is therefore not caught by the hybrid financial instrument rule. This result should be contrasted with **Example 1.1** where the payee jurisdiction exempts only foreign dividend payments. In that case, the exemption on foreign source income applies only to a particular category of income (i.e. dividends) so that the tax exemption turns not only on the source of the payment but the character of the instrument under the laws of the payee jurisdiction and, accordingly, the terms of the instrument itself.

Recommendation 1.4 - Scope of the rule

99. In order to strike a balance between a rule that is clear and comprehensive and that is properly targeted and administrable, Recommendation 1.4 limits the scope of the hybrid financial instrument rule to payments made to related persons and under structured arrangements. See Recommendations 10 and 11 regarding the definition of structured arrangements and related persons.

Recommendation 1.5 - Exceptions to the rule

100. Recommendation 1.5 provides an exception for entities where the tax policy of the deduction under the laws of the payer jurisdiction is to preserve tax neutrality for the payer and payee.

Entities entitled to deduct dividends not within the scope of the hybrid financial instrument rule

101. In order to preserve its tax neutrality, a jurisdiction may grant an investment vehicle, such as a mutual fund or real estate investment trust (REIT), the right to deduct dividend payments. Although the payment of a deductible dividend is likely to give rise to a mismatch in tax outcomes, such a payment will not generally give rise to a hybrid mismatch under Recommendation 1 provided any resulting mismatch will be attributable to the payer's tax status rather than the ordinary tax treatment of dividends under the laws of that jurisdiction. As noted in **Example 1.10**, however, under Recommendation 2.1 of the report the payee jurisdiction should not permit a taxpayer to claim an exemption or equivalent relief from double taxation in respect of a deductible dividend paid by such an entity.

Application of the exception to securitisation vehicles and other investment funds

102. In certain cases, the tax neutrality of an investment vehicle depends not on the particular tax status of the vehicle but on assumptions as to the tax treatment of the instruments issued by the vehicle. One example of this is a securitisation vehicle or an infrastructure investment fund that is financed almost entirely by way of borrowing and where all, or substantially all, of the income is paid out to lenders in the form of deductible interest. The exception to the hybrid financial instrument rule set out in Recommendation 1.5 is intended to protect the tax neutrality of these vehicles while ensuring that they cannot be used to defer or avoid tax at the level of the payee. Accordingly, the exception applies where the regulatory and tax framework in the establishment jurisdiction has the effect that the financial instruments issued by the investment vehicle will result in all or substantially all of the income of the vehicle being paid and distributed to holders within a reasonable period of time and where the tax policy of the establishment jurisdiction is that such payments will be subject to tax in the hands of investors. Recommendation 1.5 specifically notes that the defensive rule in Recommendation 1.1(b) should continue to apply to such payments on receipt.

Chapter 2

Specific recommendations for the tax treatment of financial instruments

Recommendation 2

1. Denial of dividend exemption for deductible payments

In order to prevent D/NI outcomes from arising under a financial instrument, a dividend exemption that is provided for relief against economic double taxation should not be granted under domestic law to the extent the dividend payment is deductible by the payer. Equally, jurisdictions should consider adopting similar restrictions for other types of dividend relief granted to relieve economic double taxation on underlying profits.

2. Restriction of foreign tax credits under a hybrid transfer

In order to prevent duplication of tax credits under a hybrid transfer, any jurisdiction that grants relief for tax withheld at source on a payment made under a hybrid transfer should restrict the benefit of such relief in proportion to the net taxable income of the taxpayer under the arrangement.

3. Scope of the rule

There is no limitation as to the scope of these recommendations.

Overview

103. Recommendation 2 sets out two specific recommendations for changes to the tax treatment cross-border financial instruments.

(a) Under Recommendation 2.1 the report recommends that countries do not grant a dividend exemption or equivalent tax relief for payments that are treated as deductible by the payer.

(b) Under Recommendation 2.2 the report recommends limiting the ability of a taxpayer to claim relief from foreign withholding tax on instruments that are held subject to a hybrid transfer.

104. Rather than simply adjusting the tax treatment of a payment in order to align it with the tax consequences in another jurisdiction, the purpose of these recommendations goes further by seeking to bring the treatment of these instruments into line with the tax policy outcomes that will generally apply to the same instruments in the wholly-domestic context.

105. The domestic law changes required to implement Recommendation 2 will depend on the current state of a country's domestic law. There are a number of different ways of

restricting the benefit of double taxation relief and these recommendations only set out recommended outcomes rather than specifying how such changes ought to be implemented.

Recommendation 2.1 - Denial of dividend exemption for deductible payments

106. The purpose of a dividend exemption is generally to avoid imposing an additional layer of taxation at the shareholder level on income that has already been subject to tax at the entity level. Recommendation 2.1 recommends that jurisdictions that provide payees with an exemption for dividends, as a mechanism for relieving economic double taxation on corporate profits, do not extend that exemption to payments that have not borne tax at the entity level.

107. The operation of this Recommendation is set out in **Example 1.1**. In that example a taxpayer borrows money under an interest bearing loan from a related taxpayer in another jurisdiction. The issuer of the loan is allowed a deduction for the interest while the holder treats the payment as a dividend. Any mismatch in tax outcomes, however, is eliminated if the payee jurisdiction prevents the payee from taking advantage of a dividend exemption in respect of a payment that is deductible under the laws of the payer jurisdiction. Similar outcomes are identified in **Example 1.2**, **Example 1.3** and **Example 1.4**.

Recommendation extends to other types of dividend relief

108. Recommendation 2.1 also encourages countries to consider introducing restrictions on the availability of other types of double taxation relief for dividends. **Example 1.3** illustrates the potential application of the Recommendation to a deductible dividend subject to a reduced tax rate, **Example 1.4** illustrates the application of the Recommendation to a payment that is eligible for an underlying foreign tax credit and **Example 2.1** illustrates the possible application of the Recommendation to a payment that is eligible for a domestic tax credit.

Recommendation applies only to payments characterised as dividends

109. The Recommendation only affects payments that would otherwise qualify for a dividend exemption or equivalent tax relief and does not deal with other types of non-inclusion (such as a payment that is treated as a return of capital under a share). This principle is illustrated in **Example 1.13** where a taxpayer treats a loan from its parent as having been issued at a discount and accrues this discount as an expense over the life of the loan. The parent jurisdiction, however, does not adopt the same accounting treatment as its subsidiary and treats all the payments on the instrument as loan principal or a return of share capital. A rule limiting double taxation relief on deductible dividend payments will not apply to the facts of that example, because the payment is not treated as a dividend under the domestic laws of the payee jurisdiction.

Recommendation applies only to dividends that are deductible by the issuer

110. In determining whether a dividend is deductible for the purposes of Recommendation 2.1 a taxpayer will generally look to the instrument under which the payment was made and whether the issuer of that instrument was entitled to a deduction for such payment. The fact that a dividend triggers a deduction in another jurisdiction for separate taxpayer due to the existence of a hybrid entity structure or under a hybrid

transfer, will not generally trigger a denial of the dividend exemption in the payee jurisdiction.

111. This principle is illustrated in **Example 1.31** where the payment of a dividend on shares that have been subject to a repo triggers a deduction for the repo counterparty in a third jurisdiction. The payment, however, does not trigger a deduction for the issuer of the shares so that the recommended changes to domestic law in Recommendation 2.1 would not be expected to restrict the holder's entitlement to an exemption on the dividend. The principle is further illustrated in **Example 1.23** where a hybrid entity borrows money from a related person in the same jurisdiction under an instrument that is treated as equity under local law. The hybrid entity is treated as making a non-deductible payment for local law purposes but the payment under the instrument is treated as deductible under the laws of the parent jurisdiction. Recommendation 2.1 would not be expected to restrict the holder's entitlement to an exemption on the dividend as the payment under the hybrid financial instrument does not trigger a deduction for the issuer of the shares.

Recommendation 2.2 - Restriction of foreign tax credits under a hybrid transfer

112. A hybrid transfer exploits differences between two countries in their rules for attributing income from an asset with the effect that the same payment is treated as derived simultaneously by different taxpayers resident in different jurisdictions. Because there is only one underlying payment, however, the economic benefit of that payment will be shared between the parties under the terms of the hybrid transfer. Recommendation 2.2 sets out a rule that aligns the rules for granting of foreign withholding tax relief with the economic benefit of the payment as shared under the terms of the hybrid transfer. It does this by restricting the amount of the credit in proportion to the net taxable income of the taxpayer under the arrangement.

113. The operation of this Recommendation is set out in **Example 2.2**. In that example a taxpayer borrows securities under an arrangement that generally includes the requirement to make "manufactured payments" to the lender of any amounts paid on the underlying securities during the period of the loan. A hybrid transfer arises because the lender is treated as continuing to receive payments on the underlying securities. The borrower, however, also treats itself as receiving the same income on the underlying asset and is allowed a deduction for the manufactured payments made to the lender. The hybrid transfer therefore permits both parties to claim withholding tax credits on the payment which has the effect of lowering their effective tax burden under the instrument. By limiting the amount of the credit in proportion to the taxpayer's net income under the arrangement the tax treatment is brought into line with the tax treatment of a non-hybrid financing transaction.

Recommendation 2.3 - Scope

114. The report recommends that those countries applying Recommendations 2.1 and 2.2 should be able to deny the benefit of the exemption or tax credit without any qualification as to scope

Chapter 3

Disregarded hybrid payments rule

Recommendation 3

1. Neutralise the mismatch to the extent the payment gives rise to a D/NI outcome

The following rule should apply to a disregarded payment made by a hybrid payer that results in a hybrid mismatch:

(a) The payer jurisdiction will deny a deduction for such payment to the extent it gives rise to a D/NI outcome.

(b) If the payer jurisdiction does not neutralise the mismatch then the payee jurisdiction will require such payment to be included in ordinary income to the extent the payment gives rise to a D/NI outcome.

(c) No mismatch will arise to the extent that the deduction in the payer jurisdiction is set-off against income that is included in income under the laws of both the payee and the payer jurisdiction (i.e. dual inclusion income).

(d) Any deduction that exceeds the amount of dual inclusion income (the excess deduction) may be eligible to be set-off against dual inclusion income in another period.

2. Rule only applies to disregarded payments made by a hybrid payer

For the purpose of this rule:

(a) A disregarded payment is a payment that is deductible under the laws of the payer jurisdiction and is not recognised under the laws of the payee jurisdiction.

(b) A person will be a hybrid payer where the tax treatment of the payer under the laws of the payee jurisdiction causes the payment to be a disregarded payment.

3. Rule only applies to payments that result in a hybrid mismatch

A disregarded payment made by a hybrid payer results in a hybrid mismatch if, under the laws of the payer jurisdiction, the deduction may be set-off against income that is not dual inclusion income.

4. Scope of the rule

This rule only applies if the parties to the mismatch are in the same control group or where the payment is made under a structured arrangement and the taxpayer is a party to that structured arrangement.

Overview

115. A deductible payment can give rise to a D/NI outcome where the payment is made by a hybrid entity that is disregarded under the laws of the payee jurisdiction. Such disregarded payments can give rise to tax policy concerns where that deduction is available to be set-off against an amount that is not treated as income under the laws of the payee jurisdiction (i.e. against income that is not "dual inclusion income"). The purpose of the disregarded hybrid payments rule is to prevent a taxpayer from entering into structured arrangements, or arrangements with members of the same control group, that exploit differences in the tax treatment of payer to achieve such outcomes.

116. The primary recommendation under the deductible hybrid payments rule is that the payer jurisdiction should restrict the amount of the deduction that can be claimed for a disregarded payment to the total amount of dual inclusion income. The defensive rule requires the payee jurisdiction to include an equivalent amount in ordinary income.

117. An item of income should be treated as dual inclusion income if it is taken into account as income under the laws of both the payer and payee jurisdictions. It may be possible to undertake a line by line comparison of each item of income in straightforward cases where the hybrid payer is party to only a few transactions. In more complex cases however, countries may wish to adopt a simpler implementation solution for tracking deductions and items of dual inclusion income, which is based, as much as possible, on existing domestic rules, administrative guidance, presumptions and tax calculations while continuing to meet the basic policy objectives of the disregarded hybrid payments rule. Examples of possible implementation solutions are identified in Chapters 3, 6 and 7 and described in further detail in the examples.

118. Jurisdictions use different tax accounting periods and have different rules for recognising when items of income or expenditure have been derived or incurred. These timing and quantification differences should not be treated as giving rise to mismatches in tax outcomes under Recommendation 3. Excess deductions that are subject to restriction in the payer jurisdiction under the disregarded hybrid payments rule may be carried over to another period, in accordance with the ordinary rules for the treatment of net losses, and applied against dual inclusion income in that period.

Recommendation 3.1 - Neutralise the mismatch to the extent the payment gives rise to a D/NI outcome

119. The Recommendation for disregarded hybrid payments is to neutralise the effect of the mismatch through the adoption of a linking rule that aligns the tax outcomes for the payer and payee. This report recommends that the primary response should be to deny the payer a deduction for payments made under a disregarded payment with the payee jurisdiction applying a defensive rule that would require a disregarded payment to be included in ordinary income in the event the payer was located in a jurisdiction that did not apply the disregarded hybrid payments rule.

120. The hybrid mismatch rule does not apply, however, to the extent the deduction for the disregarded payment is set-off against "dual inclusion income", which is income that is taken into account as income under the laws of both the payer and payee jurisdictions. In order to address timing differences in the recognition of deductions for disregarded payments and dual inclusion income any excess deduction (i.e. net loss) from such disregarded payments that cannot be set-off against dual inclusion income in the current

period remains eligible to be set-off against dual inclusion income that arises in another period under the ordinary rules that allow for the carry-forward (or back) of losses to other taxable periods.

Deductible payments caught by the rule

121. In order to be a disregarded payment, the payment must be deductible under the laws of the payer jurisdiction. The meaning of deductible and deduction is the same as that used in the other recommendations in the report and generally covers items of current expenditure such as service payments, rents, royalties, interest and other amounts that may be set-off directly against ordinary income. The term does not cover the cost of acquiring a capital asset or an allowance for depreciation or amortisation.

122. Unlike the hybrid financial instrument rule, which focuses only on the tax treatment of the instrument, and not on the status of the counterparty or the context in which the instrument is held, the disregarded hybrid payments rule should only operate to the extent that the payer is actually entitled to a deduction for a payment under local law. Accordingly the rule will not apply to the extent the taxpayer is subject to transaction or entity specific rules that prevent the payment from being deducted (including the hybrid financial instrument rule).

123. The interaction between Recommendations 1 and 3 is explained in **Example 3.2** where a PE in the payer jurisdiction borrows money from the parent of the group. Both the loan and the interest payment are disregarded under the laws of the payee jurisdiction. In the example the payer jurisdiction first applies the hybrid financial instrument rule to determine whether interest on the loan is deductible before any adjustment is made under the disregarded hybrid payments rule.

No mismatch to the extent the deduction does not exceed dual inclusion income

124. A deductible payment will not be treated as giving rise to a mismatch in tax outcomes if the deduction does not exceed dual inclusion income. This is illustrated in **Example 3.1** where a hybrid entity (an entity that is treated as a separate taxpayer in its jurisdiction of establishment but as transparent under the laws of its parent) makes an interest payment to its non-resident parent that is disregarded under the laws of the parent jurisdiction. The adjustment under the disregarded hybrid payments rule only operates to the extent that the interest payment exceeds dual inclusion income for the hybrid entity in the payer jurisdiction.

Dual inclusion income

125. An item will be dual inclusion income if it is included in income under the laws of both the payer and payee jurisdictions. The identification of whether an item should be treated as dual inclusion income is primarily a legal question that requires an comparison of the treatment of the income under the laws of the payer and payee jurisdictions. An amount should be treated as dual inclusion income if it is included in income under the laws of both jurisdictions even if there are differences in the way those jurisdictions value that item or in the accounting period in which the income is derived. In **Example 6.1**, which considers the application of the deductible hybrid payments rule, the parent and subsidiary jurisdictions use different timing and valuation rules for recognising the income and expenses of a hybrid entity. In that case, both jurisdictions apply their own timing and valuation rules for calculating the amount of dual inclusion income and

duplicate deductions arising in each period and the resulting timing difference does not impact on the operation of the rule.

126. Double taxation relief, such as a domestic dividend exemption granted by the payer jurisdiction or a foreign tax credit granted by the payee jurisdiction should not prevent an item from being treated as dual inclusion income where the effect of such relief is simply to avoid subjecting the income to an additional layer of taxation in either jurisdiction. Thus, while a payment of dual inclusion income will generally be recognised as ordinary income under the laws of both jurisdictions, an equity return should still qualify as dual inclusion income if the payment is subject to an exemption, exclusion, credit of other type of double taxation relief in the payer or payee jurisdiction that relieves the payment from economic double taxation. An example of this type of dual inclusion income is given in **Example 6.3** in respect of a structure that produces DD outcomes and **Example 7.1** in respect of the dual resident payer rule. In **Example 6.3** the expenses of a hybrid entity are funded by an intra-group dividend that is exempt from taxation in the hands of jurisdiction where the dividend is received but included as income under the laws of its parent. Allowing the hybrid entity a deduction against this type of exempt or excluded equity return preserves the intended tax policy outcomes in both jurisdictions and, accordingly, the dividend should be treated as dual inclusion income for the purposes of disregarded hybrid payments rule even where such dividend carries an entitlement to an underlying foreign tax credit in the payee jurisdiction. Such double taxation relief may give rise to tax policy concerns, however, if it has the effect of generating surplus tax relief that can be used to reduce or offset the tax on non-dual inclusion income. In determining whether to treat an item of income, which benefits from such double-taxation relief, as dual-inclusion income, countries should seek to strike a balance between rules that minimise compliance costs, preserve the intended effect of such double taxation relief and prevent taxpayers from entering into structures that undermine the integrity of the rules.

127. A tax administration may treat the net income of a controlled foreign company that is attributed to a shareholder of that company under a CFC or other offshore inclusion regime as dual inclusion income if the taxpayer can satisfy the tax administration that the effect of the CFC regime is to bring such income into tax at the full rate under the laws of both jurisdictions. **Example 6.4** sets out a simplified calculation to illustrate how income attributed under a CFC regime can be taken into account in determining the amount of dual inclusion income under a hybrid structure.

Primary response and defensive rule

128. Where a payment gives rise to a D/NI outcome the payer jurisdiction should apply the recommended response and deny the deduction for the payment to the extent that the deduction exceeds dual inclusion income. The defensive rule is the mirror image of the primary recommendation in that the payee jurisdiction recognises the same amount as ordinary income. The operation of the primary and secondary rules are described in further detail in **Example 3.2**.

Carry-forward of deductions to another period

129. Because the hybrid mismatch rules are generally not intended to impact on, or be affected by, timing differences, the disregarded hybrid payment rules contain a mechanism that allows the payer jurisdiction to carry-forward (or back if permitted under local law) a hybrid deduction to a period where it can be set-off against surplus dual

inclusion income. The Recommendation contemplates that the ordinary domestic rules governing the utilisation of losses would apply to such deductions. **Example 6.1** sets out an example of the operation of the carry-forward of excess deductions.

Implementation solution based on existing domestic rules

130. The disregarded hybrid payments rule caps the aggregate amount of hybrid deductions that can be claimed to the aggregate amount of dual inclusion income. In principle Recommendation 3 requires the taxpayer to individually identify the items of income that arise under the laws of both jurisdictions and to determine which of them have given rise to dual inclusion income. In those cases where the taxpayer has entered into a large number of transactions this approach could result in a significant compliance burden for taxpayers. In order to facilitate implementation and minimise compliance costs, tax administrations will wish to consider simpler implementation solutions. These solutions should be designed to produce substantially similar results to those described in this Chapter while avoiding unnecessary complexity.

131. In the case of the kind of structures covered by Recommendation 3 it will generally be the case that accounts showing the income and expenditure of the taxpayer will have been prepared under the laws of both jurisdictions. These accounts will generally be prepared under local law using domestic tax concepts. Tax administrations should use these existing sources of information and tax calculations as a starting point for identifying dual inclusion income. For instance, **Example 3.2** contemplates that the payer jurisdiction might prohibit a hybrid entity from surrendering the benefit of any net loss to another group member to the extent the entity has made deductible payments that were disregarded under the laws of payee jurisdiction and introduce other transaction specific rules that prevent that entity entering into arrangements that stream non-dual inclusion income to the hybrid entity in order to soak-up unused losses. **Example 3.2** further suggests that the payee jurisdiction could use the accounts prepared by the hybrid payer as a starting point and (after making transaction specific adjustments to determine the amount of dual inclusion income derived by the hybrid payer) require the payee to recognise, as ordinary income in each accounting period, the amount of any deductible intra-group payments to the extent these payments generate a net loss under the laws of the payer jurisdiction.

Recommendation 3.2 - Rule only applies to disregarded payments made by a hybrid payer

132. The disregarded hybrid payments rule applies where the reason the deductible payment is not recognised by the payee is because of the way the payer is treated under the laws of the payee jurisdiction. Recommendation 3 restricts the scope of the rule to *disregarded payments* made by a *hybrid payer*.

Disregarded payment

133. A disregarded payment is a payment that is not treated as a payment under the laws of the payee jurisdiction or that is not otherwise taken into account as a receipt for tax purposes. **Example 3.1** and **Example 3.2** both provide examples of disregarded payments. In **Example 3.1** the payment is made by a hybrid entity that is disregarded under the laws of the payee jurisdiction so that a deductible payment made by the hybrid entity to its immediate owner is similarly disregarded for tax purposes and does not give rise to income in the hands of the payee. In **Example 3.2** the payment is made within the

confines of a tax consolidation regime that treats all transactions and payments between consolidated group members as disregarded for tax purposes.

Hybrid payer

134. A person making a payment will be treated as a hybrid payer in circumstances where the tax treatment of the payer, under the laws of the payee jurisdiction, results in the payment being disregarded for tax purposes in the hands of the payee. The kinds of arrangements that cause a person to be a hybrid payer under Recommendation 3 will also generally cause that person to be a hybrid payer under Recommendation 6, which applies to DD outcomes using hybrid entities.

Recommendation 3.3 - Rule only applies to payments that result in a hybrid mismatch

135. A deduction for a disregarded payment made by a hybrid payer will give rise to tax policy concerns where the laws of the payer jurisdiction permit that deduction to be set-off against an amount that is not dual inclusion income. Accordingly, Recommendation 3.3 restricts the application of the disregarded hybrid payments rule to those cases where the deduction may be set-off against dual inclusion income.

136. There are a number of different techniques that a taxpayer can use in the payer jurisdiction to set-off a double deduction against non-dual inclusion income. The most common mechanism used to offset a deduction against non-dual inclusion income will be the use of a tax consolidation or grouping regime that allows the payer to apply the benefit of a deduction against the income of another entity within the same group. An example of this technique is set out in **Example 3.2**. Other techniques include making an investment through a reverse hybrid (an entity that is only treated as transparent under the laws of the payer jurisdiction) so that the resulting income is only brought into account under the laws of the payer jurisdiction. An example of such a structure is set out in **Example 6.1**. Alternatively, as explained in further detail in **Example 3.1**, the taxpayer may enter into a financial instrument or other arrangement where payments are only included in income in the payer jurisdiction. Non-dual inclusion income can also be set-off via merger-type transactions.

137. Regardless of the mechanism used to achieve the offset, if the effect of the structure is to create the opportunity for a deduction under a disregarded payment to be set-off against income that will not be brought into account as ordinary income under the laws of the payee jurisdiction, this will be sufficient to bring the payment within the scope of the disregarded hybrid payments rule.

Recommendation 3.4 - Scope of the rule

138. Recommendation 3.4 limits the scope of the rule to structured arrangements and mismatches that arise within a control group. See Recommendations 10 and 11 regarding the definition of structured arrangements and control group.

Chapter 4

Reverse hybrid rule

> **Recommendation 4**
>
> **1. Neutralise the mismatch to the extent the payment gives rise to D/NI outcome**
>
> In respect of a payment made to a reverse hybrid that results in a hybrid mismatch the payer jurisdiction should apply a rule that will deny a deduction for such payment to the extent it gives rise to a D/NI outcome.
>
> **2. Rule only applies to payment made to a reverse hybrid**
>
> A reverse hybrid is any person that is treated as a separate entity by an investor and as transparent under the laws of the establishment jurisdiction.
>
> **3. Rule only applies to hybrid mismatches**
>
> A payment results in a hybrid mismatch if a mismatch would not have arisen had the accrued income been paid directly to the investor.
>
> **4. Scope of the rule**
>
> The recommendation only applies where the investor, the reverse hybrid and the payer are members of the same control group or if the payment is made under a structured arrangement and the payer is party to that structured arrangement.

Overview

139. A deductible payment made to a reverse hybrid may give rise to a mismatch in tax outcomes where that payment is not included in ordinary income in the jurisdiction where the payee is established (the establishment jurisdiction) or in the jurisdiction of any investor in that payee (the investor jurisdiction). The recommended rule neutralises those mismatches that arise under a reverse hybrid structure where the mismatch is a result of both the establishment jurisdiction and the investor jurisdiction treating the payment to the reverse hybrid as owned by a taxpayer in the other jurisdiction. As for the other hybrid entity payments rules, the reverse hybrid rule can apply to a broad range of deductible payments (including interest, royalties, rents and payments for services). The rule only applies, however:

(a) to payments that are made to a reverse hybrid (as defined under Recommendation 4); and

(b) where the mismatch in tax outcomes would not have arisen had the payment been made directly to the investor.

140. A reverse hybrid is any person (including any unincorporated body of persons) that is treated as transparent under the laws of the jurisdiction where it is established but as a separate entity (i.e. opaque) under the laws of the jurisdiction of the investor. The transparency or opacity of an entity must be tested by reference to the payment that is subject to the reverse hybrid rule. A person will be treated as tax transparent in respect of a payment where the reverse hybrid attributes or allocates a payment that it has received to an investor and the effect of such attribution or allocation under the laws of the establishment jurisdiction is to treat the payment as it would have been treated had it been paid directly to that investor. The same person will be treated as opaque, from the perspective of the investor jurisdiction, if the effect of such attribution or allocation is ignored for tax purposes in the investor jurisdiction.

141. The mismatch in tax outcomes that arises in respect of a payment to a reverse hybrid will only be treated as a hybrid mismatch where that mismatch would not have arisen had the attributed payment been made directly to the investor. In order to prevent a reverse hybrid being inserted into a structure to circumvent the operation of the hybrid financial instrument rule, the reverse hybrid rule will also apply to the extent a direct payment would have been subject to adjustment under the primary rule in Recommendation 1.

142. The recommended response under the reverse hybrid rule is to deny the deduction on the payment to the extent of any hybrid mismatch.

143. The reverse hybrid rule will only apply where the payer, the reverse hybrid and the investor are part of the same control group or the payer is a party to a structured arrangement.

Recommendation 4.1 - Neutralise the mismatch to the extent the payment gives rise to a D/NI outcome

144. The response recommended in this report is to neutralise the effect of hybrid mismatches that arise under payments made to reverse hybrids through the adoption of a linking rule that denies a deduction for such payments to the extent they give rise to a D/NI outcome. This report only recommends the adoption of the primary response of denying the payer a deduction for payments made to a reverse hybrid. A defensive rule is unnecessary given the specific recommendations in Chapter 5 for changes CFC rules and other offshore investment regimes that would require payments to a reverse hybrid to be included in income in the investor jurisdiction.

Payment

145. The definition of payment is set out in further detail in Recommendation 12 and includes any amount that is capable of being paid including a distribution, credit or accrual. A payment will be treated as "deductible" if it is applied, or can be applied, to reduce a taxpayer's net income. Deductible payments generally include current expenditures such as rents, royalties, interest, payments for services and other payments that may be set-off against ordinary income under the laws of the payer jurisdiction in the period they are treated as made. The term would not typically cover the cost of acquiring a capital asset and would not extend to an allowance for a depreciation or amortisation.

146. A "payment" will give rise to a D/NI outcome under a reverse hybrid rule if it is deductible under the laws of the payer jurisdiction and if it is allocated or attributed by the reverse hybrid to the investor in circumstances that give rise to a mismatch in tax

outcomes. The payment does not incorporate any distribution or right to distribution from the reverse hybrid that occurs as a consequence of making a payment to a reverse hybrid. While the effect of allocating or attributing a payment to an investor may trigger an obligation on the part of the reverse hybrid to make a further payment to the investor (for example, in the form of a distribution), the tax treatment of that distribution will not generally be relevant to whether a D/NI outcome arises under the rule.

D/NI outcome in respect of a payment to a reverse hybrid

147. A D/NI outcome will arise in respect of a payment to a reverse hybrid to the extent that the payment is deductible under the laws of one jurisdiction (the payer jurisdiction) and not included in ordinary income by a taxpayer under the laws of any other jurisdiction where the payment is treated as being received (the payee jurisdiction).

Deduction in any jurisdiction sufficient to trigger application of the rule

148. In certain cases, where the payer is transparent or has a taxable presence in more than one jurisdiction, a payment may be treated as made from more than one jurisdiction. In these cases, however, the deduction of the payment in the other jurisdiction is not relevant to the question of whether the payment gives rise to a D/NI outcome under the laws of the jurisdiction applying the reverse hybrid rule. This principle is illustrated in **Example 4.4** where a payment to a reverse hybrid is made by a hybrid entity. In this case the example concludes that the hybrid mismatch rule in Recommendation 4 should be applied in both the parent and subsidiary jurisdictions to neutralise the effect of the mismatch and the application of the reverse hybrid rule in one jurisdiction does not impact on its application in the other.

Inclusion in any jurisdiction sufficient to discharge application of the rule

149. If the payment is brought into account as ordinary income in at least one jurisdiction then there will be no mismatch for the rule to apply to. A payment to a reverse hybrid will not be treated as giving rise to a D/NI outcome if the mismatch is neutralised by the investor or the establishment jurisdiction adopting a specific rule designed to bring into account items of ordinary income paid to a reverse hybrid. This will include any rules, consistent with Recommendation 5.1, that require a taxpayer in the investor jurisdiction to take into account, for tax purposes, any item of ordinary income allocated to that taxpayer by a reverse hybrid (including under a CFC regime) and any rules in the establishment jurisdiction, consistent with Recommendation 5.2, that deny the benefit of tax transparency to a non-resident investor or group of investors if they are not required to take into account, for tax purposes, an item of ordinary income that is allocated to them by the transparent entity.

CFC inclusion

150. A payment that has been fully attributed to the ultimate parent of the group under a CFC regime and has been subject to tax at the full rate should be treated as having been included in ordinary income for the purposes of the reverse hybrid rule. As for Recommendation 1 and Recommendation 3, the burden is on the taxpayer to establish, to the satisfaction of the tax administration, the extent to which the payment:

(a) Has been fully included under the laws of the investor jurisdiction and is subject to tax at the full rate.

(b) Has not been treated as reduced or offset by any deduction or other relief other than in respect of expenditure incurred by the investor under the laws of the investor jurisdiction.

(c) Does not carry an entitlement to any credit or other relief.

(d) Does not give rise to an imported mismatch.

151. In **Example 4.3** an intra-group services fee is paid to a reverse hybrid, but the ultimate parent of the group brings the full amount of that payment into account as ordinary income under its CFC rules. The example concludes that, provided the taxpayer can establish, to the satisfaction of the tax administration, that the full amount of the payment has been included in income under the CFC regime of the investor jurisdiction and is not subject to any deduction, credit or other relief, then the reverse hybrid rule does not apply because the payment has not given rise to a mismatch in tax outcomes.

Other types of inclusion

152. The same principle is illustrated in **Example 1.8** where interest is paid to a branch of a company that is resident in another jurisdiction. In determining whether the payment has given rise to a D/NI outcome, **Example 1.8** looks to the tax treatment of the payment under the laws of both the residence and the branch jurisdiction. While **Example 1.8** concerns the identification of D/NI outcomes under the hybrid financial instrument rule, the issues are the same in respect of a determination of D/NI outcomes under the reverse hybrid rule, and a similar interpretation would apply if the reverse hybrid maintained a branch in a third jurisdiction and the payment is brought into ordinary income in that jurisdiction.

Taxation in the establishment jurisdiction on the basis of source

153. Frequently, in the case of transparent intermediaries such as trusts and partnerships, the establishment jurisdiction will not treat the intermediary as a taxpayer in its own right. Rather, payments that are made to the intermediary will be treated as having been made directly by the underlying partners or beneficiaries in accordance with the allocation mechanics set out in the partnership agreement or trust deed. In these cases such payments may, nevertheless, be brought into account as ordinary income in the establishment jurisdiction because the payments are treated as being sourced in that jurisdiction, either because the payment is made by a person who is a taxpayer in the establishment jurisdiction or because the partnership or trust has a sufficient taxable presence in the establishment jurisdiction to give that income a domestic source. In such cases, provided the establishment jurisdiction taxes such payments on an ordinary basis, the payments should not generally give rise to a D/NI outcome under the reverse hybrid rules.

Demonstrating that a payment has not given rise to a D/NI outcome

154. It will be the taxpayer who has the burden of establishing, to the reasonable satisfaction of the tax administration, how the tax treatment of the payment in the payee jurisdiction impacts on the amount of the adjustment required under the rule. The initial burden of proof may be discharged by the taxpayer demonstrating that the payment has actually been recorded as ordinary income on the tax return in the other jurisdiction.

Deduction should only be denied to the extent of the mismatch

155. The adjustment should be no more than is necessary to neutralise the hybrid effect that results from inserting the reverse hybrid between the payer and the investor. If part of the payment remains subject to tax in the investor or establishment jurisdiction then that part of the payment should not be subject to adjustment under the hybrid financial instrument rule. This is illustrated in **Example 4.2** where a taxpayer makes a payment of interest to a reverse hybrid, only part of which is treated as exempt income under the laws of establishment jurisdiction. The example concludes that the payer jurisdiction should not deny a deduction for that part of the payment that remains subject to tax as ordinary income under the laws of the establishment jurisdiction.

Treatment of distributions from a reverse hybrid

156. The reverse hybrid rule will apply even if the investor is ultimately taxed on distributions made by the reverse hybrid. The mere fact that the accrued income of the reverse hybrid will be taxable as ordinary income when it is distributed to the investor will not be sufficient to show that the payment does not give rise to a mismatch. The reverse hybrid rule is intended to neutralise the D/NI outcome that arises at the time the payment is made to the reverse hybrid. The tax treatment of a separate payment that the reverse hybrid makes to the investor at some point in the future (and which may or may not be funded out of the payments caught by the reverse hybrid rule) will generally be too remote from the mismatch to be taken into account for the purposes of the rule.

Recommendation 4.2 - Rule only applies to payment made to a reverse hybrid

157. A reverse hybrid is any person (which includes an unincorporated body of persons such as a trust) that is treated as transparent under the laws of the jurisdiction where it is established but as a separate entity by an investor in that reverse hybrid.

158. An investor is not confined to persons that subscribe money for an interest in a reverse hybrid and includes any person to whom the reverse hybrid allocates or attributes a payment.

Establishment jurisdiction

159. The establishment jurisdiction will, in the case of entities that are formed by incorporation or registration, be the jurisdiction where that person is registered or established. For entities that can be formed without formal incorporation or registration requirements (such as partnerships and trusts) the establishment jurisdiction will be the jurisdiction under which the entity has been created and/or where the directors (or equivalent) perform their functions.

Transparent treatment in the establishment jurisdiction

160. A person will be treated as transparent under the laws of the establishment jurisdiction if the laws of that jurisdiction permit or require the person to allocate or attribute ordinary income to an investor and such allocation or attribution has the effect that the payment is not included in the income of any other taxpayer.

161. The most basic example of a transparent person is a trust or partnership, which is not treated as a taxpayer in its own right but where the income derived by that person is allocated or attributed to the partners or beneficiaries and those partners or beneficiaries

are liable to tax on that income as if they had received it directly. Other tax transparency regimes, however, may achieve the same effect without triggering a direct tax liability for the investor. For example, an establishment jurisdiction may permit or require an intermediary to allocate or attribute items of income to an investor but pay the tax on that allocated income on the investor's behalf and at the investor's marginal rate. Alternatively the regime in the establishment jurisdiction may exempt certain payments from tax on the grounds that the income is foreign source income allocated or attributed to a non-resident investor that would not have been subject to tax if the payment had been received by the investor directly.

162. The types of regimes described above should be treated as transparency regimes if the effect of allocating or attributing a payment of ordinary income to the investor results in the payment being taxed under the laws of the establishment jurisdiction as if it had been paid directly to that investor. **Example 4.2** provides an illustration of a transparency regime where the tax liability falls on the reverse hybrid rather than the investor. In that example the payee is entitled to claim an exemption for a payment of foreign source interest on the basis that the interest payment has accrued to the benefit of a non-resident. The example concludes that the payee is a reverse hybrid and the payment gives rise to a hybrid mismatch to the extent such payment would have been included in ordinary income if it had been paid directly to the investor.

Separate entity treatment in the investor jurisdiction

163. In most cases the allocation or attribution of ordinary income by the intermediary will not have any tax consequences for the investor under the laws of the investor jurisdiction. If this is the case then the intermediary should be considered opaque under the laws of the investor jurisdiction.

Recommendation 4.3 - Rule only applies to hybrid mismatches

164. A payment made to a reverse hybrid that gives rise to a D/NI outcome will only be subject to adjustment under the reverse hybrid rule if that D/NI outcome constitutes a hybrid mismatch under Recommendation 4.3

165. The identification of a mismatch as a hybrid mismatch under a reverse hybrid structure is primarily a legal question that requires the general rules in the investor jurisdiction to be applied to the payment that is made to the reverse hybrid to determine the character, amount and tax treatment of that payment and whether it would have been treated as ordinary income if it had been paid directly to the investor.

166. Unlike in the hybrid financial instrument rule, which applies whenever the terms of the instrument were sufficient to bring about a mismatch in tax outcomes, the reverse hybrid rule will not apply unless the payment attributed to the investor would have been included as ordinary income if it had been paid directly to the investor (i.e. the interposition of the reverse hybrid must have been necessary to bring about the mismatch in tax outcomes). This is illustrated in **Example 4.1** where income is allocated by a reverse hybrid to a tax exempt entity. In that case the payment would not have been taxable even if it had been made directly to the investor and the reverse hybrid rule will not apply to deny the deduction.

Reverse hybrids cannot be used to circumvent the application of Recommendation 1

167. In order to prevent a reverse hybrid being used to circumvent the operation of the hybrid financial instrument rule, the reverse hybrid rule will continue to apply to the extent a direct payment would have been subject to adjustment under the primary rule in Recommendation 1. An example where this principle might apply is set out in **Example 4.4** where the payment to a reverse hybrid is made under a financial instrument. In this case, the payer will continue to deny the deduction for the payment because the hybrid financial instrument rule would have applied *in the payer jurisdiction* to neutralise the mismatch in tax outcomes if the payment had been made directly to the investor. The mismatch in tax outcomes therefore still falls within the language and intent of the rule.

Recommendation 4.4 - Scope of the rule

168. Recommendation 4.4 limits the scope of the reverse hybrid rule to structured arrangements and mismatches that arise within a control group. See Recommendations 10 and 11 regarding the definition of structured arrangements and control group.

Chapter 5

Specific recommendations for the tax treatment of reverse hybrids

Recommendation 5

1. Improvements to CFC and other offshore investment regimes

Jurisdictions should introduce, or make changes to, their offshore investment regimes in order to prevent D/NI outcomes from arising in respect of payments to a reverse hybrid. Equally jurisdictions should consider introducing or making changes to their offshore investment regimes in relation to imported mismatch arrangements.

2. Limiting the tax transparency for non-resident investors

A reverse hybrid should be treated as a resident taxpayer in the establishment jurisdiction if the income of the reverse hybrid is not brought within the charge to taxation under the laws of the establishment jurisdiction and the accrued income of a non-resident investor in the same control group as the reverse hybrid is not brought within the charge to taxation under the laws of the investor jurisdiction.

3. Information reporting for intermediaries

Jurisdictions should introduce appropriate tax filing and information reporting requirements on persons established within their jurisdiction in order to assist both taxpayers and tax administrations to make a proper determination of the payments that have been attributed to that non-resident investor.

Overview

169. Recommendation 5 sets out three specific recommendations for the tax treatment of reverse hybrids. These recommendations cover the tax treatment of payments made to a reverse hybrid under the laws of the investor and establishment jurisdiction and recommendations on tax filing and information requirements in order to assist both taxpayers and tax administrations to make a proper determination of the payments that have been attributed to that non-resident investor.

170. These specific recommendations are not hybrid mismatch rules. That is, they do not adjust the tax consequences of a payment because of differences in its tax treatment in another jurisdiction. Rather, Recommendation 5 sets out improvements that jurisdictions could make to their domestic law that will reduce the frequency of hybrid mismatches by bringing the tax treatment of cross-border payments made to transparent entities into line with the tax policy outcomes that would generally be expected to apply to payments between domestic taxpayers.

Recommendation 5.1 - Improvements to CFC and other offshore investment regimes

171. Payments made through a reverse hybrid structure will not result in D/NI outcomes if the income is fully taxed under a CFC, foreign investment fund (FIF) or a similar anti-deferral rule in the investor jurisdiction that requires the investor to include its allocated share of any payment of ordinary income made to the intermediary on a current basis. Recommendation 5.1 therefore recommends that jurisdictions introduce or extend their offshore investment regimes to require a taxpayer to take into account, for tax purposes, any item of ordinary income allocated to that taxpayer by a reverse hybrid.

172. There are a number of ways a jurisdiction could go about aligning the tax treatment of the payment in the investor jurisdiction with its treatment in the establishment jurisdiction. A jurisdiction may use one or a combination of measures that could include changes to residency rules, CFC rules and rules that tax a resident investor on changes in the market value of the investment. When considering changes to their offshore investment regime, jurisdictions should also take into account the effect of existing exemptions, safe harbours and thresholds that may reduce the effectiveness of those regimes in bringing into account income of a reverse hybrid.

173. A reverse hybrid will be transparent under the laws of the establishment jurisdiction. Such transparency means that the laws of the establishment jurisdiction permit or require the reverse hybrid to allocate or attribute payments to an investor in such a way that the payment is not included in the income of any other taxpayer. An offshore investment regime in the investor jurisdiction could isolate this requirement and tax investors on the amount of income allocated to that investor. Treating income allocated by a reverse hybrid as taxable under the laws of the investor jurisdiction would have the effect of neutralising any hybrid mismatch under a payment to a transparent entity. Such a rule would ensure that the payer jurisdiction could suspend the application of the hybrid mismatch rule insofar as payments were allocated to investors in the investor jurisdiction.

Recommendation 5.2 - Limiting the tax transparency for non-resident investors

174. Tax transparency is an effective way for collective investment vehicles to ensure tax neutrality of outcomes for different investors that are subject to different marginal rates of taxation. Tax transparency proceeds on the assumption, however, that the income allocated to the investor will be taxable in the hands of the investor. In the cross-border context this is not always the case. Recommendation 5.2 is intended to prevent a non-resident taking advantage of a person's tax transparency in order to achieve a mismatch in tax outcomes.

175. Recommendation 5.2 of the report applies where a tax transparent person is controlled or otherwise owned by a non-resident investor and that investor is not required to take into account payments of ordinary income allocated to them by that person. The rule effectively encourages jurisdictions to turn off their transparency rules when those rules are primarily used to achieve hybrid mismatches. The Recommendation only applies in circumstances where:

(a) the person is tax transparent under the laws of the establishment jurisdiction;

(b) the person derives foreign source income or income that is not otherwise subject to taxation in the establishment jurisdiction;

(c) all or part of that income is allocated under the laws of the establishment jurisdiction to a non-resident investor that is in the same control group as that person.

In these circumstances Recommendation 5.2 provides that the establishment jurisdiction should treat the reverse hybrid as if it were a resident taxpayer. By treating the entity as a resident taxpayer, this will eliminate the need to apply the reverse hybrid rule to such entities and the investor jurisdiction could continue to include such payments in income under Recommendation 5.1 but provide a credit for any taxes paid in the establishment jurisdiction on the income that is brought into account under such rules.

Recommendation 5.3 - Information reporting for intermediaries

176. Recommendation 5.3 is intended to encourage jurisdictions to maintain appropriate reporting and filing requirements for tax transparent entities that are established within that jurisdiction. This would involve the maintenance of accurate records of who their investors are, how much of an investment each investor holds in the entity and the amount of income and expenditure allocated to those investors. These records should be made available, on request, to both investors and to the tax administration in the establishment jurisdiction.

177. In Brisbane, the G20 Leaders endorsed the *Standard for Automatic Exchange of Financial Account Information in Tax Matters* (the AEOI Standard, OECD 2014a). As part of this standard, investment entities will be required to provide their local tax administration with certain information about their investors including the value of each investor's holding at the end of the relevant reporting period. This information will be automatically exchanged with the tax administration in the investor jurisdiction making it easier for tax authorities to identify (and identify the amount of) offshore investments held by resident investors.

178. The legal basis for information exchange between tax administrations is generally Article 26 of the *OECD Model Tax Convention on Income and on Capital* (OECD Model Tax Convention, OECD, 2014b) or *The Multilateral Convention on Mutual Administrative Assistance in Tax Matters, Amended by the 2010 Protocol* (Multilateral Convention, OECD, 2010). This Multilateral Convention provides for all possible forms of administrative co-operation between States and contains strict rules on confidentiality and proper use of the information.

179. Furthermore, tax authorities are encouraged to require intermediaries established in their jurisdiction to maintain records on the investors holding interests in those intermediaries and the amounts of income and expenditure allocated to those investors (including the categories of income and expenditure as determined under the relevant tax or accounting standard).

Bibliography

OECD (2014a), *Standard for Automatic Exchange of Financial Account Information in Tax Matters,* OECD Publishing, Paris, http://dx.doi.org/10.1787/9789264216525-en.

OECD (2014b), Model Tax Convention on Income and on Capital, condensed version, OECD Publishing, Paris, http://dx.doi.org/10.1787/mtc_cond-2014-en.

OECD (2010), *The Multilateral Convention on Mutual Administrative Assistance in Tax Matters, Amended by the 2010 Protocol,* OECD Publishing, Paris, http://dx.doi.org/10.1787/9789264115606-en.

Chapter 6

Deductible hybrid payments rule

Recommendation 6

1. Neutralise the mismatch to the extent the payment gives rise to a DD outcome

The following rule should apply to a hybrid payer that makes a payment that is deductible under the laws of the payer jurisdiction and that triggers a duplicate deduction in the parent jurisdiction that results in a hybrid mismatch:

(a) The parent jurisdiction will deny the duplicate deduction for such payment to the extent it gives rise to a DD outcome.

(b) If the parent jurisdiction does not neutralise the mismatch, the payer jurisdiction will deny the deduction for such payment to the extent it gives rise to a DD outcome.

(c) No mismatch will arise to the extent that a deduction is set-off against income that is included in income under the laws of both the parent and the payer jurisdictions (i.e. dual inclusion income).

(d) Any deduction that exceeds the amount of dual inclusion income (the excess deduction) may be eligible to be set-off against dual inclusion income in another period. In order to prevent stranded losses, the excess deduction may be allowed to the extent that the taxpayer can establish, to the satisfaction of the tax administration, that the excess deduction in the other jurisdiction cannot be set-off against any income of any person under the laws of the other jurisdiction that is not dual inclusion income.

2. Rule only applies to deductible payments made by a hybrid payer

A person will be treated as a hybrid payer in respect of a payment that is deductible under the laws of the payer jurisdiction where:

(a) the payer is not a resident of the payer jurisdiction and the payment triggers a duplicate deduction for that payer (or a related person) under the laws of the jurisdiction where the payer is resident (the parent jurisdiction); or

(b) the payer is resident in the payer jurisdiction and the payment triggers a duplicate deduction for an investor in that payer (or a related person) under the laws of the other jurisdiction (the parent jurisdiction).

3. Rule only applies to payments that result in a hybrid mismatch

A payment results in a hybrid mismatch where the deduction for the payment may be set-off, under the laws of the payer jurisdiction, against income that is not dual inclusion income.

4. Scope of the rule

The defensive rule only applies if the parties to the mismatch are in the same control group or where the mismatch arises under a structured arrangement and the taxpayer is party to that structured arrangement. There is no limitation on scope in respect of the recommended response.

Overview

180. Where a taxpayer makes a payment through a cross-border structure, such as a dual resident, a foreign branch or a hybrid person, that payment may trigger a DD outcome where:

(a) the expenditure is required to be taken into account in calculating the taxpayer's net income under the laws of two or more jurisdictions; or

(b) in the case of a payment made by a hybrid person that is treated as transparent by one of its investors, the payment is also treated as deductible in calculating the net income of that investor.

181. A DD outcome will give rise to tax policy concerns where the laws of both jurisdictions permit that deduction to be set-off against an amount that is not treated as income under the laws of the other jurisdiction (i.e. against income that is not "dual inclusion income"). The policy of the deductible hybrid payments rule is to limit a taxpayer's deduction to the amount of dual inclusion income in circumstances where the deduction that arises in the other jurisdiction is not subject to equivalent restrictions on deductibility.

182. Recommendation 6 applies to DD outcomes in respect of expenditure incurred through a foreign branch or hybrid person. The definition of "hybrid payer" means that the deductible hybrid payments rule only applies where a deductible payment in one jurisdiction (the payer jurisdiction) triggers a duplicate deduction in another jurisdiction (the parent jurisdiction) because:

(a) the payer is resident in the parent jurisdiction (i.e. the expenditure has been incurred through a branch); or

(b) an investor in the parent jurisdiction claims a deduction for the same payment (i.e. the expenditure has been incurred by a hybrid person that is treated as transparent under the laws of the parent jurisdiction).

183. The primary recommendation under the deductible hybrid payments rule is that the parent jurisdiction should restrict the amount of duplicate deductions to the total amount of dual inclusion income. There is no limitation on the scope of the primary response. The defensive rule, which imposes the same type of restriction in the payer jurisdiction, will only apply in the event that the effect of mismatch is not neutralised in the parent jurisdiction and is limited to those cases where the parties to the mismatch are in the same control group or the taxpayer is party to a structured arrangement.

184. Determining which payments have given rise to a double deduction and which items are dual inclusion income requires a comparison between the domestic tax treatment of these items and their treatment under the laws of the other jurisdiction. It may be possible to undertake a line by line comparison of each item of income or expense in straightforward cases where the hybrid payer is party to only a few transactions. In more complex cases, however, where the taxpayer has entered into a significant number of transactions which give rise to different types of income and expense, countries may wish to adopt a simpler implementation solution for tracking double deductions and dual inclusion income. The way in which DD outcomes will arise will differ from one jurisdiction to the next and countries should choose an implementation solution that is based, as much as possible, on existing domestic rules, administrative guidance, presumptions and tax calculations while still meeting the basic policy objectives of the

deductible hybrids payments rule. Examples of possible implementation solutions are identified in this guidance at **Example 6.1** to **Example 6.5**.

185. Jurisdictions use different tax accounting periods and have different rules for recognising when items of income or expenditure have been derived or incurred. These timing differences should not be treated as giving rise to mismatches in tax outcomes under Recommendation 6. Recommendation 6.1(d) therefore allows excess deductions that are subject to restriction under the deductible hybrid payments rule to be carried-forward to another period, in accordance with a jurisdiction's ordinary rules for the treatment of net losses, and applied against dual inclusion income in that period. In order to prevent stranded losses, jurisdictions may further permit excess deductions to be set-off against non-dual inclusion income if a taxpayer can show that such deductions cannot be offset against any income under the laws of the other jurisdiction that is not dual inclusion income.

Recommendation 6.1- Neutralise the mismatch to the extent the payment gives rise to a DD outcome

186. The response recommended in this report is to neutralise the effect of hybrid mismatches through the adoption of a linking rule that aligns the tax outcomes in the payer and parent jurisdictions. The hybrid mismatch rule isolates the hybrid element in the structure by identifying a deductible payment made by a hybrid payer in the payer jurisdiction and the corresponding "duplicate deduction" generated in the parent jurisdiction. The primary response is that the duplicate deduction cannot be claimed in the parent jurisdiction to the extent it exceeds the claimant's dual inclusion income (income brought into account for tax purposes under the laws of both jurisdictions). A defensive rule applies in the payer jurisdiction to prevent the hybrid payer claiming the benefit of a deductible payment against non-dual inclusion income if the primary rule does not apply.

187. In the case of both the primary and defensive rules, the excess deductions can be offset against dual inclusion income in another period. In order to prevent stranded losses, it is recommended that excess duplicate deductions should be allowed to the extent that the taxpayer can establish, to the satisfaction of the tax administration, that the deduction cannot be set-off against the income of any person under the laws of the other jurisdiction.

Deductible payments caught by the rule

188. The meaning of deductible payment is the same as that used in other recommendations in the report and generally covers a taxpayer's current expenditures such as service payments, rents, royalties, interest and other amounts that may be set-off against ordinary income under the laws of the payer jurisdiction in the period they are treated as made.

189. The determination of whether a payment is deductible requires a proper assessment of the character and treatment of the payment under the laws of both the payer and parent jurisdiction. The approach that should be taken to analysing the tax treatment of the payment is similar to that used for determining mismatches under a financial instrument, except that Recommendation 6 requires a comparison between the jurisdictions where the payment is made, rather than the jurisdictions where the payment is made and received.

190. Unlike the hybrid financial instrument rule, which focuses only on the tax treatment of the instrument, and not on the status of the counterparty or the context in which the instrument is held, the deductible hybrid payments rule should only operate to the extent a taxpayer is actually entitled to a deduction for a payment under local law. Accordingly the rule will not apply to the extent the taxpayer is subject to transaction or entity specific rules under the parent or payer jurisdiction that prevent the payment from being deducted. These restrictions on deductibility may include hybrid mismatch rules that deny the taxpayer a deduction in order to neutralise a direct or indirect D/NI outcome.

191. The interaction between Recommendation 6 and other rules that govern the deductibility of payments is illustrated in **Example 6.3** where the parent company establishes a hybrid subsidiary in another jurisdiction that incurs employment expenses. **Example 6.3** notes that, if the parent is tax exempt under the laws of its own jurisdiction and it is unable to claim deductions for any of its expenditure then no DD outcome will arise on these facts. In **Example 4.4** a hybrid person makes an interest payment to a reverse hybrid in the same group. In this case the example concludes that the reverse hybrid rule in Chapter 3 of the report will apply to the arrangement to deny the deduction so that there is no scope for the operation of the deductible hybrid payments rule.

Extending the principles of Recommendation 6 to other deductible items

192. As illustrated in **Example 6.1**, the kind of structures that give rise to DD outcomes in respect of payments can also be used to generate double deductions for non-cash items such as depreciation or amortisation. A DD outcome raises the same tax policy issues, regardless of how the deduction has been triggered, and distinguishing between deductible items on the basis of whether they are attributable to a payment would complicate rather than simplify the implementation of these recommendations. Accordingly when implementing the hybrid mismatch rules into domestic law countries may wish to apply the principles of Recommendations 6 and 7 to all deductible items regardless of whether they are attributable to a payment. **Example 6.1** provides an example of the application of the deductible hybrid payments rule to a depreciation deduction where both the payer and the parent jurisdiction provide for a depreciation allowance in respect of the same asset.

Determining the existence and amount of a DD outcome

193. The question of whether a payment has given rise to a "DD outcome" is primarily a legal question that should be determined by an analysis of the character and tax treatment of the payment under the laws of the payer and the parent jurisdiction. If the laws of both jurisdictions grant a deduction for the same payment (or an allowance in respect of the same asset) then that deduction can be said to give rise to a DD outcome.

194. This principle is applied in **Example 6.3** where a taxpayer claims a deduction for salary and other employment benefits paid to an employee. In order to determine whether these payments have given rise to a DD outcome, the taxpayer must make a proper assessment of the facts and circumstances that gave rise to the deduction under local law and determine whether a deduction has been granted on the same basis in the other jurisdiction. If, for example, one jurisdiction allows taxpayers a deduction for the value of share options granted under an employee incentive scheme, but the other jurisdiction does not, then this item of deductible expenditure will not give rise to a DD outcome. On the other hand, if one jurisdiction treats a travel subsidy as a deductible allowance, while the

other simply categorises the payment as part of the taxpayer's (deductible) salary or wages, then the payment will still be treated as giving rise to a DD outcome notwithstanding the different ways in which the payment is described under the laws of each jurisdiction.

Differences in valuation should not affect the amount treated as giving rise to a DD outcome

195. If a payment has triggered a deduction under the laws of two or more jurisdictions then differences between the payer and parent jurisdictions as to the value of that payment will not generally impact on the extent to which a payment has given rise to a mismatch in tax outcomes. This principle is illustrated in **Example 6.3** where a hybrid payer allocates share options to an employee. The example concludes that the grant of the share options should be treated as giving rise to a DD outcome if the laws of the payer and parent jurisdiction both allow a deduction for the grant of such options. The example notes that differences between the jurisdictions in the amount of value they ascribe to the share options will not generally prevent the deductible hybrid payments rule applying to the entire amount of the deduction under the laws of either jurisdiction.

Differences in timing should not affect the amount treated as giving rise to a DD outcome

196. The hybrid mismatch rules are not generally intended to impact on mismatches in the timing of income and expenditure. Equally the operation of the rules is not dependant on the timing of the deduction or receipt in the other jurisdiction. If a payment will be deductible under the laws of the other jurisdiction (or if an item of income will be included under the laws of another jurisdiction) it will be treated as a double deduction (or dual inclusion income) at the moment it is treated as incurred (or derived) under local law. This principle is illustrated in **Example 6.1** where both the hybrid person and its immediate parent are entitled to a deduction for the same interest payment. Differences in timing rules, however, mean that one jurisdiction requires the taxpayer to defer a deduction for part of the accrued interest expense to the next accounting period. The resulting difference in timing between the jurisdictions does not prevent the deductible hybrid payments rule from applying to the whole interest payment in both jurisdictions.

Dual inclusion income

197. An item of income will be dual inclusion income if the same item is included in income under the laws of the jurisdictions where the DD outcome arises. As for deductions, the identification of whether an item should be treated as dual inclusion income is primarily a legal question that requires a comparison of the treatment of that item under the laws of both jurisdictions. An amount should still be treated as dual inclusion income even if there are differences between jurisdictions in the way they value that item or in the accounting period in which that item is recognised for tax purposes. This principle is applied in **Example 6.1** and **Example 6.3** where the laws of the parent and the payer jurisdiction use different timing and valuation rules in the recognition of the income of a hybrid entity. In this case, both countries apply their own rules for calculating the amount of dual inclusion income arising in each period and the resulting difference in measurement does not impact on the operation of the rule.

198. Double taxation relief, such as a domestic dividend exemption granted by the payer jurisdiction or a foreign tax credit granted by the payee / parent jurisdiction should

not prevent an item from being treated as dual inclusion income where the effect of such relief is simply to avoid subjecting that item to an additional layer of taxation in either jurisdiction. Thus, while a payment must generally be recognised as ordinary income under the laws of both jurisdictions before it can be treated as dual inclusion income, an equity return should still qualify as dual inclusion income if the payment is subject to an exemption, exclusion, credit of other type of double taxation relief in the payer or parent jurisdiction that relieves the payment from economic double taxation. An example of this type of dual inclusion income is given in **Example 6.3** where the expenses of a hybrid entity are funded by an intra-group dividend that is exempt from taxation in the jurisdiction where the dividend is received but included as income under the laws of its parent. Allowing the hybrid entity a deduction against this type of exempt or excluded equity return preserves the intended tax policy outcomes in both jurisdictions. The dividend should be treated as dual inclusion income for the purposes of deductible hybrid payments rule even where such dividend carries an entitlement to an underlying foreign tax credit in the parent jurisdiction. Such double taxation relief may give rise to tax policy concerns, however, if it has the same net effect as allowing for a DD outcome. In determining whether to treat an item of income, which benefits from such double-taxation relief, as dual-inclusion income, countries should seek to strike a balance between rules that minimise compliance costs, preserve the intended effect of such double taxation relief and prevent taxpayers from entering into structures that undermine the integrity of the rules.

199. A tax administration may treat the net income of a CFC that is attributed to a shareholder of that company under a CFC or other offshore inclusion regime as dual inclusion income if the taxpayer can satisfy the tax administration that such income has been brought into account as income and subject to tax at the full rate under the laws of both jurisdictions. **Example 6.4** sets out a simplified calculation that illustrates how income attributed under a CFC regime can be taken into account in determining the amount of dual inclusion income under a hybrid structure.

To the extent of the mismatch

200. The adjustment should be no more than is necessary to neutralise the hybrid mismatch and should result in an outcome that is proportionate and that does not lead to double taxation. When applying the defensive rule, however, the amount of the deduction that must be denied in order to neutralise the mismatch may exceed the amount of the deduction that would have been disallowed by the parent jurisdiction in respect of the same payment. This will be the case, for example, where deductible interest accrued by a hybrid person is treated as allocated to a number of investors in accordance with their proportionate interest in the entity. As explained in **Example 6.5** a deduction must be denied for the full amount of the interest payment under the defensive rule in order to eliminate any mismatch in tax outcomes even though only a portion of the interest payment is treated as giving rise to a duplicate deduction under the laws of the investor's jurisdiction.

Excess deductions

Carry-forward of deductions to another period

201. Because the hybrid mismatch rules are generally not intended to impact on, or be affected by, timing differences, the deductible hybrids payment rules contain a mechanism that allows jurisdictions to carry-forward (or back if permitted under local

law) double deductions to a period where they can be set-off against surplus dual inclusion income. The Recommendation contemplates that the ordinary domestic rules governing the utilisation of losses would apply to such deductions. **Example 6.1** sets out an example of the operation of the carry-forward of excess deductions.

Stranded losses

202. In certain cases the rule may operate to restrict a deduction in the payer or parent jurisdiction even though the deduction that arises in the other jurisdiction cannot be used to offset income in that jurisdiction (because, for example, the business in that jurisdiction is in a net loss position). In this case it is possible for the rule to generate "stranded losses" that cannot be used in one jurisdiction for practical and commercial reasons and that cannot be used in the other jurisdiction due to the fact that they are caught by Recommendation 6. Recommendation 6.1(d) provides that a tax administration may permit those excess deductions to be set-off against non-dual inclusion income if the taxpayer can establish that the deduction in the other jurisdiction cannot be offset against any income that is not dual inclusion income. The treatment of stranded losses is discussed in **Example 6.2** where a taxpayer incurs losses in a foreign branch. In that example, the deductible hybrid payments rule has the potential to generate "stranded losses" if the taxpayer abandons its operations in the payer jurisdiction and winds up the branch at a time when it still has unused carry-forward losses from a prior period. The example notes that the tax administration may permit the taxpayer to set-off any excess against non-dual inclusion income provided the taxpayer can establish that the winding up of the branch will prevent the taxpayer from using those losses anywhere else. Stranded losses are discussed further in respect of dual resident entities at **Example 7.1**.

Implementation solution based on existing domestic rules

203. In principle, Recommendation 6 requires the taxpayer to identify the items of deductible expenditure under the laws of both jurisdictions and to determine which of those items have given rise to DD outcomes. The rule then caps the aggregate amount of duplicate deductions that can be claimed to the aggregate amount of dual inclusion income. Dual inclusion income should, in principle, be identified in the same way (i.e. by identifying each item of income in the domestic jurisdiction and determining whether and to what extent those items have been included in income in the other jurisdiction).

204. It may be possible to undertake such a line by line comparison in straightforward cases, where the hybrid payer or foreign branch is party to only a few transactions, but in more complex cases, where the taxpayer has entered into a large number transactions which could all potentially give rise to DD outcomes or dual inclusion income, this kind of approach could entail a significant compliance burden. In order to facilitate implementation and minimise compliance costs, tax administrations will wish to consider an implementation solution that preserves the policy objectives of the deductible hybrids payments rule and arrives at a substantially similar result but is based, as much as possible, on existing domestic rules, administrative guidance, presumptions and tax calculations.

205. In the case of the kind of structures covered by Recommendation 6, it will generally be the case that accounts have been prepared in both jurisdictions that will show the income and expenditure of the taxpayer. These accounts will generally be prepared under local law using domestic tax concepts. Tax administrations should use these

existing sources of information and tax calculations as a starting point for identifying duplicate deductions and dual inclusion income.

206. For example, a parent jurisdiction that requires the preparation of separate branch accounts could restrict the ability of the taxpayer to deduct any resulting branch loss from the income of the parent or parent affiliate. Alternatively the parent jurisdiction could require the branch to make adjustments to the accounts that have been prepared under the laws of the payer jurisdiction (eliminating items of income and expenditure that are not recognised under the law of the parent jurisdiction) to determine whether the activities of the branch have resulted in a net loss (as determined under parent jurisdiction's rules).

207. When applying the defensive rule, and subject to concerns about compliance and administration costs (especially when numerous items of income and expenditure are involved), a payer jurisdiction could adjust the income and expenditure of a hybrid person or branch to eliminate any material items of income or deduction that are not recognised under the laws of the parent jurisdiction. The payer jurisdiction could deny a deduction to the extent of any adjusted net loss and prevent the net loss being carried-forward to a subsequent period in the event of a change in control. Examples of implementation solutions to address DD outcomes are set out further in **Example 6.1** to **Example 6.5**.

Recommendation 6.2 - Rule only applies to deductible payments made by a hybrid payer

208. Recommendation 6.2 confines the operation of the deductible hybrid payments rule to DD outcomes that arise through the use of a foreign branch or hybrid entity.

209. Recommendation 6 does not presuppose that the person making the payment is regarded as transparent in one jurisdiction and opaque in the other. Paragraph (a) of the definition of "hybrid payer" applies in cases such as foreign branch structures where the payer is treated as transparent under the laws of both jurisdictions. The application of the deductible hybrid payments rule to a branch is set out in **Example 6.2**.

210. Paragraph (b) of Recommendation 6.2 covers those cases where the payer is a hybrid person, that is to say where the payer is treated as transparent by one of its investors so that a duplicate deduction arises for that investor in another jurisdiction. A transparent person in this case can include a disregarded person or one that is treated as if it were a partnership under the laws of the parent jurisdiction. **Example 6.3** sets out an instance where the rule applies to deductible payment made by a disregarded person and **Example 6.5** illustrates the application of the rule to entities that are treated as partnerships.

Recommendation 6.3 - Rule only applies to payments that result in a hybrid mismatch

211. A DD outcome will give rise to tax policy concerns where the laws of both jurisdictions permit a deduction for the same payment to be set-off against an amount that is not dual inclusion income (see **Example 6.2**). Recommendation 6.3 restricts the application of the deductible hybrid payments rule to those cases where the deduction may be set-off against dual inclusion income. It is not necessary for a tax administration to know whether the deduction has actually been applied against non-dual inclusion income in the other jurisdiction before it is subject to restriction under the rule.

212. In general, the deduction that arises in the parent jurisdiction will be available to be set-off against non-dual inclusion income (i.e. other income of the taxpayer) unless the parent jurisdiction has implemented the deductible hybrid payments rule.

213. The most common mechanism used to offset a double deduction that arises in the payer jurisdiction will be the use of a tax consolidation or grouping regime that allows a domestic taxpayer to apply the benefit of a deduction against the income of another person within the same group. There are a number of ways of achieving this offset. Some countries permit taxpayers to transfer losses, deductions, income and gains to other group members. Other jurisdictions simply treat all the group members as a single taxpayer. Some consolidation regimes permit taxpayers in the same group to make taxable intra-group payments in order to shift net income around the group. Regardless of the mechanism used to achieve tax grouping or consolidation, if its effect is to allow a double deduction to be set-off against income that will not be brought into account under the laws of the parent jurisdiction that will be sufficient to bring the double deduction within the scope of the hybrid deductible payments rule.

214. There are a number of other different techniques that a taxpayer can use in the payer jurisdiction to set-off a double deduction against non-dual inclusion income. These techniques include having the taxpayer:

(a) make an investment through a reverse hybrid so that the income of the reverse hybrid is only brought into account under the laws of the payer jurisdiction. An example of such a structure is set out in **Example 6.1**.

(b) enter into a financial instrument or other arrangement where payments are included in ordinary income in the payer jurisdiction but not included in income in the parent jurisdiction. An example of such a structure is set out in **Example 3.1** in respect of an adjustment under the disregarded hybrid payments rule.

(c) enter into a merger transaction or other corporate re-organisation that permits losses that have been carried-forward to be offset against the income of other entities.

Recommendation 6.4 - Scope of the rule

215. Recommendation 6.4 limits the scope of the defensive rule to structured arrangements and mismatches that arise within a control group. See Recommendations 10 and 11 regarding the definition of structured arrangements and control group.

Chapter 7

Dual-resident payer rule

> **Recommendation 7**
>
> **1. Neutralise the mismatch to the extent the payment gives rise to a DD outcome**
>
> The following rule should apply to a dual resident that makes a payment that is deductible under the laws of both jurisdictions where the payer is resident and that DD outcome results in a hybrid mismatch:
>
> (a) Each resident jurisdiction will deny a deduction for such payment to the extent it gives rise to a DD outcome.
>
> (b) No mismatch will arise to the extent that the deduction is set-off against income that is included as income under the laws of both jurisdictions (i.e. dual inclusion income).
>
> (c) Any deduction that exceeds the amount of dual inclusion income (the excess deduction) may be eligible to be set-off against dual inclusion income in another period. In order to prevent stranded losses, the excess deduction may be allowed to the extent that the taxpayer can establish, to the satisfaction of the tax administration, that the excess deduction cannot be set-off against any income under the laws of the other jurisdiction that is not dual inclusion income.
>
> **2. Rule only applies to deductible payments made by a dual resident**
>
> A taxpayer will be a dual resident if it is resident for tax purposes under the laws of two or more jurisdictions.
>
> **3. Rule only applies to payments that result in a hybrid mismatch**
>
> A deduction for a payment results in a hybrid mismatch where the deduction for the payment may be set-off, under the laws of the other jurisdiction, against income that is not dual inclusion income.
>
> **4. Scope of the rule**
>
> There is no limitation on the scope of the rule.

Overview

216. A payment made by a dual resident taxpayer will trigger a DD outcome where the payment is deductible under the laws of both jurisdictions where the taxpayer is resident. Such a DD outcome will give rise to tax policy concerns where one jurisdiction permits that deduction to be set-off against an amount that is not treated as income under the laws of the other jurisdiction (i.e. against income that is not "dual inclusion income").

217. Recommendation 6 applies to DD outcomes in respect of expenditure incurred through a foreign branch or hybrid person where it is possible to distinguish between the jurisdiction where the expenditure is actually incurred (the payer jurisdiction) and the jurisdiction where the duplicate deduction arises due to the resident status or the tax transparency of the payer (the parent jurisdiction). The distinction between the parent/payer jurisdictions is not possible in the context of dual resident taxpayers because it is not possible to reliably distinguish between where the payment is actually made and where the duplicate deduction has arisen. In this case, therefore, the dual resident payer rule provides that both jurisdictions should apply the primary rule to restrict the deduction to dual inclusion income. There is no limitation on the scope of the response under the dual resident payer rule as the deduction that arises in each jurisdiction is being claimed by the same taxpayer.

218. As for Recommendation 6, determining which payments have given rise to a double deduction and which items are dual inclusion income requires a comparison between the domestic tax treatments of these items in each jurisdiction where the payer is resident. As discussed in Recommendation 6, countries should choose an implementation solution that is based, as much as possible, on existing domestic rules, administrative guidance, presumptions and tax calculations while still meeting the basic policy objectives of the dual resident payer rule.

219. Jurisdictions use different tax accounting periods and have different rules for recognising when items of income or expenditure have been derived or incurred. These timing differences should not be treated as giving rise to mismatches in tax outcomes under Recommendation 7. Recommendation 7.1(c) allows excess deductions that are subject to restriction under the deductible hybrid payments rule to be carried over to another period and jurisdictions may further permit excess losses to be set-off against non-dual inclusion income if a taxpayer can show that such losses have become stranded.

Recommendation 7.1 - Neutralise the mismatch to the extent it gives rise to a DD outcome

220. Recommendation 7.1 identifies the hybrid element in the structure as a deductible payment made by a dual resident that gives rise to a corresponding "duplicate deduction" in the other jurisdiction where the payer is resident. The primary response is that the deduction cannot be claimed for such payment to the extent it exceeds the payer's dual inclusion income (income brought into account for tax purposes under the laws of both jurisdictions). As both jurisdictions will apply the primary response there is no need for a defensive rule.

221. As with other structures that generate DD outcomes, the excess deductions can be offset against dual inclusion income in another period. In order to prevent stranded losses, it is recommended that excess duplicate deductions should be allowed to the extent that the taxpayer can establish, to the satisfaction of the tax administration, that the deduction cannot be set-off against any income under the laws of the other jurisdiction that is not dual inclusion income.

Deductible payments caught by the rule

222. The meaning of deductible payment is the same as that used in other recommendations in the report and generally covers a taxpayer's current expenditures such as service payments, rents, royalties, interest and other amounts that may be set-off

against ordinary income under the laws of the payer jurisdiction in the period they are treated as made.

223. As for Recommendation 6, the determination of whether a payment is deductible requires a proper assessment of the character and treatment of the payment under the laws of each jurisdiction where the taxpayer is resident. The rule will not apply to the extent the taxpayer is subject to transaction or entity specific rules under the laws of either jurisdiction that prevent the payment from being deducted. These restrictions on deductibility may include hybrid mismatch rules in one jurisdiction that deny the taxpayer a deduction in order to neutralise a direct or indirect D/NI outcome.

Extending the principles of Recommendation 7 to other deductible items

224. Dual resident payers can also be used to generate double deductions for non-cash items such as depreciation or amortisation. As discussed in the guidance to Recommendation 6.1, DD outcomes raise the same tax policy issues regardless of how the deduction has been triggered. Distinguishing between deductible items on the basis of whether or not they are attributable to a payment may complicate rather than simplify the implementation of these recommendations. Accordingly, when implementing the hybrid mismatch rules into domestic law, countries may wish to apply the principles of Recommendation 7 to all deductible items regardless of whether the deduction that arises is attributable to a payment.

Determining the existence and amount of a DD outcome and dual inclusion income

225. As discussed in the guidance to Recommendation 6.1, the question of whether a payment has given rise to a "DD outcome" is primarily a legal question that should be determined by an analysis of the character and tax treatment of the payment under the laws of each residence jurisdiction. If both jurisdictions grant a deduction for the same payment (or an allowance respect of the same asset) then that deduction can be said to give rise to a DD outcome. Differences between jurisdictions as to the quantification and timing of a deduction will not generally impact on the extent to which a payment has given rise to a mismatch in tax outcomes. A payment should be treated as giving rise to a double deduction (or dual inclusion income) at the moment it is treated as incurred (or derived) under local law regardless of when such payment has been treated incurred (or derived) under the laws of the other jurisdiction.

226. While a payment must generally be recognised as ordinary income under the laws of both jurisdictions before it can be treated as dual inclusion income, an equity return should still qualify as dual inclusion income if the payment is subject to an exemption, exclusion, credit of other type of double taxation relief that relieves the payment from economic double taxation. An example of this type of dual inclusion income is given in **Example 7.1** in respect of the dual resident payer rule. Such double taxation relief may give rise to tax policy concerns, however, if it has the same net effect as allowing for a DD outcome. In determining whether to treat an item of income, which benefits from such double-taxation relief, as dual-inclusion income, countries should seek to strike a balance between rules that minimise compliance costs, preserve the intended effect of such double taxation relief and prevent taxpayers from entering into structures that undermine the integrity of the rules. As discussed in the guidance to Recommendation 6.1, a tax administration may also treat the net income of a CFC that is attributed to a shareholder of that company under a CFC or other offshore inclusion regime as dual

inclusion income if the taxpayer can satisfy the tax administration that the CFC regime brings that amount of income into account so that it is subject to tax at the full rate under the laws of both jurisdictions.

Recommended response

227. Where a payment by a dual resident payer gives rise to a DD outcome, the jurisdiction where the payer is resident should apply the recommended response to neutralise the effect of the mismatch by denying the deduction to the extent it gives rise to a mismatch in tax outcomes. A DD outcome will give rise to a mismatch in tax outcomes to the extent it is set-off against income that is not dual inclusion income. The adjustment should be no more than is necessary to neutralise the hybrid mismatch and should result in an outcome that is proportionate and that does not lead to double taxation. **Example 7.1** illustrates a situation where the simultaneous application of the dual resident payer rules in both residence jurisdictions has the potential to create double taxation. As noted in that example, however, structuring opportunities will usually be available to avoid the risk of double taxation.

Excess deductions

Carry-forward of deductions to another period

228. Because the hybrid mismatch rules are generally not intended to impact on, or be affected by, timing differences both Recommendations 6 and 7 allow jurisdictions to carry-forward (or -back if permitted under local law) double deductions to a period where they can be set-off against surplus dual inclusion income. The Recommendations contemplate that the ordinary domestic rules governing the utilisation of losses would apply to such deductions.

Stranded losses

229. In certain cases the rule may operate simultaneously to restrict a deduction in both jurisdictions. In this case it is possible for the rule to generate "stranded losses" that cannot be used in either jurisdiction. Recommendation 7.1(c) provides that a tax administration may permit those excess deductions to be set-off against non-dual inclusion income if the taxpayer can establish that the deduction that has arisen in the other jurisdiction cannot be offset against any income that is not dual inclusion income. **Example 7.1** discusses allowances for the use of stranded losses in respect of dual resident payers.

Recommendation 7.2 - Rule only applies to deductible payments made by a dual resident

230. Recommendation 7.2 confines the operation of the deductible hybrid payments rule to DD outcomes that arise through the use of dual resident structures.

231. A person should be treated as a resident of a jurisdiction for tax purposes if it qualifies as tax resident or is taxable in that jurisdiction on their worldwide net income. As discussed in **Example 7.1**, a person will be treated as a resident of a jurisdiction even if that person forms part of a tax consolidation group which treats that person as disregarded for local law purposes.

Recommendation 7.3 - Rule only applies to payments that result in a hybrid mismatch

232. As for Recommendation 6.3, the dual resident payer rule restricts the application of the deductible hybrid payments rule to those cases where the other jurisdiction permits the deduction to be set-off against income that is not dual inclusion income. It is not necessary for a tax administration to know whether the deduction has actually been applied against non-dual inclusion income in the other jurisdiction before it applies the rule in Recommendation 7.

233. The same techniques that a taxpayer can use to trigger a DD outcome that falls within the scope of Recommendation 6 can also be used to generate hybrid mismatches under Recommendation 7. These techniques include: the use of tax consolidation regimes, having the taxpayer make an investment through a reverse hybrid and entering into a financial instrument or other arrangement where payments are included in income in one jurisdiction but not the other. An example of the use of a consolidation regime and of the use of a reverse hybrid structure involving a dual resident entity is given in **Example 7.1**.

Chapter 8

Imported mismatch rule

Recommendation 8

1. Deny the deduction to the extent the payment gives rise to an indirect D/NI outcome

The payer jurisdiction should apply a rule that denies a deduction for any imported mismatch payment to the extent the payee treats that payment as set-off against a hybrid deduction in the payee jurisdiction.

2. Definition of hybrid deduction

Hybrid deduction means a deduction resulting from:

(a) a payment under a financial instrument that results in a hybrid mismatch;

(b) a disregarded payment made by a hybrid payer that results in a hybrid mismatch;

(c) a payment made to a reverse hybrid that results in a hybrid mismatch; or

(d) a payment made by a hybrid payer or dual resident that triggers a duplicate deduction resulting in a hybrid mismatch;

and includes a deduction resulting from a payment made to any other person to the extent that person treats the payment as set-off against another hybrid deduction.

3. Imported mismatch payment

An imported mismatch payment is a deductible payment made to a payee that is not subject to hybrid mismatch rules.

4. Scope of the rule

The rule applies if the taxpayer is in the same control group as the parties to the imported mismatch arrangement or where the payment is made under a structured arrangement and the taxpayer is party to that structured arrangement.

Overview

234. The policy behind the imported mismatch rule is to prevent taxpayers from entering into structured arrangements or arrangements with group members that shift the effect of an offshore hybrid mismatch into the domestic jurisdiction through the use of a non-hybrid instrument such as an ordinary loan. The imported mismatch rule disallows deductions for a broad range of payments (including interest, royalties, rents and payments for services) if the income from such payments is set-off, directly or indirectly, against a deduction that arises under a hybrid mismatch arrangement in an offshore jurisdiction (including arrangements that give rise to DD outcomes). The key objective of imported mismatch rule is to maintain the integrity of the other hybrid mismatch rules by

removing any incentive for multinational groups to enter into hybrid mismatch arrangements. While these rules involve an unavoidable degree of co-ordination and complexity, they only apply to the extent a multinational group generates an intra-group hybrid deduction and will not apply to any payment that is made to a taxpayer in a jurisdiction that has implemented the full set of recommendations set out in the report.

235. The imported mismatch rule applies to both structured and intra-group imported mismatch arrangements and can be applied to any payment that is directly or indirectly set-off against any type of hybrid deduction. This guidance sets out three tracing and priority rules to be used by taxpayers and administrations to determine the extent to which a payment should be treated as set-off against a deduction under an imported mismatch arrangement. These rules start by identifying the payment that gives rise to a hybrid mismatch under one of the other chapters in this report (a "direct hybrid deduction") and then determine the extent to which the deductible payment made under that hybrid mismatch arrangement has been funded (either directly or indirectly) out of payments made by taxpayers that are subject to the imported mismatch rule ("imported mismatch payments"). The tracing and priority rules are summarised below, in the order in which they should be applied.

Structured imported mismatches

236. If the hybrid deduction is attributable to a payment made under a *structured arrangement* it will be treated as giving rise to an imported mismatch to the extent that deduction is funded out of the *payments made under that structured arrangement*. This rule applies a tracing approach to determine to what extent an imported mismatch payment made under a structured arrangement has been set-off (directly or indirectly) against a hybrid deduction under the same arrangement.

Direct imported mismatches

237. If the structured imported mismatch rule does not fully neutralise the effect of the mismatch, the direct imported mismatch rule treats the hybrid deduction as giving rise to an imported mismatch to the extent that it is directly set-off against payments received from other members of the group that are subject to the imported mismatch rule. This rule applies an apportionment approach which prevents the same hybrid deduction giving rise to an imported mismatch under the laws of more than one jurisdiction.

Indirect imported mismatch rule

238. Finally, if the structured or direct imported mismatch rule does not fully neutralise the effect of the mismatch, the indirect imported mismatch rule treats any surplus hybrid deduction as being set-off against imported mismatch payments received indirectly from members of the same control group. This rule applies a *tracing methodology* to determine to what extent the expenditure that gave rise to a surplus hybrid deduction has been indirectly funded by imported mismatch payments from other group members and an *apportionment approach*, which prevents the same surplus hybrid deduction being treated as set-off against an imported mismatch payment under the laws of more than one jurisdiction.

239. These three rules are designed to co-ordinate the operation of the imported mismatch rule within and between jurisdictions so that they can be applied consistently by each jurisdiction to neutralise the effect of imported mismatch arrangements while avoiding double taxation and ensuring predictable and transparent outcomes for

taxpayers. The rules contemplate that each member of the group will calculate the amount of imported mismatch payments and hybrid deductions on the same basis, in order to prevent differences in the calculation, timing and quantification of payments giving rise to the risk of over- or under-taxation.

Recommendation 8.1 - Deny the deduction to the extent the payment gives rise to an indirect D/NI outcome

240. Imported mismatches rely on the absence of effective hybrid mismatch rules in offshore jurisdictions in order to generate the mismatch in tax outcomes which can then be imported into the payer jurisdiction. Therefore the most reliable protection against imported mismatches will be for all jurisdictions to introduce rules recommended in this report. Such rules will neutralise the effect of the hybrid mismatch arrangement in the jurisdiction where it arises and prevent its effect being imported into a third jurisdiction.

241. In order to protect the integrity of the recommendations, however, this report further recommends the adoption of linking rule that requires the payer jurisdiction to deny a deduction for a payment to the extent the income from such payment is offset against a hybrid deduction in the counterparty jurisdiction. The imported mismatch rule has three basic elements:

(a) a deductible payment, made by a taxpayer that is subject to the hybrid mismatch rules, and which is included in ordinary income under the laws of the payee jurisdiction (an "imported mismatch payment");

(b) a deductible payment made by a person that is not subject to the hybrid mismatch rules which directly gives rise to a hybrid mismatch (a "direct hybrid deduction");

(c) a nexus between the imported mismatch payment and the direct hybrid deduction that shows how the imported mismatch payment has been set-off (whether directly or indirectly) against that hybrid deduction.

Imported mismatch payment

242. The definition of payment used in the imported mismatch rule is the same as that used for the other recommendations. It is generally broad enough to capture any transfer of value from one person to another but it does not include payments that are only deemed to be made for tax purposes and that do not involve the change of any economic rights between the parties. A payment will only be treated as an imported mismatch payment if it is both deductible under the laws of the payer jurisdiction and gives rise to ordinary income under the laws of the payee jurisdiction. Imported mismatch payments will therefore include rents, royalties, interest and fees paid for services but will not generally include amounts that are treated as consideration for the disposal of an asset. A payment made to a person who is not a taxpayer in any jurisdiction 9such as in **Example 1.6**) will not be treated as an imported mismatch payment.

Hybrid deduction

243. A person's hybrid deduction can come from two sources:

(a) payments that directly give rise to a D/NI or DD outcome under one of the hybrid mismatch arrangements identified in the other chapters in this report. These types of hybrid deductions are referred to in this guidance as "direct hybrid deductions".

(b) hybrid deductions that are surrendered to a group member under a tax grouping regime or arise as a consequence of making taxable payments to a group member with surplus hybrid deductions. These types of hybrid deductions are referred to in this guidance as "indirect hybrid deductions".

A hybrid deduction does not arise, however, to the extent a disregarded or deductible hybrid payment is set-off against dual inclusion income (see **Example 8.11** and **Example 8.12**). The method for calculating a person's hybrid deductions is set out further below.

Nexus between hybrid deduction and imported mismatch payment

244. The third element of the imported mismatch rule is that there must be a nexus, or chain of transactions and payments, that connects the hybrid deduction of one person with the imported mismatch payment made by another. This will be relatively easy to establish in the case of direct imported mismatches where the imported mismatch payment is made to the person who has the direct hybrid deduction. The tracing exercise will become more complex, however, where the imported mismatch payment must be traced through a chain of taxable payments or offsets under a tax grouping regime in order to determine whether the imported mismatch payment has been set-off against an indirect hybrid deduction under the indirect imported mismatch rule.

245. A number of different approaches could be adopted for determining whether, and to what extent, the hybrid deduction has been used to shelter the income on an imported mismatch payment. Countries applying the imported mismatch rules should, however, adopt a uniform approach that is clear, easy to administer and apply and that avoids the risk of double taxation.

Tracing and priority rules

246. This guidance sets out three tracing and priority rules that a jurisdiction should apply to determine the extent of the adjustment required under the imported mismatch rule. The rules should be applied (in the following order) by each jurisdiction that has an imported mismatch rule:

(a) The first rule (the "structured imported mismatch rule") identifies whether a direct hybrid deduction is part of a structured arrangement and, if so, treats that hybrid deduction as being set-off against any imported mismatch payment that forms part of the same arrangement and that funds (directly or indirectly) the expenditure that gave rise to the hybrid deduction.

(b) To the extent the mismatch in tax outcomes has not been neutralised by a jurisdiction applying the structured imported mismatch rule, the second rule then looks to see whether the taxpayer's hybrid deduction can be directly set-off against an imported mismatch payment made by a taxpayer that is a member of the same control group (the direct imported mismatch rule).

(c) Finally the jurisdiction should determine the extent to which any surplus hybrid deductions can be treated as being indirectly set-off against imported mismatch payments from other group members under the indirect imported mismatch rule.

247. Each of these rules applies a different approach to determining the nexus between the imported mismatch payment and the hybrid deduction. The structured imported mismatch rule applies a tracing approach that starts with the imported mismatch payment in one jurisdiction and follows the path of payments under the structured arrangement,

through the interconnected entities and payments that make up the arrangement, to identify whether that imported mismatch payment has directly or indirectly funded expenditure that gives rise to the hybrid deduction. The direct imported mismatch rule applies an apportionment rule that looks to the aggregate amount of imported mismatch payments received by a group member and the aggregate amount of hybrid deductions incurred by that group member and treats the hybrid deduction as being set-off against the imported mismatch payment in the same proportion. The indirect imported mismatch rule applies a combination of tracing and apportionment approaches to determine whether, and to what extent, an imported mismatch payment made by a taxpayer in one part of the group can be said to be indirectly set-off against a hybrid deduction of a taxpayer in another part of the group.

Structured imported mismatch arrangements

248. Where a hybrid deduction has arisen under a structured arrangement it is necessary to identify all the steps and transactions that form part of the same arrangement and to identify whether the taxpayer has made a deductible payment under that arrangement that has been set-off (directly or indirectly) against that hybrid deduction. The structured imported mismatch rule is applied first because it has a wider scope and applies to all the payments made under a structured arrangement even if those payments are not intra-group. The structured imported mismatch arrangement should be applied, however, whenever a hybrid deduction forms part of a structured arrangement even where the mismatch in tax outcomes occurs within the confines of a wholly-owned group. For example, in **Example 8.1**, a multinational group puts in place a group financing structure where the first link in the chain of intra-group loans is designed to produce a hybrid mismatch. In that case, all the intra-group loans and imported mismatch payment flows under the financing arrangement are treated as part of the same structured arrangement.

249. The tracing approach under the structured imported mismatch rule requires taxpayers to follow the flow of payments under the structured arrangement through the tiers of entities and transactions that make up the arrangement to determine if the taxpayer's imported mismatch payment has been directly or indirectly offset against a hybrid deduction arising under the same arrangement. In general it is expected that a tax administration will respect both a taxpayer's decision to treat a transaction that gives rise to a hybrid mismatch as forming part of a structured arrangement and the taxpayer's definition of the scope of that structured arrangement provided that treatment and definition is applied consistently by all the parties to that structured arrangement.

250. **Example 8.1**, **Example 8.2** and **Example 10.5** illustrate the operation of the structured imported mismatch rule.

Intra-group mismatches

251. Although a hybrid mismatch arrangement that is entered into between two members of a wholly-owned group may not be designed to shelter income of any taxpayer other than the immediate parties to the arrangement, any such mismatch has the net effect of lowering the aggregate tax burden of the group and the combination of intra-group payment flows and the fungible nature of income and expenses for tax purposes can make it difficult, if not impossible, to determine, which taxpayer in the group has derived a tax advantage under a hybrid mismatch arrangement. In order to neutralise the effect of such intra-group mismatches, without giving rise to economic double taxation,

this guidance sets out a direct and indirect imported mismatch rule which should be applied (in that order) to neutralise the effect of such intra-group mismatches.

Direct imported mismatches

252. The direct imported mismatch rule applies an apportionment approach that compares the amount of the taxpayer's hybrid deductions (including any indirect hybrid deductions) to the total amount of imported mismatch payments made to that taxpayer by group entities (as calculated under the law of the taxpayer's jurisdiction) and treats each imported mismatch payment as being set-off against those hybrid deductions in accordance with that ratio. Calculating the limitation by reference to a ratio determined under the laws of the payee jurisdiction ensures that each jurisdiction applies the direct imported mismatch rule on the same basis. The direct imported mismatch rule provides countries with a simple and comprehensive solution for neutralising the effect of intra-group mismatches while avoiding the risk of economic double taxation. Any remaining hybrid deductions that are not treated as set-off against direct imported mismatch payments will be treated as "surplus hybrid deductions" and allocated in accordance with the indirect imported mismatch rule described in further detail below.

253. The mechanical steps in the application of the structured and direct imported mismatch rule are as follows:

(a) The tax manager of the group should determine whether any group entity has direct hybrid deductions.

(b) If the direct hybrid deduction arises under a transaction that forms part of a structured arrangement, then those hybrid deductions should be treated as directly or indirectly set-off against imported mismatch payments made under the same arrangement.

(c) Any remaining hybrid deductions, together with any indirect hybrid deductions allocated to that group member in accordance with the indirect imported mismatch rule (see below), should be treated as directly set-off (pro-rata) against imported mismatch payments made by a group member.

(d) Hybrid deductions that are not neutralised under the structured or direct imported mismatch rules are treated as surplus hybrid deductions.

254. **Example 8.2** to **Example 8.4**, and **Example 8.6**, **Example 8.7** and **Example 8.10**, illustrate the operation of the direct imported mismatch rule.

Indirect imported mismatches

255. If the effect of the hybrid deduction has not been fully neutralised through the operation of the direct imported mismatch rule, the final step is to determine whether the surplus hybrid deduction should be allocated to another group member under the indirect imported mismatch rule.

256. The indirect imported mismatch rule applies a waterfall approach (described below) to determine to what extent the surplus hybrid deduction has been indirectly funded from imported mismatch payments made by members of the same group. This approach incorporates an allocation and tracing methodology to match a taxpayer's surplus hybrid deductions with imported mismatch payments within the group while ensuring that the rule will not result in the same hybrid deduction being set-off against an imported mismatch payment under the laws of more than one jurisdiction.

257. The group member's surplus hybrid deductions are allocated proportionately around the group in accordance with taxable payment flows within the group and in a way that takes into account the extent to which such taxable payments have been funded, directly or indirectly, out of imported mismatch payments. The resulting offset gives rise to an indirect hybrid deduction for the group member making the taxable payment. That indirect hybrid deduction can, in turn, be treated as set-off against an imported mismatch payment under the direct imported mismatch rule or give rise to a further surplus hybrid deduction that can be allocated to another group member.

258. The approach starts with a group member's "surplus hybrid deductions", which are the total of that group member's direct and indirect hybrid deductions that have not been neutralised by a jurisdiction applying the structured or direct imported mismatch rule. The group member's surplus hybrid deductions are treated as set-off against any taxable payments received. Taxable payments received by a group member will include any intra-group payment that is included in ordinary income by that group member and that is deductible under the laws of the payer jurisdiction (other than an imported mismatch payment).

259. A taxable payment should be treated as fully set-off against a surplus hybrid deduction of each group member unless the amount of a payee's "funded taxable payments" exceeds the amount of the payee's surplus hybrid deductions. A funded taxable payment is any taxable payment that is directly funded out of imported mismatch payments made by other group entities. In a case where the amount of a payee's "funded taxable payments" exceeds the amount of the payee's surplus hybrid deductions, the payee's surplus hybrid deductions should be treated as set-off against such funded taxable payments on a pro-rata basis.

260. The mechanical steps in the application of the indirect imported mismatch rule are as follows:

(a) The tax manager of the group should determine whether any group member has surplus hybrid deductions.

(b) The surplus hybrid deductions of that group member should be treated as surrendered to another member of the same tax group or set-off against a taxable payment made by another group member in accordance with the allocation and tracing methodology of the waterfall approach. This means that:

- In the event the amount of funded taxable payments exceeds the amount of surplus hybrid deductions, the surplus hybrid deductions should only be treated as set-off pro rata to the amount of funded taxable payments.

- In all other cases the surplus hybrid deduction should be treated as fully surrendered under the tax grouping regime or fully set-off against each taxable payment;

(c) The group entity that made the taxable payment or received the benefit of the group surrender (the payer entity) should then apply the direct imported mismatch rule and treat those hybrid deductions as set-off against any imported mismatch payments received from other group members;

(d) Both group entities will have a surplus hybrid deduction to the extent the mismatch in tax outcomes is not addressed through the application of the direct imported mismatch rule as described in paragraph (c) above.

261. The calculation of a group entity's surplus hybrid deduction under paragraph (d) should be adjusted as necessary to ensure that the application of the indirect imported mismatch rule does not result in the same hybrid deduction being treated as indirectly set-off against more than one imported mismatch payment.

262. **Example 8.5** and **Example 8.7** to **Example 8.15** illustrate the operation of the indirect imported mismatch rules.

Losses

263. In order to account for timing differences between jurisdictions and to prevent groups manipulating that timing in order to avoid the effect of the imported mismatch rule, a hybrid deduction should be taken to include any net loss that has been carried-forward to a subsequent accounting period, to the extent that loss results from a hybrid deduction. An example showing the application of the imported mismatch rule to losses which have been carried-forward from a prior period is set out in **Example 8.11** and **Example 8.16**. In order to reduce the complexity associated with the need to identify hybrid deductions that arose prior to the publication of this report any carry-forward loss from periods ending on or before 31 December 2016, should be excluded from the operation of this rule.

Co-ordination of imported mismatch rule between jurisdictions

264. In order to limit compliance costs and the risk of double taxation each country that implements the recommendations set out in the report should make reasonable endeavours to implement an imported mismatch rule that adheres to the methodology set out in this guidance and to apply this methodology in the same way. This will allow the adjustments required under the imported mismatch rules in each jurisdiction to be calculated consistently for the whole group and in a way that avoids any unnecessary duplication of compliance obligations.

265. It will be the domestic taxpayer who has the burden of establishing, to the reasonable satisfaction of the tax administration, that the imported mismatch rule has been properly applied in that jurisdiction. This initial burden may be discharged by providing the tax administration with copies of the group calculations together with supporting evidence of the adjustments that have been made under the imported mismatch rules in other jurisdictions. Tax administrations will generally be relying on the taxpayer to provide them with these calculations and supporting evidence. In the absence of such information, a tax administration may consider issuing its own assessment of the extent to which income from an imported mismatch payment has been directly or indirectly set-off against a hybrid deduction of another group member.

Recommendation 8.2 - Rule only applies to payments that are set-off against a deduction under a hybrid mismatch arrangement

266. Recommendation 8.2 defines when a deduction will be treated as a hybrid deduction for the purposes of the imported mismatch rule.

267. The definition of hybrid deduction includes a payment by a hybrid payer or dual resident that triggers a duplicate deduction resulting in a hybrid mismatch (i.e. a deduction that arises under a DD structure). When applying the imported mismatch rule in the intra-group context the rule applies in such a way that ensures there is no

double-counting of the hybrid deductions that are generated under such a DD structure. An illustration of a hybrid deduction involving a DD structure is set out in **Example 8.12**.

Recommendation 8.3 – Definition of imported mismatch payment

268. As noted above, the most reliable protection against imported mismatches will be for jurisdictions to introduce hybrid mismatch rules recommended in this report. Such rules will address the effect of the hybrid mismatch arrangement in the jurisdiction where it arises, and therefore prevent the effect of such mismatch being imported into a third jurisdiction. The imported mismatch rule therefore will not apply to any payment that is made to a taxpayer in a jurisdiction that has implemented the full set of recommendations set out in the report.

Recommendation 8.4 – Scope of the rule

269. The imported mismatch rule targets both structured arrangements and imported mismatch arrangements that arise within a control group.

270. An imported mismatch should be treated as structured if the hybrid deduction and the imported mismatch payment arise under the same arrangement. The definition of arrangement is set out in Recommendation 12 and includes any agreement, plan or understanding and all the steps and transactions by which it is carried into effect. A structured imported mismatch arrangement therefore includes not only those payments and transactions that give rise to the mismatch but also all the other transactions and imported mismatch payments that are entered into as part of the same scheme plan or agreement.

271. An example of the application of the imported mismatch rule to a structured arrangement is set out in **Example 10.5**. In that example, a fund that is in the business of providing loans to medium-sized enterprises enters into negotiations to provide a company with an unsecured loan that will be used to meet the companies working capital requirements. The fund uses a subsidiary in a third jurisdiction to make the loan and finances that loan through the use of a hybrid financial instrument. Neither the fund nor the subsidiary is resident in a jurisdiction that has introduced the hybrid mismatch rules. In that example, the financing arrangement is conceived as a single plan that includes both the loan by the subsidiary to the taxpayer and the transaction between the subsidiary and the fund that gives rise to the hybrid deduction. The arrangement is therefore a structured arrangement and the taxpayer should be treated as a party to that structured arrangement if it is involved in the design or has sufficient information about the arrangement to understand its operation and effect.

Chapter 9

Design principles

Recommendation 9

1. Design principles

The hybrid mismatch rules have been designed to maximise the following outcomes:

(a) neutralise the mismatch rather than reverse the tax benefit that arises under the laws of the jurisdiction;

(b) be comprehensive;

(c) apply automatically;

(d) avoid double taxation through rule co-ordination;

(e) minimise the disruption to existing domestic law;

(f) be clear and transparent in their operation;

(g) provide sufficient flexibility for the rule to be incorporated into the laws of each jurisdiction;

(h) be workable for taxpayers and keep compliance costs to a minimum; and

(i) minimise the administrative burden on tax authorities.

Jurisdictions that implement these recommendations into domestic law should do so in a manner intended to preserve these design principles.

2. Implementation and co-ordination

Jurisdictions should co-operate on measures to ensure these recommendations are implemented and applied consistently and effectively. These measures should include:

(a) the development of agreed guidance on the recommendations;

(b) co-ordination of the implementation of the recommendations (including timing);

(c) development of transitional rules (without any presumption as to grandfathering of existing arrangements);

(d) review of the effective and consistent implementation of the recommendations;

(e) exchange of information on the jurisdiction treatment of hybrid financial instruments and hybrid entities;

(f) endeavouring to make relevant information available to taxpayers (including reasonable endeavours by the OECD); and

(g) consideration of the interaction of the recommendations with other Actions under the BEPS Action Plan including Actions 3 and 4.

Overview

272. The domestic law changes and hybrid mismatch rules recommended in Part I of the report are designed to be co-ordinated with those in other jurisdictions. Co-ordination of the rules is important because it ensures predictability of outcomes for taxpayers and avoids the risk of double taxation. Co-ordination can be achieved by ensuring that countries implement the recommendations set out in the report consistently and that tax administrations interpret and apply those rules in the same way.

273. In order to achieve that consistency, Recommendation 9 calls on countries to implement and apply the rules in a manner that preserves the underlying policy objectives of the report. The Recommendation further calls on countries to:

(a) agree guidance on how the rules ought to be applied;

(b) co-ordinate the implementation on the rules (primarily as to timing);

(c) agree how the rules should apply to existing instruments and entities that are caught by the rules when they are first introduced (i.e. transitional arrangements);

(d) undertake a review of the operation of the rules as necessary to determine whether they are operating as intended;

(e) agree procedures for exchanging information on the domestic tax treatment of instruments and entities in order to assist tax administrations in applying their rules to hybrid mismatch arrangements within their jurisdiction;

(f) endeavour to make such information available to taxpayers; and

(g) provide further commentary on the interaction between the recommendations in the report and the other Items in the *BEPS Action Plan* (OECD, 2013).

274. The guidance on Recommendation 9.1 sets out and explains the design principles in further detail and the guidance on Recommendation 9.2 sets out further detail on achieving co-ordination in the implementation and application of the rules summarised in the paragraph above.

Recommendation 9.1 - Design principles

275. Although the recommendations in the report are drafted in the form of rules, it is not intended that countries transcribe them directly into domestic law without adjustment. It is expected that the recommendations will be incorporated into domestic tax legislation using existing local law definitions and concepts in a manner that takes into account the existing legislative and tax policy framework. At the same time, countries should seek to ensure that these domestic rules, once implemented, will apply to the same arrangements and entities, and provide for the same tax outcomes, as those set out in the report.

276. The recommendations set out in this report are intended to operate as a comprehensive and coherent package of measures to neutralise mismatches that arise from the use of hybrid instruments and entities without imposing undue burdens on taxpayers and tax administrations.

277. In practice, many of these design principles are complementary. For example, hybrid mismatch rules that apply automatically will be more clear and transparent in their operation and reduce administration costs for tax authorities. Rules that minimise disruption to domestic law will be easier for countries to implement and reduce

compliance costs for taxpayers. Each of these design principles and their implications for the domestic implementation and application of the rules is discussed in further detail below.

Rules should target the mismatch rather than focusing on establishing in which jurisdiction the tax benefit arises

278. The Action Plan simply calls for the elimination of mismatches without requiring the jurisdiction applying the rule to establish that it has "lost" tax revenue under the arrangement. While neutralising the effect of hybrid mismatch arrangements will address the risks to a jurisdiction's tax base, this will not be achieved by capturing additional revenue under the hybrid mismatch rules themselves, rather the rules are intended to drive taxpayers towards less complicated and more transparent tax structuring that is easier for jurisdictions to address with more orthodox tax policy tools. Accordingly the hybrid mismatch rules apply automatically and without regard for whether the arrangement has eroded the tax base of the country applying the rule. This approach assures consistency in the application of the rules (and their outcomes) between jurisdictions and also avoids the practical and conceptual difficulties in distinguishing between acceptable and unacceptable mismatches or trying to allocate taxing rights based on the extent to which a country's tax base has been eroded through the hybrid mismatch arrangement.

Comprehensive

279. Hybrid mismatch rules that are not comprehensive will create further tax planning opportunities and additional compliance costs for taxpayers without achieving their intended policy outcomes. The rules should avoid leaving gaps that would allow a taxpayer to structure around them. This report recommends that every jurisdiction introduces a complete set of rules that are sufficient to neutralise the effect of the hybrid mismatch on a stand-alone basis, without the need to rely on hybrid mismatch rules in the counterparty jurisdiction.

280. Hybrid mismatch rules that are both comprehensive and widespread will be subject to some degree of jurisdictional overlap; while it is important to have rules that are comprehensive and effective, such overlap should not result in double taxation of the same economic income. For this reason the rules recommended in the report are organised in a hierarchy that switches-off the effect of one rule where there is another rule operating in the counterparty jurisdiction that will be sufficient to address the mismatch. Both primary recommendations and defensive rules are required, however, in order to comprehensively address the mismatch; the hierarchy simply addresses the risk of over-taxation in the event the same hybrid mismatch rules apply to the same arrangement in different jurisdictions.

281. The hybrid mismatch rules apply automatically to a hybrid mismatch arrangement if it gives rise to a mismatch in tax outcomes that can be attributed to the hybrid element in the arrangement. Automatic rules are more effective than those that only apply subject to the exercise of administrative discretion and avoid the need for co-ordination of responses between tax authorities, which would increase complexity and make the rules less efficient and consistent in their operation.

Co-ordination of rules to avoid double taxation

282. Rules that are comprehensive and apply automatically need:

(a) an agreed ordering rule to ensure that they apply consistently and proportionately in situations where the counterparty jurisdiction does, or does not, have a similar set of hybrid mismatch rules;

(b) to apply consistently with other rules of the domestic tax system so that the interaction does not result in double taxation of the same economic income;

(c) to co-ordinate with the rules in a third jurisdiction (such as CFC rules) which subject payments to taxation in the residence state of the investor.

283. In order to achieve the first of these design outcomes, these recommendations contain an ordering rule so that one rule is turned-off when the counterparty jurisdiction with the same set of rules can neutralise the effect of the hybrid mismatch arrangement in a more efficient and practical way. This ordering rule avoids the need for an express tie-breaker and achieves the necessary degree of co-ordination without resorting to the competent authority procedure.

284. Just as the hybrid mismatch rules require co-ordination with hybrid mismatch rules in other jurisdictions they also must be co-ordinated as between themselves and with other specific anti-abuse and re-characterisation rules.

Co-ordination between specific recommendations and hybrid mismatch rules

285. The hybrid financial instrument rule and the reverse hybrid rule only operate to the extent the arrangement gives rise to a D/NI outcome. Such an outcome will not arise if, after a proper determination of the character and treatment of the payment under the laws of the payer and payee jurisdictions, a mismatch in tax outcomes has not arisen. This consideration of the tax consequences in each jurisdiction should include the introduction of measures to implement the specific recommendations for improvements in domestic law under Recommendations 2 and 5 respectively.

Co-ordinating the interaction between the hybrid mismatch rules

286. The hybrid mismatch rules set out in this report should generally be applied in the following order:

(a) Hybrid financial instrument rule (Recommendation 1);

(b) Reverse hybrid rule (Recommendation 4) and disregarded hybrid payments rule (Recommendation 3);

(c) Imported mismatch rule (Recommendation 8); and

(d) Deductible hybrid payments rule (Recommendation 6) and dual resident entity rule (Recommendation 7).

287. In **Example 4.4** a hybrid entity makes an interest payment to a reverse hybrid in the same group. The example concludes that the reverse hybrid rule will apply to the arrangement to deny the deduction so that there is no scope for the operation of the deductible hybrid payments rule.

288. In **Example 3.2** the payer borrows money from its parent and the loan is attributed to the payer's foreign branch. The payment of interest on the loan is deductible under the laws of the foreign jurisdiction but is not recognised by the payee. The example considers whether the disregarded hybrid payments rule or the hybrid financial instrument rule should be applied to neutralise the D/NI outcome. The example concludes that the

payer jurisdiction should apply the hybrid financial instrument rule to deny a deduction for the interest if the mismatch in the tax treatment of the interest payment can be attributed to the terms of the instrument between the parties. If the interest payment is not treated, under the laws of the payer jurisdiction as subject to adjustment under the hybrid financial instrument rule then the payer jurisdiction should then apply the disregarded hybrid payments rule to deny the payer a deduction for the interest payment to the extent the interest expense exceeds the dual inclusion income of the branch.

Co-ordinating the interaction between hybrid mismatch rules and other transaction specific and other anti-abuse rules

289. The hybrid financial instrument rule applies whenever the mismatch can be attributed to the terms of the instrument. The fact that the mismatch can also be attributed to other factors (such as the fact that payee is tax exempt) will not prevent the rule from applying provided the mismatch would have arisen even in respect of the same payment between taxpayers of ordinary status. Because the hybrid financial instrument rule is confined to looking at the tax treatment of the instrument under the laws of the payer and payee jurisdictions, the rule will operate to make an adjustment in respect of an expected mismatch in tax outcomes and it will not be necessary for the taxpayer or tax administration to know precisely how the payments under a financial instrument have actually been taken into account in the calculation of the counterparty's taxable income in order to apply the rule. This means that transaction specific rules that adjust the tax treatment of payment based on the status of the taxpayer or the context in which the instrument is held, will not typically impact on the outcome under the hybrid financial instrument rule. For example, a taxpayer may be denied a deduction under local law in respect of interest on a loan, because the proceeds are used to acquire an asset that generates a tax exempt return. This tax treatment in the payer jurisdiction will not affect whether the payment is required to be included in income by the payee under the secondary rule.

290. The hybrid entity rules (Recommendations 3 to 7), however, only operate to the extent a taxpayer is actually entitled to a deduction for a payment under local law. Accordingly these rules will not apply to the extent the taxpayer is subject to transaction or entity specific rules under the parent or payer jurisdiction that prevent the payment from being deducted.

Interaction between hybrid mismatch rule and general limitations on deductibility

291. In addition to transaction and entity specific rules, jurisdictions may impose further restrictions on deductibility that limit the overall deduction that can be claimed by a taxpayer. Such limitations would include a general limitation on interest deductibility such as a fixed-ratio rule. The hybrid mismatch rules make adjustments in respect of particular items that are taken into account for the purposes of calculating a taxpayer's overall income or expense and therefore, as a matter of logic, would generally apply before any such general or overall limitation. This principle is illustrated in **Example 9.2** where the loan made to a subsidiary results in the subsidiary becoming subject to an interest limitation rule in the subsidiary's jurisdiction so that a portion of the interest expense on the loan is no longer deductible. The tax position of the borrower under a general interest limitation rule is not relevant to a determination of whether the payment is deductible for the purposes of the hybrid financial instrument rule. Accordingly the hybrid mismatch rule treats the interest payments as giving rise to a D/NI outcome,

notwithstanding the partial disallowance of the interest expense under the laws of the payer jurisdiction.

292. The interaction between the interest limitation rule and the hybrid mismatch rules should be co-ordinated under domestic law to achieve an overall outcome that avoids double taxation and is proportionate on an after-tax basis. The mechanism for co-ordinating the interaction between the two rules will depend on how the interest limitation rule operates; however, the interaction between these rules should not have the net effect of denying a deduction twice for the same item of expenditure. Double counting can generally be avoided by the taxpayer applying the hybrid mismatch rules first and then applying the interest limitation rule to the extent the remaining deductible interest expense exceeds the statutory ratio.

CFC inclusion

293. Domestic hybrid mismatch rules that deny a deduction for a payment that is not includible in income by the recipient should take appropriate account of the fact that the payment may be subject to taxation under the CFC or other rules operating in the jurisdiction of the recipient's investor.

294. When introducing the hybrid mismatch rules into local law, countries may choose to set materiality thresholds that a taxpayer must meet before a taxpayer can treat a CFC inclusion as reducing the amount of adjustments required under the rule. These thresholds could be based on the percentage of shareholding or the amount of income included under a CFC regime.

Rules should minimise disruption under existing domestic law

295. The hybrid mismatch rules seek to align the tax treatment of the arrangement in the affected jurisdictions with as little disruption to domestic law as possible. In order to minimise the impact on other domestic rules, the hybrid mismatch rules are intended to do no more than simply reconcile the tax consequences under the arrangement. They do not need to address the characterisation of the hybrid entity or instrument itself.

296. A country adopting hybrid mismatch rules could choose to go further under domestic law and re-characterise an instrument, entity or arrangement to achieve consistency with domestic law outcomes, however, such a re-characterisation approach is not necessary to align the ultimate tax outcome in both jurisdictions.

Rules should be clear and transparent

297. The outcome envisaged by the report is that each country will adopt a single set of integrated linking rules that provides for clear and transparent outcomes under the laws of all jurisdictions applying the same rules. The rules must therefore be drafted as simply and clearly as possible so that they can be consistently and easily applied by taxpayers and tax authorities operating in different jurisdictions. This will make it easier for multinationals and other cross-border investors to interpret and apply the hybrid mismatch rules, reducing both compliance costs and transactional risk for taxpayers.

Rules should achieve consistency while providing implementation flexibility

298. The rules must be the same in each jurisdiction while being sufficiently flexible and robust to fit within existing domestic tax systems. To achieve this, hybrid mismatch rules must strike a balance between providing jurisdiction neutral definitions that can be

applied to the same entities and arrangements under the laws of two jurisdictions while avoiding a level of detail that would make them impossible to implement under the domestic laws of a particular jurisdiction.

299. If the same hybrid mismatch rules are to be applied to the same arrangement by two jurisdictions and they are to co-ordinate the response between them, it will generally be necessary to ensure that the rules in both jurisdictions operate on the same entities and payments. For this reason, the implementing legislation should use (where appropriate) jurisdiction neutral terminology that describes the arrangement by reference to the mismatch in tax outcomes rather than the mechanism used to achieve it. For example, there are a number of different mechanisms that can be used to offset a double deduction against non-dual inclusion income and, in order to achieve consistency in the application of the hybrid entity rules across all jurisdictions, the deductible or disregarded hybrid payment rule needs to be articulated without reference to the mechanism by which the double deduction is achieved.

Rules should minimise compliance costs

300. One of the fundamental principles in the design of any tax rule is that it keeps compliance costs for taxpayers to a minimum. One of the intended outcomes of the report is to address any potential compliance costs by dealing with hybrid mismatch arrangements on a multilateral and co-ordinated basis. For example, in the context of deductible hybrid payments, rule co-ordination and ordering ensures that the limitation on deductibility needs to be applied in only one jurisdiction to neutralise the effect of the hybrid mismatch.

301. Similarly, if countries move from unilateral measures to protect their tax bases to a more co-ordinated approach, that will not only have the effect of reducing the risk posed by these structures to the tax base of all countries but it should also lead to an overall decrease in transaction costs and tax risks for cross-border investors who might otherwise find themselves exposed to the risk of economic double taxation under a unilateral hybrid mismatch measure adopted by an individual jurisdiction.

Rules should be easy for tax authorities to administer

302. Once the hybrid mismatch rules are in place they will be applied automatically by taxpayers when determining their tax liability, and should not raise significant on-going administration costs for tax authorities. It is expected that in many cases these types of arrangements will disappear which should reduce the costs associated with identifying and responding to these structures. The costs to tax administrations in applying and enforcing the rule will depend, however, on having rules that are clear and transparent so that they apply automatically with minimal need for the taxpayer or tax administration to make qualitative judgments about whether an arrangement is within scope.

303. In general the rules are intended to improve the coherence of the international tax system and remove the incentive for taxpayers to exploit gaps in the international tax architecture. This should lead to a reduction in tax administration costs. For example, in the case of the hybrid financial instruments, the alignment of tax outcomes should take some pressure off the distinction between the use of debt and equity in cross-border investment. A multilateral and co-ordinated approach also reduces administration costs as it enables one tax authority to quickly understand the rule being applied in the other jurisdiction. The work undertaken as part of Action Item 12 on mandatory disclosure and information exchange (*Mandatory Disclosure Rules*, OECD, 2015a) should also make it

easier for tax authorities to collect and exchange information on both the structure of arrangements and the payments made under them.

Recommendation 9.2 - Implementation and co-ordination

304. Recommendation 9.2 sets out further actions that countries should take to ensure that the rules are interpreted and applied consistently on a cross-border basis.

Guidance

305. This report sets out agreed guidance on the interpretation and application of the hybrid mismatch rules. Implementing and applying the recommendations in accordance with this guidance should ensure predictable and proportionate outcomes. This consistency is important for achieving the overall design objectives, which are to create a network of domestic rules that comprehensively and automatically neutralise the effect of cross-border hybrid mismatch arrangements in a way that minimises disruption to domestic laws and the risk of double taxation. The guidance set out in this report is intended to provide both taxpayers and tax administrations with a clear and consistent understanding of how the technical elements of the recommendations are intended to achieve these outcomes. It is expected that the guidance will be reviewed periodically to determine whether there is a need for any additions, clarifications, updates or amendments to the recommendations or the guidance.

Co-ordination of timing in application of the rules

306. Recommendation 9.2(b) calls for countries to develop standards that will allow them to better co-ordinate the implementation of the recommendations particularly with regards to the timing issues that can arise where the implementation of hybrid mismatch rules in one jurisdiction has tax consequences in the counterparty jurisdiction. These include situations where the introduction of hybrid mismatch rules in the payer jurisdiction has the effect of releasing the payee from the burden of making adjustments under the secondary rule or where rules the introduction of new rules governing the taxation of deductible dividends or reverse hybrids in the payee jurisdiction relieve the payer from the restrictions on the ability to deduct payments under a hybrid mismatch arrangement.

307. Complications in determining the amount of the payment caught by the primary and secondary rule during the switch-over period can be minimised by ensuring that, when the recommendations are introduced into domestic law they take effect prospectively and from the beginning of a taxpayer's accounting period. In cases where the parties to the hybrid mismatch arrangement have the same accounting period and recognise income and expenditure on a similar basis, the switch-over from the secondary to the primary rule should not generally raise significant issues. However, complexity, and the risk of double taxation, can arise where the accounting period for the counterparty commences on a date that is part-way through an existing accounting period (referred to in this guidance as the "switch-over period") and/or there are differences between the two jurisdictions in the rules for recognising the timing of income and expenditure. In this case, unless the primary and secondary rules are properly co-ordinated, there is a risk that both jurisdictions could apply the hybrid mismatch rules to the same payment or to part of the same payment.

308. When determining the amount of income or expenditure subject to adjustment under the hybrid financial instrument rule: the secondary rule should apply to any payment that is treated as made prior to the switch-over period and the primary rule should apply to any payment that is treated as made during or after the switch-over period. This approach gives priority to the primary response, while ensuring that the taxpayer in the secondary jurisdiction does not need to re-open a prior return for a period when the primary rule was not in effect.

309. This application of the co-ordination rule is illustrated in **Example 9.1** where the payee jurisdiction applies the defensive rule under Recommendation 3.1(b) to include a disregarded hybrid payment in income. In that example, the payer jurisdiction introduces hybrid mismatch rules from the beginning of the payer's accounting period. Because the payer's accounting period commences part-way through the accounting period of the payee (the switch-over period), the payee jurisdiction will only apply the secondary rule during the switch-over period to the extent the mismatch in tax treatment has not been eliminated under the primary rule in the payer jurisdiction. **Example 2.3** provides an example of how to co-ordinate the hybrid financial instrument rules with rules denying the benefit of a dividend exemption to a deductible payment. In the example a payment of interest on a bond issued by a foreign subsidiary is treated as an exempt dividend by the parent jurisdiction and the subsidiary jurisdiction denies a deduction for this payment under the hybrid financial instrument rule. However the hybrid financial instrument rule ceases to apply to the extent the payments are included in ordinary income as a consequence of the parent jurisdiction amending its domestic law consistent with Recommendation 2.1.

Transitional rules

310. Recommendation 9.2(c) provides that countries will identify the need for any transitional measures. The report expressly, however, that there will be no presumption as to the need to grandfather any existing arrangements.

311. When the hybrid mismatch rules are introduced they should generally apply to all payments under hybrid mismatch arrangements that are made after the effective date of the legislation or regulation. This would include applying the rules to arrangements that are structured even if such structuring occurred before the introduction of the rules. The effective date for the hybrid mismatch rules should be set far enough in advance to give taxpayers sufficient time to determine the likely impact of the rules and to restructure existing arrangements to avoid any adverse tax consequences associated with hybridity. In order to avoid unnecessary complication and the risk of double taxation, the rules should generally take effect from the beginning of a taxpayer's accounting period and include the co-ordination rules described above.

312. In general the need for transitional arrangements can be minimised by ensuring taxpayers have sufficient notice of the introduction of the rules. Given the hybrid mismatch rules apply to related parties, members of a control group and structured arrangements it is expected that in most cases taxpayers will be able to avoid any unintended effects by restructuring their existing arrangements. Jurisdiction specific grandfathering of existing arrangements should generally be avoided because of its potential to complicate the rules and lead to inconsistencies in their application. The effect of such jurisdiction specific grandfathering is also likely to be limited in the absence of similar carve-outs being put in place in the counterparty jurisdiction.

Review

313. The recommendations in the report are intended to tackle the problem of hybrid mismatches on a multilateral and co-ordinated basis. All of the hybrid mismatch rules are linking rules that depend on tax outcomes in the other jurisdiction and certain rules contain a defensive rule that only applies when the mismatch has not been neutralised by the primary recommendation in the counterparty jurisdiction. Therefore, when applying these rules under their domestic laws, tax administrations will be implicitly relying on the tax outcomes (including any hybrid mismatch rules) applying under the laws of the other jurisdiction in order to arrive at the right legal and policy outcome. Furthermore, when it comes to co-ordinating the interaction between the hybrid mismatch rules of two jurisdictions, tax administrations will need a clear understanding of what the rules in the counterparty jurisdiction are and how they are intended to operate. This process can be facilitated by each country that introduces the rules, providing other countries with notification that they have introduced the rule and information on how they are intended to operate in the context of their domestic tax system. This information may need to be updated, from time to time, to reflect changes in domestic law.

Exchange of information

314. Countries have recognised that, in order for the implementation of the hybrid mismatch rules to be effective, tax administrations will need to have efficient and effective information exchange processes and to increase the frequency and quality of their co-operative cross border collaboration. Applying the recommendations in this report, particularly the imported mismatch rule in Recommendation 8, may require countries to undertake multi-lateral interventions in relation to cases involving hybrid mismatch arrangements.

315. Countries have also recognised the need to engage in early and spontaneous exchanges of information that are foreseeably relevant to the administration or enforcement of the hybrid mismatch rules. The information that will need to be exchanged will typically be taxpayer specific and be based on existing legal instruments, including Double Tax Conventions and Tax Information Exchange Agreements entered into by the participating countries and the *Convention on Mutual Administrative Assistance in Tax Matters* (OECD 2010). The Forum on Tax Administration's (FTA) Joint International Tax Shelter Information and Collaboration (JITSIC) network also provides a forum for countries to work more closely and collaboratively on areas of mutual interest such as hybrid mismatch arrangements including through the sharing of information about the cross-border tax treatment of entities and instruments and increased bi-lateral and multi-lateral intervention activity.

Information to taxpayers

316. Publication of this guidance is intended to provide both taxpayers and tax administrations with a clear and consistent understanding of how the rules are intended to operate. Countries will continue to make reasonable endeavours to ensure taxpayers have accurate information on the tax treatment of entities and financial instruments under the laws of their jurisdiction.

Interaction with Action 4

317. Where a country has introduced a fixed ratio rule, the potential base erosion and profit shifting risk posed by hybrid mismatch arrangements is reduced, as the overall

level of net interest deductions an entity may claim is restricted. However, this risk is not eliminated. Within the limits imposed by a fixed ratio rule, there may still be significant scope for an entity to claim interest deductions in circumstances where a hybrid financial instrument or hybrid entity is used to give rise to a double deduction or deduction/no inclusion outcome. Where a group ratio rule applies, there is also a risk that hybrid mismatch arrangements could be used to increase a group's net third party interest expense, supporting a higher level of net interest deductions across the group. In order to address these risks, a country should implement all of the recommendations in this report, alongside the best practice approach agreed under Action 4 (OECD, 2015b). Rules to address hybrid mismatch arrangements should be applied by an entity before the fixed ratio rule and group ratio rule to determine an entity's total net interest expense. Once this total net interest expense figure has been determined, the fixed ratio rule and group ratio rule should be applied to establish whether the full amount may be deducted, or to what extent net interest expense should be disallowed.

Bibliography

OECD (2015a), *Mandatory Disclosure Rules, Action 12 - 2015 Final Report*, OECD/G20 Base Erosion and Profit Shifting Project, OECD Publishing, Paris, http://dx.doi.org/10.1787/9789264241442-en.

OECD (2015b), *Limiting Base Erosion Involving Interest Deductions and Other Financial Payments, Action 4 - 2015 Final Report*, OECD/G20 Base Erosion and Profit Shifting Project, OECD Publishing, Paris, http://dx.doi.org/10.1787/9789264241176-en.

OECD (2014), *Neutralising the Effects of Hybrid Mismatch Arrangements*, OECD Publishing, Paris, http://dx.doi.org/10.1787/9789264218819-en.

OECD (2013), *Action Plan on Base Erosion and Profit Shifting*, OECD Publishing, Paris, http://dx.doi.org/10.1787/9789264202719-en.

OECD (2010), *Convention on Mutual Administrative Assistance in Tax Matters, Amended by the 2010 Protocol*, OECD Publishing, Paris, http://dx.doi.org/10.1787/9789264115606-en.

Chapter 10

Definition of structured arrangement

Recommendation 10

1. General Definition

Structured arrangement is any arrangement where the hybrid mismatch is priced into the terms of the arrangement or the facts and circumstances (including the terms) of the arrangement indicate that it has been designed to produce a hybrid mismatch.

2. Specific examples of structured arrangements

Facts and circumstances that indicate that an arrangement has been designed to produce a hybrid mismatch include any of the following:

(a) an arrangement that is designed, or is part of a plan, to create a hybrid mismatch;

(b) an arrangement that incorporates a term, step or transaction used in order to create a hybrid mismatch;

(c) an arrangement that is marketed, in whole or in part, as a tax-advantaged product where some or all of the tax advantage derives from the hybrid mismatch;

(d) an arrangement that is primarily marketed to taxpayers in a jurisdiction where the hybrid mismatch arises;

(e) an arrangement that contains features that alter the terms under the arrangement, including the return, in the event that the hybrid mismatch is no longer available; or

(f) an arrangement that would produce a negative return absent the hybrid mismatch.

3. When taxpayer is not a party to a structured arrangement

A taxpayer will not be treated as a party to a structured arrangement if neither the taxpayer nor any member of the same control group could reasonably have been expected to be aware of the hybrid mismatch and did not share in the value of the tax benefit resulting from the hybrid mismatch.

Overview

318. The hybrid mismatch rules apply to any person who is a party to a structured arrangement. The purpose of the structured arrangement definition is to capture those taxpayers who enter into arrangements that have been designed to produce a mismatch in tax outcomes while ensuring taxpayers will not be required to make adjustments under

the rule in circumstances where the taxpayer is unaware of the mismatch and derives no benefit from it.

319. The test for whether an arrangement is structured is objective. It applies, regardless of the parties' intentions, whenever the facts and circumstances would indicate to an objective observer that the arrangement has been designed to produce a mismatch in tax outcomes. The structured arrangement rule asks whether the mismatch has been priced into the terms of the arrangement or whether the arrangement's design and the surrounding facts and circumstances indicate that the mismatch in tax outcomes was an intended feature of the arrangement. The test identifies a set of non-exhaustive factors that indicate when an arrangement should be treated as structured.

320. The structured arrangement definition does not apply to a taxpayer who is not a party to the arrangement. A person will be a party to an arrangement when that person has sufficient involvement in the design of the arrangement to understand how it has been structured and what its tax effects might be. A person will not be a party to a structured arrangement, however, if that person (or any member of the control group) does not benefit from, and could not reasonably have been expected to be aware of, the mismatch arising under a structured arrangement.

Recommendation 10.1 - General definition

321. Recommendation 10.1 sets out the general definition of a structured arrangement. The test is objective. It is based on what can reasonably be concluded from the terms of the arrangement and the surrounding facts and circumstances. If the tax benefit of the mismatch is priced into the arrangement or if a reasonable person, looking at the facts of the arrangement, would otherwise conclude that it was designed to engineer a mismatch in tax outcomes, then the arrangement should be caught by the definition regardless of the actual intention or understanding of the taxpayer when entering into an arrangement. The fact that an arrangement is structured, however, does not mean that every person with tax consequences under that arrangement should be treated as a party to it (see Recommendation 10.3 below).

Definition of arrangement

322. The definition of arrangement will include a number of separate arrangements that all form part of the same plan or understanding and will include all the steps and transactions by which that plan or understanding is carried into effect. When looking into whether a hybrid mismatch has been "priced into the terms of the arrangement" or whether the facts and circumstances "indicate that [the arrangement] has been designed to produce a mismatch" taxpayers and tax administrations should look to the entire arrangement rather than simply to the transaction that gives rise to the mismatch in tax outcomes.

Priced into the arrangement

323. The hybrid mismatch will be priced into the terms of the arrangement if the mismatch has been factored into the calculation of the return under the arrangement. The test looks to the actual terms of the arrangement, as they affect the return on the arrangement, and as agreed between the parties, to determine whether the pricing of the transaction is different from what would have been agreed had the mismatch not arisen. This is a legal and factual test that looks only to the terms of the arrangement itself and

the allocation of risk and return under the arrangement rather than taking into account broader factors such as the relationship between the parties or the circumstances in which the arrangement was entered into. The test would not, for example, take into account the consideration paid by a taxpayer to acquire a hybrid financial instrument unless the instrument is issued and sold as part of the same arrangement.

324. **Example 10.1** illustrates a situation where the hybrid mismatch can be described as "priced into the terms of the arrangement". In that example the taxpayer subscribes for a hybrid financial instrument that provides for what would otherwise be considered a market rate of return minus an amount that is calculated by reference to the holder's tax saving on the instrument. In this case the example concludes that the mismatch in tax outcomes is priced into the terms of the instrument and that, accordingly, the arrangement is a structured arrangement.

325. The pricing of the arrangement includes more than just the return under the transaction that gives rise to the hybrid mismatch. **Example 10.2** describes a situation where back-to-back loans are structured through an unrelated intermediary in order to produce a hybrid mismatch. In that example, the tax benefit under the hybrid mismatch arrangement is returned to the parent company in the form of an above-market rate of interest. In such a case, the arrangement includes the back-to-back financing and the tax consequences of the hybrid mismatch will be considered to have been priced into the terms of the arrangement in the form of an above market rate of interest on the loan.

Facts and circumstances of the arrangement

326. The facts and circumstances test is a wider test that looks to: the relationship between the parties; the circumstances under which the arrangement was entered into; the steps and transactions that were undertaken to put the arrangement into effect; the terms of the arrangement itself and the economic and commercial benefits of the transaction; to determine whether the arrangement can be described as having been "designed to produce a hybrid mismatch". The fact that an arrangement also produces a combination of tax and commercial benefits does not prevent the arrangement from being treated as structured if an objective and well informed observer would conclude that part of the explanation for the design of the arrangement was to generate a hybrid mismatch.

327. Recommendation 10.2 sets out a list of factors that point to the existence of a structured arrangement. These factors are not exclusive or exhaustive and there may be other factors in an arrangement that would lead an objective observer to conclude that the arrangement has been designed to produce a mismatch in tax outcomes.

328. The facts and circumstances test could, for example, take into account any relationship between the parties that makes it more likely that the arrangement has been structured. For example, in **Example 1.36**, two taxpayers are joint shareholders in third company. One shareholder transfers a bond that has been issued by the subsidiary to the other shareholder. This transfer relieves the subsidiary company of liability under the hybrid financial instrument rule. The fact that the parties to the transfer were both investors in the issuer and the fact that the transaction had the effect of relieving the issuer from an impending tax liability should be taken into account in considering whether the arrangement has been designed to produce a mismatch in tax outcomes.

Recommendation 10.2 - Specific examples of structured arrangements

329. The list of factors in Recommendation 10.2 should be used as a guide for taxpayers and tax administrations as to the kinds of transactions and activities that will bring a hybrid mismatch arrangement within the structured arrangement definition. In many cases more than one of the factors may be present in the same arrangement.

Arrangement that is designed or part of a plan to produce a mismatch

330. An arrangement will be part of a plan to produce a hybrid mismatch where a person with material involvement in, or awareness of, the design of the arrangement (such as a tax advisor) has identified, before the arrangement was entered into, that it will give rise to mismatch in tax outcomes. This element will be present if there is a written or oral advice given in connection with the arrangement, or working papers or documents produced before the arrangement is entered into, that indicate that the transaction will give rise to a mismatch. This factor ensures that if a taxpayer is advised of the hybrid mismatch then the arrangement will be a structured arrangement.

331. An illustration of a structured arrangement that is part of a plan to produce a mismatch is set out in **Example 1.31**. In that example a company wishes to borrow money from an unrelated lender. The lender suggests structuring the loan as a repo transaction in order to secure a lower tax cost for the parties under the arrangement. The facts of the arrangement therefore indicate that it has been designed to produce a mismatch. Furthermore, as indicated in the example, structuring the loan in this way may result in a lower cost of funds for the borrower which will mean that that the mismatch has been priced into the terms of the arrangement.

332. In **Example 10.2** a tax advisor advises a company to loan money under a hybrid financial instrument to a subsidiary through an unrelated intermediary in order to avoid the effect of the related party test under the hybrid financial instrument rule. In this case the arrangement has been designed to avoid the effect of the related party rules in order to produce a mismatch in tax outcomes and the arrangement can therefore be described as having been designed to produce a hybrid mismatch.

An arrangement that uses a term, step or transaction to create a mismatch

333. An arrangement will be structured if it incorporates a term, step or transaction that has been inserted into the arrangement to achieve a hybrid mismatch. A term, step or transaction will be treated as inserted into an arrangement to produce a mismatch in tax outcomes if that mismatch would not have arisen in the absence of that term, step or transaction and where there was no substantial business, commercial or other reason for inserting that term into the arrangement or undertaking that step or transaction. An assessment of purpose of a transaction should take into account other reasonable alternatives that would have achieved the same effect without triggering a mismatch in tax outcomes. This factor ensures that a taxpayer does not go out of their way to create a hybrid mismatch. The factors listed in Recommendation 10.2 do not limit the scope of the general wording in Recommendation 10.1 so that a hybrid mismatch should still be treated as structured even if every step in the transaction has a non-tax justification if it is reasonable to conclude that part of the explanation for the overall design of the arrangement was to generate a hybrid mismatch.

334. The application of this factor is discussed in **Example 10.2** where a company causes its subsidiary to enter into a hybrid financial instrument with an unrelated

intermediary in order to avoid the effect of the related party test under the hybrid mismatch rules. In that case the intermediary has been inserted into the financing arrangement in an attempt to circumvent the effect of the hybrid mismatch rules. There is no substantial business, commercial or other reason that explains why the financing is routed through a third party and, accordingly, the use of the intermediary and the back-to-back financing structure has been inserted into the structure in order to produce a mismatch in tax outcomes. In **Example 4.2** two individuals wish to make a loan to a company that is wholly-owned by one of them. Instead of making the loan directly, they contribute equity to B Co, a reverse hybrid which makes the loan. The example concludes that the intermediary has been inserted into the financing arrangement in an attempt to produce a hybrid mismatch. Given the relatively simple nature of the financing arrangement, there is no substantial business, commercial or other reason for providing the financing through a reverse hybrid other than to produce a mismatch in tax outcomes.

An arrangement is marketed as a tax advantaged product

335. An arrangement will be treated as marketed as a tax advantaged product if there is written, electronic or oral communication provided to the parties to the arrangement or potential parties to the arrangement that identifies the potential tax benefits of the structure. As indicated in **Example 10.3** the marketing material need not specifically refer to the existence of the hybrid mismatch but must identify an advantage that flows from the hybrid mismatch arrangement. This could include, for example, material that points out, to an investor in a double deduction structure, that the investor will be able to claim the benefit of any losses incurred by the investment vehicle, or, in a D/NI structure that indicates that the borrower should be entitled to a tax deduction for the payments. Marketing information would include any information in a prospectus or other offering documents that are required to be provided to an investor as part of an offer of investment securities. This factor ensures that tax benefits derived from the hybrid mismatch arrangement cannot be used to market the arrangement.

An arrangement that is primarily marketed to taxpayers in a particular jurisdiction

336. In the absence of marketing material, the arrangement should still be considered structured if, in practice, the arrangement is primarily marketed to taxpayers who will benefit from the mismatch. The fact that the arrangement is also available to taxpayers in other jurisdictions who do not benefit from the mismatch will not prevent that transaction from being treated as part of a structured arrangement if the majority of the arrangements, by number or value, are entered into with taxpayers located in jurisdictions that do benefit from the mismatch.

337. In **Example 6.1** a company seeking to raise money, approaches several potential investors that are resident in the same jurisdiction inviting them to make an investment in the company on particular terms. Differences in the way the jurisdictions of the issuer and investors treat an instrument of this nature mean that payments under the instrument will give rise to a hybrid mismatch under the hybrid financial instrument rule. The potential investors are sent an investment memorandum that includes a summary of the expected tax treatment of the instrument. The arrangement will be treated as a structured arrangement because the tax advantages arising under the hybrid mismatch have been marketed to investors and the investment is primarily marketed to taxpayers in a jurisdiction that can take advantage of the mismatch. While the issuer will be subject to the hybrid mismatch rule for as long as the instrument remains outstanding, the example

notes that a subsequent purchaser of the notes may not be required to apply the hybrid mismatch rule if they do not have sufficient information about the arrangement to understand its hybrid effect.

Change to the economic return under the instrument

338. Features of an arrangement that alter the economic return for the parties in the event that the hybrid mismatch is no longer available can evidence that the benefit of the hybrid mismatch has been priced into the arrangement. The potential presence of this factor is discussed in **Example 10.2** where a company causes its subsidiary to enter into a hybrid financial instrument with an unrelated intermediary in order to avoid the effect of the related party test under the hybrid mismatch rules. In that case, it is noted that the intermediary will typically insist on the structure being unwound in the event the tax benefit is no longer available. This factor ensures that parties to the structured arrangement cannot enter into arrangements allocating the risk and benefits of an adjustment under the hybrid mismatch rules without actually triggering such an adjustment.

339. It is not unusual for financing arrangements to include provisions dealing with tax risk (particularly change of law risk). Clauses that permit a lender to increase the cost of financing due to a change in circumstances beyond the lender's control and clauses that permit a bond issuer to redeem an instrument for its face value in the event of a change in tax law, do not necessarily indicate that the parties intended to enter into a structured arrangement provided the taxpayer can show that such contractual terms would ordinarily be expected to be found in a financing arrangement of that nature. If, on the other hand, the evidence suggests that such provisions were inserted primarily to deal with the risk that the hybrid mismatch rules may apply to the arrangement, then the structured arrangement rule is likely to apply.

Pre-tax negative return

340. The fact that it would be uneconomic for the taxpayer to enter into the arrangement but for the benefit under the hybrid mismatch may be evidence that the arrangement is a structured arrangement. This factor is also related to the pricing of the arrangement and is intended to prevent a taxpayer from passing the tax benefits under a hybrid mismatch arrangement to another contracting party. An example of pre-tax negative return transaction is given in **Example 10.2** in respect of a back-to-back loan structure. In that example, the tax benefit under the hybrid mismatch arrangement is returned to the parent company in the form of an above-market rate of interest so that, on the facts of that case, the intermediary is borrowing money at a more expensive rate than it is earning under the hybrid financial instrument.

Recommendation 10.3 - When taxpayer is not a party to a structured arrangement

341. Recommendation 10.3 excludes a taxpayer from the structured arrangement rule where the taxpayer is not a party to the structured arrangement.

342. A person will be a party to a structured arrangement when that person has a sufficient level of involvement in the arrangement to understand how it has been structured and what its tax effects might be. A taxpayer will not be treated as a party to a structured arrangement, however, where neither the taxpayer nor any member of the same

control group was aware of the mismatch in tax outcomes or obtained any benefit from the mismatch.

343. The test for whether a person is a party to structured arrangement is intended to capture situations where the taxpayer or any member of the taxpayer's control group was aware of the mismatch in tax outcomes and should apply to any person with knowledge of the arrangement and its tax effects regardless of whether that person has derived a tax advantage under that arrangement. The policy of the hybrid mismatch rules is to neutralise the mismatch in tax outcomes by adjusting the tax outcomes in the payer or payee jurisdiction without the need to consider whether, or to what extent, the person subject to the adjustment has benefited from that mismatch. While a taxpayer must be aware of the existence of the hybrid mismatch arrangement in order to make the adjustment, a tax administration should not be required to establish that the taxpayer has benefited from the mismatch before requiring that the adjustment be made. The knowledge test is an objective test based on the information available to the taxpayer and should not impose an obligation on a taxpayer to undertake additional due diligence on a commercial transaction over and above what would be expected of a reasonable and prudent person.

344. Whether a taxpayer is a party to a structured arrangement is likely to have the most practical significance in the context of payments made to a reverse hybrid or under an imported mismatch arrangement. In the cases of a reverse hybrid, for example, the relationship between the investor and the reverse hybrid will often satisfy the conditions of a structured arrangement. This is particularly the case in respect of investment funds where investors may look to invest in vehicles that are tax neutral under the laws of the establishment jurisdiction and to ensure that the investment return will only be taxable on distribution. While fund structures such as this could be described as having been designed to create a mismatch in tax outcomes, the payer will not be considered a party to such an arrangement if it did not benefit from the mismatch (i.e. the payment was at fair market value) and the payer could not reasonably have been expected to be aware of the mismatch in tax treatment.

345. This principle is illustrated in **Example 4.1** where the use of a reverse hybrid as a single-purpose lending entity prima facie indicates that the arrangement between the investor and the reverse hybrid has been engineered to produce a mismatch in tax outcomes. In that case, however, the payer is not treated as a party to the structured arrangement because it pays a market rate of interest under the loan and would not have been expected, as part of its ordinary commercial due diligence, to take into consideration the tax position of the underlying investor or the tax treatment of the interest payment under the laws of the investor jurisdiction when making the decision to borrow money from the reverse hybrid..

346. The outcome described in **Example 4.1** can be contrasted with that described below in **Example 10.5** where the hybrid element is introduced into the structure after financing discussions between the investor and the payer have commenced. In that example a fund that is in the business of providing loans to medium-sized enterprises enters into negotiations to provide a company with an unsecured loan that will be used to meet the company's working capital requirements. The fund uses a subsidiary in a third jurisdiction to make the loan and finances that loan through the use of a hybrid financial instrument. Neither the fund nor the subsidiary is resident in a jurisdiction that has introduced the hybrid mismatch rules. The financing arrangement is conceived as a single plan that includes both the transaction that gives rise to the original hybrid deduction (the

hybrid financial instrument) and the loan by the subsidiary to the taxpayer. The taxpayer will be treated as a party to that structured arrangement if it is involved in the design or has sufficient information about the arrangement to understand its operation and effect. A taxpayer will not be treated as a party to a structured arrangement, however, where neither the taxpayer nor any member of the taxpayer's control group obtained any benefit under a hybrid mismatch arrangement or had sufficient information about the arrangement to be aware of the fact that it gave rise to a mismatch in tax outcomes. The principle is further illustrated in **Example 10.3** where a hybrid financial instrument is sold to a taxpayer. The example notes that, while the purchaser can be taken to be aware of its own tax treatment under the financial instrument it would not typically be expected to enquire into the tax position of the issuer and, provided the instrument was acquired for its fair market value (and not under the same arrangement that gave rise to the hybrid mismatch) such a person would not typically be brought within the scope of the structured arrangement rules.

Arrangements entered into on behalf of a taxpayer

347. When applying the structured arrangement rule, the actions of a taxpayer's agent should be attributed to the taxpayer. Where a transparent entity enters into a hybrid mismatch arrangement and the tax consequences of a payment under that arrangement are attributed to the investor, the structured arrangement rule should be applied to the investor as if the investor was a direct party to that structured arrangement and had entered into that arrangement on the same basis as the transparent entity. In **Example 10.4** a trust subscribes for an investment in the company on particular terms. Differences in the way the jurisdiction of the issuer and the jurisdiction of the investors treat an instrument of this nature mean that payments under the instrument will give rise to a hybrid mismatch under the hybrid financial instrument rule. Potential investors, including the trust, are sent an investment memorandum that includes a summary of the expected tax treatment of the instrument. The payment under the instrument is allocated by the trust to a beneficiary who has no knowledge of the investment made by the trustee. In this case, the trust's status as a party to a structured arrangement is attributed to the beneficiary, together with the payment, so that the payment to the beneficiary is caught by the hybrid financial instrument rule.

Chapter 11

Definitions of related persons, control group and acting together

Recommendation 11

1. General definition

For the purposes of these recommendations:

(a) Two persons are related if they are in the same control group or the first person has a 25% or greater investment in the second person or there is a third person that holds a 25% or greater investment in both.

(b) Two persons are in the same control group if:

(i) they are consolidated for accounting purposes;

(ii) the first person has an investment that provides that person with effective control of the second person or there is a third person that holds investments which provides that person with effective control over both persons;

(iii) the first person has a 50% or greater investment in the second person or there is a third person that holds a 50% or greater investment in both; or

(iv) they can be regarded as associated enterprises under Article 9.

(c) A person will be treated as holding a percentage investment in another person if that person holds directly or indirectly through an investment in other persons, a percentage of the voting rights of that person or of the value of any equity interest in that person.

2. Aggregation of interests

For the purposes of the related party rules a person who acts together with another person in respect of ownership or control of any voting rights or equity interests will be treated as owning or controlling all the voting rights and equity interests of that person.

3. Acting together

Two persons will be treated as acting together in respect of ownership or control of any voting rights or equity interests if:

(a) they are members of the same family;

(b) one person regularly acts in accordance with the wishes of the other person;

(c) they have entered into an arrangement that has material impact on the value or control of any such rights or interests; or

(d) the ownership or control of any such rights or interests are managed by the same person or group of persons.

If a manager of a collective investment vehicle can establish to the satisfaction of the tax authority, from the terms of any investment mandate, the nature of the investment and the circumstances that the hybrid mismatch was entered into, that the two funds were not acting together in respect of the investment then the interest held by those funds should not be aggregated for the purposes of the acting together test.

Overview

348. The report treats hybrid financial instruments and hybrid transfers between related parties as within the scope of the hybrid mismatch rules. Other hybrid mismatch arrangements are generally treated as within scope of the recommendations where the parties to the mismatch are members of the same control group.

349. The related party and control group tests apply regardless of the circumstances in which the hybrid mismatch arrangement was entered into. The principle is illustrated in **Example 1.1** where it is noted that a debt instrument that is acquired by the issuer's parent in an unrelated transaction will still constitute a financial instrument between related parties and is potentially subject to the application of the hybrid financial instrument rule notwithstanding that it was not caught by the rule at the time it was originally issued.

350. Two persons will be treated as related if they form part of the same control group or if one person has a 25% investment in the other person or a third person has a 25% investment in both. The test measures both direct and indirect investment, which includes both voting rights and the value of any equity interests. Persons who are acting together in respect of the ownership or control of an investment in certain circumstances are required to aggregate their ownership interests for the purposes of the related party test.

351. Parties will be treated as members of the same control group if:

(a) they form part of the same consolidated group for accounting purposes or the provision between them can be regarded as a provision between associated enterprises under Article 9 of the *OECD Model Tax Convention* (OECD, 2014);

(b) one person has a 50% investment or effective control of the other person (or a third person has a 50% or effective control of both).

352. The hybrid mismatch rules also apply to any person who is a party to a "structured" arrangement that has been designed to produce a mismatch. For the discussion of structured arrangements see the guidance to Recommendation 10.

Recommendation 11.1 - General definition

353. Recommendation 11.1 sets out the general definition of related persons and control group.

Related parties

354. Persons are treated as related parties for the purposes of the hybrid mismatch rules if they are in the same control group or one person holds a 25% investment in the other or the same person holds a 25% investment in both. A person's investment in another person is determined by looking to the percentage of voting rights or of the value of any equity interests that the first person holds in the second person. The terms "voting rights" and "equity interests" are defined in Recommendation 12.

Voting interests

355. While the measurement of voting interests will be easiest in the context of corporate entities that issue equity share capital, the term also includes equivalent control rights in other types of investment vehicles such as partnerships, joint ventures and trusts.

A person's voting interest is the right of that person to participate in the decision-making concerning a distribution by that person, a change in that person's constitutional structure or in the appointment of a director. The term director refers to any person who has power, under the constitutional documents, to manage and control a person (such as the trustee of a trust).

356. The right to participate in any one of the decision-making functions of a person is sufficient to constitute a voting right in that person but the right must be conferred under the constitutional documents of the entity itself. **Example 11.1** concerns a trust where the settlor has the right, under the trust deed, to appoint trustees but has no right to distributions or to amend the trust deed. In this case the settlor is, nevertheless, treated as a related party of the trust as the settlor effectively holds 100% of the decision-making rights concerning any trustee appointment.

357. **Example 11.2** concerns a partnership formed between four individuals. All partners have the same voting rights and an equal share in the profits of the partnership. In this case each partner should be treated as having a 25% investment in the partnership and will be considered related to the partnership. The partners will not, however, be considered related to each other.

358. The rights must be actual decision-making rights rather than rights that might arise at some point in the future, although contingencies that are procedural in nature and within the control of the holder can be ignored for these purposes. Thus a convertible bond holder who can elect, at any time, to convert such bonds into ordinary shares should be treated as holding voting interests in the issuer on a diluted basis, while a lender who has the right to appoint a receiver in the event of default under a loan will not be treated as holding voting rights in the borrower as such rights are contingent on default by the borrower and are not conferred under the articles of association of the company but by the terms of the security granted under the loan.

Value of equity interests

359. An instrument should be treated as giving rise to an equity interest if it provides the holder with an equity return. An equity return means an entitlement to profits or eligibility to participate in distributions. While the definition of "equity return" in Recommendation 12 also includes derivative equity returns, this extended definition does not apply in the measurement of equity interests for the purposes of the related party and control tests. An instrument may be treated as an equity interest, even if it is in the form of a debt instrument, if it confers a right to participate in the profits of the issuer or in any surplus on liquidation.

360. In the case of a company with only one class of ordinary shares on issue, it should generally be the case that voting interests and equity interests are held in the same proportions. Non-voting shares, bonds, warrants or other financial instruments that carry an entitlement to an equity return and that are widely-held or regularly traded may be excluded from the measurement of the value of equity interests where the way these instruments are issued, held or traded does not give rise to significant structuring concerns.

Indirect holding

361. A person that holds voting rights or equity interest in another person will be treated as holding a proportionate amount of the voting rights or equity interests held by

that person. Indirect holdings should be measured on a dilution basis so that if Individual A holds 50% of the voting or equity interests in B Co and B Co holds 50% of the voting or equity interests in C Co, then A should be treated as holding 25% of the interests C Co. A more detailed example setting out the calculation of indirect voting rights is set out in **Example 11.3**. In that example, A Co owns 100% of voting rights in C Co and 20% of voting rights in D Co. F Co is owned 20% by C Co and 40% by D Co. A Co is therefore related to C Co and F Co and F Co is related to D Co, but A Co is not related to D Co (unless it can be shown that they are members of the same control group).

Control group

362. Two persons should be treated as being in the same control group if they meet one of the conditions listed in Recommendation 11.1(b).

Consolidation

363. A subsidiary entity should be treated as related to its ultimate parent if the subsidiary is required to be consolidated, on a line-by-line basis in the parent's consolidated financial statements prepared under International Financial Reporting Standards (IFRS) or applicable local Generally Accepted Accounting Principles (GAAP).

Effective control

364. Persons are members of the same control group if the first person can effectively control the second person through an investment in that person or if there is a third person that has a sufficiently significant investment in both persons that gives it an effective control over both of them. This will be the case, for example, where a person is a substantial shareholder in a widely-held company and that shareholding gives that person effective control over the appointment of directors.

Voting or equity interests

365. Persons are treated as part of the same control group if one person holds at least a 50% investment in the other or the same person holds at least a 50% investment in both. A percentage investment in another person is to be determined by reference to the percentage voting rights of that person or of the value of any equity interests of that person. The measurement of voting and value rights is discussed above.

Associated enterprises

366. Two persons should be regarded as members of the same control group if they are treated as associated enterprises under Article 9 of the *OECD Model Tax Convention* (OECD, 2014). According to Article 9.1 "associated enterprises" are found where:

(a) An enterprise of a Contracting State participates directly or indirectly in the management, control or capital of an enterprise of the other Contracting State, or

(b) The same persons participate directly or indirectly in the management control or capital enterprise of a Contracting State and an enterprise of the other Contracting State.

367. The *OECD Model Tax Convention* (OECD, 2014) and the Commentaries do not establish the threshold or criteria to determine when participation in capital, management or control is sufficient to make two enterprises "associated enterprises" within the scope

of Article 9. It is left for countries to set the criteria to assess when the transfer pricing rules will apply under domestic law and especially as to the meaning of "control". The effect of including associated enterprises within the definition of control group is that the hybrid mismatch rules should apply to any transaction that is also subject to adjustment under a country's transfer pricing rules.

Recommendation 11.2 - Aggregation of interests

368. Recommendation 11.2 defines when a person's equity interests should be aggregated with those of another person for the purposes of the related party or control group tests.

Recommendation 11.3 - Acting together

369. The purpose of the "acting together" requirement is to prevent taxpayers from avoiding the related party or control group requirements by transferring their voting interest or equity interests to another person, who continues to act under their direction in relation to those interests. The other situation targeted by the acting together requirement is where a taxpayer or group of taxpayers who individually hold minority stakes in an entity, enter into arrangements that would allow them to act together (or under the direction of a single controlling mind) to enter into a hybrid mismatch arrangement with respect to one of them.

370. The acting together test covers voting rights or equity interests held by a single economic unit such as a family and covers the following three basic scenarios:

(a) where one person is required, or can be expected to act, in accordance with the wishes of another person in respect of the voting rights or equity interests held by that first person;

(b) where two or more people agree to act together in respect of voting rights or equity interests that they hold;

(c) where a person (or people) agree that a third person can act on their behalf in respect of voting rights or equity interests that they hold.

Members of the same family

371. A person will be deemed to hold any equity or voting interests that are held by the members of that person's family. Family is defined in Recommendation 12. This test would include a person's spouse (including civil partner), the relatives of that person and their spouses. A relative includes grandparents, parents, children, grandchildren and brothers and sisters (including adopted persons and step-siblings) but it would not include indirect or non-lineal descendants such as a person's nephew or niece.

Regularly acts in accordance with the wishes of the other person

372. A person will be treated as acting in accordance with the wishes of another person where the person is legally bound to act in accordance with another's instructions or if it can be established that one person is expected to act, or typically acts, in accordance with another's instructions. The focus of the test is on the actions of that person in relation to the voting rights or equity interests. The equity interests or voting rights held by a lawyer for example, will not be treated as held by the lawyer's client under the acting together

test, unless it can be established that such rights or interest are held as part of the lawyer – client relationship.

Entered into an arrangement that has material impact on the value or control of any such rights or interests

373. One person will be treated as holding the equity or voting interests of another person if they have entered into an arrangement regarding the ownership or control of those rights or interests. The test covers both arrangements concerning the exercise of voting interests (such as the right to participate in any decision-making) and or regarding beneficial entitlements (such as entitlement to profits or eligibility to participate in distributions) or arrangements concerning the ownership of those rights (such as agreements or options to sell such rights). The test is intended to capture arrangements that are entered into with other investors and does not cover arrangements that are simply part of the terms of the equity or voting interest or operate solely between the holder and issuer.

374. The arrangement regarding the ownership or control of voting rights or interests must have a material impact on the value of those rights or interests. The materiality threshold prevents an investor having their equity or voting interests treated as part of a common holding arrangement simply because the investor is a party to a commercially standard shareholder or investor agreement that does not have a material impact on the ability of a holder to exercise ownership or control over its equity or voting interest.

375. This point is illustrated in **Example 11.4** where an investor is a party to a shareholder's agreement that requires the investor to first offer his equity interest to existing investors (at market value) before selling to a third party. Such an agreement will not generally have a material impact on the value of the holder's equity interest and should not be taken into account for the purposes of the acting together requirement.

376. The acting together test does not impose any definitional limits on the content of the common control arrangement and the acting together test can capture transactions between otherwise unrelated taxpayers even if the common control arrangement has not played any direct role in the transaction that has given rise to the mismatch. This is illustrated by **Example 11.4**. In that example an unrelated investor acquires a listed financial instrument issued by a company. Payments under that instrument give rise to a hybrid mismatch. The fact that an investor is also a minority investor in that company and has entered into a voting rights agreement with a majority shareholder automatically brings that investor within the scope of the hybrid financial instrument rule.

The ownership or control of any such rights or interests are managed by the same person or group of persons

377. This element of the acting together test treats investors as acting together if their interests are managed by the same person or group of persons. This requirement would pick up a number of investors whose investments were managed under a common investment mandate or partners in an investment partnership.

378. This element of the acting together test contains an exception for investors that are collective investment vehicles where the nature of the investment mandate and the investment means that two funds under the common control of the same investment manager will not be treated as acting together if the circumstances in which they make the investment (including the terms of the investment mandate) mean that the funds should

not be treated as acting together for the purposes of the test. The application of this exception is illustrated in **Example 11.5**.

Bibliography

OECD (2014), *Model Tax Convention on Income and on Capital*, condensed version, OECD Publishing, Paris, http://dx.doi.org/10.1787/mtc_cond-2014-en.

Chapter 12

Other definitions

Recommendation 12

1. Definitions

For the purpose of these recommendations:

Accrued income	Accrued income, in relation to any payee and any investor, means income of the payee that has accrued for the benefit of that investor.
Arrangement	Arrangement refers to an agreement, contract, scheme, plan, or understanding, whether enforceable or not, including all steps and transactions by which it is carried into effect. An arrangement may be part of a wider arrangement, it may be a single arrangement, or it may be comprised of a number of arrangements.
Collective investment vehicle	Collective investment vehicle means a collective investment vehicle as defined in paragraph 4 of the *Granting of Treaty Benefits with Respect to the Income of Collective Investment Vehicles* (2010, OECD).
Constitution	Constitution, in relation to any person, means the rules governing the relationship between the person and its owners and includes articles of association or incorporation.
D/NI outcome	A payment gives rise to a D/NI outcome to the extent the payment is deductible under the laws of the payer jurisdiction but is not included in ordinary income by any person in the payee jurisdiction. A D/NI outcome is not generally impacted by questions of timing in the recognition of payments or differences in the way jurisdictions measure the value of that payment. In some circumstances however a timing mismatch will be considered permanent if the taxpayer cannot establish to the satisfaction of a tax authority that a payment will be brought into account within a reasonable period of time (see Recommendation 1.1(c)).
DD outcome	A payment gives rise to a DD outcome if the payment is deductible under the laws of more than one jurisdiction.
Deduction	Deduction (including deductible), in respect of a payment, means that, after a proper determination of the character and treatment of the payment under the laws of the payer jurisdiction, the payment is taken into account as a deduction or equivalent tax relief under the laws of that jurisdiction in calculating the taxpayer's net income.
Director	Director, in relation to any person, means any person who has the power under the constitution to manage and control that person and includes a trustee.
Distribution	Distribution, in relation to any person, means a payment of profits or gains by that person to any owner.

Recommendation 12 (*continued*)

Dual inclusion income	Dual inclusion income, in the case of both deductible payments and disregarded payments, refers to any item of income that is included as ordinary income under the laws of the jurisdictions where the mismatch has arisen. An item that is treated as income under the laws of both jurisdictions may, however, continue to qualify as dual inclusion income even if that income benefits from double taxation relief, such as a foreign tax credit (including underlying foreign tax credit) or a domestic dividend exemption, to the extent such relief ensures that income, which has been subject to tax at the full rate in one jurisdiction, is not subject to an additional layer of taxation under the laws of either jurisdiction.
Equity interest	Equity interest means any interest in any person that includes an entitlement to an equity return.
Equity return	Equity return means an entitlement to profits or eligibility to participate in distributions of any person and, in respect of any arrangement is a return on that arrangement that is economically equivalent to a distribution or a return of profits or where it is reasonable to assume, after consideration of the terms of the arrangement, that the return is calculated by reference to distributions or profits.
Establishment jurisdiction	Establishment jurisdiction, in relation to any person, means the jurisdiction where that person is incorporated or otherwise established.
Family	A person (A) is a member of the same family as another person (B) if B is: • the spouse or civil partner of A; • a 'relative' of A (brother, sister, ancestor or lineal descendant); • the spouse or civil partner of a relative of A; • a relative of A's spouse or civil partner; • the spouse or civil partner of a relative of A's spouse or civil partner; or • an adopted relative.
Financing return	Financing return, in respect of any arrangement is a return on that arrangement that is economically equivalent to interest or where it is reasonable to assume, after consideration of the terms of the arrangement, that the return is calculated by reference to the time value of money provided under the arrangement.
Hybrid mismatch	A hybrid mismatch is defined in paragraph 3 in Recommendations 1, 3, 4, 6 and 7 for the purposes of those recommendations.
Included in ordinary income	A payment will be treated as included in ordinary income to the extent that, after a proper determination of the character and treatment of the payment under the laws of the relevant jurisdiction, the payment has been incorporated as ordinary income into a calculation of the payee's income under the law of that jurisdiction.
Investor	Investor, in relation to any person, means any person directly or indirectly holding voting rights or equity interests in that person.
Investor jurisdiction	Investor jurisdiction is any jurisdiction where the investor is a taxpayer.

Recommendation 12 (*continued*)

Mismatch	A mismatch is a DD outcome or a D/NI outcome and includes an expected mismatch.
Money	Money includes money in any form, anything that is convertible into money and any provision that would be paid for at arm's length.
Offshore investment regime	An offshore investment regime includes controlled foreign company and foreign investment fund rules and any other rules that require the investor's accrued income to be included on a current basis under the laws of the investor's jurisdiction.
Ordinary income	Ordinary income means income that is subject to tax at the taxpayer's full marginal rate and does not benefit from any exemption, exclusion, credit or other tax relief applicable to particular categories of payments (such as indirect credits for underlying tax on income of the payer). Income is considered subject to tax at the taxpayer's full marginal rate notwithstanding that the tax on the inclusion is reduced by a credit or other tax relief granted by the payee jurisdiction for withholding tax or other taxes imposed by the payer jurisdiction on the payment itself.
Payee	Payee means any person who receives a payment under an arrangement including through a permanent establishment of the payee.
Payee jurisdiction	Payee jurisdiction is any jurisdiction where the payee is a taxpayer.
Payer	Payer means any person who makes a payment under an arrangement including through a permanent establishment of the payer.
Payer jurisdiction	Payer jurisdiction is any jurisdiction where the payer is a taxpayer.
Payment	Payment includes any amount capable of being paid including (but not limited to) a distribution, credit, debit, accrual of money but it does not extend to payments that are only deemed to be made for tax purposes and that do not involve the creation of economic rights between parties.
Person	Person includes any natural or legal person or unincorporated body of persons and a trust.
Taxpayer	Taxpayer, in respect of any jurisdiction, means any person who is subject to tax in that jurisdiction whether as a resident or by virtue of applicable source rules (such as maintaining a permanent establishment in that jurisdiction).
Trust	Trust includes any person who is a trustee of a trust acting in that capacity.
Voting rights	Voting rights means the right to participate in any decision-making concerning a distribution, a change to the constitution or the appointment of a director.

Overview

379. The recommendations in the report set out requirements for the design of domestic laws. The language of the recommendations is not meant to be translated directly into domestic legislation. Rather countries are expected to implement these recommendations into domestic law using their own concepts and terminology. At the same time, in order for the recommended rules to be effective and to avoid double taxation, they need to be co-ordinated with the rules in other countries. To this end,

Recommendation 12 sets out a common set of defined terms intended to ensure consistency in the application of the rules.

Recommendation 12.1 - Other definitions

Accrued income

380. The definition of *accrued income* is used as part of the definition of *offshore investment regime* and in Recommendation 5, which sets out specific recommendations on the treatment of reverse hybrids. The concept of accrued income, in relation to any investor, includes any amount that is paid to an investment entity that increases the value of that investor's interest in that entity.

Arrangement

381. The term *arrangement* is used as part of the definition of *financial instrument,* in Recommendation 1.2, and as part of the definition of *structured arrangement* in Recommendation 10.

Collective investment vehicle

382. The rules on aggregation of ownership interests set out in Recommendation 11.3 of the report, state that two persons will be treated as *acting together* in respect of their ownership interest in an entity if the ownership interests are managed by the same person or group of persons. The rule does not, however, apply to any person that is a *collective investment vehicle* if the investment manager can establish to the satisfaction of the tax authority, from the terms of the investment mandate and the circumstances in which the investment was made, that two funds were not acting together in respect of the investment. The definition of collective investment vehicle cross-refers to the definition set out in the 2010 Report on the Granting of Treaty Benefits with Respect to the Income of Collective Investment Vehicles.

Constitution

383. The term *constitution* is used in the definition of *director* and *voting rights*. These terms are used for determining the amount of investment held by one person in another person for the purposes of the related party and control group tests in Recommendation 11.

D/NI outcome

384. The hybrid mismatch rules in Chapters 1, 3 and 4 of the report neutralise the effects of *mismatches* that are *D/NI outcomes*. A D/NI outcome arises where a payment is deductible under the laws of one jurisdiction (the payer jurisdiction) and is not *included in ordinary income* under the laws of any other jurisdiction where the payment is treated as being received (the payee jurisdiction).

Differences in valuation

385. A D/NI outcome can arise from differences between tax jurisdictions in the way they measure the value ascribed to a payment. This principle is illustrated in **Example 1.13** and **Example 1.16** where a taxpayer treats a loan from its parent as having been issued at a discount and accrues this discount as an expense over the life of the loan. A mismatch could arise, on the facts of these examples, if the parent adopted the same

accounting treatment as the subsidiary but attributed a lower value to the discount. In such a case the amount accrued as a deduction in each accounting period would not be matched by the same inclusion in the parent jurisdiction.

386. If however, both jurisdictions characterise the payment in the same way and arrive at the same monetary value for a payment then there will generally be no mismatch in tax outcomes within the scope of the recommendations (see **Example 1.15**). While there may be differences in tax outcomes that arise from the valuation of a payment or in translating a payment into local currency, these differences in will not give rise to a D/NI outcome. This principle is illustrated in **Example 1.17** where payments of interest and principal under the loan are payable in a foreign currency. A fall in the value of the local currency results in the payments under the loan becoming more expensive in local currency terms. Under local law, the payer is entitled to a deduction for this increased cost. This deduction, however, is not reflected by a corresponding inclusion in the payee jurisdiction. The difference in tax treatment does not give rise to a D/NI outcome, however, as the proportion of the interest and principal payable under the loan is the same under the laws of both jurisdictions.

Entity located in a no tax jurisdiction

387. The recommendations in the report with respect to D/NI arrangements are not intended to capture payments made to a person resident in a no-tax jurisdiction. As illustrated in **Example 1.6** a payment will not be treated as giving rise to a D/NI outcome if it is received by a person who is not subject to tax in any jurisdiction.

DD outcome

388. The hybrid mismatch rules in Chapter 6 and 7 of the report neutralise the effects of *mismatches* that are *DD outcomes*. A DD outcome arises where a payment that is deductible under the laws of one jurisdiction (the payer jurisdiction) triggers a duplicate deduction under the laws of another jurisdiction.

Deduction

389. The concept of "deduction" and "deductible" refer to an item of expenditure that is eligible to be offset against a taxpayer's *ordinary income* when that person's liability to income tax under the laws of the taxpayer's jurisdiction. The definition should include any tax relief that is economically equivalent to a deduction such as a tax credit for dividends paid.

390. The recommendations focus on whether a payment falls into the category of a "deductible" item under the laws of the relevant jurisdiction and the jurisdiction specific details of the taxpayer's net income calculation should not generally affect the question of whether a payment is deductible for tax purposes. Interest that is capitalised into the cost of an asset should, for example, be treated as deductible for the purposes of this rule.

391. Under the hybrid mismatch rules a deduction must arise in respect of a "payment". Therefore the starting point in applying the hybrid mismatch rules is to look for the legal basis for the deduction to determine whether the deduction relates to actual expenditure or transfer or value rather than it being a purely notional amount for tax purposes.

Director

392. A "director" includes a director of a company. The term also applies to anyone, such as a trustee of a trust, who has been formally appointed under the constituent documents to manage and control another person. The ability to appoint a director is used as part of the determination of "voting rights". These terms are used for determining the amount of investment held by one person in another for the purposes of the related party and control group tests in Recommendation 11.

Distribution

393. The term distribution is used to determine a person's *voting rights* under the related party and control group tests in Recommendation 11 and as part of the definition of *equity return,* which is used for calculating the amount of a person's equity interest and for defining what arrangements should be treated as a *financial instrument* in Recommendation 1.3.

Dual inclusion income

394. The measurement of dual inclusion income is relevant to determining the amount of deduction restricted under the hybrid mismatch rules in Chapters 3, 6 and 7 of the report.

Equity interest

395. An amount of a person's equity interest is used to determine whether they fall within the related party or control group tests in Recommendation 11.

Equity return

396. The definition of *equity return* is used for calculating the amount of a person's equity interest in another person in order to determine whether they fall within the related party or control group tests in Recommendation 11. The definition is also used to determine the scope of the term *financial instrument* in Recommendation 1.2(c).

Establishment jurisdiction

397. The term establishment jurisdiction is used in Recommendation 1.5 in describing an exception to the hybrid financial instrument rule and in Recommendation 4 in respect of the definition of a reverse hybrid. The term refers to the jurisdiction where a person is incorporated or otherwise established. For entities such as companies that are established by formal registration this will be the jurisdiction where the entity is registered. For entities such as partnerships or trusts that may not require formal registration, this will be the jurisdiction under whose laws the entity is created or operates.

Family

398. The rules on aggregation of ownership interests set out in Recommendation 11.3 of the report, state that two persons will be treated as *acting together* in respect of their interest in an entity if they are members of the same family.

399. When introducing this test into domestic law, jurisdictions should ensure that the applicable test for family captures:

(a) a person's spouse (including civil partner);

(b) a person's brother, sister, child, parent, grandparent or grandchild (i.e. a relative);

(c) anyone who is a relative of that person's spouse or a spouse of a relative.

400. The test should include adopted persons but does not extend to indirect and non-lineal descendants (such as a person's nephew or niece).

Financing return

401. The definition of *financing return* is used to determine the scope of the term *financial instrument* in Recommendation 1.2(c). It includes any arrangement that is designed to provide a person with a return for the time value of money.

Hybrid mismatch

402. Each recommendation for hybrid mismatch rules contains its own definition of when a mismatch constitutes a hybrid mismatch. The definition in Recommendation 12 serves as a collective definition for the specific definitions set out in each of the recommendations.

Included in ordinary income

403. A payment that is *included in ordinary income* under the laws of the payee jurisdiction will not give rise to D/NI outcome.

404. The requirement that the payment be *included as ordinary income* by the payee means that the payment is required to be incorporated into the payee's income tax calculation as *ordinary income*. The concept of ordinary income is discussed further below.

405. A consideration of whether a payment has been included in ordinary income requires a proper determination of the character and treatment of the payment under the laws of the counterparty jurisdiction.

A payment treated as included in ordinary income if offset against losses

406. A payment that is offset against deductible expenditure or losses that have been carried-forward would, on this definition, be treated as having been included in income.

Withholding taxes

407. A country will continue to levy withholding taxes on payments that are subject to adjustment under the hybrid mismatch rules in accordance with its domestic law and consistent with its treaty obligations. The function of withholding taxes under the laws of the payer jurisdiction is generally not to address mismatches in tax outcomes and a payment should not be treated as included in ordinary income simply because it has been subject to withholding at source. The primary rule denying the deduction may apply in cases in which the payer jurisdiction also imposes a withholding tax on the payment as it is still important to neutralise the hybrid mismatch in those cases. Withholding taxes alone do not neutralise the hybrid mismatch as withholding taxes, where applicable, often are imposed with respect to equity instruments.

Investor

408. The definition of investor is incorporated into the recommendations dealing with hybrid entities as follows:

(a) An entity will be treated as a reverse hybrid under Recommendation 5 where it is treated as transparent under the laws of its own jurisdiction but as a separate entity by an investor.

(b) Further a D/NI outcome that arises in respect of a payment made to that reverse hybrid will be treated as a hybrid mismatch if the D/NI outcome would not have arisen had the accrued income been paid directly to the investor.

Money

409. The definition of money forms part of the definition of payment. The broad definition of money means that the term payment will generally include the transfer of anything that has exchangeable value.

410. A D/NI outcome can arise from differences between tax jurisdictions in the way they measure the value ascribed to a payment, however, if both jurisdictions arrive at the same monetary value for a payment then the value attributed to that payment will be the same. Differences in the valuation of money itself (such as gains and losses from foreign currency fluctuations) will not give rise to a D/NI outcome provided the proportion of the interest and principal payable under the loan is the same under the laws of both jurisdictions.

Offshore investment regime

411. Recommendation 5.1 provides that jurisdictions should introduce, or make changes to their, *offshore investment regimes* in order to prevent *D/NI outcomes* from arising in respect of payments to a *reverse hybrid.*

Ordinary income

412. The definition of ordinary income is used to both identify hybrid mismatch arrangements that produce D/NI outcomes and to neutralise their effect.

A payment will not qualify as ordinary income unless it is taxed at the full marginal rate

413. A payment will not treated as included in ordinary income if the payee jurisdiction does not tax the payment at the taxpayer's full marginal rate. The definition of "ordinary income" excludes any type of income that is subject to preferential tax treatment regardless of the form in which the tax relief is provided.

414. A payment will not be treated as ordinary income if tax on the payment is relieved by excluding or exempting all or part of a payment from taxation (see **Example 1.1**) or the full payment is subject to tax but at a lower rate (see **Example 1.3**). Alternatively, the entire amount of the payment may be taxed at the full tax rate but the jurisdiction may permit the taxpayer to claim some other form of tax relief that attaches to a payment of that nature, such as a credit for underlying foreign taxes (see **Example 1.4**) or a deemed deduction. Income is considered subject to tax at the taxpayer's full marginal rate, however, notwithstanding that the tax on the inclusion is reduced by a credit or other tax

relief granted by the payee jurisdiction for withholding tax or other taxes imposed by the source jurisdiction on the payment itself.

A taxpayer's full marginal rate is the expected rate of tax on ordinary income under that arrangement.

415. In the context of the hybrid financial instrument rule, the payee's *full marginal rate* is the tax the payee would be expect to pay on ordinary income derived under a financial instrument, so that a mismatch will not arise, for the purposes of the hybrid financial instrument rule, simply because the payee jurisdiction taxes financial instruments at a lower rate from other types of income.

Treating a payment as ordinary income under the secondary rule

416. If the arrangement gives rise to a mismatch and the hybrid mismatch rule calls for an adjustment to be made under the secondary rule, the adjustment is confined to adjusting the taxation of the payment itself. Changing the tax treatment of the payment will not necessarily result in an increased tax liability for the payee. As illustrated in **Example 1.5** and **Example 1.8** no additional tax liability will arise under the secondary rule if the payee is not subject to tax on ordinary income or exempt from tax on income from particular sources.

Payee

417. A payee means any person who receives a payment. The payee will generally be the person with the legal right to the payment. There may be cases, however, where, due to tax transparency of the direct recipient, the payment is not included in ordinary income by the direct payee but is included in the income of an underlying investor. In this case the taxpayer will have the burden of establishing, to the reasonable satisfaction of the tax administration, how the tax transparency of the direct recipient and the tax treatment of the payment by the underlying investor impacts on the amount of the adjustment required under the rule.

Payee jurisdiction

418. The payee jurisdiction includes any jurisdiction where the payee is a taxpayer. It therefore includes a non-resident receiving a payment through a PE in the payee jurisdiction. As illustrated in **Example 1.8**, a person may therefore receive the same payment in more than one jurisdiction (i.e. there can be one payee that receives the payment in two jurisdictions). In such cases the taxpayer will generally have the burden of establishing, to the reasonable satisfaction of the tax administration, how the tax treatment in the third jurisdiction impacts on the amount of the adjustment required under the rule.

419. Although D/NI outcomes most commonly arise where the payer and payee jurisdictions are different, this is not a requirement of the hybrid mismatch rules. **Example 1.10** illustrates a case where the payer and payee are in the same jurisdiction, but the arrangement still gives rise to a hybrid mismatch owing to differences in the way payments are accounted for under the arrangement. **Example 1.21** also illustrates a case where the payer and payee are in the same jurisdiction.

Payer

420. A payer means any person who makes a payment. This will generally be the person with the legal obligation to the payment. There may be cases, however, where, due to tax transparency of the direct payer, the payment is treated as made by an underlying investor. In this case the taxpayer will have the burden of establishing, to the reasonable satisfaction of the tax administration, how the tax transparency of the payer and the tax treatment of the payment by the underlying investor impacts on the amount of the adjustment required under the rule.

Payer jurisdiction

421. The payer jurisdiction includes any jurisdiction where the payer is a taxpayer. It therefore includes a non-resident making a payment through a PE in the payer jurisdiction. As illustrated in **Example 1.23** and **Example 4.4**, and as is evident in the context of DD outcomes a payment may be treated as made by taxpayers in more than one jurisdiction (i.e. there can be one payer that is treated as making the same payment). In such cases, the taxpayer will generally have the burden of establishing, to the reasonable satisfaction of the tax administration, how the tax treatment in the other payer jurisdiction impacts on the amount of the adjustment required under the rule.. Although, in the context of DD outcomes, there are, in effect, two payer jurisdictions, Recommendation 6 uses the terms "payer jurisdiction" and "parent jurisdiction" to distinguish between the jurisdictions where the deduction and the duplicate deduction arises.

422. Although mismatches in tax outcomes most commonly arise in cross-border situations, this is not a requirement of the hybrid mismatch rules. The restrictions on double deductions apply equally to residents and non-residents and, as discussed above, in respect of the definition of *payee jurisdiction*, D/NI outcomes can also arise in circumstances where the payer and payee are residents of the same jurisdiction.

Payment

423. Payment means a payment of money (which includes money's worth) made under the financing instrument and includes a distribution, credit or accrual. It includes an amount that is *capable of being paid* and includes any future or contingent obligation to make a payment. The definition of payment includes notional amounts that accrue in respect of a future payment obligation even when the amount accrued does not correspond to any increase in the payment obligation during that period. Where the context requires, payment should include part of any payment.

424. A payment will be treated as having been made when the relevant payment obligation is incurred under the laws of the payer jurisdiction or the payment is derived under the laws of the recipient jurisdiction.

Taxpayer

425. A reference to "taxpayer" in respect of a jurisdiction should generally include a person who is tax resident in that jurisdiction and any other person to the extent they are subject to net income taxation in that jurisdiction through a PE. A person established in a jurisdiction that does not impose a corporate income tax will not be treated as a taxpayer of that jurisdiction.

Voting rights

426. An amount of a person's voting rights is used to determine whether they fall within the related party or control group tests in Recommendation 11.

Bibliography

OECD (2010), *Granting of Treaty Benefits with Respect to the Income of Collective Investment Vehicles* , OECD Publishing, Paris, www.oecd.org/tax/treaties/45359261.pdf.

Part II

Recommendations on treaty issues

Introduction to Part II

427. Part II of this report complements Part I and deals with the parts of Action 2 that indicate that the outputs of the work on that action item may include "changes to the *OECD Model Tax Convention* (OECD, 2014) to ensure that hybrid instruments and entities (as well as dual resident entities) are not used to obtain the benefits of treaties unduly" and that stress that "[s]pecial attention should be given to the interaction between possible changes to domestic law and the provisions of the *OECD Model Tax Convention*."[1]

428. This part first examines treaty issues related to dual resident entities (Chapter 13). It then includes a proposal for a new treaty provision dealing with transparent entities (Chapter 14). Chapter 15 addresses the issue of the interaction between the recommendations included in Part I of this report and the provisions of tax treaties.

429. At the outset, it should be noted that a number of treaty provisions resulting from the work on Action 6 (Preventing Treaty Abuse) may play an important role in ensuring "that hybrid instruments and entities (as well as dual resident entities) are not used to obtain the benefits of treaties unduly". The following provisions included in the report on Action 6 may be of particular relevance:

(a) limitation-on-benefits rules;[2]

(b) rule aimed at arrangements one of the principal purposes of which is to obtain treaty benefits;[3]

(c) rule aimed at dividend transfer transactions (i.e. to subject the lower rate of tax provided by Art. 10(2)a) or by a treaty provision applicable to pension funds to a minimum shareholding period);[4]

(d) rule concerning a Contracting State's right to tax its own residents;[5]

(e) anti-abuse rule for permanent establishments situated in third States.[6]

Notes

1. See Action 2 – Neutralise the effects of hybrid mismatch arrangements (BEPS Action Plan, OECD 2013), pp. 15-16.
2. See paragraph 25 of the report Action 6: *Preventing the Granting of Treaty Benefits in Inappropriate Circumstances* (OECD, 2015).
3. Paragraph 26 of the report on Action 6 (OECD, 2015).
4. Paragraph 36 of the report on Action 6 (OECD, 2015).
5. Paragraph 63 of the report on Action 6 (OECD, 2015).
6. Paragraph 52 of the report on Action 6 (OECD, 2015).

Bibliography

OECD (2015), *Preventing the Granting of Treaty Benefits in Inappropriate Circumstances, Action 6 - 2015 Final Report*, OECD/G20 Base Erosion and Profit Shifting Project, OECD Publishing, Paris, http://dx.doi.org/10.1787/9789264241695-en.

OECD (2014), *Model Tax Convention on Income and on Capital: Condensed Version 2014,* OECD Publishing, Paris, http://dx.doi.org/ DOI:10.1787/mtc_cond-2014-en.

Chapter 13

Dual-resident entities

430. Action 2 refers expressly to possible changes to the *OECD Model Tax Convention* (OECD, 2014) to ensure that dual resident entities are not used to obtain the benefits of treaties unduly.

431. The change to Art. 4(3) of the *OECD Model Tax Convention* (OECD, 2014) that will result from the work on Action 6[1] will address some of the BEPS concerns related to the issue of dual resident entities by providing that cases of dual treaty residence would be solved on a case-by-case basis rather than on the basis of the current rule based on place of effective management of entities, which creates a potential for tax avoidance in some countries. The new version of Art. 4(3) reads as follows:

> *3. Where by reason of the provisions of paragraph 1 a person other than an individual is a resident of both Contracting States, the competent authorities of the Contracting States shall endeavour to determine by mutual agreement the Contracting State of which such person shall be deemed to be a resident for the purposes of the Convention, having regard to its place of effective management, the place where it is incorporated or otherwise constituted and any other relevant factors. In the absence of such agreement, such person shall not be entitled to any relief or exemption from tax provided by this Convention except to the extent and in such manner as may be agreed upon by the competent authorities of the Contracting States.*

432. This change, however, will not address all BEPS concerns related to dual resident entities. It will not, for instance, address avoidance strategies resulting from an entity being a resident of a given State under that State's domestic law whilst, at the same time, being a resident of another State under a tax treaty concluded by the first State, thereby allowing that entity to benefit from the advantages applicable to residents under domestic law without being subject to reciprocal obligations (*e.g.* being able to shift its foreign losses to another resident company under a domestic law group relief system while claiming treaty protection against taxation of its foreign profits). That issue arises from a mismatch between the treaty and domestic law concepts of residence and since the treaty concept of residence cannot simply be aligned on the domestic law concept of residence of each Contracting State without creating situations where an entity would be a resident of the two States for the purposes of the treaty, the solution to these avoidance strategies must be found in domestic law. Whilst such avoidance strategies may be addressed through domestic general anti-abuse rules, States for which this is a potential problem may wish to consider inserting into their domestic law a rule, already found in the domestic law of some States,[2] according to which an entity that is considered to be a resident of another State under a tax treaty will be deemed not to be a resident under domestic law.

433. Also, the change to Art. 4(3) will not address BEPS concerns that arise from dual-residence where no treaty is involved. **Example 7.1** of the report illustrates a dual consolidation structure where BEPS concerns arise from the fact that two States consider the same entity as a resident to which each country applies its consolidation regime. In such a case, the same BEPS concerns arise whether or not there is a tax treaty between the two States, which indicates that the solution to such a case needs to be found in domestic laws. It should be noted, however, that if a treaty existed between the two States and the domestic law of each State included the provision referred to in the preceding paragraph, the entity would likely be a resident under the domestic law of only one State, i.e. the State of which it would be a resident under the treaty.

Notes

1. Paragraph 48 of the report on Action 6, *Preventing the Granting of Treaty Benefits in Inappropriate Circumstances* (OECD, 2015).
2. See subsection 250(5) of the Income Tax Act of Canada and section 18 of the Corporation Tax Act 2009 of the United Kingdom.

Bibliography

OECD (2015), *Preventing the Granting of Treaty Benefits in Inappropriate Circumstances, Action 6 - 2015 Final Report*, OECD/G20 Base Erosion and Profit Shifting Project, OECD Publishing, Paris, http://dx.doi.org/10.1787/9789264241695-en.

OECD (2014), *Model Tax Convention on Income and on Capital: Condensed Version 2014*, OECD Publishing, Paris. http://dx.doi.org/ DOI:10.1787/mtc_cond-2014-en.

Parliament of the United Kingdom (2009), *Corporation Tax Act 2009,* United Kingdom. Available at: www.legislation.gov.uk/ukpga/2009/4/contents (accessed on 15 September 2015).

Chapter 14

Treaty provision on transparent entities

434. The 1999 OECD report on *The Application of the OECD Model Tax Convention to Partnerships* (the Partnership Report, OECD, 1999)[1] contains an extensive analysis of the application of treaty provisions to partnerships, including in situations where there is a mismatch in the tax treatment of the partnership. The main conclusions of the Partnership Report, which have been included in the Commentary of the *OECD Model Tax Convention* (OECD, 2014), seek to ensure that the provisions of tax treaties produce appropriate results when applied to partnerships, in particular in the case of a partnership that constitutes a hybrid entity.

435. The Partnership Report (OECD, 1999), however, did not expressly address the application of tax treaties to entities other than partnerships. In order to address that issue, as well as the fact that some countries have found it difficult to apply the conclusions of the Partnership Report, it was decided to include in the *OECD Model Tax Convention* (OECD, 2014), the following provision and Commentary, which will ensure that income of transparent entities is treated, for the purposes of the Convention, in accordance with the principles of the Partnership report. This will ensure not only that the benefits of tax treaties are granted in appropriate cases but also that these benefits are not granted where neither Contracting State treats, under its domestic law, the income of an entity as the income of one of its residents.

Replace Article 1 of the Model Tax Convention by the following (additions to the existing text appear in **bold italics**):

Article 1

PERSONS COVERED

1. This Convention shall apply to persons who are residents of one or both of the Contracting States.

2. For the purposes of this Convention, income derived by or through an entity or arrangement that is treated as wholly or partly fiscally transparent under the tax law of either Contracting State shall be considered to be income of a resident of a Contracting State but only to the extent that the income is treated, for purposes of taxation by that State, as the income of a resident of that State.

Add the following paragraphs 26.3 to 26.16 to the Commentary on Article 1 (other consequential changes to the Commentary on Article 1 would be required):

Paragraph 2

26.3 This paragraph addresses the situation of the income of entities or arrangements that one or both Contracting States treat as wholly or partly fiscally transparent for tax purposes. The provisions of the paragraph ensure that income of such entities or arrangements is treated, for the purposes of the Convention, in accordance with the

principles reflected in the 1999 report of the Committee on Fiscal Affairs entitled "The Application of the OECD Model Tax Convention to Partnerships".[2] That report therefore provides guidance and examples on how the provision should be interpreted and applied in various situations.

26.4 The report, however, dealt exclusively with partnerships and whilst the Committee recognised that many of the principles included in the report could also apply with respect to other non-corporate entities, it expressed the intention to examine the application of the Model Tax Convention to these other entities at a later stage. As indicated in paragraph 37 of the report, the Committee was particularly concerned with "cases where domestic tax laws create intermediary situations where a partnership is partly treated as a taxable unit and partly disregarded for tax purposes." According to the report

> ***Whilst this may create practical difficulties with respect to a very limited number of partnerships, it is a more important problem in the case of other entities such as trusts. For this reason, the Committee decided to deal with this issue in the context of follow-up work to this report.***

26.5 Paragraph 2 addresses this particular situation by referring to entities that are "wholly or partly" treated as fiscally transparent. Thus, the paragraph not only serves to confirm the conclusions of the Partnership Report but also extends the application of these conclusions to situations that were not directly covered by the report (subject to the application of specific provisions dealing with collective investment vehicles, see paragraphs 6.17 to 6.34 above).

26.6 The paragraph not only ensures that the benefits of the Convention are granted in appropriate cases but also ensures that these benefits are not granted where neither Contracting State treats, under its domestic law, the income of an entity or arrangement as the income of one of its residents. The paragraph therefore confirms the conclusions of the report in such a case (see, for example, example 3 of the report). Also, as recognised in the report, States should not be expected to grant the benefits of a bilateral tax convention in cases where they cannot verify whether a person is truly entitled to these benefits. Thus, if an entity is established in a jurisdiction from which a Contracting State cannot obtain tax information, that State would need to be provided with all the necessary information in order to be able to grant the benefits of the Convention. In such a case, the Contracting State might well decide to use the refund mechanism for the purposes of applying the benefits of the Convention even though it normally applies these benefits at the time of the payment of the relevant income. In most cases, however, it will be possible to obtain the relevant information and to apply the benefits of the Convention at the time the income is taxed (see for example paragraphs 6.29 to 6.31 above which discuss a similar issue in the context of collective investment vehicles).

26.7 The following example illustrates the application of the paragraph:

> ***Example: State A and State B have concluded a treaty identical to the Model Tax Convention. State A considers that an entity established in State B is a company and taxes that entity on interest that it receives from a debtor resident in State A. Under the domestic law of State B, however, the entity is treated as a partnership and the two members in that entity, who share equally all its income, are each taxed on half of the interest. One of the members is a resident of State B and the other one is a resident of a country with which States A and B do not have a***

treaty. The paragraph provides that in such case, half of the interest shall be considered, for the purposes of Article 11, to be income of a resident of State B.

26.8 The reference to "income derived by or through an entity or arrangement" has a broad meaning and covers any income that is earned by or through an entity or arrangement, regardless of the view taken by each Contracting State as to who derives that income for domestic tax purposes and regardless of whether or not that entity or arrangement has legal personality or constitutes a person as defined in subparagraph 1 a) of Article 3. It would cover, for example, income of any partnership or trust that one or both of the Contracting States treats as wholly or partly fiscally transparent. Also, as illustrated in example 2 of the report, it does not matter where the entity or arrangement is established: the paragraph applies to an entity established in a third State to the extent that, under the domestic tax law of one of the Contracting States, the entity is treated as wholly or partly fiscally transparent and income of that entity is attributed to a resident of that State.

26.9 The word "income" must be given the wide meaning that it has for the purposes of the Convention and therefore applies to the various items of income that are covered by Chapter III of the Convention (Taxation of Income), including, for example, profits of an enterprise and capital gains.

26.10 The concept of "fiscally transparent" used in the paragraph refers to situations where, under the domestic law of a Contracting State, the income (or part thereof) of the entity or arrangement is not taxed at the level of the entity or the arrangement but at the level of the persons who have an interest in that entity or arrangement. This will normally be the case where the amount of tax payable on a share of the income of an entity or arrangement is determined separately in relation to the personal characteristics of the person who is entitled to that share so that the tax will depend on whether that person is taxable or not, on the other income that the person has, on the personal allowances to which the person is entitled and on the tax rate applicable to that person; also, the character and source, as well as the timing of the realisation, of the income for tax purposes will not be affected by the fact that it has been earned through the entity or arrangement. The fact that the income is computed at the level of the entity or arrangement before the share is allocated to the person will not affect that result.[3] *States wishing to clarify the definition of "fiscally transparent" in their bilateral conventions are free to include a definition of that term based on the above explanations.*

26.11 In the case of an entity or arrangement which is treated as partly fiscally transparent under the domestic law of one of the Contracting States, only part of the income of the entity or arrangement might be taxed at the level of the persons who have an interest in that entity or arrangement as described in the preceding paragraph whilst the rest would remain taxable at the level of the entity or arrangement. This, for example, is how some trusts and limited liability partnerships are treated in some countries (i.e. in some countries, the part of the income derived through a trust that is distributed to beneficiaries is taxed in the hands of these beneficiaries whilst the part of that income that is accumulated is taxed in the hands of the trust or trustees; similarly, in some countries, income derived through a limited partnership is taxed in the hands of the general partner as regards that partner's share of that income but is considered to be the income of the limited partnership as regards the limited partners' share of the income). To the extent that the entity or arrangement qualifies as a resident of a Contracting State, the paragraph will ensure that the benefits of the treaty also apply to the share of the income that is attributed to the entity or arrangement under the domestic law of that State (subject to any anti-abuse provision such as a limitation-on-benefits rule).

26.12 As with other provisions of the Convention, the provision applies separately to each item of income of the entity or arrangement. Assume, for example, that the document that establishes a trust provides that all dividends received by the trust must be distributed to a beneficiary during the lifetime of that beneficiary but must be accumulated afterwards. If one of the Contracting States considers that, in such a case, the beneficiary is taxable on the dividends distributed to that beneficiary but that the trustees are taxable on the dividends that will be accumulated, the paragraph will apply differently to these two categories of dividends even if both types of dividends are received within the same month.

26.13 By providing that the income to which it applies will be considered to be income of a resident of a Contracting State for the purposes of the Convention, the paragraph ensures that the relevant income is attributed to that resident for the purposes of the application of the various allocative rules of the Convention. Depending on the nature of the income, this will therefore allow the income to be considered, for example, as "income derived by" for the purposes of Articles 6, 13 and 17, "profits of an enterprise" for the purposes of Articles 7, 8 and 9 (see also paragraph 4 of the Commentary on Article 3) or dividends or interest "paid to" for the purposes of Articles 10 and 11. The fact that the income is considered to be derived by a resident of a Contracting State for the purposes of the Convention also means that where the income constitutes a share of the income of an enterprise in which that resident holds a participation, such income shall be considered to be the income of an enterprise carried on by that resident (e.g. for the purposes of the definition of enterprise of a Contracting State in Article 3 and paragraph 2 of Article 21).

26.14 Whilst the paragraph ensures that the various allocative rules of the Convention are applied to the extent that income of fiscally transparent entities is treated, under domestic law, as income of a resident of a Contracting State, the paragraph does not prejudge the issue of whether the recipient is the beneficial owner of the relevant income. Where, for example, a fiscally transparent partnership receives dividends as an agent or nominee for a person who is not a partner, the fact that the dividend may be considered as income of a resident of a Contracting State under the domestic law of that State will not preclude the State of source from considering that neither the partnership nor the partners are the beneficial owners of the dividend.

26.15 The paragraph only applies for the purposes of the Convention and does not, therefore, require a Contracting State to change the way in which it attributes income or characterises entities for the purposes of its domestic law. In the example in paragraph 26.7 above, whilst paragraph 2 provides that half of the interest shall be considered, for the purposes of Article 11, to be income of a resident of State B, this will only affect the maximum amount of tax that State A will be able to collect on the interest and will not change the fact that State A's tax will be payable by the entity. Thus, assuming that the domestic law of State A provides for a 30 per cent withholding tax on the interest, the effect of paragraph 2 will simply be to reduce the amount of tax that State A will collect on the interest (so that half of the interest would be taxed at 30 per cent and half at 10 per cent under the treaty between States A and B) and will not change the fact that the entity is the relevant taxpayer for the purposes of State A's domestic law. Also, the provision does not deal exhaustively with all treaty issues that

may arise from the legal nature of certain entities and arrangements and may therefore need to be supplemented by other provisions to address such issues (such as a provision confirming that a trust may qualify as a resident of a Contracting State despite the fact that, under the trust law of many countries, a trust does not constitute a "person").

26.16 As confirmed by paragraph 3, paragraph 2 does not restrict in any way a State's right to tax its own residents. This conclusion is consistent with the way in which tax treaties have been interpreted with respect to partnerships (see paragraph 6.1 above).This, however, does not restrict the obligation to provide relief of double taxation that is imposed on a Contracting State by Articles 23 A and 23 B where income of a resident of that State may be taxed by the other State in accordance with the Convention, taking into account the application of the paragraph].[4]

Notes

1. OECD (1999), *The Application of the OECD Model Tax Convention to Partnerships*, Issues in International Taxation, No. 6, OECD Publishing, Paris.
2. Reproduced in Volume II of the full-length version of the *OECD Model Tax Convention* (OECD, 2014) at page R(15)-1.
3. See paragraphs 37-40 of the Partnership Report.
4. [Double taxation issues related to the transparent entity provision will be addressed as part of the work that will be done on the draft proposal included in paragraph 64 of the report on Action 6.]

Bibliography

OECD (2014), *Model Tax Convention on Income and on Capital: Condensed Version 2014*, OECD Publishing, Paris, http://dx.doi.org/ DOI:10.1787/mtc_cond-2014-en.

OECD (2014), *Model Tax Convention on Income and on Capital: Full Version 2014*, OECD Publishing, Paris, http://dx.doi.org/10.1787/9789264239081-en.

OECD (1999), *The Application of the OECD Model Tax Convention to Partnerships*, Issues in International Taxation, No. 6, OECD Publishing, Paris, http://dx.doi.org/10.1787/9789264173316-en.

Chapter 15

Interaction between part I and tax treaties

436. Part I of this report includes various recommendations for the domestic law treatment of hybrid financial instruments and hybrid entity payments. Since Action 2 provides that "[s]pecial attention should be given to the interaction between possible changes to domestic law and the provisions of the *OECD Model Tax Convention*", it is necessary to examine treaty issues that may arise from these recommendations.

Rule providing for the denial of deductions

437. Chapter 1 of Part I includes a recommended hybrid mismatch rule under which "the payer jurisdiction will deny a deduction for such payment to the extent it gives rise to a D/NI outcome" to neutralise the effects of hybrid mismatches with respect to a payment under a financial instrument. This raises the question of whether tax treaties, as currently drafted, would authorise such a denial of deduction.

438. Apart from the rules of Articles 7 and 24, the provisions of tax treaties do not govern whether payments are deductible or not and whether they are effectively taxed or not, these being matters of domestic law. The possible application of the provisions of Article 24 with respect to the recommendations set out in Part I of this report is discussed below; as regards Article 7, paragraph 30 of the Commentary on that Article is particularly relevant:

> *30. Paragraph 2 [of Article 7] determines the profits that are attributable to a permanent establishment for the purposes of the rule in paragraph 1 that allocates taxing rights on these profits. Once the profits that are attributable to a permanent establishment have been determined in accordance with paragraph 2 of Article 7, it is for the domestic law of each Contracting State to determine whether and how such profits should be taxed as long as there is conformity with the requirements of paragraph 2 and the other provisions of the Convention. Paragraph 2 does not deal with the issue of whether expenses are deductible when computing the taxable income of the enterprise in either Contracting State. The conditions for the deductibility of expenses are a matter to be determined by domestic law, subject to the provisions of the Convention and, in particular, paragraph 3 of Article 24 ...*

Defensive rule requiring the inclusion of a payment in ordinary income

439. Chapter 1 of Part I also includes a recommended "defensive" rule under which "[i]f the payer jurisdiction does not neutralise the mismatch then the payee jurisdiction will require such payment to be included in ordinary income to the extent the payment gives rise to a D/NI outcome". The provisions of tax treaties could be implicated if such a

rule would seek the imposition of tax on a non-resident whose income would not, under the provisions of the relevant tax treaty, be taxable in that State. By virtue of the combination of the definitions of "payee" and "taxpayer" in the recommendations (Part I, Chapter 12), that rule contemplates the imposition of tax by a jurisdiction only in circumstances where the recipient of the payment is a resident of that jurisdiction or maintains a permanent establishment in that jurisdiction. Since the allocative rules of tax treaties generally do not restrict the taxation rights of the State in such circumstances, any interaction between the recommendation and the provisions of tax treaties will therefore appear to relate primarily to the rules concerning the elimination of double taxation (Articles 23 A and 23 B of the *OECD Model Tax Convention*, OECD, 2014).

440. The following two recommendations included in Part I of this report deal with the elimination of double taxation by the State of residence:

(a) "In order to prevent D/NI outcomes from arising under a financial instrument, a dividend exemption that is provided for relief against economic double taxation should not be granted under domestic law to the extent the dividend payment is deductible by the payer. Equally, jurisdictions should consider adopting similar restrictions for other types of dividend relief granted to relieve economic double taxation on underlying profits." [Recommendation 2.1].

(b) "In order to prevent duplication of tax credits under a hybrid transfer, any jurisdiction that grants relief for tax withheld at source on a payment made under a hybrid transfer should restrict the benefit of such relief in proportion to the net taxable income of the taxpayer under the arrangement." [Recommendation 2.2].

441. As explained below, these recommendations do not appear to raise any issues with respect to the application of Articles 23 A and Articles 23 B of the *OECD Model Tax Convention* (OECD, 2014).

Exemption method

442. As regards Articles 23 A (Exemption Method), paragraph 2 of that Article provides that in the case of dividends (covered by Article 10 of the *OECD Model Tax Convention*, OECD, 2014), it is the credit method, and not the exemption method, that is applicable. The Recommendation that "a dividend exemption that is provided for relief against economic double taxation should not be granted under domestic law to the extent the dividend payment is deductible by the payer" should not, therefore, create problems with respect to bilateral tax treaties that include the wording of Article 23 A.

443. It is recognised, however, that a number of bilateral tax treaties depart from the provisions of Article 23 A and provide for the application of the exemption method with respect to dividends received from foreign companies in which a resident company has a substantial shareholding. This possibility is expressly acknowledged in the *OECD Model Tax Convention* (OECD, 2014)(see paragraphs 49 to 54 of the Commentary on Articles 23 A and 23 B).

444. Problems arising from the inclusion of the exemption method in tax treaties with respect to items of income that are not taxed in the State of source have long been recognised in the *OECD Model Tax Convention* (OECD, 2014) (see, for example, paragraph 35 of the Commentary on Articles 23 A and 23 B). Whilst paragraph 4 of Article 23 A[1] may address some situations of hybrid mismatch arrangements where a dividend would otherwise be subject to the exemption method, many tax treaties do not

include that provision. At a minimum, therefore, States that wish to follow the above recommendations included in Part I of this report but that enter into tax treaties providing for the application of the exemption method with respect to dividends should consider the inclusion of paragraph 4 of Article 23 A in their tax treaties, although these States should also recognise that the provision will only provide a partial solution to the problem. A more complete solution that should be considered by these States would be to include in their treaties rules that would expressly allow them to apply the credit method, as opposed to the exemption method, with respect to dividends that are deductible in the payer State. These States may also wish to consider a more general solution to the problems of non-taxation resulting from potential abuses of the exemption method, which would be for States not to include the exemption method in their treaties. Under that approach, the credit method would be provided for in tax treaties, thereby ensuring the relief of juridical double taxation, and it would be left to domestic law to provide whether that should be done through the credit or exemption method (or probably through a combination of the two methods depending on the nature of the income, as is the case of the domestic law of many countries). The issue that may arise from granting a credit for underlying taxes (which is not a feature of Articles 23 A and 23 B of the *OECD Model Tax Convention,* OECD, 2014) is discussed below.

Credit method

445. As regards the application of the credit method provided for by paragraph 2 of Article 23 A and by Article 23 B, the recommendation that relief should be restricted "in proportion to the net taxable income under the arrangement" appears to conform to the domestic tax limitation provided by that method. As noted in paragraphs 60 and 63 of the Commentary on Articles 23 A and 23 B, Article 23 B leaves it to domestic law to determine the domestic tax against which the foreign tax credit should be applied (the "maximum deduction") and one would normally expect that this would be the State of residence's tax as computed after taking into account all relevant deductions:

> *60. Article 23 B sets out the main rules of the credit method, but does not give detailed rules on the computation and operation of the credit. ... Experience has shown that many problems may arise. Some of them are dealt with in the following paragraphs. In many States, detailed rules on credit for foreign tax already exist in their domestic laws. A number of conventions, therefore, contain a reference to the domestic laws of the Contracting States and further provide that such domestic rules shall not affect the principle laid down in Article 23 B.*
>
> *63. The maximum deduction is normally computed as the tax on net income, i.e. on the income from State E (or S) less allowable deductions (specified or proportional) connected with such income...*

446. It is recognised, however, that double non-taxation situations may arise in the application of the credit method by reasons of treaty or domestic law provisions that either supplement, or depart from, the basic approach of Article 23 B (Credit Method) of the *OECD Model Tax Convention* (OECD, 2014). One example would be domestic law provisions that allow the foreign tax credit applicable to one item of income to be used against the State of residence's tax payable on another item of income. Another example would be where treaty or domestic law provisions provide for an underlying foreign tax credit with respect to dividends, which may create difficulties with respect to the part of Recommendation 2.1 according to which "jurisdictions should consider adopting similar restrictions for other types of dividend relief granted to relieve economic double taxation

on underlying profits". These are other situations where Contracting States should ensure that their tax treaties provide for the elimination of double taxation without creating opportunities for tax avoidance strategies.

Potential application of anti-discrimination provisions in the OECD Model Tax Convention

447. The basic thrust of the recommendations set out in Part I of this report is to ensure that payments are treated consistently in the hands of the payer and the recipient and, in particular, to prevent a double deduction or deduction without a corresponding inclusion. These recommendations do not appear to raise any issue of discrimination based on nationality (Art. 24(1)). They also do not appear to treat permanent establishments differently from domestic enterprises (Art. 24(3), to provide different rules for the deduction of payments made to residents and non-residents (Art. 24(4)) or to treat domestic enterprises differently based on whether their capital is owned or controlled by residents or non-residents (Art. 24(5)).

448. Some of the domestic law recommendations to neutralise the effects of hybrid mismatch arrangements that are included in Part I may impact payments to non-residents more than they will impact payments to residents. This, however, is not relevant for the purposes of Article 24 as long as the distinction is based on the treatment of the payments in the hands of the payers and recipients. The fact that a mismatch in the tax treatment of an entity or payment is less likely in a purely domestic context (i.e. one would expect a country to be consistent in the way it characterises domestic payments and entities) cannot be interpreted as meaning that rules that are strictly based on the existence of such a mismatch are treating payments to non-residents, or to non-resident owned enterprises, differently from the way payments to residents, or resident-owned enterprises, are treated under domestic law.

449. The following excerpts from the Commentary on Article 24 are of particular relevance in that context:

(a) *As regards all the provisions of Art. 24:* "The non-discrimination provisions of the Article seek to balance the need to prevent unjustified discrimination with the need to take account of these legitimate distinctions. For that reason, the Article should not be unduly extended to cover so-called "indirect" discrimination." (paragraph 1)

> "Also, whilst the Article seeks to eliminate distinctions that are solely based on certain grounds, it is not intended to provide foreign nationals, non-residents, enterprises of other States or domestic enterprises owned or controlled by non-residents with a tax treatment that is better than that of nationals, residents or domestic enterprises owned or controlled by residents …" (paragraph 3)

(b) *As regards Art. 24(3)*: "That principle, therefore, is restricted to a comparison between the rules governing the taxation of the permanent establishment's own activities and those applicable to similar business activities carried on by an independent resident enterprise. It does not extend to rules that take account of the relationship between an enterprise and other enterprises (e.g. rules that allow consolidation, transfer of losses or tax-free transfers of property between companies under common ownership) since the latter rules do not focus on the taxation of an enterprise's own business activities similar to those of the permanent establishment but, instead, on the taxation of a resident enterprise as part of a group of associated enterprises." (paragraph 41)

(c) *As regards Art 24(4):* "This paragraph is designed to end a particular form of discrimination resulting from the fact that in certain countries the deduction of interest, royalties and other disbursements allowed without restriction when the recipient is resident, is restricted or even prohibited when he is a non-resident." (paragraph 73)

(d) *As regards Art. 24(5):* "Since the paragraph relates only to the taxation of resident enterprises and not to that of the persons owning or controlling their capital, it follows that it cannot be interpreted to extend the benefits of rules that take account of the relationship between a resident enterprise and other resident enterprises (e.g. rules that allow consolidation, transfer of losses or tax-free transfer of property between companies under common ownership)." (paragraph 77)

> "…it follows that withholding tax obligations that are imposed on a resident company with respect to dividends paid to non-resident shareholders but not with respect to dividends paid to resident shareholders cannot be considered to violate paragraph 5. In that case, the different treatment is not dependent on the fact that the capital of the company is owned or controlled by non-residents but, rather, on the fact that dividends paid to non-residents are taxed differently." (paragraph 78)

450. For these reasons, and subject to an analysis of the precise wording of the domestic rules that would be drafted to implement the recommendations, the recommendations set out in Part I of this report would not appear to raise concerns about a possible conflict with the provisions of Article 24 of the *OECD Model Tax Convention* (OECD, 2014).

Notes

1. "4. The provisions of paragraph 1 [of Article 23 A] shall not apply to income derived or capital owned by a resident of a Contracting State where the other Contracting State applies the provisions of this Convention to exempt such income or capital from tax or applies the provisions of paragraph 2 of Article 10 or 11 to such income."

Bibliography

OECD (2014), *Model Tax Convention on Income and on Capital: Condensed Version 2014*, OECD Publishing, Paris, http://dx.doi.org/ DOI:10.1787/mtc_cond-2014-en.

Annex A

List of Part I Recommendations

Recommendations

Recommendation 1	Hybrid Financial Instrument Rule
Recommendation 2	Specific Recommendations for the Tax Treatment of Financial Instruments
Recommendation 3	Disregarded Hybrid Payments Rule
Recommendation 4	Reverse Hybrid Rule
Recommendation 5	Specific Recommendations for The Tax Treatment of Reverse Hybrids
Recommendation 6	Deductible Hybrid Payments Rule
Recommendation 7	Dual Resident Payer Rule
Recommendation 8	Imported Mismatch Rule
Recommendation 9	Design Principles
Recommendation 10	Definition of Structured Arrangement
Recommendation 11	Definition of Related Persons, Control Group and Acting Together
Recommendation 12	Other Definitions

Recommendation 1

Hybrid financial instrument rule

1. Neutralise the mismatch to the extent the payment gives rise to a D/NI outcome

The following rule should apply to a payment under a financial instrument that results in a hybrid mismatch and to a substitute payment under an arrangement to transfer a financial instrument:

(a) The payer jurisdiction will deny a deduction for such payment to the extent it gives rise to a D/NI outcome.

(b) If the payer jurisdiction does not neutralise the mismatch then the payee jurisdiction will require such payment to be included in ordinary income to the extent the payment gives rise to a D/NI outcome.

(c) Differences in the timing of the recognition of payments will not be treated as giving rise to a D/NI outcome for a payment made under a financial instrument, provided the taxpayer can establish to the satisfaction of a tax authority that the payment will be included as ordinary income within a reasonable period of time.

2. Definition of financial instrument and substitute payment

For the purposes of this rule:

(a) A financial instrument means any arrangement that is taxed under the rules for taxing debt, equity or derivatives under the laws of both the payee and payer jurisdictions and includes a hybrid transfer.

(b) A hybrid transfer includes any arrangement to transfer a financial instrument entered into by a taxpayer with another person where:

(i) the taxpayer is the owner of the transferred asset and the rights of the counterparty in respect of that asset are treated as obligations of the taxpayer; and

(ii) under the laws of the counterparty jurisdiction, the counterparty is the owner of the transferred asset and the rights of the taxpayer in respect of that asset are treated as obligations of the counterparty.

Ownership of an asset for these purposes includes any rules that result in the taxpayer being taxed as the owner of the corresponding cash-flows from the asset.

(c) A jurisdiction should treat any arrangement where one person provides money to another in consideration for a financing or equity return as a financial instrument to the extent of such financing or equity return.

(d) Any payment under an arrangement that is not treated as a financial instrument under the laws of the counterparty jurisdiction shall be treated as giving rise to a mismatch only to the extent the payment constitutes a financing or equity return.

(e) A substitute payment is any payment, made under an arrangement to transfer a financial instrument, to the extent it includes, or is payment of an amount representing, a financing or equity return on the underlying financial instrument where the payment or return would:

Recommendation 1 (*continued*)

(i) not have been included in ordinary income of the payer;

(ii) have been included in ordinary income of the payee; or

(iii) have given rise to hybrid mismatch;

if it had been made directly under the financial instrument.

3. Rule only applies to a payment under a financial instrument that results in a hybrid mismatch

A payment under a financial instrument results in a hybrid mismatch where the mismatch can be attributed to the terms of the instrument. A payment cannot be attributed to the terms of the instrument where the mismatch is solely attributable to the status of the taxpayer or the circumstances in which the instrument is held.

4. Scope of the rule

This rule only applies to a payment made to a related person or where the payment is made under a structured arrangement and the taxpayer is party to that structured arrangement.

5. Exceptions to the rule

The primary response in in Recommendation 1.1(a) should not apply to a payment by an investment vehicle that is subject to special regulation and tax treatment under the laws of the establishment jurisdiction in circumstances where:

(a) The tax policy of the establishment jurisdiction is to preserve the deduction for the payment under the financial instrument to ensure that:

(i) the taxpayer is subject to no or minimal taxation on its investment income; and

(ii) that holders of financial instruments issued by the taxpayer are subject to tax on that payment as ordinary income on a current basis.

(b) The regulatory and tax framework in the establishment jurisdiction has the effect that the financial instruments issued by the investment vehicle will result in all or substantially all of the taxpayer's investment income being paid and distributed to the holders of those financial instruments within a reasonable period of time after that income was derived or received by the taxpayer.

(c) The tax policy of the establishment jurisdiction is that the full amount of the payment is:

(i) included in the ordinary income of any person that is a payee in the establishment jurisdiction; and

(ii) not excluded from the ordinary income of any person that is a payee under the laws of the payee jurisdiction under a treaty between the establishment jurisdiction and the payee jurisdiction.

(d) The payment is not made under a structured arrangement.

The defensive rule in Recommendation 1.1(b) will continue to apply to any payment made by such an investment vehicle.

Recommendation 2

Specific recommendations for the tax treatment of financial instruments

1. Denial of dividend exemption for deductible payments

In order to prevent D/NI outcomes from arising under a financial instrument, a dividend exemption that is provided for relief against economic double taxation should not be granted under domestic law to the extent the dividend payment is deductible by the payer. Equally, jurisdictions should consider adopting similar restrictions for other types of dividend relief granted to relieve economic double taxation on underlying profits.

2. Restriction of foreign tax credits under a hybrid transfer

In order to prevent duplication of tax credits under a hybrid transfer, any jurisdiction that grants relief for tax withheld at source on a payment made under a hybrid transfer should restrict the benefit of such relief in proportion to the net taxable income of the taxpayer under the arrangement.

3. Scope of the rule

There is no limitation as to the scope of these recommendations.

Recommendation 3

Disregarded hybrid payments rule

1. Neutralise the mismatch to the extent the payment gives rise to a D/NI outcome

The following rule should apply to a disregarded payment made by a hybrid payer that results in a hybrid mismatch:

(a) The payer jurisdiction will deny a deduction for such payment to the extent it gives rise to a D/NI outcome.

(b) If the payer jurisdiction does not neutralise the mismatch then the payee jurisdiction will require such payment to be included in ordinary income to the extent the payment gives rise to a D/NI outcome.

(c) No mismatch will arise to the extent that the deduction in the payer jurisdiction is set-off against income that is included in income under the laws of both the payee and the payer jurisdiction (i.e. dual inclusion income).

(d) Any deduction that exceeds the amount of dual inclusion income (the excess deduction) may be eligible to be set-off against dual inclusion income in another period.

2. Rule only applies to disregarded payments made by a hybrid payer

For the purpose of this rule:

(a) A disregarded payment is a payment that is deductible under the laws of the payer jurisdiction and is not recognised under the laws of the payee jurisdiction.

(b) A person will be a hybrid payer where the tax treatment of the payer under the laws of the payee jurisdiction causes the payment to be a disregarded payment.

3. Rule only applies to payments that result in a hybrid mismatch

A disregarded payment made by a hybrid payer results in a hybrid mismatch if, under the laws of the payer jurisdiction, the deduction may be set-off against income that is not dual inclusion income.

4. Scope of the rule

This rule only applies if the parties to the mismatch are in the same control group or where the payment is made under a structured arrangement and the taxpayer is a party to that structured arrangement.

Recommendation 4

Reverse hybrid rule

1. Neutralise the mismatch to the extent the payment gives rise to D/NI outcome

In respect of a payment made to a reverse hybrid that results in a hybrid mismatch the payer jurisdiction should apply a rule that will deny a deduction for such payment to the extent it gives rise to a D/NI outcome.

2. Rule only applies to payment made to a reverse hybrid

A reverse hybrid is any person that is treated as a separate entity by an investor and as transparent under the laws of the establishment jurisdiction.

3. Rule only applies to hybrid mismatches

A payment results in a hybrid mismatch if a mismatch would not have arisen had the accrued income been paid directly to the investor.

4. Scope of the rule

The recommendation only applies where the investor, the reverse hybrid and the payer are members of the same control group or if the payment is made under a structured arrangement and the payer is party to that structured arrangement.

Recommendation 5

Specific recommendations for the tax treatment of reverse hybrids

1. Improvements to CFC and other offshore investment regimes

Jurisdictions should introduce, or make changes to, their offshore investment regimes in order to prevent D/NI outcomes from arising in respect of payments to a reverse hybrid. Equally jurisdictions should consider introducing or making changes to their offshore investment regimes in relation to imported mismatch arrangements.

2. Limiting the tax transparency for non-resident investors

A reverse hybrid should be treated as a resident taxpayer in the establishment jurisdiction if the income of the reverse hybrid is not brought within the charge to taxation under the laws of the establishment jurisdiction and the accrued income of a non-resident investor in the same control group as the reverse hybrid is not brought within the charge to taxation under the laws of the investor jurisdiction.

3. Information reporting for intermediaries

Jurisdictions should introduce appropriate tax filing and information reporting requirements on persons established within their jurisdiction in order to assist both taxpayers and tax administrations to make a proper determination of the payments that have been attributed to that non-resident investor.

Recommendation 6

Deductible hybrid payments rule

1. Neutralise the mismatch to the extent the payment gives rise to a DD outcome

The following rule should apply to a hybrid payer that makes a payment that is deductible under the laws of the payer jurisdiction and that triggers a duplicate deduction in the parent jurisdiction that results in a hybrid mismatch:

(a) The parent jurisdiction will deny the duplicate deduction for such payment to the extent it gives rise to a DD outcome.

(b) If the parent jurisdiction does not neutralise the mismatch, the payer jurisdiction will deny the deduction for such payment to the extent it gives rise to a DD outcome.

(c) No mismatch will arise to the extent that a deduction is set-off against income that is included in income under the laws of both the parent and the payer jurisdictions (i.e. dual inclusion income).

(d) Any deduction that exceeds the amount of dual inclusion income (the excess deduction) may be eligible to be set-off against dual inclusion income in another period. In order to prevent stranded losses, the excess deduction may be allowed to the extent that the taxpayer can establish, to the satisfaction of the tax administration, that the excess deduction in the other jurisdiction cannot be set-off against any income of any person under the laws of the other jurisdiction that is not dual inclusion income.

2. Rule only applies to deductible payments made by a hybrid payer

A person will be treated as a hybrid payer in respect of a payment that is deductible under the laws of the payer jurisdiction where:

(a) the payer is not a resident of the payer jurisdiction and the payment triggers a duplicate deduction for that payer (or a related person) under the laws of the jurisdiction where the payer is resident (the parent jurisdiction); or

(b) the payer is resident in the payer jurisdiction and the payment triggers a duplicate deduction for an investor in that payer (or a related person) under the laws of the other jurisdiction (the parent jurisdiction).

3. Rule only applies to payments that result in a hybrid mismatch

A payment results in a hybrid mismatch where the deduction for the payment may be set-off, under the laws of the payer jurisdiction, against income that is not dual inclusion income.

4. Scope of the rule

The defensive rule only applies if the parties to the mismatch are in the same control group or where the mismatch arises under a structured arrangement and the taxpayer is party to that structured arrangement. There is no limitation on scope in respect of the recommended response.

Recommendation 7

Dual resident payer rule

1. Neutralise the mismatch to the extent the payment gives rise to a DD outcome

The following rule should apply to a dual resident that makes a payment that is deductible under the laws of both jurisdictions where the payer is resident and that DD outcome results in a hybrid mismatch:

(a) Each resident jurisdiction will deny a deduction for such payment to the extent it gives rise to a DD outcome.

(b) No mismatch will arise to the extent that the deduction is set-off against income that is included as income under the laws of both jurisdictions (i.e. dual inclusion income).

(c) Any deduction that exceeds the amount of dual inclusion income (the excess deduction) may be eligible to be set-off against dual inclusion income in another period. In order to prevent stranded losses, the excess deduction may be allowed to the extent that the taxpayer can establish, to the satisfaction of the tax administration, that the excess deduction cannot be set-off against any income under the laws of the other jurisdiction that is not dual inclusion income.

2. Rule only applies to deductible payments made by a dual resident

A taxpayer will be a dual resident if it is resident for tax purposes under the laws of two or more jurisdictions.

3. Rule only applies to payments that result in a hybrid mismatch

A deduction for a payment results in a hybrid mismatch where the deduction for the payment may be set-off, under the laws of the other jurisdiction, against income that is not dual inclusion income.

4. Scope of the rule

There is no limitation on the scope of the rule.

Recommendation 8

Imported mismatch rule

1. Deny the deduction to the extent the payment gives rise to an indirect D/NI outcome

The payer jurisdiction should apply a rule that denies a deduction for any imported mismatch payment to the extent the payee treats that payment as set-off against a hybrid deduction in the payee jurisdiction.

2. Definition of hybrid deduction

Hybrid deduction means a deduction resulting from:

(a) a payment under a financial instrument that results in a hybrid mismatch;

(b) a disregarded payment made by a hybrid payer that results in a hybrid mismatch;

(c) a payment made to a reverse hybrid that results in a hybrid mismatch; or

(d) a payment made by a hybrid payer or dual resident that triggers a duplicate deduction resulting in a hybrid mismatch;

and includes a deduction resulting from a payment made to any other person to the extent that person treats the payment as set-off against another hybrid deduction.

3. Imported mismatch payment

An imported mismatch payment is a deductible payment made to a payee that is not subject to hybrid mismatch rules.

4. Scope of the rule

The rule applies if the taxpayer is in the same control group as the parties to the imported mismatch arrangement or where the payment is made under a structured arrangement and the taxpayer is party to that structured arrangement.

Recommendation 9

Design principles

1. Design principles

The hybrid mismatch rules have been designed to maximise the following outcomes:

(a) neutralise the mismatch rather than reverse the tax benefit that arises under the laws of the jurisdiction;

(b) be comprehensive;

(c) apply automatically;

(d) avoid double taxation through rule co-ordination;

(e) minimise the disruption to existing domestic law;

(f) be clear and transparent in their operation;

(g) provide sufficient flexibility for the rule to be incorporated into the laws of each jurisdiction;

(h) be workable for taxpayers and keep compliance costs to a minimum; and

(i) minimise the administrative burden on tax authorities.

Jurisdictions that implement these recommendations into domestic law should do so in a manner intended to preserve these design principles.

2. Implementation and co-ordination

Jurisdictions should co-operate on measures to ensure these recommendations are implemented and applied consistently and effectively. These measures should include:

(a) the development of agreed guidance on the recommendations;

(b) co-ordination of the implementation of the recommendations (including timing);

(c) development of transitional rules (without any presumption as to grandfathering of existing arrangements);

(d) review of the effective and consistent implementation of the recommendations;

(e) exchange of information on the jurisdiction treatment of hybrid financial instruments and hybrid entities;

(f) endeavouring to make relevant information available to taxpayers (including reasonable endeavours by the OECD); and

(g) consideration of the interaction of the recommendations with other Actions under the BEPS Action Plan including Actions 3 and 4.

Recommendation 10

Definition of structured arrangement

1. General Definition

Structured arrangement is any arrangement where the hybrid mismatch is priced into the terms of the arrangement or the facts and circumstances (including the terms) of the arrangement indicate that it has been designed to produce a hybrid mismatch.

2. Specific examples of structured arrangements

Facts and circumstances that indicate that an arrangement has been designed to produce a hybrid mismatch include any of the following:

(a) an arrangement that is designed, or is part of a plan, to create a hybrid mismatch;

(b) an arrangement that incorporates a term, step or transaction used in order to create a hybrid mismatch;

(c) an arrangement that is marketed, in whole or in part, as a tax-advantaged product where some or all of the tax advantage derives from the hybrid mismatch;

(d) an arrangement that is primarily marketed to taxpayers in a jurisdiction where the hybrid mismatch arises;

(e) an arrangement that contains features that alter the terms under the arrangement, including the return, in the event that the hybrid mismatch is no longer available; or

(f) an arrangement that would produce a negative return absent the hybrid mismatch.

3. When taxpayer is not a party to a structured arrangement

A taxpayer will not be treated as a party to a structured arrangement if neither the taxpayer nor any member of the same control group could reasonably have been expected to be aware of the hybrid mismatch and did not share in the value of the tax benefit resulting from the hybrid mismatch.

Recommendation 11

Definitions of related persons, control group and acting together

1. General definition

For the purposes of these recommendations:

(a) Two persons are related if they are in the same control group or the first person has a 25% or greater investment in the second person or there is a third person that holds a 25% or greater investment in both.

(b) Two persons are in the same control group if:

(i) they are consolidated for accounting purposes;

(ii) the first person has an investment that provides that person with effective control of the second person or there is a third person that holds investments which provides that person with effective control over both persons;

(iii) the first person has a 50% or greater investment in the second person or there is a third person that holds a 50% or greater investment in both; or

(iv) they can be regarded as associated enterprises under Article 9.

(c) A person will be treated as holding a percentage investment in another person if that person holds directly or indirectly through an investment in other persons, a percentage of the voting rights of that person or of the value of any equity interest in that person.

2. Aggregation of interests

For the purposes of the related party rules a person who acts together with another person in respect of ownership or control of any voting rights or equity interests will be treated as owning or controlling all the voting rights and equity interests of that person.

3. Acting together

Two persons will be treated as acting together in respect of ownership or control of any voting rights or equity interests if:

(a) they are members of the same family;

(b) one person regularly acts in accordance with the wishes of the other person;

(c) they have entered into an arrangement that has material impact on the value or control of any such rights or interests; or

(d) the ownership or control of any such rights or interests are managed by the same person or group of persons.

If a manager of a collective investment vehicle can establish to the satisfaction of the tax authority, from the terms of any investment mandate, the nature of the investment and the circumstances that the hybrid mismatch was entered into, that the two funds were not acting together in respect of the investment then the interest held by those funds should not be aggregated for the purposes of the acting together test.

Recommendation 12

Other definitions

1. Definitions

For the purpose of these recommendations:

Accrued income	Accrued income, in relation to any payee and any investor, means income of the payee that has accrued for the benefit of that investor.
Arrangement	Arrangement refers to an agreement, contract, scheme, plan, or understanding, whether enforceable or not, including all steps and transactions by which it is carried into effect. An arrangement may be part of a wider arrangement, it may be a single arrangement, or it may be comprised of a number of arrangements.
Collective investment vehicle	Collective investment vehicle means a collective investment vehicle as defined in paragraph 4 of the *Granting of Treaty Benefits with Respect to the Income of Collective Investment Vehicles* (2010, OECD).
Constitution	Constitution, in relation to any person, means the rules governing the relationship between the person and its owners and includes articles of association or incorporation.
D/NI outcome	A payment gives rise to a D/NI outcome to the extent the payment is deductible under the laws of the payer jurisdiction but is not included in ordinary income by any person in the payee jurisdiction. A D/NI outcome is not generally impacted by questions of timing in the recognition of payments or differences in the way jurisdictions measure the value of that payment. In some circumstances however a timing mismatch will be considered permanent if the taxpayer cannot establish to the satisfaction of a tax authority that a payment will be brought into account within a reasonable period of time (see Recommendation 1.1(c)).
DD outcome	A payment gives rise to a DD outcome if the payment is deductible under the laws of more than one jurisdiction.
Deduction	Deduction (including deductible), in respect of a payment, means that, after a proper determination of the character and treatment of the payment under the laws of the payer jurisdiction, the payment is taken into account as a deduction or equivalent tax relief under the laws of that jurisdiction in calculating the taxpayer's net income.
Director	Director, in relation to any person, means any person who has the power under the constitution to manage and control that person and includes a trustee.
Distribution	Distribution, in relation to any person, means a payment of profits or gains by that person to any owner.

Recommendation 12 (*continued*)

Dual inclusion income	Dual inclusion income, in the case of both deductible payments and disregarded payments, refers to any item of income that is included as ordinary income under the laws of the jurisdictions where the mismatch has arisen. An item that is treated as income under the laws of both jurisdictions may, however, continue to qualify as dual inclusion income even if that income benefits from double taxation relief, such as a foreign tax credit (including underlying foreign tax credit) or a domestic dividend exemption, to the extent such relief ensures that income, which has been subject to tax at the full rate in one jurisdiction, is not subject to an additional layer of taxation under the laws of either jurisdiction.
Equity interest	Equity interest means any interest in any person that includes an entitlement to an equity return.
Equity return	Equity return means an entitlement to profits or eligibility to participate in distributions of any person and, in respect of any arrangement is a return on that arrangement that is economically equivalent to a distribution or a return of profits or where it is reasonable to assume, after consideration of the terms of the arrangement, that the return is calculated by reference to distributions or profits.
Establishment jurisdiction	Establishment jurisdiction, in relation to any person, means the jurisdiction where that person is incorporated or otherwise established.
Family	A person (A) is a member of the same family as another person (B) if B is: • the spouse or civil partner of A; • a 'relative' of A (brother, sister, ancestor or lineal descendant); • the spouse or civil partner of a relative of A; • a relative of A's spouse or civil partner; • the spouse or civil partner of a relative of A's spouse or civil partner; or • an adopted relative.
Financing return	Financing return, in respect of any arrangement is a return on that arrangement that is economically equivalent to interest or where it is reasonable to assume, after consideration of the terms of the arrangement, that the return is calculated by reference to the time value of money provided under the arrangement.
Hybrid mismatch	A hybrid mismatch is defined in paragraph 3 in Recommendations 1, 3, 4, 6 and 7 for the purposes of those recommendations.
Included in ordinary income	A payment will be treated as included in ordinary income to the extent that, after a proper determination of the character and treatment of the payment under the laws of the relevant jurisdiction, the payment has been incorporated as ordinary income into a calculation of the payee's income under the law of that jurisdiction.
Investor	Investor, in relation to any person, means any person directly or indirectly holding voting rights or equity interests in that person.
Investor jurisdiction	Investor jurisdiction is any jurisdiction where the investor is a taxpayer.
Mismatch	A mismatch is a DD outcome or a D/NI outcome and includes an expected mismatch.

Recommendation 12 (*continued*)

Money	Money includes money in any form, anything that is convertible into money and any provision that would be paid for at arm's length.
Offshore investment regime	An offshore investment regime includes controlled foreign company and foreign investment fund rules and any other rules that require the investor's accrued income to be included on a current basis under the laws of the investor's jurisdiction.
Ordinary income	Ordinary income means income that is subject to tax at the taxpayer's full marginal rate and does not benefit from any exemption, exclusion, credit or other tax relief applicable to particular categories of payments (such as indirect credits for underlying tax on income of the payer). Income is considered subject to tax at the taxpayer's full marginal rate notwithstanding that the tax on the inclusion is reduced by a credit or other tax relief granted by the payee jurisdiction for withholding tax or other taxes imposed by the payer jurisdiction on the payment itself.
Payee	Payee means any person who receives a payment under an arrangement including through a permanent establishment of the payee.
Payee jurisdiction	Payee jurisdiction is any jurisdiction where the payee is a taxpayer.
Payer	Payer means any person who makes a payment under an arrangement including through a permanent establishment of the payer.
Payer jurisdiction	Payer jurisdiction is any jurisdiction where the payer is a taxpayer.
Payment	Payment includes any amount capable of being paid including (but not limited to) a distribution, credit, debit, accrual of money but it does not extend to payments that are only deemed to be made for tax purposes and that do not involve the creation of economic rights between parties.
Person	Person includes any natural or legal person or unincorporated body of persons and a trust.
Taxpayer	Taxpayer, in respect of any jurisdiction, means any person who is subject to tax in that jurisdiction whether as a resident or by virtue of applicable source rules (such as maintaining a permanent establishment in that jurisdiction).
Trust	Trust includes any person who is a trustee of a trust acting in that capacity.
Voting rights	Voting rights means the right to participate in any decision-making concerning a distribution, a change to the constitution or the appointment of a director.

Annex B

Examples

List of examples

Hybrid financial instrument rule

Specific recommendations for the tax treatment of financial instruments

Disregarded hybrid payments rule

Reverse hybrid rule

Deductible hybrid payments rule

Dual-resident payer rule

Imported mismatch rule

Design principles

Definition of structured arrangements

Definition of related persons, control group and acting together

Example 1.1

Interest payment under a debt/equity hybrid

Facts

1. In the example illustrated in the figure below, A Co (a company resident in Country A) owns all the shares in B Co (a company resident in Country B). A Co lends money to B Co. The loan carries a market rate of interest which is payable every six months in arrears. Payments of interest and principal under the loan are subordinated to the ordinary creditors of B Co and can be suspended in the event B Co fails to meet certain solvency requirements.

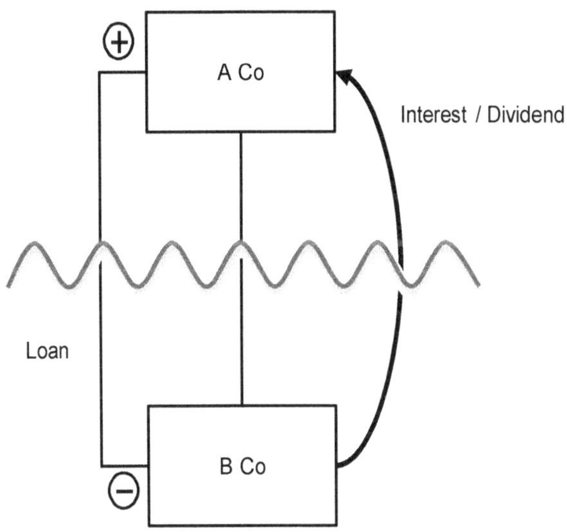

2. The loan is treated as a debt instrument under the laws of Country B but as an equity instrument (i.e. a share) under the laws of Country A and interest payments on the loan are treated as a deductible expense under Country B law but as dividends under Country A law. Country A exempts dividends paid by a foreign company if that shareholder has held more than 10% of the shares in the company in the 12 month period immediately prior to when the dividend is paid.

Question

3. Whether the interest payments fall within the scope of the hybrid financial instrument rule and, if so, to what extent an adjustment is required in accordance with that rule.

Answer

4. If Country A applies Recommendation 2.1 to deny A Co the benefit of tax exemption for a deductible dividend then no mismatch will arise for the purposes of the hybrid financial instrument rule.

5. If Country A does not apply Recommendation 2.1 then the payment of interest will give rise to a hybrid mismatch within the scope of the hybrid financial instrument rule and Country B should deny B Co a deduction for the interest paid to A Co. If Country B does not apply the recommended response, then Country A should treat the interest payments as ordinary income.

Analysis

Recommendation 2.1 will apply to deny A Co the benefit of the dividend exemption for the payment

6. Recommendation 2.1 states that a dividend exemption, which is granted by the payee jurisdiction to relieve double taxation, should not apply to payments that are deductible by the payer. As, in this case, the entire interest payment is deductible under Country B law, no part of the interest payment should be treated as eligible for exemption under Country A law.

7. If the dividend exemption in Country A does not extend to deductible dividends then no mismatch will arise for the purposes of the hybrid financial instrument rule. The determination of whether a payment gives rise to a D/NI outcome requires a proper consideration of the character of the payment and its tax treatment in both jurisdictions. This will include the effect of any rules in Country A, consistent with Recommendation 2.1, excluding deductible dividends from the benefit of a tax exemption.

If Country A does not apply Recommendation 2.1 then the payment will give rise to a hybrid mismatch that is within the scope of the hybrid financial instrument rule

8. Assuming that Country A has not implemented Recommendation 2.1, and the dividend exemption continues to apply in Country A, then the payment of interest will give rise to a D/NI outcome, which can be attributed to differences in the tax treatment of the subordinated loan under Country A and Country B law.

9. The subordinated loan meets the definition of a *financial instrument* under Recommendation 1 because it is characterised and taxed as a debt instrument in Country B and as an equity instrument in Country A.

10. A Co and B Co are also related parties (A Co owns 100% of B Co) so that the hybrid financial instrument falls within the scope of the hybrid financial instrument rule. Note that, because A Co and B Co are related parties, the circumstances in which the parties enter into the financial instrument does not affect whether the hybrid financial instrument rule is within the scope of Recommendation 1. If, for example, the subordinated loan was purchased by A Co from an unrelated party in an unconnected transaction, the mismatch in tax outcomes under the loan would still be treated as a hybrid mismatch between related parties for the purposes of Recommendation 1.

Primary recommendation – deny the deduction in the payer jurisdiction

11. Country B should deny the deduction to the extent the interest payment is not included in ordinary income under the laws of Country A. The adjustment is limited to neutralising the mismatch in tax outcomes. Recommendation 1 does not further require, for example, that Country B change the tax character of the payment in order to align it with the tax outcomes in the payee jurisdiction by treating it as a dividend for tax purposes.

Defensive rule – require income to be included in the payee jurisdiction

12. If Country B does not apply the recommended response, then the Country A should treat the deductible payment as ordinary income. As with the primary recommendation, the adjustment required under the defensive rule is limited to neutralising the mismatch in tax outcomes and does not require Country A to re-characterise the loan as debt or treat the payment as interest for tax purposes.

Example 1.2

Interest payment under a debt/equity hybrid eligible for partial exemption

Facts

1. The facts of this example are the same as **Example 1.1** except that Country A provides a partial tax exemption for foreign dividends paid by a controlled foreign entity. A table summarising the tax treatment of the instrument is set out below. In this table it is assumed that B Co has 100 of income for the period and makes a payment of 50 to A Co. A Co has no income for the period other than the payment under the subordinated loan. The corporate tax rate in both countries is 30%.

A Co			B Co		
	Tax	Book		Tax	Book
Income			Income		
Dividend received	5	50	Other income	100	100
Expenditure			Expenditure		
			Interest paid	(50)	(50)
Net return		**50**	**Net return**		**50**
Taxable income	**5**		**Taxable income**	**50**	
Tax to pay (30%)		(1.5)	Tax to pay (30%)		(15)
After-tax return		**48.5**	**After-tax return**		**35**

2. Under Country B law, the payment to A Co is treated as a deductible interest which means that B Co's taxable income is equal to its pre-tax net return. Under Country A law, however, the payment is treated as a dividend and A Co is entitled to a tax exemption for 90% of the payment received. The net effect of this difference in the characterisation of the instrument for tax purposes can be illustrated by comparing it to the tax treatment of an ordinary interest or dividend payment under the laws of Country A and B.

		Loan	Share	Hybrid
B Co	Income	100	100	100
	Expenditure	(50)	(50)	(50)
	Tax (at 30%)	(15)	(30)	(15)
	After-tax return	**35**	**20**	**35**
A Co	Income	50	50	50
	Expenditure	-	-	-
	Tax (at 30%)	(15)	(1.5)	(1.5)
	After-tax return	**35**	**48.5**	**48.5**
	Combined after-tax return	**70**	**68.5**	**83.5**

3. This comparison shows the net tax benefit to the parties of making a payment under the subordinated loan is between 13.5 and 15 (depending on whether the final outcome is compared to a dividend or interest payment).

Question

4. Whether the tax treatment of the payments under the subordinated loan falls within the scope of the hybrid financial instrument rule and, if so, to what extent an adjustment is required under that rule?

Answer

5. The payment under the subordinated loan will give rise to a mismatch in tax outcomes unless Country A applies Recommendation 2.1 to prevent A Co claiming the benefit of a partial dividend exemption in respect of a deductible payment.

6. Country B should deny B Co a deduction for a portion of the interest payable under the subordinated loan equal to the amount that is fully exempt from taxation under Country A law. If Country B does not apply the recommended response, then Country A should treat the entire payment as ordinary income.

Analysis

If Country A does not apply Recommendation 2.1 then the payment will give rise to a hybrid mismatch

7. Assuming Country A has not applied Recommendation 2.1 to prevent A Co claiming the benefit of the partial exemption, the payment will give rise to a mismatch in tax outcomes. This mismatch is attributable to the terms of the instrument because it is attributable to a difference in the way the loan is characterised under Country A and Country B laws.

Primary recommendation – deny the deduction in the payer jurisdiction

8. The primary recommendation under the hybrid financial instrument rule is that Country B deny the deduction to the extent it gives rise to a D/NI outcome. The effect of the adjustment should be to align the tax treatment of the payments made under the instrument so that the amounts that are treated as a financing expense in the payer jurisdiction are limited to the amounts that are fully taxed in the payee jurisdiction. The adjustment should result in a proportionate outcome that minimises the risk of double taxation. This can be achieved by only denying a deduction for the portion of the interest payment that is effectively exempt from taxation in the payee jurisdiction. Because 10% of the payment made to A Co is taxed at A Co's full marginal rate, B Co may continue to deduct an equivalent portion of the interest payment under Country B law. A table setting out the amount of the required adjustment is set out below.

A Co			B Co		
	Tax	**Book**		**Tax**	**Book**
Income			Income		
Dividend received	5	50	Other income	100	100
Expenditure			Expenditure		
			Interest paid	(5)	(50)
Net return		**50**	**Net return**		**50**
Taxable income	**5**		**Taxable income**	**95**	
Tax to pay		(1.5)	Tax to pay		(28.5)
After-tax return		**48.5**	**After-tax return**		**21.5**

9. Under Country B law the deduction is denied to the extent the payment is treated as exempt in Country A. Because the exemption granted in Country A only extends to 90% of the payment made under the instrument, the hybrid financial instrument rule still allows B Co to deduct 10% of the payment made to A Co. The adjustment has the net effect of bringing a sufficient amount of income into tax, under the laws of the payer and payee jurisdictions, to ensure that all the income under the arrangement is subject to tax at the taxpayer's full marginal rate.

Defensive rule – require income to be included in the payee jurisdiction

10. If Country B does not apply the recommended response, then A Co should treat the entire amount of the deductible payment as ordinary income under Country A law. A table setting out the amount of the required adjustment is set out below.

A Co			B Co		
	Tax	Book		Tax	Book
Income			Income		
Dividend received	50	50	Other income	100	100
Expenditure			Expenditure		
			Interest paid	(50)	(50)
Net return		**50**	**Net return**		**50**
Taxable income	**50**		**Taxable income**	**50**	
Tax to pay		(15)	Tax to pay		(15)
After-tax return		**35**	**After-tax return**		**35**

11. Under Country A law the entire amount of the payment is treated as ordinary income and subject to tax at the taxpayer's full marginal rate. As with the adjustment made under the primary recommendation this has the net effect of bringing the total amount of the income under the arrangement into tax under the laws of either the payer or payee jurisdiction and, because the tax rates in Country A and B are the same, produces the same net tax outcome as an adjustment under the primary rule.

Example 1.3

Interest payment under a debt/equity hybrid that is subject to a reduced rate

Facts

1. The facts of this example are the same as **Example 1.1** except that amounts that are characterised as dividends under Country A law are subject to tax at a reduced rate. A table summarising the tax treatment of the interest payment under the laws of Country A and Country B is set out below.

2. In this table it is assumed that B Co has income of 100 for the period and makes a payment of 40 under the subordinated loan. A Co has no income for the period other than the payment under the loan. The corporate tax rate is 20% in Country B and 40% in Country A, however Country A taxes dividends at 10% of the normal corporate rate (i.e. 4%).

A Co				B Co		
	Tax		Book		Tax	Book
	4%	40%				
Income				Income		
Dividend received	40		40	Other income	100	100
Expenditure				Expenditure		
				Interest paid	(40)	(40)
Net return			**40**	**Net return**		**60**
Income taxable at full rate		**4**		**Taxable income**	**60**	
Tax to pay			(1.6)	Tax to pay		(12)
After-tax return			**38.4**	**After-tax return**		**48**

3. Under Country B law, the payment to A Co is treated as deductible interest, which means that B Co's taxable income and pre-tax net return are the same. Under Country A law, however, the payment is treated as a dividend. A Co is subject to a reduced rate of taxation on dividend income (4%), which leaves A Co with an after-tax return of 38.4. The net effect of this difference in the characterisation of the instrument for tax purposes can be illustrated by comparing the tax treatment of this payment to that of an ordinary interest or dividend payment under the laws of Country A and B.

		Loan	Share	Hybrid
B Co	Income	100	100	100
	Expenditure	(40)	(40)	(40)
	Tax (at 20%)	(12)	(20)	(12)
	After-tax return	48	40	48
A Co	Income	40	40	40
	Expenditure	-	-	-
	Tax (at 40%)	(16)	(1.6)	(1.6)
	After-tax return	**24**	**38.4**	**38.4**
	Combined after-tax return	**72**	**78.4**	**86.4**

4. This comparison shows the net tax benefit to the parties of making a payment under the subordinated loan is between 8 and 14.4 (depending on whether the final outcome is compared to a dividend or interest payment).

Question

5. Whether the tax treatment of the payments under the subordinated loan falls within the scope of the hybrid financial instrument rule and, if so, to what extent an adjustment is required under that rule?

Answer

6. No mismatch will arise for the purposes of the hybrid financial instrument rule (and therefore no adjustment will be required under that rule) if the reduced rate of taxation applicable to the payment under the subordinated loan is the same rate that is applied to ordinary income derived by A Co under all types of financial instruments.

7. Assuming, however, that the reduced rate in Country A is less than the general rate applied to other types of income under a financial instrument then, unless Country A applies Recommendation 2.1 to prevent A Co claiming the benefit of the reduced rate for dividends, the payment under the loan will give rise to a mismatch in tax outcomes. The mismatch will be a hybrid mismatch because it is attributable to the way the subordinated loan is characterised under Country A and Country B laws.

8. Country B should therefore deny B Co a deduction for a portion of the interest payable under the subordinated loan. The amount that remains eligible to be deducted should equal the amount of income that is effectively subject to tax at the full marginal rate in the payee jurisdiction. If Country B does not apply the recommended response, then Country A should treat the entire payment as ordinary income subject to tax at the full rate.

Analysis

A payment made under the financial instrument will not give rise to a mismatch if the payment is subject to tax at A Co's full marginal rate

9. Ordinary income means "income that is subject to tax at the taxpayer's full marginal rate and does not benefit from any exemption, exclusion, credit or other tax relief applicable to particular categories of payments." Accordingly, the payment under the subordinated loan will not give rise to a mismatch in tax treatment if the payment is subject to tax at A Co's full marginal rate.

10. In the context of the hybrid financial instrument rule, A Co's *full marginal rate* is the rate of tax A Co would be expected to pay on ordinary income derived under a financial instrument. A mismatch will not arise, for the purposes of the hybrid financial instrument rule, simply because Country A taxes income from financial instruments at a lower rate than other types of income.

11. If, therefore, the reduced rate of taxation applicable to the payment under the subordinated loan applies to all payments of ordinary income under a financial instrument, then no mismatch arises for the purposes of the hybrid financial instrument rule and no adjustment is required to be made to the tax treatment of the payment under Country A or B laws.

12. If, however, the reduced rate of 4% applies only to dividends then, assuming Country A has not applied Recommendation 2.1 to prevent A Co claiming the benefit of the reduced rate, the payment will give rise to a mismatch in tax outcomes that is attributable to the terms of the instrument.

Primary recommendation – deny the deduction in the payer jurisdiction

13. The primary recommendation under the hybrid financial instrument rule is that Country B deny the deduction to the extent it gives rise to a D/NI outcome. This can be achieved by denying a deduction for a portion of the interest payment up to the amount that is effectively exempt from taxation in the payee jurisdiction. Because of the reduced rate in Country A, only 10% of the payment made to A Co is effectively taxed at the full rate and B Co's deduction should be restricted to a corresponding amount. A table showing the amount of the required adjustment is set out below.

A Co				B Co		
	Tax		Book		Tax	Book
	4%	40%				
Income				Income		
Dividend received	40		40	Other income	100	100
Expenditure				Expenditure		
				Interest paid	(4)	(40)
Net return			**40**	**Net return**		**60**
Income taxable at full rate		**4**		**Taxable income**	**96**	
Tax to pay			(1.6)	Tax to pay		(19.2)
After-tax return			**38.4**	**After-tax return**		**40.8**

14. Country B should deny a deduction for 90% of the payment made under the instrument because the reduced rate of tax is only sufficient to cover 10% of the payment at normal corporate rates. This adjustment has the net effect of bringing a sufficient amount of income into tax, under the laws of the payer and payee jurisdictions, to ensure that all the income under the arrangement is subject to tax at the taxpayer's full marginal rate.

Defensive rule – require income to be included in the payee jurisdiction

15. If Country B does not apply the recommended response, then A Co should be required to treat the entire amount of the deductible payment as ordinary income under Country A law. A table setting out the amount of the required adjustment is set out below.

A Co				B Co		
	4% Tax	40% Tax	Book		Tax	Book
Income				Income		
Dividend received		40	40	Other income	100	100
Expenditure				Expenditure		
				Interest paid	(40)	(40)
Net return			**40**	**Net return**		**60**
Income subject to tax at effective rate of 40%		**40**		**Taxable income**	**60**	
Tax to pay			(16)	Tax to pay		(12)
After-tax return			**24**	**After-tax return**		**48**

16. Under Country A law the entire amount of the payment is treated as ordinary income and subject to tax at the taxpayer's full marginal rate (40%). The adjustment has the net effect of bringing a sufficient amount of income into tax, under the laws of the payer and payee jurisdictions, to ensure that all the income under the arrangement is subject to tax at the taxpayer's full marginal rate in each jurisdiction.

17. The differences between the total aggregate tax liability under the primary and secondary rule are explained by reference to different amounts of income brought into account in each jurisdiction under the rule and differences in tax rate between the payer and payee jurisdictions.

Example 1.4

Interest payment eligible for an underlying foreign tax credit

Facts

1. The facts of this example are the same as **Example 1.1** except that the tax relief granted by Country A is in the form of a tax credit for underlying foreign taxes paid by its subsidiary. The credit is granted in proportion to the amount of pre-tax retained earnings that are distributed to the shareholder by way of dividend. A table summarising the treatment of a payment under the laws of Country A and Country B is set out below. In this table it is assumed that B Co derives income of 100 for the period. B Co makes a payment of 40 to A Co under the subordinated loan. A Co has no other income for the period. The corporate tax rate in Country B is 20% and in Country A is 35%.

A Co			B Co		
	Tax	Book		Tax	Book
Income			Income		
Dividend received	40	40	Other income	100	100
Expenditure			Expenditure		
			Interest paid	(40)	(40)
Net return		**40**	**Net return**		**60**
Taxable income	**40**		**Taxable income**	**60**	
Tax (35%)	(14)				
Tax credit	4.8				
Tax to pay		(9.2)	Tax to pay (at 20%)		(12)
After-tax return		**30.8**	**After-tax return**		**48**

2. Under Country B law, the payment to A Co is treated as deductible interest which means that B Co's taxable income is equal to its net return. Under Country A law, however, the payment is treated as a dividend and A Co is entitled to a foreign tax credit for the underlying foreign tax paid on the dividend. The formula for determining the amount of the credit granted under Country A law for underlying foreign taxes can be expressed as follows:

$$\text{Total amount of tax paid by B Co} \quad \times \quad \frac{\text{Total amount of dividend from B Co}}{\text{B Co's retained earnings + taxes paid + B Co distributions}}$$

Assuming the B Co has no historical earnings and has not previously made any distributions, the simplified formula set out above produces an underlying foreign tax credit that is equal to 4.8 (= 12 x 40/100) leaving A Co with a total Country A tax to pay of 9.2.

3. Note that this formula for calculating foreign taxes has been simplified for the purpose of demonstrating the effect of the hybrid financial instrument rule in the context of a dividend that qualifies for a credit for underlying foreign taxes. In practice, the amount of underlying foreign tax paid on distributions of retained earnings can be more accurately calculated by determining the historical amount of tax paid on the subsidiary's *after-tax* retained earnings. The jurisdiction granting the credit will treat the dividend as grossed-up by the amount of the foreign tax credit attached to the dividend and may operate a tax credit pooling system that tracks the retained earnings of each subsidiary and the amount of tax that has been borne by those earnings and treats the foreign tax credits attached to previous dividends as reducing the available pool of foreign tax credits.

4. The net effect of the difference in the characterisation of the payment made under the instrument can be illustrated by comparing it to the tax treatment of an ordinary interest or dividend payment under the laws of Country A and B. This comparison shows the net tax benefit to the parties of making a payment under the subordinated loan is 4.8.

		Loan	Share	Hybrid
B Co	Income	100	100	100
	Expenditure	(40)	(40)	(40)
	Tax (at 20%)	(12)	(20)	(12)
	After-tax return	**48**	**40**	**48**
A Co	Income	40	40	40
	Expenditure			
	Tax (at 35%)	(14)	(6)	(9.2)
	After-tax return	**26**	**34**	**30.8**
Combined after-tax return		**74**	**74**	**78.8**

5. In theory, because a credit for underlying foreign taxes only imposes incremental tax on distributed profit, the aggregate tax burden borne by a dividend and an interest payment is the same regardless of the difference in tax rates between the payer and payee jurisdictions. Hence, in this simplified example, the total retained earnings of A Co and B Co are unaffected by whether the payment is characterised as a dividend or as interest. In practice, however, differences in the way the payer and payee jurisdictions calculate income for tax and foreign tax credit purposes and restrictions on the utilisation of tax credits in the payee jurisdiction will impact on the amount of tax paid on the dividend in the payee jurisdiction (and therefore on the equality of tax treatment between dividends

and interest) in much the same way as they will under a partial exemption or reduced rate system.

Question

6. Whether the tax treatment of the payments under the subordinated loan falls within the scope of the hybrid financial instrument rule and, if so, what adjustments are required under the rule?

Answer

7. If Country A applies Recommendation 2.1 to deny A Co the benefit of tax credit for a deductible dividend then no mismatch will arise for the purposes of the hybrid financial instrument rule.

8. If Country A does not apply Recommendation 2.1 then the payment under the subordinated loan will give rise to a mismatch in tax outcomes to the extent that the credit shelters the dividend from tax under the laws of Country A.

9. Country B should deny B Co a deduction for a portion of the interest payable under the subordinated loan. The amount that remains eligible to be deducted following the adjustment should equal the amount of income that will be effectively subject to tax at the full marginal rate in the payee jurisdiction after application of the tax credit.

10. If Country B does not apply the recommended response, then A Co should treat the entire payment as ordinary income under the secondary rule and deny A Co the benefit of any tax credit.

Analysis

Recommendation 2.1 will apply to deny A Co the benefit of the tax credit

11. Credits, such as those granted by Country A, which are designed to relieve the payee from economic double taxation of dividend income, fall within Recommendation 2.1. That Recommendation states that jurisdictions should consider denying the benefit of such double taxation relief in the case of payments that are deductible by the payer. Accordingly, no part of the interest payment should be treated as eligible for a credit for underlying taxes in the payee jurisdiction where that payment is deductible under the laws of the payer jurisdiction. If Country A maintains a pooling system for foreign tax credits then any credits that are denied under the application of the defensive rule should be left in the pool.

12. The determination of whether a payment gives rise to a D/NI outcome requires a proper consideration of the character of the payment and its tax treatment in both jurisdictions. This will include the effect of any rules in Country A, consistent with Recommendation 2.1, that exclude deductible dividends from the benefit of any double tax relief. Therefore, if Country A withdraws the benefit of the underlying foreign tax credit for the dividends paid by B Co, on the grounds that such dividend payments are deductible under Country B law, then no mismatch will arise for the purposes of the hybrid financial instrument rule.

A payment made under the financial instrument will give rise to a hybrid mismatch

13. On the assumption that Country A has not implemented the restrictions on double-tax relief that are called for under Recommendation 2.1, the payments of interest under the subordinated loan will give rise to a D/NI outcome as the payments are deductible under the laws of Country B and not included in ordinary income in the payee jurisdiction (because such payments benefit from a credit under Country A law). This mismatch will be a hybrid mismatch because the tax treatment in Country A that gives rise to the D/NI outcome is attributable to a difference in the characterisation of the loan under Country A and B laws.

Primary recommendation – deny the deduction in the payer jurisdiction

14. The primary recommendation under the hybrid financial instrument rule is that Country B deny the deduction for a payment to the extent it gives rise to a D/NI outcome. The effect of the adjustment should be to align the tax treatment of the payments made under the instrument so that amounts that are treated as a financing expense in the payer jurisdiction do not exceed the amounts that are taxed as ordinary income in the payee jurisdiction. The adjustment should result in an outcome that is proportionate and minimises the risk of double taxation.

15. This can be achieved by denying a deduction for the interest payment to the extent it is fully sheltered from tax under the laws of Country A. Of the payment made to A Co, 65.7% (i.e. 9.2/14) is taxed at the full rate of tax applicable to ordinary income in Country A and Country B should allow for a similar portion of the interest payment to be deducted. A table setting out the effect of this adjustment is set out below.

A Co			B Co		
	Tax	Book		Tax	Book
Income			Income		
Dividend received	40	40	Other income	100	100
Expenditure			Expenditure		
			Interest paid	(26.29)	(40)
Net return		**40**	**Net return**		**60**
Taxable income	**40**		**Taxable income**	**73.71**	
Tax (35%)	(14)				
Tax credit	4.8				
Tax to pay		(9.2)	Tax to pay (at 20%)		(14.74)
After-tax return		**30.8**	**After-tax return**		**45.26**

16. Under Country B law the deduction is denied to the extent the payment is not subject to tax at the payee's full marginal rate in the payee jurisdiction. A Co's tax liability on the payment is 9.20 which at the 35% tax rate indicates that 26.29 (i.e. 9.2/0.35) of the payment was taxable as ordinary income in Country A.

17. The adjustment has the net effect of bringing a sufficient amount of income into tax, under the laws of the payer and payee jurisdictions, to ensure that all the income under the arrangement is subject to tax at the taxpayer's full marginal rate. While the adjustment results in a lower overall effective tax rate for the arrangement than would have occurred under a normal dividend this is explained by reference to the different amounts of income brought into account, and differences in tax rate between, the payer and payee jurisdictions.

18. In this simplified example it is assumed that the effect of the increase in taxation in Country B, resulting from the application of the hybrid financial instrument rule, is not taken into account for the purposes of calculating the amount of the tax credit in Country A. This may be because Country A expressly prohibits the crediting of increased foreign taxes that arise due to the application of the hybrid financial instrument rule or because, in practice, the incremental tax increase does not have a material impact on the amount of the payment brought into taxation as ordinary income in Country A.

Defensive rule – require income to be included in the payee jurisdiction

19. If Country B does not apply the recommended response, then Country A should treat the entire amount of the deductible payment as ordinary income and deny A Co the benefit of the foreign tax credit. A table setting out the amount of the required adjustment is set out below.

A Co			B Co		
	Tax	**Book**		**Tax**	**Book**
Income			Income		
Dividend received	40	40	Other income	100	100
Expenditure			Expenditure		
			Interest paid	(40)	(40)
Net return		**40**	**Net return**		**60**
Taxable income	**40**		**Taxable income**	**60**	
Tax (35%)	(14)				
Tax credit	-				
Tax to pay		(14)	Tax to pay (at 20%)		(12)
After-tax return		**26**	**After-tax return**		**48**

20. Under Country A law the entire amount of the payment is treated as ordinary income and subject to tax at the taxpayer's full marginal rate without a credit for underlying taxes. The adjustment has the net effect of bringing a sufficient amount of income into tax, under the laws of the payer and payee jurisdictions, to ensure that all the income under the arrangement is subject to tax at the taxpayer's full marginal rate. As for the adjustment under Recommendation 2.1, Country A should treat any credits that are denied under the application of the defensive rule as left in the pool and available for distribution at a future date.

Example 1.5

Interest payment to an exempt person

Facts

1. In this example the facts are the same as in **Example 1.1** except that both jurisdictions treat the subordinated loan as a debt instrument. A Co is a sovereign wealth fund established under Country A law that is exempt from tax on all income. A Co is therefore not taxable on the interest payment.

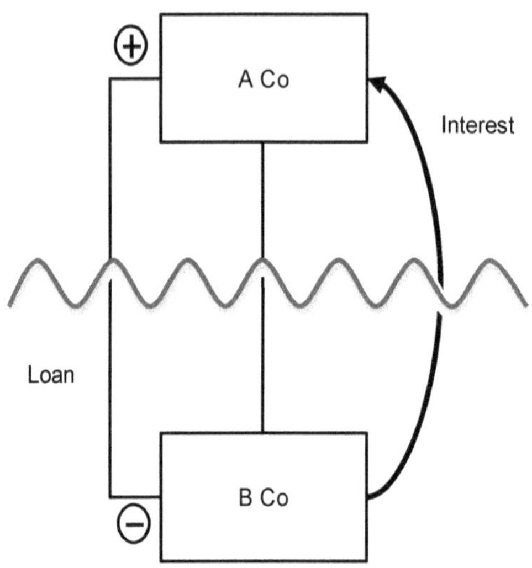

Question

2. Whether the tax treatment of the payments under the subordinated loan falls within the scope of the hybrid financial instrument rule and, if so, what adjustments are required under the rule?

Answer

3. The payment of interest under the loan gives rise to a mismatch in tax outcomes as it is deductible under Country B law but is not included in ordinary income under Country A law. This D/NI outcome will not, however, be treated as a *hybrid mismatch* unless it can be attributed to the terms of the instrument.

4. If the mismatch in tax outcomes would not have arisen had the interest been paid to a taxpayer of ordinary status, then the mismatch will be solely attributable to A Co's status as a tax exempt entity, and cannot be attributable to the terms of the instrument

itself. In such a case the mismatch in tax outcomes will not be caught by the hybrid financial instrument rule. If the terms of the instrument would have been sufficient, on their own, to bring about a mismatch in tax outcomes (i.e. the payment would not have been included in interest even if it had been made to an ordinary taxpayer) then the mismatch will be treated as a hybrid mismatch and subject to adjustment under the hybrid financial instrument rule.

5. While the application of the hybrid financial instrument rule could result in the denial of a deduction under Country B law, the application of the secondary rule in Country A will not result in any additional tax liability for A Co because A Co is not taxable on ordinary income.

Analysis

A payment made under the financial instrument may give rise to a hybrid mismatch

6. The mismatch in tax outcomes under the instrument will be treated as a *hybrid* mismatch when the outcome is attributable to the tax treatment of the instrument, rather than the tax treatment of the entity receiving the payment or the circumstances under which it is held. On the facts of this example the exemption is most likely to be attributable to A Co's special status as a tax exempt entity, however, if the terms of the instrument would have been sufficient, on their own, to bring about a D/NI outcome, then the mismatch should be treated as a "hybrid mismatch" for the purposes of these rules.

7. The guidance to Recommendation 1 notes that one way of testing for whether a mismatch is attributable to the terms of the instrument is to ask whether the same mismatch would have arisen between taxpayers of ordinary status. The test looks to what the tax treatment of the instrument would have been if both the payer and payee were ordinary resident taxpayers that computed their income and expenditure in accordance with the rules applicable to all taxpayers of the same type. If the payment of interest would not have been expected to be treated as ordinary income under this counterfactual then the mismatch should be treated as attributable to the terms of the instrument and potentially subject to adjustment under the hybrid financial instrument rule.

Primary recommendation – deny the deduction in the payer jurisdiction

8. In the event the mismatch is determined to be a hybrid mismatch, Country B should apply its hybrid mismatch rule to deny B Co a deduction for the payment made under the hybrid financial instrument to the extent of that mismatch. This deduction would be denied notwithstanding that the D/NI outcome would have arisen if the instrument had not been a hybrid financial instrument.

Defensive rule – require income to be included in the payee jurisdiction

9. While Country A should also treat the loan as a hybrid financial instrument the application of the defensive rule will not have any tax impact on A Co. Although, in theory A Co would be required to treat the interest payments as "ordinary income", this will not result in any additional tax liability for A Co because A Co is exempt from tax on all income.

Example 1.6

Interest payment to a person established in a no-tax jurisdiction

Facts

1. The facts of this example are the same as in **Example 1.1** except that Country A (the laws under which A Co is established) does not have a corporate tax system and A Co does not have a taxable presence in any other jurisdiction. A Co is therefore not liable to tax in any jurisdiction on payments of interest under the loan.

Question

2. Whether the interest payments under the loan fall within the scope of the hybrid financial instrument rule?

Answer

3. The interest payment does not give rise to a mismatch within the language or intended scope of the hybrid financial instrument rule.

Analysis

4. Recommendation 1 only applies to payments that give rise to a D/NI outcome. While the interest payment is deductible under the laws of Country B, a mismatch will only arise in respect of that payment if it is not included in income by a payee in a payee jurisdiction. In this case, however, the recipient of the interest payment is not a taxpayer in any jurisdiction and, accordingly, there is no payee jurisdiction where the payment can be included in income. The payment of interest under the loan therefore does not fall within the language or intended scope of the hybrid financial instrument rule.

Example 1.7

Interest payment to a taxpayer resident in a territorial tax regime

Facts

1. The facts of this example are the same as in **Example 1.1** except that Country A administers a pure territorial tax system and does not tax income unless it has a domestic source. Interest income paid by a non-resident is treated as foreign source income and is exempt from taxation unless the payment can be attributed to a PE maintained by B Co in Country A. As B Co has no PE in Country A, the interest is not subject to tax in the hands of A Co.

Question

2. Whether the interest payments under the loan fall within the scope of the hybrid financial instrument rule?

Answer

3. The mismatch is not attributable to the terms of the instrument but to the fact that A Co is exempt from tax on foreign source income of any description. The mismatch is thus not caught by the hybrid financial instrument rule.

Analysis

A payment made under the financial instrument gives rise to a mismatch

4. The payment of interest is deductible under the laws of the payer jurisdiction (Country B) but not included in income under the laws of the payee jurisdiction (Country A). Note that this outcome is to be contrasted with that under **Example 1.6** where the payment is made to an entity established in a no-tax jurisdiction. In that case the payment does not give rise to a mismatch in tax outcomes as the payment is not treated as received under the laws of any "payee jurisdiction". In this case Country A does maintain a corporate tax system and A Co is a taxpayer in that jurisdiction. There is therefore both payer and a payee jurisdictions that can be tested for the purposes of determining whether a D/NI outcome has arisen.

Mismatch is not a hybrid mismatch

5. Although the payment gives rise to a D/NI outcome the resulting mismatch is not a hybrid mismatch because it is not attributable to the terms of the instrument but to the fact that A Co is exempt on foreign source income of any description. There is no change that could be made to the terms of the instrument that would result in payments under the

instrument becoming taxable. Note that this outcome is to be contrasted with **Example 1.1** where the payee jurisdiction exempts only dividend payments. In that case, it is both the source of the payment and the terms of the instrument that give rise to the dividend treatment (and hence the exemption) in the payee jurisdiction.

Example 1.8

Interest payment to a tax exempt PE

Facts

1. In the example illustrated below, A Co, a company resident in Country A lends money to C Co (a wholly-owned subsidiary) through a PE in Country B. Country A, B and C all treat the loan as a debt instrument for tax purposes. Payments of interest under the loan are deductible under Country C law but not included in income under Country A law. Country A provides an exemption for income derived through a foreign PE.

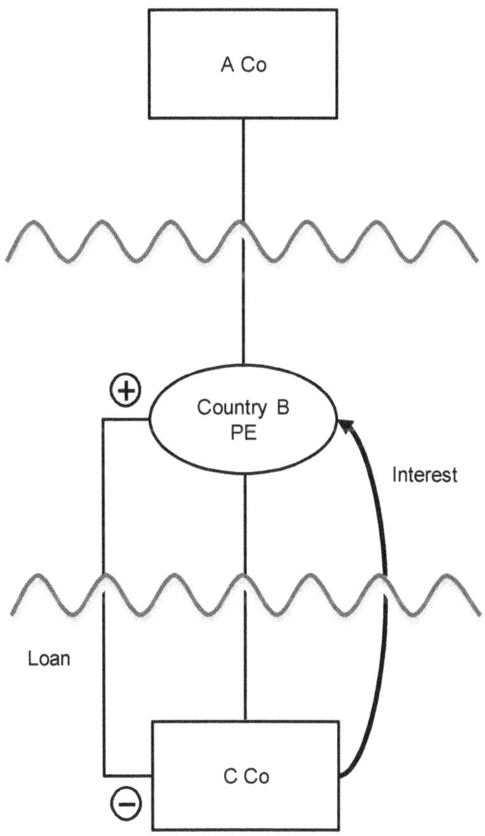

Question

2. In what circumstances will the payment of interest under the loan be treated as giving rise to a hybrid mismatch subject to adjustment under the hybrid financial instrument rule?

Answer

3. The payment of interest under the loan will only give rise to a D/NI outcome if the payment is not treated as ordinary income under both Country A and Country B laws. If a payment of deductible interest is not expected to be included in ordinary income under the laws of one of the payee jurisdictions (either Country A or B) then a tax administration may treat the payment as giving rise to a D/NI outcome unless the taxpayer can satisfy the tax authority that the payment has been included in ordinary income in the other jurisdiction.

4. A deductible payment that gives rise to a mismatch in tax outcomes will be treated as within the scope of the hybrid financial instrument rule if the mismatch can be attributed to the tax treatment of the instrument under the laws of either Country A or Country B. If, for example, the mismatch could be attributed to the fact that either jurisdiction treats the interest on the loan as an exempt dividend then the hybrid financial instrument rule would apply to the instrument. The arrangement should not be treated as falling within the scope of the hybrid financial instrument rule, however, if the mismatch would not have arisen in respect of a loan that had been entered into directly by a payee resident in either Country A or B.

5. If the interest payment falls within the scope of the hybrid financial instrument rule then the recommended response is to deny the deduction for that payment under Country C law. The application of the secondary rule in Country A will not, however, result in any additional tax liability if A Co is not taxable on ordinary income derived through a foreign PE.

Analysis

No mismatch arises if the interest payment is included in ordinary income under either Country A or Country B law

6. A D/NI outcome will only arise where a payment that is deductible under the laws of one jurisdiction (the payer jurisdiction) is not included in ordinary income under the laws of any other jurisdiction where the payment is treated as being received (the payee jurisdiction). In order for a jurisdiction to link the tax treatment of a payment in one jurisdiction with the tax consequences in another it is therefore necessary to identify the taxpayers and jurisdictions where the payment is made and received. In most cases the payee will be the legal entity with the right to receive the payment (in this case, A Co) and the payee jurisdiction will be the jurisdiction where that entity is resident (in this case, Country A). However where the payment is received through a tax transparent structure such as a PE, it will be necessary to look to the laws of the PE jurisdiction (in this case, Country B) to definitively establish whether a mismatch has arisen.

7. The facts of the example do not state whether the interest payment is treated as included in ordinary income under Country B law. Assuming, however, the tax treatment of the payment in Country B cannot be established, the deductible interest payments on the loan should be treated as giving rise to a D/NI outcome to the extent such payments are not included in ordinary income under the laws of Country A. It will be the taxpayer who has the burden of establishing, to the reasonable satisfaction of the tax administration, how the tax treatment in Country B impacts on the amount of the adjustment required under the rule. If the taxpayer can establish, to the satisfaction of its own tax administration, that the full amount of the interest payment is expected to be

included in ordinary income under the laws of another jurisdiction then the taxpayer should not be required to make an adjustment under the hybrid financial instrument rule.

Mismatch may be a hybrid mismatch

8. The mismatch will be treated as a hybrid mismatch to the extent it can be attributed to differences in the tax treatment of the instrument under the laws of the payer and payee jurisdictions. The test for hybridity, in the financial instrument context, looks to whether the terms of the instrument were sufficient to bring about the mismatch under the laws of the relevant jurisdictions. Thus, if the mismatch arose because either Country A or B treated the interest on the loan as an exempt dividend, then the hybrid financial instrument rule would apply.

9. A mismatch in outcomes will not be treated as a hybrid mismatch, however, if it is solely attributable to the circumstances in which the instrument is held. If, for example, the interest payment is exempt in Country A only because A Co has made the loan through the foreign PE then the resulting mismatch in tax outcomes will not be treated a hybrid mismatch for the purposes of the rule.

10. One way of testing whether the mismatch is attributable to the terms of the instrument, rather than the status of the taxpayer or the context in which the instrument is held, is to ask whether the mismatch would have arisen had the instrument been held directly by an ordinary taxpayer that computed its income and expenditure under the ordinary rules applicable to taxpayers of the same type. If a mismatch would still have arisen in these circumstances then the mismatch should be treated as a hybrid mismatch within the scope of the rule.

Application of the hybrid financial instrument rule under Country C law

11. If Country C determines that the loan is caught by the rule, then Country C should apply the primary recommendation and deny C Co a deduction for the interest to the extent of that mismatch.

12. C Co may be able to establish, however, that, notwithstanding the hybrid mismatch between Country A and C, the payment has, in fact, been included in income under the laws of a third jurisdiction (Country B). If the taxpayer can reasonably satisfy the tax administration that the interest payments are in fact included in income under Country B law, then, in fact, no D/NI outcome arises and the hybrid financial instrument rule should not apply.

Application of the hybrid financial instrument rule under Country B law

13. If Country C does not apply the recommended response, Country B may treat the interest payment as ordinary income under the secondary rule.

Application of the hybrid financial instrument rule under Country A law

14. In no event will the hybrid financial instrument rule in Country A result in any additional tax liability for A Co. This is either because:

(a) the mismatch will not be attributable the terms of the instrument but to the special tax treatment granted under Country A law for income derived through a foreign PE (in which case the instrument is not a hybrid financial instrument under Country A law); or

(b) the instrument will be treated as a hybrid financial instrument but the response under the hybrid financial instrument rule (treating the payment as ordinary income) will not result in any increase in tax liability for A Co as all ordinary income derived through a foreign PE is exempt from income under Country A law.

Example 1.9

Interest payment to a person holding instrument through tax-exempt account

Facts

1. In the example illustrated in the figure below, A is an individual resident in Country A and B Co is a company resident in Country B. Individual A subscribes for a bond issued by B Co that pays regular interest.

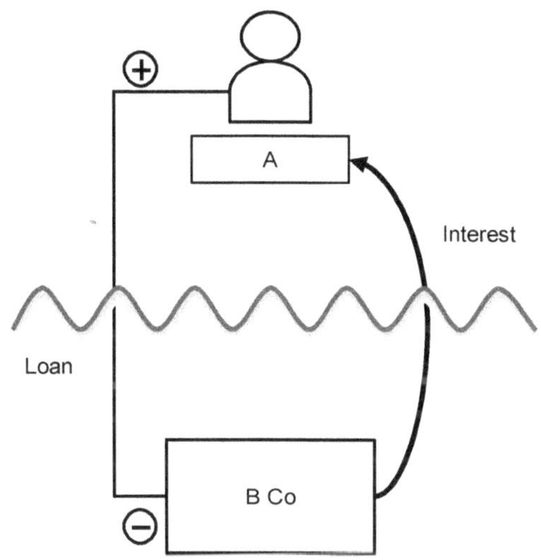

2. The bond is treated as a debt instrument under the laws of both Country A and B. B Co is entitled to a deduction for the interest payments and these payments would usually be treated as ordinary income in Country A. In this case, however, the bond is held by A through a tax exempt personal savings account that entitles A to an exemption on any income and gains in respect of assets held in the account. The saving account is available only to individuals and there are limits on the amount and type of assets that can be put into the account.

Question

3. Whether the arrangement falls within the scope of the hybrid financial instrument rule?

Answer

4. The instrument does not fall within the scope of the hybrid financial instrument rule because the mismatch is attributable to the circumstances in which the bond is held and cannot be attributed to the terms of the instrument.

Analysis

There is no payment made under the financial instrument that gives rise to a hybrid mismatch

5. The hybrid financial instrument rule only applies where the mismatch can be attributed to terms of the instrument. In this example B Co's interest payments result in D/NI outcome, however this mismatch is caused by the fact that A holds the instrument through a savings account that, under Country A law, entitles A to an exemption in respect of the interest payment on the bond. The mismatch would not have arisen if the bond was held directly by A, rather than through the savings account. Because the mismatch is attributable to the context in which the instrument is held rather than the nature of the instrument itself, it falls outside the intended scope of the hybrid financial instrument rule.

Example 1.10

Deductible dividends paid by a special purpose entity

Facts

1. In the example illustrated in the figure below, A Co (a company resident in Country A) owns 25% of the shares in B Co. B Co is a Real Estate Investment Trust (REIT) that earns most of its income from real estate investments. B Co pays a dividend to A Co. The dividend is not required to be included in ordinary income under Country A law.

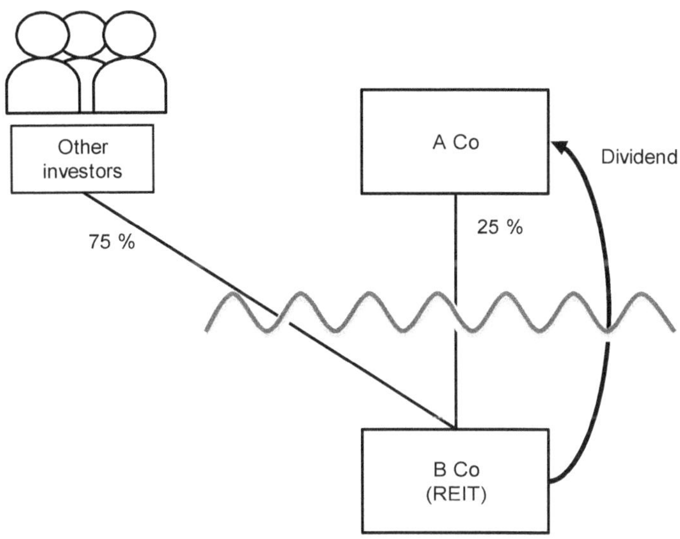

2. Under the laws of Country B, a REIT is granted a special tax status, which is only available to entities that invest in certain classes of assets and that derive certain kinds of income. Entities that meet the criteria to become a REIT and have elected to take advantage of this special tax status are entitled to a deduction for the dividends they pay their investors. This dividend deduction is intended to ensure that there is only one level of taxation (at the shareholder level) in respect of the investments made by the REIT.

3. The REIT will generally be required to meet certain distribution requirements (intended to ensure that all the income of the REIT is distributed to investors within a reasonable period of time) and there may also be restrictions on the type of persons that can invest in the REIT and the amount of shares of the REIT that the investor can hold.

Question

4. Whether the dividend payment falls within the scope of the hybrid financial instrument rule?

Answer

5. The deductibility of the dividend turns on B Co's special tax status as REIT not on the terms of the instrument. Therefore the dividend does not fall within the scope of the hybrid financial instrument rule.

Analysis

Recommendation 2.1 will apply to the dividend

6. Recommendation 2.1 states that a dividend exemption, which is granted by the payee jurisdiction to relieve double taxation, should not apply to payments that are deductible by the payer. As, in this case, the entire interest payment is deductible by B Co, no part of the interest payment should be treated as eligible for exemption under Country A law. Recommendation 2.1 should apply notwithstanding the payment will not be treated as subject to adjustment under the hybrid financial instrument rule (see below).

Deductible dividend does not give rise to a hybrid mismatch as deduction attributable to special status of REIT

7. The payment of a deductible dividend will not give rise to a hybrid mismatch under Recommendation 1 provided the deduction is attributable to the tax status of the REIT rather than the ordinary tax treatment of dividends under the laws of that jurisdiction.

8. The guidance to Recommendation 1 notes that one way of testing for whether a mismatch is attributable to the terms of the instrument is to ask whether the same mismatch would have arisen between taxpayers of ordinary status. If dividend payments are not ordinarily deductible under Country B law, then the mismatch that arises in this case should be treated as attributable to the particular status of the payer rather than the tax treatment of the instrument.

Example 1.11

Tax relief equivalent to a deduction

Facts

1. In this example A Co, a company resident in Country A owns all the shares of B Co a company resident in Country B. B Co derives operating income which is subject to corporation tax under the laws of Country B. B Co pays a dividend to A Co. A Co is not subject to tax on the dividend under the laws of Country B (as A Co is not a Country B taxpayer) and Country A provides for an exemption for dividends paid by a foreign company. A Co is therefore not subject to tax on the dividend under either Country A or Country B law.

2. Under Country B law, the payment of a dividend triggers a tax credit equal to 90% of the corporate tax paid on the distributed income. This refund may be in the form of a credit against B Co's tax liability or may be paid as an additional amount directly to the shareholder. The figure below illustrates the tax consequences where Country B provides B Co with a tax credit for dividends paid.

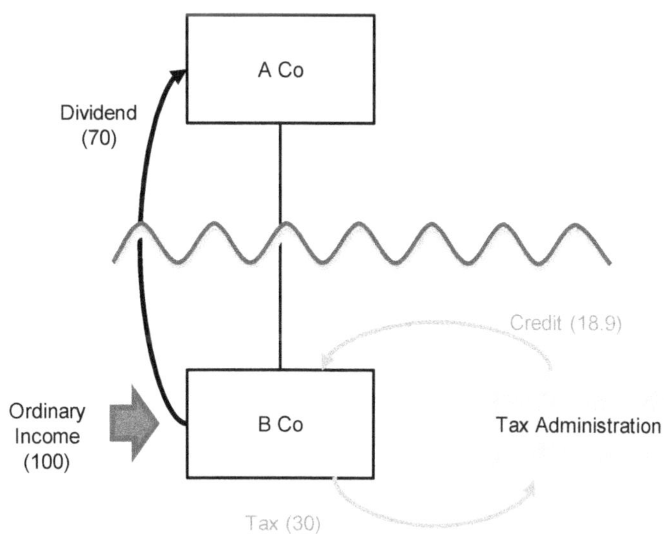

3. As illustrated in the figure above, B Co derives 100 of operating income which is subject to tax at a 30% corporate rate and that the remaining income is distributed as a dividend. Payment of the dividend, however, allows B Co to claim a tax credit equal to 90% of the corporate tax rate on the dividend. The table below sets out the net tax consequences for both A Co and B Co where Country B law provides for a tax credit in respect of dividends paid.

A Co			B Co		
	Tax	Book		Tax	Book
Income			Income		
			Ordinary income	100	100
Dividend received		70			
Expenditure			Expenditure		
			Dividend paid		(70)
Net return		**70**	**Net return**		**30**
Taxable income	**0**		**Taxable income**	**100**	
Tax on net income		0	Tax on net income (30%)	(30)	
			Credit	18.9	
			Tax to pay		(11.1)
After-tax return		**70**	**After-tax return**		**18.9**

4. As can be seen from the above table the net effect of the tax credit granted under Country B law is that B Co pays 30% tax on the undistributed income (0.3 x 30 = 9) and 3% tax on the amount that has been distributed (0.03 x 70 = 2.1).

5. The figure and table below illustrate the tax consequences that apply where Country B provides A Co with a refundable credit in respect of the dividend paid by B Co.

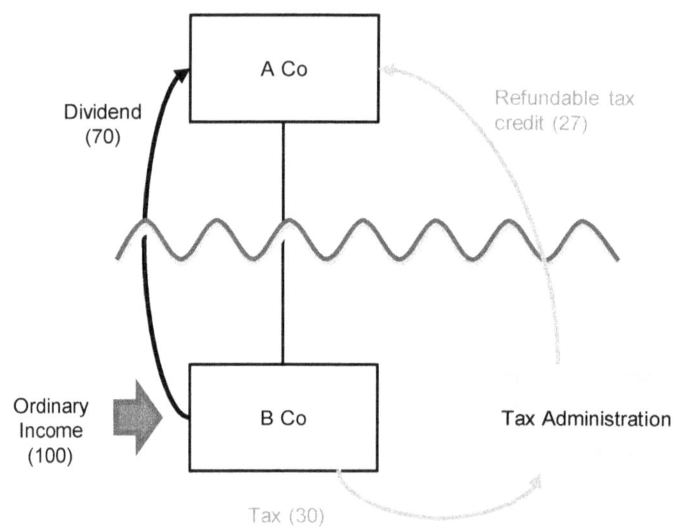

6. As in the fact pattern illustrated in the first page of this example, B Co derives 100 of operating income which is subject to tax at a 30% corporate rate with the remainder of the income distributed to A Co as a dividend. In this case, however, Country B provides A Co with a refundable tax credit in respect of the dividend paid. As A Co is not subject to tax on the dividend under the laws of Country B, it is entitled to claim a full refund for the unutilised credit. The formula for calculating the amount of the refundable credit that can be attached to the dividend is as follows:

$$0.9 \times \text{tax rate in Country B} \quad \times \quad (\text{amount of distribution} \times \frac{1}{1 - \text{tax rate in Country B}})$$

7. Applying this formula to the distribution, A Co is entitled to a credit equal to (0.27 x (70 x 1/0.7) = 27. The table below illustrates the net tax consequences for both A Co and B Co where Country B law provides shareholders with a refund of 90% of the corporate tax paid on a dividend distribution.

A Co			B Co		
	Tax	Book		Tax	Book
Income			Income		
Dividend received	-	70	Ordinary income	100	100
Refundable Tax Credit	-	27			
			Expenditure		
			Dividend paid		(70)
Net return		**97**	**Net return**		**30**
Taxable income	**0**		**Taxable income**	**100**	
Tax on net income		0	Tax on net income		(30)
After-tax return		**97**	**After-tax return**		**0**

8. This refundable credit mechanism ensures that the net amount of Country B tax paid on B Co's distributed income is 3% (i.e. 10% of the normal corporate rate). Because the dividend is not subject to tax in Country A the net effect of this credit is that only 3% of the income under the arrangement is subject to tax under either Country A or B law.

Question

9. Whether the dividend falls within the scope of the hybrid financial instrument rule and, if so, to what extent an adjustment is required to be made in accordance with the rule.

Answer

10. In either case, the dividend gives rise to tax relief that is equivalent to a deduction under Country B law and the dividend payment should, therefore, be treated as falling within the scope of the hybrid financial instrument rule.

11. When making an adjustment under Country A law, A Co should take into account the fact that only 10% of the amount distributed has been subject to tax as ordinary income due to the tax relief granted under Country B law.

Analysis

Tax credit or refund treated as equivalent tax relief under Country B law

12. A payment will be treated as deductible under the laws of the payer jurisdiction if it is applied, or can be applied, to reduce a taxpayer's net income. While B Co's dividend payment cannot be deducted directly from B Co's income, the concept of "deductible", for the purposes of the hybrid mismatch rules, also extends to payments that trigger other types of "equivalent tax relief". The tax credit or refund granted to B Co or its shareholder is equivalent to granting B Co a deduction for a dividend payment because it has the same net effect of reducing the overall amount of tax payable on B Co's net operating income.

13. The laws of some countries permit domestic companies to attach imputation or franking credits to dividends that have been paid out of tax-paid income. Taxpayers in the same jurisdiction can then apply this credit against the resulting tax liability on the dividend in order to protect themselves from economic double taxation. In such a case, however, the recognition of the credit is premised on the dividend being treated as taxable income in that jurisdiction. In this example the dividend is not subject to tax under the laws of Country B, so that allowing B Co or its shareholder to take the benefit of the credit in these circumstances has the effect, not of avoiding double taxation, but of cancelling the corporation tax previously paid on the underlying income.

Mismatch in tax outcomes arises under a financial instrument

14. The dividend gives rise to a D/NI outcome that is attributable to the terms of the instrument. In contrast to **Example 1.10**, where the difference in tax treatment is a result of the special tax status of the payer, the refund or credit is part of the ordinary rules governing the tax treatment of dividends in Country B and, accordingly, the mismatch is one that would arise between taxpayers of ordinary status.

Adjustment required

15. When determining the amount of adjustment required under the hybrid financial instrument rule under Country A law, Country A should take into account all amounts received (including the amount of any refunds paid directly to A Co) and should adjust the amount of income eligible to benefit from the dividend exemption consistently with the principles set out in **Example 1.2** to **1.4** so that the amount of the payment that remains eligible for tax relief in Country A should equal the amount of income that is effectively subject to tax at the full marginal rate in Country B.

16. In this case 10% of the payment remains subject to tax at the full corporate rate under Country B law and therefore 90% of the payment should be treated as ordinary income under Country A law. The table below sets out the adjustment required where Country B law provides B Co with a tax credit for dividends paid.

17. For the purposes of this calculation it is assumed that the corporate tax rate in Country A is 30%. A Co is required to treat 90% of the dividend paid as taxable income which results in a 18.9 tax liability.

A Co			B Co		
	Tax	Book		Tax	Book
Income			Income		
			Ordinary income	100	100
Dividend received	63	70			
Expenditure			Expenditure		
			Dividend paid		(70)
Net return		**70**	**Net return**		**30**
Taxable income	**63**		**Taxable income**	**100**	
Tax on net income	(18.9)		Tax on net income	(30)	
			Tax credit	18.9	
Tax to pay		(18.9)	Tax to pay		(11.1)
After-tax return		**51.1**	**After-tax return**		**18.9**

18. The table below sets out the adjustment for A Co where Country B law permits B Co to attach a refundable tax credit to the dividend paid to A Co.

A Co			B Co		
	Tax	Book		Tax	Book
Income			Income		
Dividend received	90	70	Ordinary income	100	100
Refundable Tax Credit	-	27			
Expenditure			Expenditure		
			Dividend paid		(70)
Net return		**97**	**Net return**		**30**
Taxable income	**90**		**Taxable income**	**100**	
Tax to pay		(27)	Tax to pay		(30)
After-tax return		**70**	**After-tax return**		**0**

Example 1.12

Debt issued in proportion to shares re-characterised as equity

Facts

1. In the example illustrated in the figure below, B Co 2 is a company resident in Country B whose shares are held by B Co 1 (another entity resident in Country B) and A Co (an entity resident in Country A). A Co owns 75% of the ordinary shares in B Co 2 with B Co 1 owning the remaining 25%.

2. B Co 2 is in need of 2 000 of additional financing. Both of its shareholders agreed to debt finance B Co 2 in proportion to their shareholding, i.e. A Co and B Co 1 subscribed 1 500 and 500 respectively for a loan that pays regular interest at a fixed rate.

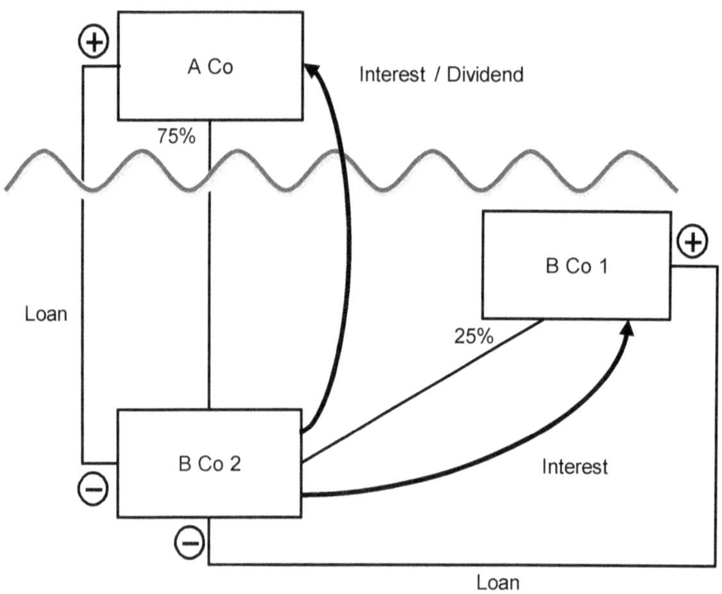

3. Country B treats the loan in accordance with its form and allows B Co 2 a deduction for the interest payments in accordance with the normal rules applicable to debt financing in Country B. B Co 2 is allowed a deduction for these interest payments and B Co 1 includes those payments in its ordinary income.

4. The laws of Country A, however, re-characterise a debt instrument as equity (i.e. shares) when the debt is issued by a company to its shareholder for an amount that is calculated by reference to the shareholder's equity in the issuer. Accordingly, the loan held by A Co is treated as a share in Country A and the interest payments on the loan are treated as an exempt dividend.

Question

5. Whether the mismatch in tax outcomes that arises in respect of the interest payments from B Co 2 to A Co, fall within the scope of the hybrid financial instrument rule?

Answer

6. The interest payment will give rise to a mismatch unless Country A denies the benefit of the dividend exemption for the deductible interest payments in accordance with Recommendation 2.1.

7. The fact that the debt is issued to each holder in proportion to their equity in the company is a commercially significant element of the debt financing transaction that impacts on the tax treatment of the payments made under it. These circumstances in which the debt was issued should therefore be considered to be part of the terms of the instrument and the resulting mismatch should be treated as a hybrid mismatch within the scope of the rule.

Analysis

Recommendation 2.1 will apply to deny A Co the benefit of the dividend exemption for the payment

8. The loan is treated as a share under the domestic laws of Country A and interest payments on the loan are treated as exempt dividends. Recommendation 2.1 states that, in order to prevent D/NI outcomes arising under a debt / equity hybrid, countries should deny the benefit of a dividend exemption for deductible payments. Accordingly, in this case, A Co should tax the interest payments from B Co 2 as ordinary income.

If Country A does not apply Recommendation 2.1 then the payment will give rise to a hybrid mismatch that is within the scope of the hybrid financial instrument rule

9. If Country A does not implement Recommendation 2.1 into its domestic law, the hybrid financial instrument rule will apply.

10. Recommendation 1 only applies to *a financial instrument* entered into with a *related party*. The loan meets the definition of financial instrument as it is treated as a debt instrument in Country B and as an equity instrument in Country A. A Co and B Co 2 are related parties as A Co holds 75% of the shares in B Co 2.

A payment made under the loan will give rise to a hybrid mismatch

11. The interest paid by B Co 2 to A Co is deductible under Country B law and treated as an exempt dividend in the hands of A Co. The interest payments therefore give rise to a mismatch. This mismatch will be treated as a hybrid mismatch if the difference in tax outcomes is attributable to the *terms of the instrument*. The terms of the instrument should be construed broadly, going beyond the rights and obligations of the loan and the relationship between the parties to include the circumstances in which the instrument is issued or held if those circumstances are commercially or economically significant to the

relationship between the parties and affect the tax treatment of the payments made under the instrument.

12. The cause of the mismatch in this example is the fact that debt has been issued to shareholders in proportion to their equity. The issue of debt in proportion to equity is commercially and economically different from the issue of debt to a third party, or to shareholders in different proportions, and is likely to impact on the commercial terms of that debt. Therefore the circumstances in which the debt was issued should be treated as part of the terms of the instrument and the resulting mismatch as a hybrid mismatch.

Application of the primary and secondary response

13. Country B should deny the interest deduction to the extent that it is not included in the ordinary income of A Co. If Country B does not apply the recommended response, Country A should treat the interest payments received by A Co as ordinary income.

Example 1.13

Accrual of deemed discount on interest free loan

Facts

1. In the example illustrated in the figure below, A Co 1 (a company resident in Country A) establishes a subsidiary in the same jurisdiction (A Co 2). A Co 1 provides A Co 2 with a total capital of 40, 12.5% of which is provided in the form of share capital and the rest by way interest free loan. The loan is repayable in full at the end of five years.

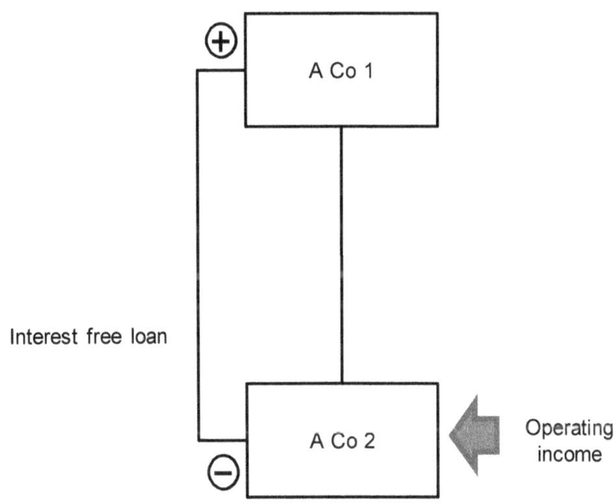

2. The loan is treated as a debt instrument under the laws of Country A. However, due to the particular tax accounting treatment adopted by A Co 2 in respect of interest free loans made by another group member, A Co 2 is required to split the loan into two separate components for accounting purposes: a non-interest bearing loan, which A Co 2 is treated as having issued to A Co 1 at a discount, and a deemed equity contribution equal to the amount of that discount. The amount that A Co 2 treats as received for the interest free loan is based on an arm's length valuation. The table below sets out a simplified illustration of how the loan and deemed equity contribution might be reflected on A Co 2's balance sheet.

	A Co 2 – Assets, Liabilities and Equity		
Year 0	**Assets**	**40**	
	Fixed assets		40
	Liabilities	**20**	
	Shareholder loan		20
	Equity	**20**	
	Share capital		5
	Other equity		15

3. In this case A Co 2 has treated the interest free loan of 35 as an equity contribution of 15 and a loan of 20. In each accounting period A Co 2 will be required to accrue a portion of the deemed discount on the loan as an expense for accounting purposes and to treat this expense as funded out of A Co 1's deemed equity contribution. The table below provides a simplified illustration of how A Co 2 might account for the accrued liability under the shareholder loan as at the end of Year 1:

	A Co 2 – Assets. Liabilities and Equity			A Co 2 - Income		
					Book / Tax	**Cash**
Year 1	**Assets**	**45**		Income		
	Current assets (cash)		5	Operating Income	5	5
	Fixed assets		40			
	Liabilities	**23**		Expenses		
	Shareholder loan		23	Accrued liability on shareholder loan	(3)	
	Equity	**22**		**Net return**	**2**	
	Share capital		5			
	Other equity		17			

4. In this case A Co 2 treats the deemed discount as accruing on a straight-line basis so that, at the end of Year 1 the shareholder loan is recorded on the balance sheet as 23 (an increase of 3). Country A law permits this deemed increase in liabilities to be treated as a current expense in Year 1 so that, while A Co has operating income of 5 in that year its accounts show a net return (and increase in equity) of only 2. Applying the same accounting treatment in each of the following years will permit the entire discount to be expensed over the life of the loan so that, at maturity, the shareholder loan will be recorded on the company's balance sheet at its face amount.

5. A Co 1 adopts a different tax accounting treatment from A Co 2 and does not split the interest-free loan into equity and debt components. Accordingly the accrued liability recorded in A Co 2's accounts in each year is not recognised by A Co 1. On repayment of the loan the entire amount paid by A Co 2 is simply treated as a non-taxable return of loan principal.

Question

6. Whether the arrangement falls within the scope of the hybrid financial instrument rule?

Answer

7. Country A should deny A Co 2 a deduction under the hybrid financial instrument rule as the amount which is expensed by A Co 2 in each accounting period gives rise to a D/NI outcome and this mismatch in tax outcomes is attributable to different approaches taken to the accounting and tax treatment of the instrument by the payer and payee under the laws of the same jurisdiction

Analysis

The accrued obligation under the loan should be treated as a payment

8. A payment includes an amount that is *capable of being paid* and includes any future or contingent obligation to make a payment. The definition specifically excludes, however, *payments that are only deemed to be made for tax purposes and that do not involve the creation of economic rights between the parties*. As described in Chapter 1 of the report, this exception for deemed payments is only intended to exclude regimes, such as those that grant deemed interest deductions for equity capital, where the tax deduction is not linked to any payment obligation of the issuer. In this example, A Co 2's deduction in each accounting period is in respect of its repayment obligation under the loan. Although the deduction granted to A Co 2 in each accounting period does not correspond to any increase in A Co 2's liabilities during that period, it does arise in respect of a repayment obligation and it therefore falls within the definition of a payment for the purposes of the rule.

Payment gives rise to a hybrid mismatch

9. The D/NI outcome that arises in this case is the result of A Co 2's entitlement to a deduction in each accounting period for the annual increase in loan liabilities recorded on its balance sheet. This deduction is not matched by a corresponding income inclusion for A Co 1 because A Co 1 does not treat the loan as having been split into equity and debt components. The ability of A Co 1 and A Co 2 to apply different accounting (and, by extension, tax) treatments to the same instrument means that the mismatch is attributable to differences in the tax treatment of the instrument under the laws of the same jurisdiction.

10. Note that a mismatch could still arise, on the facts of this example, if A Co 1 adopted the same accounting treatment as A Co 2 but attributed a lower value to the equity portion of the loan. In such a case the entitlement to a deduction in each accounting period for the annual increase in loan liabilities would not be matched by an inclusion of the same amount in Country A. While differences in the value attributed to a payment under the laws of the payer and payee jurisdictions will not generally give rise to a D/NI outcome, in this case, the valuation of the respective components of an instrument has a direct impact on the character of the payments made under it (see further the analysis in **Example 1.16**)

11. The particular accounting treatment taken by A Co 2 only applies to interest-free loans from a group member. The accounting treatment (and, by extension the mismatch in tax outcomes) would not have arisen if the loan had been entered into between unrelated taxpayers of ordinary status. The "terms of the instrument" should be given a broad meaning and may include any aspect of the relationship between the parties. The fact that a loan is from a group member should therefore be treated as part of the terms of the loan notwithstanding that there may be no legal requirement for the loan to be held intra-group.

Example 1.14

Deemed interest on interest-free loan

Facts

12. The facts of this Example are the same as Example 1.13 except that the interest free loan is made to a foreign subsidiary (B Co) and the laws of Country B allow B Co to claim a deduction for tax purposes as if it had paid interest on the loan at a market rate.

13. The laws of Country A treat the loan as a debt instrument or equity instrument and there is no corresponding adjustment in Country A. On repayment of the loan the entire amount is treated as a non-taxable return of loan principal or return of capital.

Question

14. Whether the arrangement falls within the scope of the hybrid financial instrument rule?

Answer

15. The arrangement does not fall within the scope of the hybrid financial instrument rule because there is no payment under the loan that gives rise to a deduction for tax purposes in Country B.

Analysis

There is no payment made under the financial instrument that gives rise to a hybrid mismatch

16. Recommendation 1 only applies to D/NI outcomes that arise in respect of payments. The definition specifically excludes payments that are only deemed to be made for tax purposes and that do not involve the creation of economic rights between the parties. In this example B Co's deduction in each accounting period arises in respect of an amount that is not capable of being paid. Accordingly there is no payment under the financial instrument that gives rise to a D/NI outcome.

Example 1.15

Differences in value attributable to share premium paid under mandatory convertible note

Facts

1. In the example illustrated in the figure below, A Co (a company resident in Country A) owns all the shares in B Co (a company resident in Country B). A Co subscribes for a five year zero-coupon convertible note with a principal amount of 100.

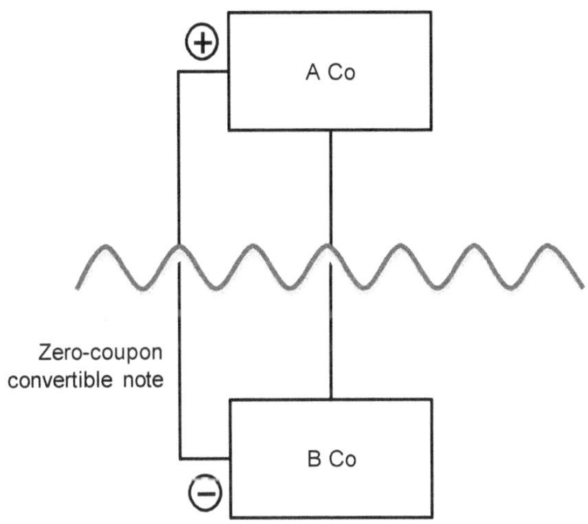

2. The zero-coupon note automatically converts into shares of B Co at the maturity date. The equity premium that arises on the conversion of the note is treated as deductible by B Co and is included in ordinary income by A Co. The value of the equity premium is calculated by Country A to be 15, while Country B values the equity premium at 30.

Question

3. Whether any portion of the deduction for the equity premium under Country B law gives rise to a hybrid mismatch within the scope of the hybrid financial instrument rule?

Answer

4. No adjustment is required under the hybrid financial instrument rule as the difference in valuation of the equity premium does not give rise to a hybrid mismatch.

Analysis

No mismatch in respect of differences in the valuation of a payment

5. The mismatch in tax outcomes in this case is not a mismatch within the meaning of the hybrid financial instrument rule. This is because the difference in outcome is merely attributable to the differences in the valuation of a payment and it does not relate to any difference in characterisation of the payment between the two countries.

Example 1.16

Differences in valuation of discount on issue of optional convertible note

Facts

1. The facts of this example are the same as those in **Example 1.15** except that zero-coupon note can be converted into shares of B Co at the option of A Co. Both Country B and Country A laws bifurcate the instrument for tax purposes. Country B treats A Co as having paid 80 for a zero-coupon note and 20 in exchange for the share option. Accordingly the note is treated as issued at a discount and B Co is entitled to accrue the amount of that discount as a deduction for tax purposes over the term of the loan. Country A adopts the same tax treatment but treats A Co as having paid 90 for the note and 10 for the share option.

Question

2. Whether the adjustment under Country B law for the deductible costs attributable to the convertible note gives rise to a hybrid mismatch within the scope of the hybrid financial instrument rule?

Answer

3. The difference in valuation has a direct impact on the characterisation of the payments made under the instrument and therefore gives rise to a hybrid mismatch.

Analysis

The accrued obligation under the loan should be treated as a payment

4. A payment includes an amount that is *capable of being paid* and includes any future or contingent obligation to make a payment. In this example, B Co's deduction in each accounting period is in respect of its contingent repayment obligation under the loan. Although the deduction does not correspond to any increase in A Co 2's liabilities during that period, it does arise in respect of a repayment obligation and it therefore falls within the definition of a payment for the purposes of the rule (see analysis in **Example 1.13**)

The difference in the valuation of the option component results in a difference in the character of the underlying payments

5. In order for the deductible payment to give rise to a D/NI outcome there must be a difference in the way the payment is measured and characterised under the laws of the payer and payee jurisdictions. If the amount of the payment is characterised and calculated in the same way under the laws of both jurisdictions, then differences in the

value attributed to that amount under the laws of the payer and payee jurisdictions will not give rise to a D/NI outcome. Differences in tax outcomes that are solely attributable to differences in the value ascribed to a payment (including through the application of transfer pricing) do not fall within the scope of the hybrid mismatch rule (see **Example 1.15**).

6. In certain cases, however, particularly in the case of more complex financial instruments that are treated as incorporating both financing and equity returns, the way the separate components of the instrument are measured, and therefore the character of the payments under local law, may be dependent on the value attributed to each of those components. In such a case, where the valuation of the components of a financial instrument has a direct impact on the characterisation of the payments made under it, differences in valuation may give rise to a mismatch.

7. In this case both the issuer and the holder treat a convertible note as being issued at discount representing its equity value. The higher valuation given to the equity value of the note in the issuer's jurisdiction, results in the issuer recognising a larger accrued discount, which, in turn, results in greater portion of the payments being treated as deductible in the issuer jurisdiction. In this case, the way in which the component elements of the note are valued has a direct impact on the way the payments under the instrument are characterised for tax purposes and, accordingly, the difference in valuation should be treated as giving rise to a mismatch in tax outcomes.

Example 1.17

No mismatch with respect to measurement of foreign exchange differences

Facts

1. In the example illustrated in the figure below, A Co (a company resident in Country A) owns all the shares in B Co (a company resident in Country B). A Co provides B Co with an ordinary loan. Interest on the loan is payable every year in arrears at a market rate and the principal on the loan is payable at maturity. The loan is treated as a debt instrument under the laws of both Country A and B and the countries take a consistent position on the characterisation of the payments made under the loan. The interest payable on the loan is deductible in Country B and included in ordinary income under the laws of Country A.

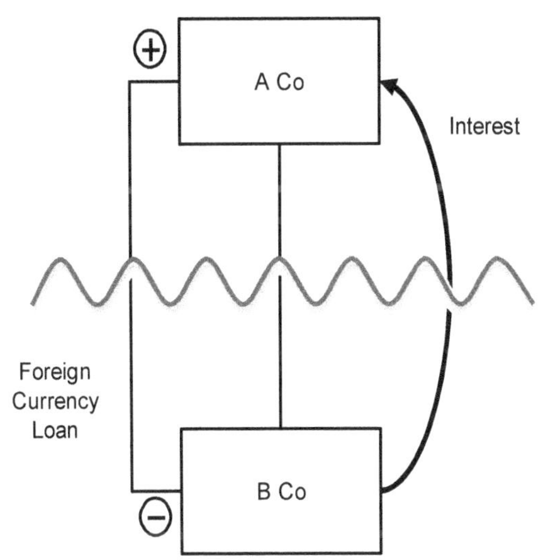

2. The interest and principal under the loan are payable in Currency A. The value of Currency B falls in relation to Currency A while the loan is still outstanding so that payments of interest and principal under the loan become more expensive in Currency B terms. Under the Country B law, B Co is entitled to a deduction for this increased cost. There is no similar adjustment required under Country A law.

Question

3. Whether the adjustment under Country B law for the increase in costs attributable to the fall in the value of Currency B gives rise to a hybrid mismatch within the scope of the hybrid financial instrument rule?

Answer

4. While the fall in the value of Currency B gives rise to a deduction under Country B law that is not reflected by a corresponding inclusion in Country A, this difference does not give rise to a D/NI outcome provided the proportion of the interest and principal payable under the loan is the same under the laws of both jurisdictions. Gains and losses that result from converting foreign exchange into local or functional currency are attributable to the way jurisdictions measure the value of money rather than the value of the payment itself.

Analysis

The foreign currency adjustment does not give rise to a mismatch

5. In this case both Country A and B characterise the payments in the same way (as either principal or interest) and take the same view as to the proportion of interest and principal payable under the loan. The difference in tax treatment in this case does not arise because the tax systems of the two countries characterise the payments in different ways or arrive at a different value for the payments made under the loan. Rather, once the character and amount have been determined, the laws of one jurisdiction require the value of the payment to be translated into local currency. This type of currency translation difference, which is a difference in the way jurisdictions measure the value of money (rather than the underlying character or amount of a payment), should not be treated as giving rise to a mismatch.

Example 1.18

Payment in consideration for an agreement to modify the terms of a debt instrument

Facts

1. In the example illustrated in the figure below B Co is a company resident in Country B. B Co borrows money from its immediate parent A Co, a company resident in Country A. The loan has a 5 year term and pays a high fixed rate of interest. B Co makes a one-off arms-length payment to A Co in consideration for A Co agreeing to lower the interest rate on the loan. The effect of this adjustment is to reduce the value of the loan as recorded in A Co's accounts.

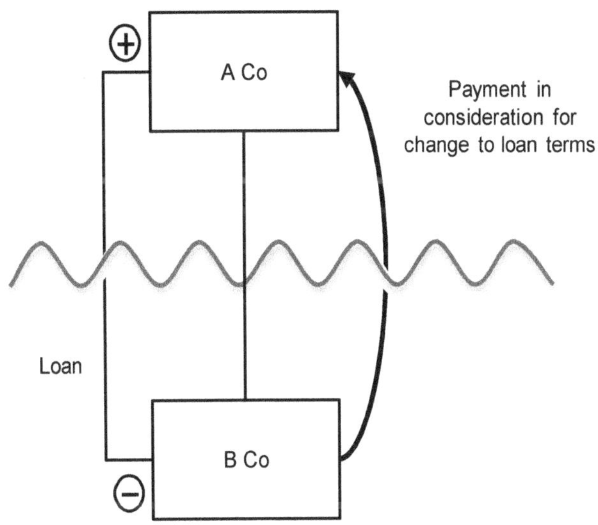

Question

2. Whether the payment in consideration for the agreement to change to the terms of the loan falls within the scope of the hybrid financial instrument rule?

Answer

3. B Co's payment should be treated as a payment made under the loan itself. The payment will give rise to a hybrid mismatch to the extent it is treated as deductible under the laws of Country B and is not included in ordinary income under Country A law. Although A Co's surrender or discharge of rights under the loan may be thought of as a

transfer of value, it should not be considered a payment under the loan within the scope of the hybrid financial instrument rule.

Analysis

The amount paid in consideration for agreeing to a change in the terms of the loan is a payment under a financial instrument

4. The determination of whether a payment is made *under a financial instrument* can usually be made by looking to the terms of the instrument and considering whether that payment is either required under the instrument or is in consideration for the release from a requirement under the instrument. In this case the payment is made in consideration for agreeing to a release from the obligation to make certain payments under the loan and should therefore be treated as a payment under the instrument.

The payment will give rise to a hybrid mismatch if it is not treated as ordinary income under Country A law

5. The payment under a financial instrument will give rise to a mismatch in tax outcomes if it is deductible under the laws of Country B and not treated as ordinary income under the laws of Country A. The example does not state whether A Co treats the one-off payment as ordinary income. If, however, Country A law does not require a taxpayer to bring this type of payment into ordinary income, the mismatch in tax outcomes should be treated as a hybrid mismatch because it arises due to differences in the way Country A and Country B laws characterise such payments for tax purposes.

6. It may be the case that A Co is not required to bring the payment into account as ordinary income until the end of the loan term. If this is the case the reasonableness of the timing difference would need to be tested in accordance with Recommendation 1.1(c).

Release of obligations under the loan is not a payment

7. A Co's agreement to surrender or modify rights under the loan may be thought of as a transfer of value to B Co but it should not be treated as a payment under the loan itself. Any deduction that A Co may claim for the reduction in the value of the loan due to such surrender or discharge does not, therefore, fall within the scope of the hybrid financial instrument rule. Accordingly, the deduction that may be granted under Country A law for the reduction in the value of the loan is not a payment under the loan and does not fall within the scope of the hybrid financial instrument rule.

Example 1.19

Payment in consideration for the cancellation of a financial instrument

Facts

1. This example illustrated in the figure below is the same as **Example 1.18** except that B Co buys the subordinated loan at premium to the amount that would have been payable on maturity. This acquisition results in a deemed cancellation of the loan. B Co treats the premium as deductible expenditure while A Co treats it as a gain on the disposal of the loan.

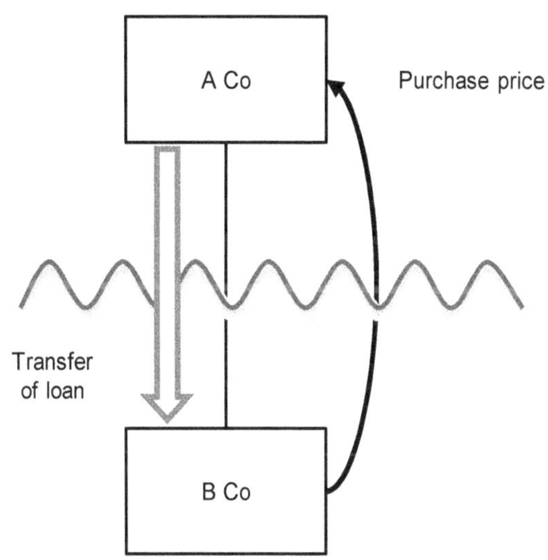

Question

2. Whether the consideration paid to acquire the loan falls within the scope of the hybrid financial instrument rule and, if so, to what extent an adjustment is required to be made in accordance with that rule.

Answer

3. The consideration for the transfer of the loan should be treated as made under a financial instrument because the transfer has the effect of discharging B Co's obligations under the loan. Unless Country A law treats the amount paid as ordinary income, the hybrid financial instrument will apply to neutralise the effect of the resulting mismatch.

Analysis

The consideration for the transfer is deemed to be a payment under a financial instrument

4. A payment made by a person to acquire an existing financial instrument will not generally be treated as a payment made under that instrument. Where, however, the payment is consideration for discharging, in whole or part, the issuer's obligations under the instrument, the payment should be treated as caught by the rule. In this case, B Co's acquisition of the loan from A Co has the effect of cancelling B Co's obligations under the instrument and, accordingly, the consideration paid for the transfer of the loan should be treated as a payment made under the instrument itself.

The payment will give rise to a hybrid mismatch

5. As the payment of a premium is deductible under the laws of Country B, the payment will give rise to a mismatch unless it is required to be included as ordinary income under Country A law. If Country A law dealing with the taxation of these types of instruments requires any gain on the disposal of such a loan to be brought into account as ordinary income for tax purposes, then the payment should not give rise to a mismatch. If, however, the gain is excluded or exempt from tax, or A Co is taxable on the proceeds of disposal solely due to its particular tax status or the context in which the instrument is held (for example, A Co holds the loan as trading asset), then the payment should be treated as giving rise to a mismatch. The mismatch that arises will be a hybrid mismatch as it is due to differences in the way in which the laws of Country A and Country B characterise redemption payments under a financial instrument.

Primary recommendation – deny the deduction in the payer jurisdiction

6. Country B should deny a deduction for the premium paid to A Co for the release of its obligations under the loan. If Country B does not apply the recommended response, then Country A should treat the premium as ordinary income.

Example 1.20

Release from a debt obligation not a payment

Facts

1. This example illustrated in the figure below is the same as **Example 1.19** except that B Co gets into financial difficulties and is unable to make payments of interest and principal on the loan. A Co agrees to forgive the loan and releases B Co from the obligation to make any further payments of principal and accrued interest. The amount of debt forgiven is treated as deductible under Country A law but is not treated as income by B Co.

Question

2. Whether the D/NI outcome, which arises with respect to the restructuring of the loan, falls within the scope of the hybrid financial instrument rule?

Answer

3. Although the forgiveness of debt is a transfer of value from A Co to B Co, it is not a payment under a financial instrument. Accordingly A Co's deduction does not fall within the scope of the hybrid financial instrument rule.

Analysis

4. The hybrid financial instrument rule applies only to payments made under a financial instrument. A payment will be treated as made *under a financial instrument* if it is made in discharge, satisfaction or release of an obligation under that financial instrument. The discharge, satisfaction or release of the obligation itself should not be treated as a payment even though such release may give rise to a transfer of value between the parties.

5. Accordingly the deduction granted under Country A law is in respect of the release of an obligation under a financial instrument, not a payment under it, and does not fall within the scope of the hybrid financial instrument rule.

Example 1.21

Mismatch resulting from accrual of contingent interest liability

Facts

1. In the example illustrated in the figure below, A Co 1 owns all the shares in A Co 2. Both companies are resident in Country A. A Co 1 provides A Co 2 with a subordinated loan. The terms of the loan provide for interest that is payable at maturity or, if earlier, at the discretion of A Co 2. The loan has a long maturity date (50 years) and A Co 1 may waive its entitlement to interest at any time prior to payment.

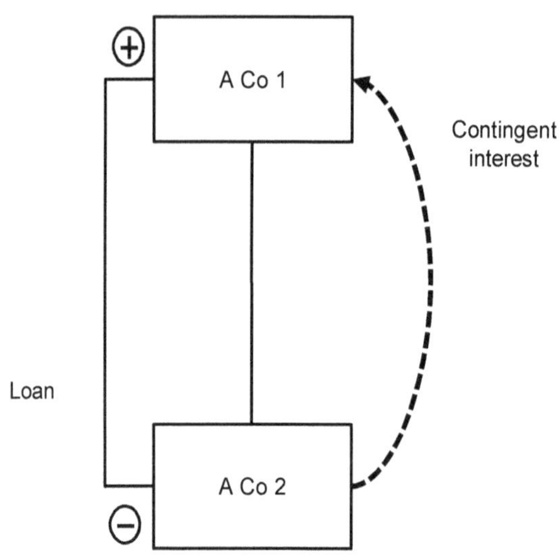

2. The loan is treated as debt under the laws of Country A but A Co 1 and A Co 2 adopt different accounting policies in respect of the loan. The effect of this difference in accounting treatment is that interest payments on the loan are treated as deductible by A Co 2 in the year the interest accrues but will only be treated as income by A Co 1 when (and if) such interest is actually paid. Furthermore, if A Co 1 waives its entitlement to accrued interest at any point prior to payment, this waiver will be treated by A Co 2 as a deemed equity contribution to A Co 2 and will therefore not trigger a recapture of interest deductions previously claimed.

Question

3. Will the accrued but unpaid interest give rise to a hybrid mismatch under the hybrid financial instrument rule?

Answer

4. The terms of the loan are such that the taxpayer will be unable establish, to the satisfaction of the tax authority, that the payment will be made, or can be expected to be made, within a reasonable period of time. Accordingly the fact that the accrued interest is deductible for A Co 2 but not included in income by A Co 1 should be treated as giving rise to a mismatch for tax purposes. This mismatch in tax outcomes arises due to different ways in which A Co 1 and A Co 2 account for the payments of interest under the loan. Accordingly the deduction for the contingent interest will be treated as giving rise to a hybrid mismatch under the hybrid financial instrument rule.

Analysis

The accrued interest is a payment under a financial instrument

5. Recommendation 1 only applies to payments made under a financial instrument. The definition of payment under the hybrid mismatch rules includes an accrual of an amount even if it is in respect of a contingent obligation.

Taxpayer unable to establish that the payment can reasonably be expected to be included in income

6. The accounting treatment adopted by A Co 2 allows A Co 2 to recognise the interest as a deductible expense (i.e. as having been paid) in the year it accrues, however the conditions under which A Co 2 is entitled to claim a deduction are not sufficient to bring the interest into ordinary income in the hands of A Co 1. The mere fact that interest is deductible by one party when it accrues, but will not be included in ordinary income by the recipient until it is actually paid, does not necessarily mean that it will be treated as giving rise to a mismatch in tax outcomes. In this case, however, the maturity date and payment terms of the instrument, together with the fact that the loan is held intra-group, indicate that the parties have placed little commercial significance on the payment of the accrued interest under the loan.

7. Even if the loan had a significantly shorter maturity date, A Co 1 still has the power to waive its entitlement to interest at any time before the interest is actually paid without such waiver giving rise to any adverse tax or economic consequences for A Co 1 or A Co 2.

8. Accordingly the taxpayers in this example will be unable to satisfy its tax administration at the time the loan is issued that it is reasonable to expect that the amounts treated as a deductible payment by A Co 2 will be included as ordinary income under the accounting method adopted by A Co 1. The mismatch in tax outcomes that arises under the loan should therefore be treated as falling within the scope of the hybrid financial instrument rule.

Mismatch in tax outcomes will be a hybrid mismatch

9. The ability of A Co 1 and A Co 2 to apply different accounting (and, by extension, tax) treatments to the same instrument means that the mismatch is attributable to differences in the tax treatment of the instrument under the laws of the same jurisdiction.

Primary response

10. Country A should deny A Co 2 a deduction for the accrued interest on the loan. If Country A introduces a rule that defers A Co 2's entitlement to a deduction until the interest is actually paid then that may have the effect of bringing such interest payments within the operation of the safe harbour described in the guidance to Recommendation 1.1 and the primary response will no longer apply.

Example 1.22

No mismatch resulting from accrual of contingent interest liability

Facts

1. In the example illustrated in the figure below, A Co 1 owns 30% of the shares in B Co (a company established and tax resident in Country B). The rest of the shares are owned by A Co 2 (an unrelated company). B Co makes an investment in an infrastructure asset that is not expected to produce returns for a number of years. As part of the funding for this arrangement, A Co 1 provides B Co with a subordinated loan.

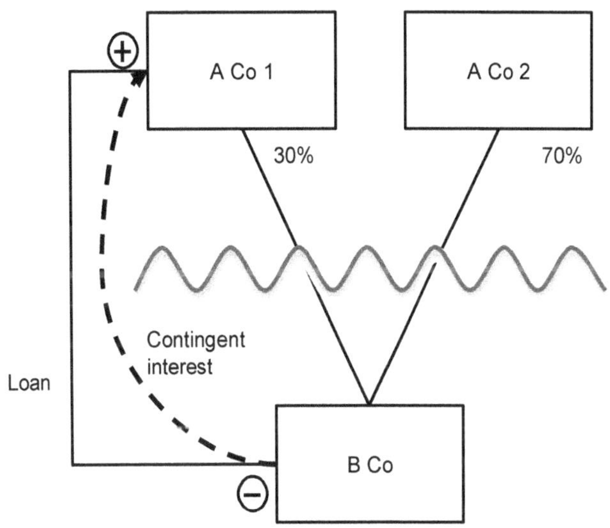

2. Interest accrues on the loan at a fixed rate. The terms of the loan, however, provide that interest will only be paid at the end of the term of the loan (15 years) or at the discretion of B Co and only if certain solvency requirements are met. Furthermore there is a 'dividend-blocker' on the shares issued by B Co that prevents B Co from making any distributions to its shareholders while there is accrued but unpaid interest on the loan.

3. The loan is treated as debt under the laws of both countries, however, due to differences in the way interest is accounted for tax purposes by the two countries, the interest is treated as deductible by B Co in the year it accrues but will only be treated as income by A Co 1 when it is actually paid.

Question

4. Will the accrued but unpaid interest give rise to a hybrid mismatch under the hybrid financial instrument rule?

Answer

5. The fact that the accrued interest can reasonably be expected to be paid and that the payment terms are reasonable in the circumstances should mean that the tax administration will not treat the accrued interest as giving rise to a hybrid mismatch.

Analysis

It can reasonably be expected that the payment will be made within a reasonable period of time

6. The hybrid financial instrument rule is not intended to pick up differences in the timing of recognition of payments under a financial instrument. A mismatch in tax outcomes will be treated as simply giving rise to a timing difference (outside the scope of the hybrid financial instrument rule) if the taxpayer can establish, to the satisfaction of the tax administration, that it is reasonable to expect payment to be made (i.e. included in ordinary income) within a reasonable period of time.

7. In this case, interest payments are not required to be made until maturity and only if the borrower meets certain solvency requirements. Although the period of maturity is long (15 years) the facts of this example, including the fact that the interests of the debt and equity holders are not aligned, suggest that, in practice, the parties have placed real commercial significance on the requirement to make payments under the loan and that they expect, at the time the arrangement is entered into, that the outstanding principal and interest under the loan will be paid.

8. The time period for the payment of interest will be treated as reasonable if it is what might be expected to be agreed between unrelated parties acting at arm's length. This determination should take into account such factors as the terms of the instrument, the circumstances in which it is held and the commercial objectives of the parties, including the nature of the accrual and any contingencies or other commercial factors affecting payment. In this case: the nature of the underlying investment (infrastructure); the competing and potentially divergent interests of the parties (bearing in mind that the holder is only a minority equity holder) and the contractual protections for the payee, such as the dividend blocker on the shares, are all factors indicative of an arrangement on arm's length terms.

Example 1.23

Payment by a hybrid entity under a hybrid financial instrument

Facts

1. In the example illustrated in the figure below B Co 1, a company resident in Country B, is a wholly-owned subsidiary of A Co, a company resident in Country A. B Co 1 is disregarded for the purposes of Country A law. B Co 1 borrows money from B Co 2 another wholly-owned subsidiary resident in the same jurisdiction.

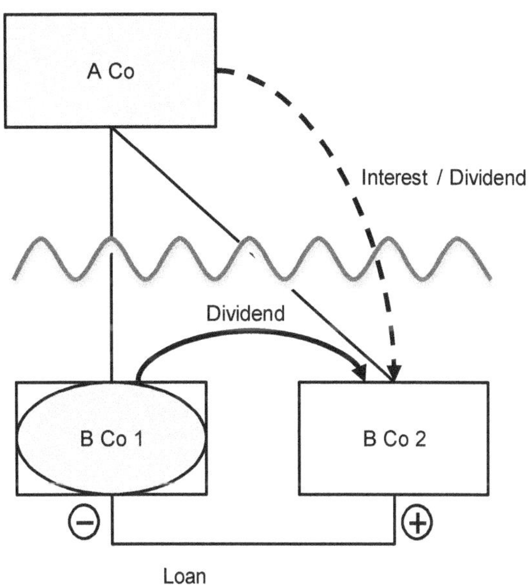

2. Country B treats the loan as an equity instrument. Accordingly it does not allow B Co 1 a deduction for the payment and treats the payment as an exempt dividend in the hands of B Co 2. The loan is, however, treated as a debt instrument under Country A law and, because B Co 1 is a disregarded entity, the interest payable on the loan is treated as deductible by A Co under the laws of Country A.

Question

3. Whether the interest payment is subject to adjustment under the hybrid financial instrument rule and, if so, what adjustments are required under the rule?

Answer

4. The interest payment is caught by the hybrid financial instrument rule.

5. Country A should deny A Co the deduction for the interest payable under the loan. If Country A does not apply the recommended response then Country B should treat the interest payments on the loan as ordinary income.

Analysis

The arrangement is a financial instrument

6. The loan meets the definition of a *financial instrument* because it is treated as an equity instrument under the laws of Country B and a debt instrument under the laws of Country A.

The payment gives rise to a hybrid mismatch

7. A D/NI outcome arises where a payment that is deductible under the laws of one jurisdiction (Country A) is not included in ordinary income under the laws of any other jurisdiction where the payment is treated as being received (Country B). The mismatch is a hybrid mismatch as it is attributable to differences in the tax treatment of the loan under the laws of the payee and payer jurisdictions.

Primary recommendation – deny the deduction in the payer jurisdiction

8. The primary recommendation under the hybrid financial instrument rule is that Country A deny the deduction to the extent it gives rise to a D/NI outcome.

Defensive rule – require income to be included in the payee jurisdiction

9. If Country A does not apply the recommended response, then Country B should treat the deductible payment as ordinary income in the hands of B Co 2, under the laws of Country B.

Example 1.24

Payment included in ordinary income under a CFC regime

Facts

1. In the example illustrated in the figure below, C Co is a company resident in Country C and a member of the ABC Group. C Co makes a payment of 30 under a hybrid financial instrument to B Co, another group company resident in Country B. In addition to receiving this payment from C Co, B Co also derives income from other sources and incurs expenses, including interest on a loan from Bank.

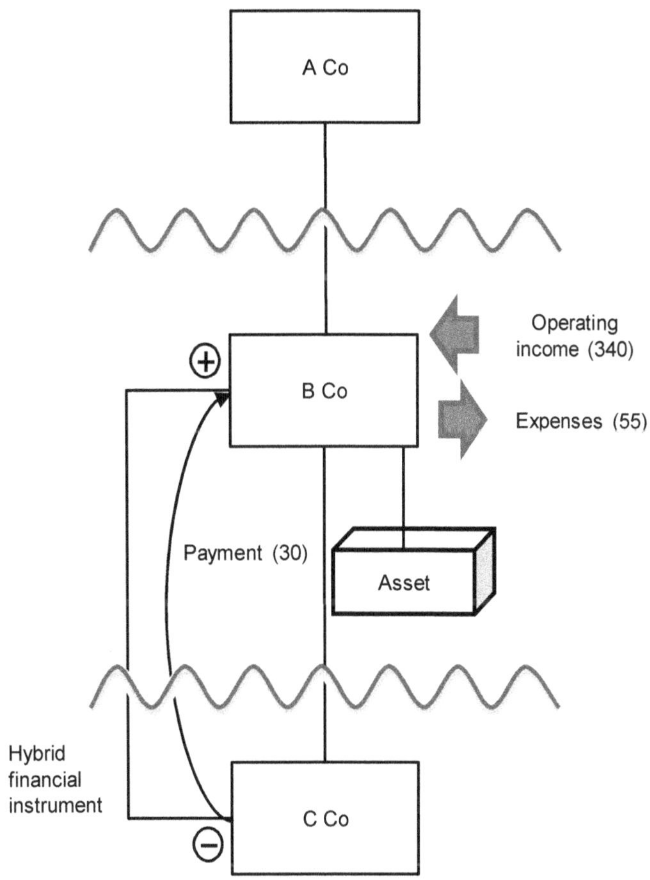

2. A Co, the parent of the group, resident in Country A, is subject to a CFC regime in Country A that attributes certain types of passive income derived by controlled foreign entities to resident shareholders in proportion to their shareholding in that entity. Countries A and C have introduced the recommendations set out in this report.

3. A simplified table below illustrates the net tax positions of A Co and B Co in the period the payment under the hybrid financial instrument was made.

B Co			A Co		
	Tax	Book		Tax	Book
Income			Income		
Active income	280	280	CFC income	80.4	
Passive income (including rents, interest and royalties)	60	60	Foreign tax credit	27.6	
Payment under hybrid financial instrument	-	30			
Expenditure			Expenditure		
Interest expense	(10)	(10)			
Depreciation	(15)	-			
Employment expenses	(45)	(45)			
Net return		315	**Net return**		0
Taxable income	**270**		**Taxable income**	**108**	
			Tax (at 30%)	(32.4)	
			Tax credit	27.6	
Tax to pay (at 40%)		(108)	Tax to pay		(4.8)
After-tax return		**207**	**After-tax return**		**(4.8)**

4. B Co derives 340 of taxable income for the period (including 60 of passive income such as rents, royalties and interest). The payment of 30 under the hybrid financial instrument is excluded from the calculation of B Co's income under Country B law. B Co incurs 70 of expenses (including tax depreciation) giving it taxable income of 270 which is taxable at the ordinary corporate rate of 40%.

5. A Co's only income for the same period is the income of B Co that is attributed under Country A's CFC regime. As set out in the table above, an amount of 80.4 is brought into account for tax purposes as ordinary income and subject to tax at the full corporate rate (30%) together with a credit of 27.6 for underlying taxes paid in Country B.

Question

6. How should the inclusion of CFC income under Country A law impact on the application of the hybrid financial instrument rule in Country C?

Answer

7. A taxpayer seeking to rely on a CFC inclusion in the parent jurisdiction, in order to avoid an adjustment under the hybrid financial instrument rule, should only be able to do so in circumstances where it can satisfy the tax administration that the payment will be

fully included under the laws of the relevant jurisdiction and subject to tax at the full rate. In this case the taxpayer will be required to establish that:

(a) the payment under the hybrid financial instrument is of a type that is required to be brought into account as ordinary income under the CFC rules in Country A (and does not benefit from any exemption under those rules, such as an active income or de-minimis exemption); and

(b) the payment is or will be brought into account as ordinary income on A Co's return under the quantification and timing rules of the CFC regime in Country A.

8. The facts of this example state that the parent of the group (A Co) is subject to a CFC regime that attributes certain types of passive income derived by controlled foreign entities to resident shareholders, The example does not, however, provide any further detail on whether, and to what extent, the payment under the hybrid financial instrument has been brought into account under the rules of that CFC regime. Accordingly, there is insufficient information, on the facts of this example, for a tax administration to conclude that relief should be provided from any adjustment under the hybrid financial instrument rule.

9. If the taxpayer can demonstrate, by reference to both the laws of Country A and the tax returns filed under Country A law that the payment is or will be included under the laws of the CFC regime in that jurisdiction then a jurisdiction in the position of Country C seeking to avoid the risk of economic double taxation under the hybrid financial instrument rule should consider whether relief should be granted from the application of the hybrid financial instrument rule in light of the CFC inclusion in Country A. Relief from the application of the hybrid financial instrument rule should only be granted, however, to the extent that the payment has not been treated as reduced or offset by any deduction incurred in the payee jurisdiction (Country B) and does not carry an entitlement to any credit or other relief under the laws of the parent jurisdiction (Country A).

10. Finally, in order for an amount that is included in ordinary income under the laws of Country A to be eligible for relief from the operation of the hybrid financial instrument rule in Country C, the taxpayer may need to establish that the income has not been set-off against a hybrid deduction under the laws of Country A. In this case the requirement will be satisfied because Country A has implemented the recommendations set out in this report.

Analysis

Inclusion of income under a CFC regime may give rise to economic double taxation

11. Recommendation 1.1 states that jurisdictions should consider how to address the mismatch in tax outcomes under the hybrid financial instrument rule in cases where the payment under a hybrid financial instrument has been included in ordinary income by the shareholder under a CFC regime and whether any relief should be granted from the operation of that rule in cases where denying a deduction for a payment that is included in income under a CFC regime may give rise to the risk of economic double taxation.

12. A CFC regime often focuses on certain categories of income derived by a foreign entity that are required to be attributed to a shareholder in a CFC. These categories, however, will often be defined by reference to the local tax law of the shareholder's

jurisdiction and will not necessarily correspond to the same categories, timing and quantification rules of the payer and payee jurisdictions. Before a payment can be treated as included in ordinary income under a CFC or other offshore inclusion regime, the taxpayer must be able to show that the payment under the hybrid financial instrument, which has given rise to the D/NI outcome, falls within a category of payments that is required to be brought into account as income of the shareholder under a CFC regime and does not qualify for any exception (such as a de-minimis exception or an exemption for active income).

13. On the face of the tax calculations above there is nothing that shows the relationship between the excluded payment received by B Co under the hybrid financial instrument and the amount included in CFC income under Country A law. In fact, the simplified accounts shown above provide no evidence that the amount of CFC income recognised by A Co is attributable to the payment made under the hybrid financial instrument. In this case, the taxpayer would therefore need to adduce additional evidence both to satisfy the tax administration that the CFC regime actually required the payment under the hybrid financial instrument to be included as CFC income and when and to what extent the payment would be recognised as CFC income in the hands of the shareholder. If, for example, all the income of a CFC from a particular period is attributed to a shareholder on the final day of the CFC's accounting period, then the shareholder would need to satisfy the tax administration that it holds or will be holding those shares on the attribution date.

Payment only treated as included to the extent it has not been reduced or offset by any deduction

14. CFC regimes typically require the net income of a CFC from particular sources or activities to be brought into account and subject to tax at the shareholder level. In this case B Co has a number of deductions that are offset against its net income. The example gives no information on whether or to what extent those deductions are also taken into account for the purposes of calculating A Co's attributed income from a CFC.

15. If Country A's CFC regime treats the amount of the payment under the hybrid financial instrument as reduced by deductible expenditure incurred by B Co then only the net amount of CFC income attributable to the payment should be treated as having been brought into account as ordinary income under the laws of the Country A.

16. For example, the CFC regime of Country A may require the full amount of passive income derived by B Co and the payment under the hybrid financial instrument to be brought into account as CFC income under Country A law (i.e. 60 + 30 = 90) but it may permit a deduction to be taken against such CFC income for a proportionate amount of B Co's expenses, other than depreciation (i.e. a deduction equal to 55 x 55/315 = 9.6) resulting in a net CFC inclusion of 80.4 (plus foreign tax credits). In this case a jurisdiction may take the view that the portion of the payment under the hybrid financial instrument actually included in income is 26.8 (= 30 – (30/90 x 9.6).

Payment only treated as included to the extent it has not been sheltered by any credit for underlying taxes

17. Country A's CFC regime further treats attributed income as carrying a right to underlying foreign tax credits. In this case the payment that is attributed CFC income

under the laws of Country A should not be treated as included in ordinary income under Country A law to the extent the payment is sheltered by such tax credits.

18. For example, the CFC regime of Country A may allow A Co to claim an underlying tax credit in proportion to the effective rate of tax on the (adjusted) income of B Co (i.e. a tax credit equal to 80.4 x (108 / 315) = 27.5). The effect of this tax credit is to shelter 85% of the tax liability on the amount of income included under the CFC regime of Country A. Applying this percentage to the amount of the payment under the hybrid financial instrument that is actually included under Country A law (26.8) a tax authority may conclude that the total amount of the payment under the hybrid financial instrument that has been included in income under this example is ((1 – 0.85) x 26.8 = 4).

Example 1.25

Payment under a lease only subject to adjustment to extent of financing return

Facts

1. The arrangement illustrated in the figure below involves a company resident in Country A (A Co) which obtains financing from a related company resident in Country B (B Co). To secure the financing A Co transfers a piece of equipment to B Co. B Co then leases that equipment back to A Co on terms that give A Co both the right and obligation to acquire the equipment for an agreed value at the end of the lease.

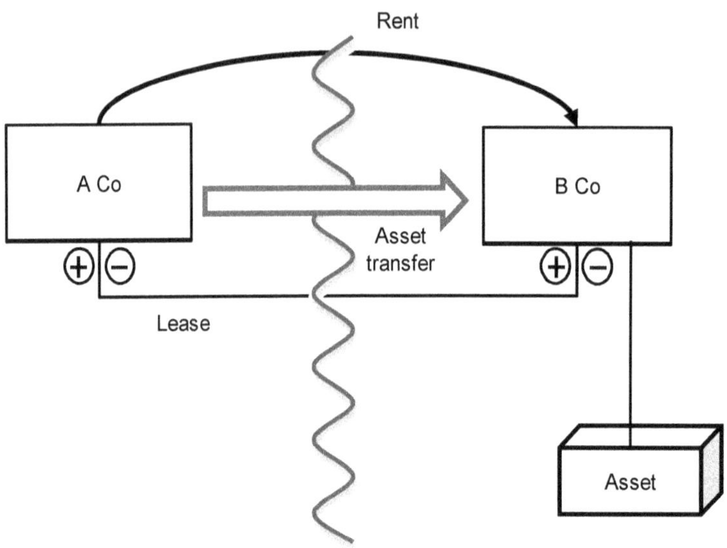

2. Country B treats the arrangement as a finance lease, pursuant to which, A Co is treated as the owner of asset and the arrangement between the parties is treated as a loan, with the payments of rental under the lease treated as payments of interest and principal on the loan.

3. Country A treats the arrangement in accordance with its form (i.e. as an ordinary lease) and the payments on the lease as deductible payments of rent. The effect of this arrangement is that a certain portion of the rental payments give rise to a D/NI outcome because they are deductible for the purposes of Country A law but are not included in ordinary income for the purposes of Country B law (because they are characterised as periodic payments of purchase price or repayments of principal).

Question

4. Is the arrangement subject to adjustment under the hybrid financial instrument rule and, if so, to what extent?

Answer

5. Under Country A law the hybrid financial instrument rule does not apply because the arrangement is not a hybrid transfer and is not otherwise treated as a financial instrument under local law.

6. The arrangement is treated as a debt instrument in Country B and B Co will therefore be required to apply the hybrid financial instrument rule to the payments under the lease. However, only the financing return is subject to adjustment under the rule. In this case the financing return is fully taxable under Country B law, so B Co should not be required to make any adjustment under the hybrid financial instrument rule.

Analysis

Whether arrangement is a financial instrument to be determined by reference to its domestic tax treatment

7. Jurisdictions are expected to use their own domestic tax concepts and terminology to define the arrangements covered by the hybrid financial instrument rule. This local law definition should generally include any financing arrangement, such a finance lease, where one party (B Co) provides money (including money's worth) to another in consideration for a financing return. On the facts of any particular case, however, the question of whether an arrangement is a financial instrument (and, therefore, potentially subject to adjustment under the hybrid financial instrument rule) should be answered solely by reference to the domestic tax treatment of that arrangement.

Rule does not apply under laws of Country A

8. In this case Country A treats the arrangement as an agreement for the supply of services (i.e. lease) and the arrangement is not taxed under the rules for taxing debt, equity or derivatives. As the agreement is not a hybrid transfer and does not give rise to a substitute payment (as it does not involve the transfer of a financial instrument) the payments under the lease will not be subject to adjustment under the hybrid financial instrument rule in Country A.

No adjustment required under laws of Country B

9. The hybrid financial instrument rule is only intended to capture mismatches that arise in respect the equity or financing return paid under a financial instrument. Accordingly, in this case, where the counterparty does not treat the payments under the arrangement as payments under a financial instrument, the hybrid financial instrument rule should only apply to the extent of the equity or financing return. Payments under the arrangement that are treated under Country B law as purchase price or repayment of principal should, therefore, not be subject to adjustment under the rule. In this case the financing return on the lease will be fully taxable in Country B under ordinary law, so the hybrid financial instrument rule will generally not result in any net adjustment for B Co.

Example 1.26

Consideration for the purchase of a trading asset

Facts

1. In the example illustrated in the figure below, A Co (a company resident in Country A) transfers shares to B Co. B Co pays fair market value for the shares. The share transfer occurs on the same day as the payment. B Co acquires the shares as part of its activities as a trader and will be able to include the purchase price as expenditure when calculating any taxable gain/loss on the disposal of the shares.

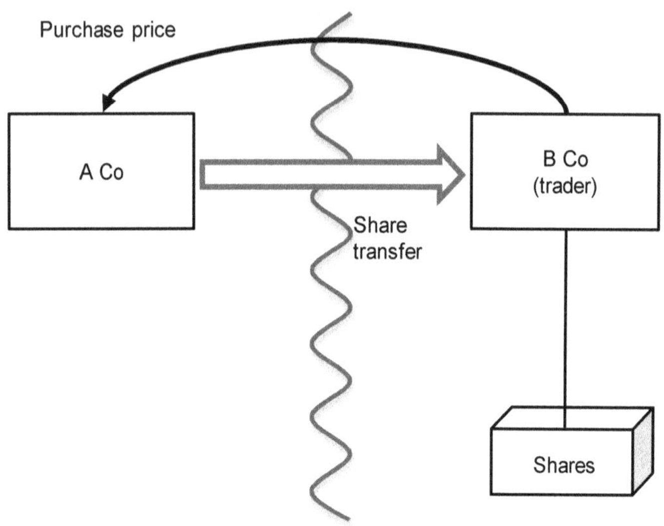

Question

2. Does the payment give rise to a D/NI outcome under the hybrid financial instrument rule?

Answer

3. The asset sale agreement is not a financial instrument as it does not provide for a financing or equity return. The payment under the asset transfer agreement is not a substitute payment as it does not include, or contain an amount representing, a financing or equity return. Accordingly the transaction does not fall within the scope of the hybrid financial instrument rule.

Analysis

The asset transfer agreement is not a financial instrument

4. The hybrid financial instrument rule is not intended to apply to asset transfers unless the transfer is a hybrid transfer or incorporates a substitute payment.

5. This asset transfer agreement does not fall within the definition of a financial instrument. It does not produce a return that is economically equivalent to interest, as the exchange of value occurs on the same day, and does not provide any party with an entitlement to an equity return (other than the return to B Co from holding the transferred asset).

6. The asset transfer agreement is not a hybrid transfer (and therefore does not fall within the extended definition of a hybrid financial instrument) as it does not give rise to a situation where both parties are treated as holding the transferred shares at the same time. Furthermore, even if the asset transfer was treated as a hybrid transfer, the purchase price deduction claimed by the trader in this case should not be treated as falling within the scope of the hybrid financial instrument rule as such a deduction is not the product of differences between jurisdictions in the tax treatment of asset transfer agreement but rather because the underlying asset is held by A Co and B Co in different capacities (i.e. by A Co as a capital asset and by B Co as a trading asset).

Purchase price does not include a substitute payment

7. Because the purchase price contains no element of an equity or financing return it should not be treated as a substitute payment under an asset transfer agreement.

Example 1.27

Interest component of purchase price

Facts

1. The example illustrated in the figure below is the same as **Example 1.26** except that the agreement provides that consideration payable under the share sale agreement will be deferred for one year. The purchase price of the shares is their fair market value on the date of the agreement plus an adjustment equivalent to a market-rate of interest on the unpaid purchase price. Country B allows B Co to treat the interest portion of the purchase price as giving rise to a separate deductible expense for tax purposes while, under Country A law, the entire purchase price (including the interest component) is treated as consideration for the transfer of the asset.

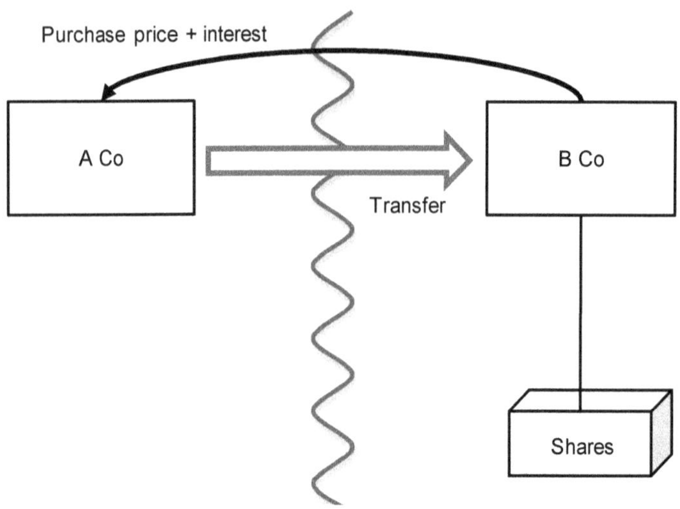

Question

2. To what extent does the hybrid financial instrument rule apply to adjust the ordinary tax consequences for A Co and B Co in respect of the purchase price?

Answer

3. The asset sale agreement is treated under Country B law as giving rise to a deductible financing expense. Country B law should therefore treat the payment as within the scope of the hybrid financial instrument rule. Country A law does not treat the payment as ordinary income under a financial instrument. The interest payment thus gives rise to a mismatch which is attributable to the different ways in which the asset transfer

agreement is characterised under the laws of Country A and Country B. Therefore B Co should be denied a deduction for the adjustment under the hybrid financial instrument rule.

4. Unless the asset transfer falls within the definition of a hybrid transfer, the hybrid financial instrument rule will not apply in Country A as Country A law does not treat the arrangement between the parties as a financial instrument.

5. The payment of interest under the asset sale agreement is not a substitute payment as the interest payment does not represent a financing or equity return on the underlying shares.

Analysis

The contract is not subject to the hybrid financial instrument rule in Country A unless it constitutes a hybrid transfer

6. While jurisdictions are encouraged to ensure that the hybrid financial instrument rules apply to any arrangement that produces a financing or equity return, the rules are not intended to standardise the categories of financial instrument or to harmonise their tax treatment and, in the present case, where the financing component of the arrangement is actually embedded into the calculation of the purchase price for an asset transfer agreement, it should be left to Country A law to determine whether the consideration paid under the share sale agreement should be taxed as a payment under a financial instrument.

7. The arrangement between the parties is treated as an asset transfer agreement under Country A law and the interest portion of the purchase price is not separately taxed under the rules for taxing debt, equity or derivatives. Accordingly the hybrid financial instrument rule will not apply in Country A.

8. The payment under the arrangement would be deemed to be a financial instrument under Country A law, however, if the way the transaction is structured results in both A Co and B Co being treated as the owner of the transferred shares at the same time. In such a case the payment of the interest component under the asset transfer agreement would be required to be treated, under Country A law as a deductible payment under a financial instrument that would give rise to a hybrid mismatch for tax purposes.

The substitute payment rule does not apply in Country A

9. The substitute payments rules in Recommendation 1.2(e) neutralise any D/NI outcome in respect of certain payments made under an asset transfer agreement. The rule only applies, however, to a taxpayer that transfers a financial instrument for a consideration that includes an amount representing a financing or equity return on the underlying instrument. In this case the interest paid under the asset transfer agreement has not been calculated by reference to the return on the underlying asset. Accordingly the interest payment does not fall within the scope of the substitute payments rule.

The interest component of the purchase price is subject to the hybrid financial instrument rule in Country B

10. B Co does not treat the interest portion of the purchase price as subsumed within the sale consideration but rather treats it as a separate and deductible financing cost. As such, the payment falls to be taxed under the rules for taxing debt or financial derivatives

in Country B and should therefore be treated as falling within the scope of the hybrid financial instrument rule.

11. The interest payment gives rise to a D/NI outcome because the payment has no independent significance under Country A law and is simply treated as a component of the purchase price paid for the shares. This mismatch in tax outcomes is attributable to the differences in the tax treatment of the share sale agreement under Country A and Country B laws and is therefore a hybrid mismatch subject to adjustment under the hybrid financial instrument rule in Country B.

12. In a case where the counterparty to the arrangement does not treat the adjustment as a payment under a financial instrument, the amount of the adjustment should be limited to the portion that is treated, under Country B law, as giving rise to a financing or equity return.

Example 1.28

Interest paid by a trading entity

Facts

1. This Example is the same as **Example 1.27** except that B Co acquires the asset as part of its activities as a trader and is entitled to include the purchase price as expenditure when calculating its (taxable) return on the asset.

Question

2. To what extent does the hybrid financial instrument rule apply to adjust the ordinary tax consequences for A Co and B Co in respect of the purchase price?

Answer

3. The adjustments required under the hybrid financial instrument rule are the same as set out in **Example 1.27**, however, denying a deduction for the interest component of the purchase price paid by B Co (i.e. the deduction that is attributable to the terms of the instrument) should not affect B Co's ability to take the full amount payable under the asset transfer agreement into account when calculating any taxable gain or loss on the acquisition and disposal of the asset.

Analysis

The interest component of the purchase price is a payment that is subject to the hybrid financial instrument rule in Country B

4. As described in further detail in the analysis part of **Example 1.27**, Country B law treats the payment as a separate and deductible financing cost and, as such, the payment should be treated as falling within the scope of the hybrid financial instrument rule to the extent it gives rise to a D/NI outcome.

The adjustment under Country B law should not affect the ability of B Co to claim a deduction for the expenditure incurred in acquiring a trading asset

5. A taxpayer's net return from trading or dealing in securities in the ordinary course of business will often be subject to tax as ordinary income. The income, expenses, profits, gains and losses from buying, holding and selling those securities will be included in, or deducted from, taxable income, as the case may be, regardless of what the ordinary rules would otherwise be for taxing payments under those instruments or how those amounts are accounted for on the balance sheet or income statement. The hybrid financial instrument rule should not prevent the trader from being able to claim a deduction for an

expense incurred in respect of the acquisition of a trading asset in the ordinary course of its business provided the taxpayer is fully taxable on the net return from those trading activities.

6. In general, therefore, the deduction that a trader is entitled to claim for the cost of acquiring an asset in the ordinary course of its trade should not be affected by the application the hybrid financial instrument rule. The deduction claimed by the trading entity will not be attributable to the terms of instrument under which payment is made but rather because the trader's particular status entitles it to bring all expenditure into account for tax purposes.

7. Even in cases where the trader would ordinarily rely on the particular tax character of the payment to determine its tax consequences (such as in respect of the payment of interest) the trader should be able to continue to deduct that payment, notwithstanding the operation of the hybrid financial instrument rule, provided that deduction is consistent with the taxpayer's status as a trader. Therefore, in the present case, the denial of the interest deduction under the hybrid financial instrument rules should not affect the ability of a trader to claim a deduction for the consideration paid to acquire the financial instrument.

Example 1.29

Interest paid to a trading entity

Facts

1. The facts of this example are the same as **Example 1.27** except that A Co sells the asset as part of its activities as a trader and is required to bring the entire amount of the payment into account as ordinary income when calculating its (taxable) return on the asset.

Question

2. To what extent does the hybrid financial instrument rule apply to adjust the ordinary tax consequences for A Co and B Co in respect of the purchase price?

Answer

3. The adjustments required under the hybrid financial instrument rule are the same as set out in **Example 1.27**. The fact that A Co may treat the amount of interest paid under the asset sale agreement as taxable gain should not affect the amount of the adjustment required under Country B law.

Analysis

The interest component of the purchase price is a deductible payment under a hybrid financial instrument

4. As described in further detail in the Analysis of **Example 1.27**, Country B law treats the interest portion of the payment as a separate and deductible financing cost and, as such, it should be treated as a deductible payment under a financial instrument for the purposes of Country B law.

The interest component of the purchase price is not included in ordinary income under Country A law

5. The interest component of the purchase price should not be treated as payment under a financial instrument that has given rise to ordinary income under the laws of Country A, even though A Co may be required to bring all or a portion of the consideration for the disposal of that asset into account as ordinary income for tax purposes.

6. In determining whether a payment under a financial instrument has given rise to a mismatch in tax outcomes the hybrid financial instrument rule looks only to the expected

tax treatment of the payment under the laws of the counterparty jurisdiction rather than its actual tax treatment in the hands of the counterparty. The fact that A Co is a trader and may include by the payment in ordinary income as proceeds from the disposal of trading assets will not impact on the determination of whether the terms of the instrument and the payments made under it are expected to give rise to a D/NI outcome.

Example 1.30

Purchase price adjustment for retained earnings

Facts

1. In the example illustrated in the figure below, A Co (a company resident in Country A) transfers shares in C Co, a wholly-owned subsidiary resident in Country C, to B Co, a company resident in Country B, under a share sale agreement. B Co pays fair market value for the shares. While the share transfer occurs on the same day as the payment the sale takes place part-way through C Co's accounting period.

2. A Co is entitled to an adjustment to the purchase price. The amount of the adjustment will be calculated by reference to the operating income of C Co at the end of the accounting period. This adjustment is treated as a deductible expense under Country B law while A Co treats the payment as consideration from the disposal of a capital asset and subject to tax at preferential rates.

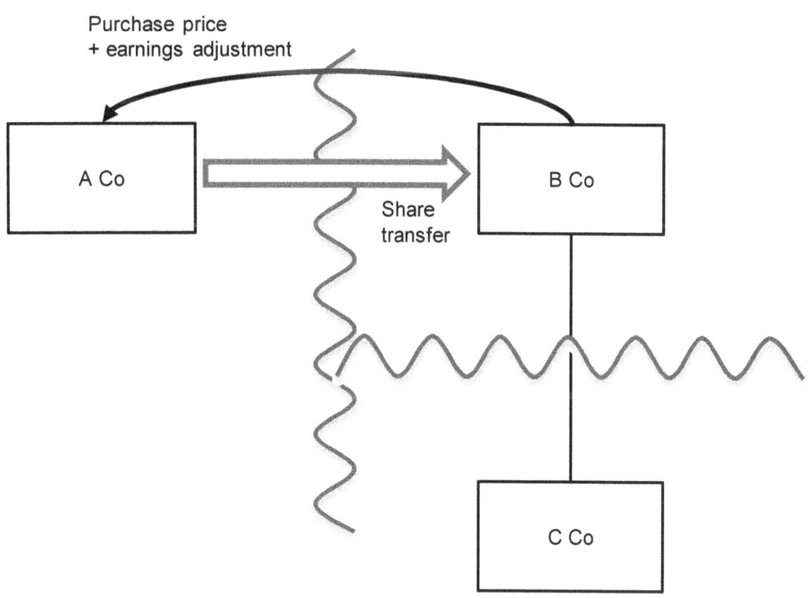

Question

3. Does the adjustment payment fall within the scope of the hybrid financial instrument rule?

Answer

4. The hybrid financial instrument rule should be applied in Country B to deny a deduction for the payment if the payment is made under a structured arrangement.

5. While the hybrid financial instrument rule will not generally apply in Country A (because A Co does not treat the payment as made under a financial instrument) the payment constitutes the payment of an equity return on the transferred shares that could be subject to adjustment under the substitute payment rules.

Analysis

Whether the asset transfer agreement should be treated as a financial instrument should be determined under local law

6. The share sale contract could fall within the definition of financial instrument for the purposes of the hybrid financial instrument rule because it provides A Co with an equity based return. The report encourages countries to take reasonable endeavours to ensure that the hybrid mismatch rules apply to instruments that produce a financing or equity return in order to ensure consistency in the application of the rules. The intention of the rules, however, is not to achieve harmonization in the way financial instruments are treated for tax purposes and, in hard cases, it should be left to local laws to determine the dividing line between financing instrument and other types of arrangement provided this is consistent with the overall intent of the rules.

Application of the hybrid financial instrument rule in Country B

7. Country B law does not treat the adjustment to the purchase price as subsumed within the consideration for the share sale but rather treats it as a separate deductible expense. The adjustment payment is in respect of an equity return under a financial instrument and should therefore be treated as a payment under a financial instrument under Country B law.

8. The adjustment payment gives rise to a D/NI outcome because the payment has no independent significance under Country A law and is simply treated as a component of the purchase price. The payment should be treated as giving rise to a D/NI outcome regardless of whether A Co is required to treat consideration from a share sale as ordinary income (see the analysis in **Example 1.29**). This mismatch in tax outcomes is attributable to the differences in the tax treatment of the share sale agreement under Country A and Country B laws and is therefore a hybrid mismatch subject to adjustment under the hybrid financial instrument rule in Country B.

9. Where, as in this case, one country treats the arrangement as a financial instrument and the other does not, the adjustment made by the country applying the rule should be limited to the portion of the payment that is treated as giving rise to the equity return.

Application of the substitute payment rule in Country A

10. A Co does not treat the payment as made under a financial instrument (because the entire amount payable is treated under Country A law as consideration for the sale of shares).

11. If the hybrid financial instrument rule does not apply in Country B to neutralise the mismatch in tax outcomes the payment may still, however, be caught by the substitute payments rule in Recommendation 1.2(e). Under this rule, a taxpayer that sells a financial instrument for a consideration that includes an amount representing an equity return on the underlying instrument (a substitute payment), is required to include such payment in income if the substitute payment is deductible under the laws of the counterparty jurisdiction and the underlying equity return would have been taxable if it had been paid directly under the financial instrument. Therefore, in this example, if A Co would have treated a dividend from C Co as ordinary income, the payment would be treated as a substitute payment and subject to adjustment under those rules.

Example 1.31

Loan structured as a share repo

Facts

1. In the example illustrated in the figure below, A Co, a company resident in Country A, wishes to borrow money from B Co, an unrelated lender resident in Country B. B Co suggests structuring the loan as a sale and repurchase transaction (repo) in order to provide B Co with security for the loan and to secure a B Co with a lower tax cost (and therefore a lower financing cost for the parties) under the arrangement.

2. Under the repo, A Co transfers shares to B Co under an arrangement whereby A Co (or an affiliate) will acquire those shares at a future date for an agreed price that represents a financing return minus any distributions received on the B Co shares during the term of the repo.

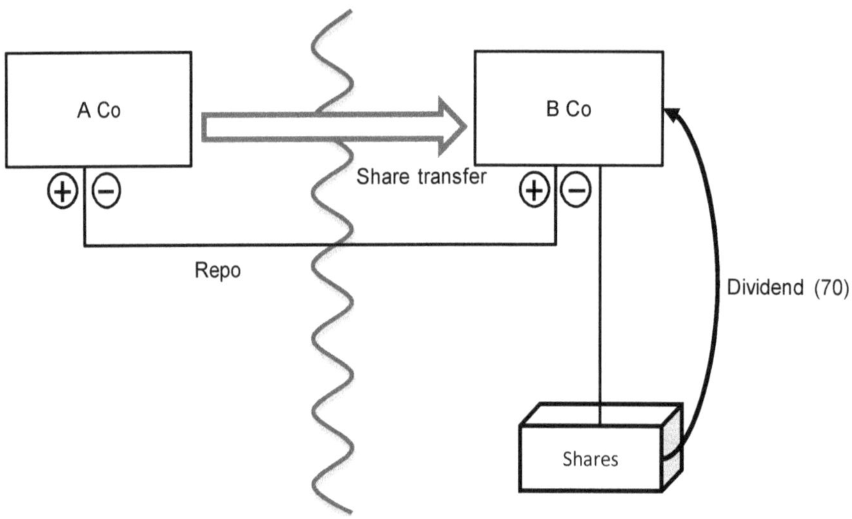

3. This type of financing arrangement can be described as a "net paying repo". This is because B Co (the lender under the arrangement and the temporary holder of the shares during the term of the repo) does not pay the dividends that it receives on the underlying shares across to A Co (the economic owner of the shares). Rather those dividends are retained by B Co as part of its overall return under the financing arrangement.

4. In this example it is assumed that Country B taxes the arrangement in accordance with its form. B Co is taxed as if it were the beneficial owner of the dividends that are paid on the underlying shares and is entitled to claim the benefit of exemption in respect of such dividends under Country B law. Country A taxes the arrangement in accordance with its economic substance. For Country A tax purposes, the repo is treated as a loan to

A Co that is secured against the transferred shares. A Co is regarded as the owner of the shares under Country A law with the corresponding entitlement to dividends that are paid on those shares during the life of the repo. Under Country A's tax system, A Co is taxed on the dividend, grossed up for underlying (deemed-paid) tax on the profits out of which the dividend is paid and credit is given for that underlying tax. Because, however, this repo is a net paying repo, where the lender retains the dividend as part of the agreed return on the loan, A Co is also treated as incurring a deductible financing expense equal to the amount of the dividend retained by B Co.

5. Assume that the amount B Co initially pays for the shares is 2 000. The term of the repo is one year and the agreed financing return is 3.5%. A Co would therefore normally be obliged to buy back the shares for 2 070. In this case, however, B Co receives and retains a dividend of 70 on the shares which means that the repurchase price of the shares is 2 000 (although the net cost of the repo for A Co is 70). Below is a table setting out the tax position of A Co and B Co under this structure.

A Co			B Co		
	Tax	Book		Tax	Book
Income			Income		
Dividend	70	70	Dividend	0	70
Gross up for deemed tax paid	30	0			
Expenditure			Expenditure		
Expenditure under repo	(70)	(70)			
Net return		**0**	**Net return**		**70**
Taxable income	**30**		**Taxable income**	**0**	
Tax (30%) on net income	(9)				
Tax credit	30				
Tax benefit		21	Tax to pay		0
After-tax return		**21**	**After-tax return**		**70**

6. As illustrated in the table above, B Co receives a dividend of 70 which is treated as tax exempt under Country B law. The dividend exactly matches B Co's contractual entitlement to the return under the repo. B Co acquires the shares and disposes of them at the same price and accordingly has no gain that might otherwise be subject to tax in Country B.

7. A Co also includes this dividend in its own income tax calculation together with an indirect foreign tax credit of 30. A Co is entitled however, to deduct the net expenditure under the repo (including the dividend retained by B Co). This deduction may be because the laws of Country A characterise the repo as a loan (i.e. a financial instrument) and treat the amount of the dividend that is paid to, and retained by, B Co as interest under that loan or because Country A law treats the net return from these types of arrangements (i.e. share repos) as giving rise to an allowable loss or taxable gain, so that, given the nature of the arrangement between the parties, the amount of the dividend that

is paid to, and retained by, B Co will be taken into account as deduction in calculating A Co's taxable income.

8. While, from A Co's perspective, the arrangement may give rise to an outcome that is not materially different from an ordinary loan, the arrangement generates a tax benefit for B Co in that, A Co's financing costs are paid for by a dividend of 70 that is not included in ordinary income by B Co due to the operation of the dividend exemption in Country B.

Question

9. Whether the arrangement falls within the scope of the hybrid financial instrument rule and, if so, to what extent an adjustment is required to be made in accordance with that rule.

Answer

10. The repo is a hybrid transfer and the payment of the dividend on the underlying shares gives rise to a D/NI outcome as between the parties to the repo. Country A treats the dividend paid on the transferred shares as a deductible expense under the repo while Country B treats the same payment as a return on the underlying shares (and, accordingly, as exempt from taxation). This resulting mismatch is a hybrid mismatch because it is attributable to the difference in the way Country A and B characterise and treat the payments made under the repo.

11. Although A Co and B Co are not related parties, the arrangement was designed to produce the mismatch in tax outcomes and therefore falls within the scope of the hybrid financial instrument rule. Accordingly Country A should deny a deduction for the financing costs under the arrangement. In the event that Country A does not apply the recommended response under the hybrid financial instrument rule, the financing return should be included in ordinary income under the laws of Country B.

Analysis

Recommendation 2.1 does not apply to the arrangement.

12. It may be the case that Country B has implemented rules, consistent with Recommendation 2.1 that would remove the benefit of a dividend exemption in cases where the payment is deductible for tax purposes. In this case, however, Recommendation 2.1 will not generally apply, as this rule only looks to the tax treatment of the payment under the laws of the issuer's jurisdiction and whether the issuer was entitled to a deduction for such payment. Because the dividend is not deductible for the issuer but for A Co (the counterparty to the repo) changes to domestic law recommended in Recommendation 2.1 would not generally restrict B Co's entitlement to an exemption on the dividend.

The arrangement is a financial instrument under Country A law

13. Country A either characterises the dividend that is paid to B Co under the terms of the repo as interest on a loan or otherwise allows taxpayers to bring into account the net expenditure under this type of arrangement as a deduction in calculating A Co's

taxable income. Accordingly the repo should be treated as falling within the hybrid financial instrument rule under Country A law.

The arrangement is a hybrid transfer under Country B law

14. The repo is a hybrid transfer because:

(a) under the laws of Country B, B Co is the owner of the shares and A Co's rights in those shares are treated as B Co's obligation to sell the shares back to A Co; and

(b) under the laws of Country A, A Co is the owner of the shares while B Co's rights in those shares are treated as a security interest under a loan.

Therefore, even if the repo is characterised as simple asset transfer agreement under the laws of Country B, the payments that are made under the repo must be treated as made under a financial instrument for purposes of the hybrid financial instrument rule in Country B and will be subject to an adjustment to the extent they give rise to a mismatch in tax outcomes that is attributable to the terms of the instrument.

The payment under the repo gives rise to a hybrid mismatch

15. The hybrid financial instrument rule applies when a deductible payment under a financial instrument is not included in ordinary income under the laws of the payee jurisdiction and the mismatch in tax outcomes is attributable to the terms of the instrument.

16. In this case, the repo transaction is treated as a financial instrument under Country A law. The payment that gives rise to the D/NI outcome is the dividend on the transferred shares that is retained by B Co under the repo. This dividend is treated as a deductible expense of A Co and is not included in ordinary income under the laws of Country B. This difference in tax outcomes is attributable to differences between Country A and B laws in the tax treatment of the repo.

17. Although, under local law, B Co would ordinarily have treated the payment that gives rise to the D/NI outcome as a separate payment on the underlying shares (and not a payment under the repo itself), because, in this case, the asset transfer arrangement constitutes a hybrid transfer, B Co is required to take into account the way that payment is characterised under the laws of Country A.

A mismatch would still arise even if dividend was treated as ordinary income under Country A law

18. On the facts of this example, the dividend on the underlying shares is treated under Country A law as carrying a right to credit for underlying taxes paid by the issuer and is therefore not included in ordinary income when it is treated as received by A Co. As with other types of financial instrument, however, the hybrid transfer rules do not take into account whether the funds A Co obtains under the repo have been invested in assets that generate ordinary income. The adjustment that is required to be made under the hybrid financial instrument rule will therefore not be affected by whether A Co treats the dividend on the transferred shares as ordinary income.

The arrangement is structured

19. The facts state that one of the reasons for structuring the loan as a repo is to secure a lower tax cost for the parties under the arrangement. The facts of the

arrangement indicate that it has been designed to produce a mismatch. In this case, where the parties to the repo are unrelated, the parties will have agreed a lower financing rate than they would have agreed if the return on the repo had been taxable in Country B.

Adjustment under Country A law

20. The primary recommendation under the hybrid financial instrument rule is that Country A should deny A Co a deduction for the financing expenses under the repo to the extent such expenses are not included in ordinary income.

Adjustment under Country B law

21. While Country B does not treat the repo as a financial instrument for domestic law purposes, the arrangement will, nevertheless, fall within the scope of the hybrid financial instrument rule under Country B law because it is a hybrid transfer. If the mismatch in tax outcomes is not neutralised by Country A denying a deduction for the financing expense under the repo then this amount should be treated as included in income under Country B law.

Example 1.32

Share lending arrangement

Facts

1. The figure below illustrates a share lending arrangement. A share loan is similar to the repo (described in **Example 1.31**) in that shares are transferred to a temporary holder (the borrower) under an arrangement to return those shares at a later date so that the transferor (the lender) continues to be exposed to the full risk and return of holding the shares through the obligations owed by the counterparty under the asset transfer agreement. The difference between a repo and a share lending arrangement is that the original transfer of the shares is not for a defined amount of consideration. Instead the borrower's obligation is to transfer the same or identical securities back to the lender at a later date.

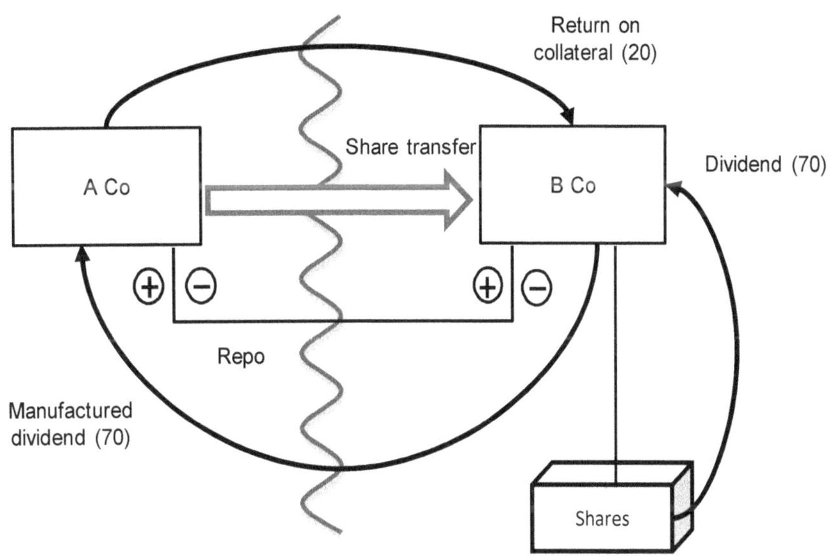

2. The lender of shares will wish to protect itself from the risk of a default by the borrower so, in most commercial share-lending transactions, the lender will require the borrower to post collateral of value at least equal to the value of the borrowed shares. Often this collateral is in the form of investment grade debt securities. Commercial securities lending arrangements will provide for the borrower to receive a return on the posted collateral and for the lender to be paid a fee which may be taken out of the income on the collateral.

3. Under both share lending and repo transactions it is possible – or even intended – that a payment of interest or dividend will arise during the course of the stock loan or repo. If the shares are not returned to the lender before a dividend is paid on the shares,

the lender will generally demand a "manufactured payment" from the borrower equivalent to what would otherwise have been payable on the underlying shares. This situation can be contrasted with that of a net-paying repo, described in **Example 1.31**, where the re-purchase price is defined in the agreement and is reduced by any dividend or interest payments paid to and retained by the temporary holder of the securities.

4. A common reason for undertaking a securities lending transaction is that the borrower has agreed to sell the shares 'short' (i.e. shares the borrower does not have) and needs to deliver these shares to the purchaser. The borrower anticipates that the shares will be able to be acquired back at a later date for a lower price and can then be transferred back to the lender realising a gain reflecting the difference between the sales proceeds and the subsequent market purchase price, as reduced by any cost of the share lending arrangement. In this example, B Co borrows shares under a share loan from A Co (a member of the same control group) intending to sell the shares 'short'. In this case, however, the subsequent disposal of the shares does not take place and B Co ends up holding the shares over a dividend payment date. B Co is therefore required to make a manufactured dividend payment to A Co equal to the amount of the dividend received on the underlying shares. A simplified illustration of the tax consequences of such an arrangement is set out below:

A Co			B Co		
	Tax	**Book**		**Tax**	**Book**
Income			Income		
Fee paid by B Co	5	5	Interest paid by A Co	25	25
Interest on collateral	25	25	Dividend on borrowed shares	-	70
Exempt dividend	-	70			
Expenditure			Expenditure		
			Fee paid to A Co	(5)	(5)
Interest paid to B Co	(25)	(25)	Manufactured dividend	(70)	(70)
Net return		**75**	**Net return**		**20**
Taxable income	**5**		**Taxable income**	**(50)**	

5. During the terms of the loan A Co earns interest on the collateral posted by B Co. A Co pays both the collateral and the interest earned on this collateral back to B Co at the end of the transaction minus a fee. B Co retains the borrowed shares over a dividend payment date and makes a manufactured payment of that dividend to A Co. B Co is entitled to claim the benefit of an exemption on the underlying dividend but is entitled to treat the manufactured dividend as a deductible expense. This deduction may be because the laws of Country B specifically grant a deduction for manufactured dividends or because Country B law treats the net return from these types of arrangements (i.e. share loans) as giving rise to an allowable loss or taxable gain, so that, given the nature of the arrangement between the parties, the amount paid to A Co under the share loan will be taken into account as deduction in calculating A Co's taxable income.

6. Country A law disregards the transfer of the shares under the arrangement and treats A Co as if it continued to hold the shares during the term of the share loan. The manufactured dividend payment is treated as if it were an exempt dividend on the

underlying share so that A Co has no net tax to pay under the arrangement (other than on the stock-lending fee it receives from B Co).

7. The net effect of this arrangement is that B Co has incurred a net deductible expense of 70 for the payment of the manufactured dividend which is not included in ordinary income by A Co. The total income under the arrangement (including the dividend received and the interest earned on the collateral) is 95, however, for tax purposes, the transaction generates a net loss of 50 for B Co and A Co is only taxable on the share lending fee.

Question

8. Whether the arrangement falls within the scope of the hybrid financial instrument rule and, if so, to what extent an adjustment is required to be made in accordance with that rule.

Answer

9. The share loan is a hybrid transfer and the payment of the manufactured dividend under the share loan gives rise to a D/NI outcome. The payments under the repo give rise to a deduction in Country B that is attributable to the terms of the arrangement between the parties, while Country A treats the same payment as a return on the underlying shares (and, accordingly, as exempt from taxation). Therefore the mismatch in tax outcomes should be treated as a hybrid mismatch because it is attributable to differences in the way Country A and B characterise and treat the payments under a share loan.

10. Furthermore, on the facts of this example the manufactured payment will be a substitute payment so that the manufactured payment will be brought within the scope of the hybrid financial instrument rule even in a case where the deduction claimed by B Co is not attributable to the tax treatment of payments on the share loan but to the acquisition and disposal of the underlying shares.

11. A Co and B Co are related parties and the arrangement therefore falls within the scope of the hybrid financial instrument rule. Accordingly Country B should deny a deduction for the financing costs under the arrangement regardless of the basis for the deduction claimed by B Co. In the event that Country B does not apply the recommended response under the hybrid financial instrument rule, the financing return should be included in ordinary income under the laws of Country A.

Analysis

Recommendation 2.1 does not apply to the arrangement

12. It may be the case that Country A has implemented rules, consistent with Recommendation 2.1 that would remove the benefit of a dividend exemption in cases where the payment is deductible for tax purposes. In this case, however, Recommendation 2.1 will not generally apply, as this rule only looks to the tax treatment of the payment under the laws of the issuer's jurisdiction and whether the issuer was entitled to a deduction for such payment. In this case the dividend is not deductible for the issuer but for B Co (the counterparty to the repo) and, accordingly, the changes to domestic law recommended in Recommendation 2.1 would not generally restrict A Co's entitlement to an exemption on the dividend.

The arrangement is a financial instrument under Country B law

13. The deduction that B Co claims for the manufactured dividend does not result from a trading loss on the borrowed shares (contrast the facts in **Example 1.34**), rather, the deduction is attributable to the tax treatment of payments under a share loan. A taxpayer in Country B will be entitled to deduct the manufactured dividend regardless of its particular status or the way it deals with the underlying shares. In such a case, where Country B specifically grants taxpayers a deduction for manufactured dividend payments, Country B should treat such amounts as paid under a financial instrument and potentially subject to adjustment under the hybrid financial instrument rule.

The arrangement is a hybrid transfer that should be treated as a financial instrument under Country A law

14. While Country A ignores the existence of the share loan and does not treat it as a financial instrument for domestic law purposes, the arrangement will, nevertheless, fall within the scope of the hybrid financial instrument rule because it is an asset transfer agreement where:

(a) under the laws of Country A, A Co is treated as the owner of the shares with B Co's rights in the shares being treated as a loan made by A Co; and

(b) under the laws of Country B, B Co is the owner of the shares under the transfer and A Co's rights in those shares are treated as B Co's obligation to transfer the shares back to A Co.

The share loan is therefore a hybrid transfer within the scope of the hybrid financial instrument rule notwithstanding that the arrangement is not treated as a financial instrument under Country A law.

The payment under the share loan gives rise to a hybrid mismatch

15. The hybrid financial instrument rule applies when a deductible payment under a financial instrument is not included in ordinary income under the laws of the payee jurisdiction and the mismatch in tax outcomes is attributable to the terms of the instrument.

16. In this case, the share lending transaction is treated as a financial instrument under Country B law. The payment that gives rise to the D/NI outcome is the manufactured dividend which is treated as a deductible expense by B Co and is not included in ordinary income under the laws of Country A. This difference in tax outcomes is attributable to differences between Country A and B laws in the tax treatment of the share loan.

17. Although under local law, A Co would ordinarily have treated the manufactured dividend payment that gives rise to the D/NI outcome as a separate payment on the underlying shares (and not a payment under the share loan itself), because, in this case, the asset transfer arrangement constitutes a hybrid transfer, A Co is required to take into account the way that payment is characterised under the laws of Country B.

A mismatch would still arise even if dividend was treated as ordinary income under Country B law

18. On the facts of this example, the dividend on the underlying shares is treated as exempt under Country B law. As with other types of financial instrument, however, the

hybrid transfer rules are not affected by whether the funding provided under the share loan has been invested in assets that generate an ordinary income return. The adjustment that is required to be made under the hybrid financial instrument rule will therefore not be dependent on the tax treatment of the dividend under the laws of Country A. This principle is illustrated in **Example 1.33**.

Tax treatment of B Co in the event payment of manufactured dividend gives rise to a trading loss

19. The adjustment that is required to be made under the hybrid financial instrument rule is generally confined to adjusting those tax consequences that are attributable to the tax treatment of the instrument itself. The adjustment is not intended to impact on tax outcomes that are solely attributable to the status of the taxpayer or the context in which the instrument is held. Thus, as set out in further detail in **Example 1.34**, the denial of the deduction in Country B under the hybrid financial instrument rule should not generally impact on the position of a financial trader in relation to the taxation of any net gain or loss in respect of its share trading business.

20. Note, however, in this case, that manufactured dividend is a substitute payment that falls within the scope of Recommendation 1.2(e) as it is a payment of an amount representing an equity return on the underlying shares. The substitute payment rules apply to any type of D/NI outcome regardless of whether such outcome is attributable to the terms of the instrument, the tax status of the parties or the context in which the asset is held. Unlike the rules applying to hybrid mismatches under a financial instrument, the substitute payment rules are only triggered, however, where differences between the tax treatment of the substitute payment and the underlying return on the instrument have the potential to undermine the integrity of the hybrid financial instrument rule. In particular, a substitute payment that gives rise to a D/NI outcome will be subject to adjustment where the underlying financing or equity return on the transferred asset is treated as exempt or excluded from income in the hands of the transferee. On these facts, therefore, where the underlying dividend paid to B Co is tax exempt, the payment of the manufactured dividend will be treated as giving rise to a mismatch in tax outcomes regardless of the basis for the deduction claimed under Country B law.

Adjustment under Country B law

21. The primary recommendation under the hybrid financial instrument rule is that Country B should deny a deduction for the manufactured dividend to the extent the dividend is not included in ordinary income under Country A law.

Adjustment under Country A law

22. While Country A does not treat the repo as a financial instrument for domestic law purposes, the arrangement will, nevertheless, fall within the scope of the hybrid financial instrument rule under Country A law, either because it is a hybrid transfer or because the dividend is a substitute payment. If the mismatch in tax outcomes is not neutralised by Country B denying a deduction for the manufactured dividend under the share loan then this amount should be treated as included in income under Country A law.

Example 1.33

Share lending arrangement where transferee taxable on underlying dividend

Facts

1. In this example the facts are the same as in **Example 1.32** except that the dividend paid on the underlying shares is treated as taxable under Country B law. A simplified illustration of the tax consequences of such an arrangement is set out below.

A Co			B Co		
	Tax	**Book**		**Tax**	**Book**
Income			Income		
Fee paid by B Co	5	5	Interest paid by A Co	25	25
Interest on collateral	25	25	Dividend on borrowed shares	70	70
Exempt dividend	-	70			
Expenditure			Expenditure		
			Fee paid to A Co	(5)	(5)
Interest paid to B Co	(25)	(25)	Manufactured dividend	(70)	(70)
Net return		**75**	**Net return**		**20**
Taxable income	**5**		**Taxable income**	**20**	

2. As in **Example 1.32**, Country A law disregards the transfer of the shares under the arrangement and treats A Co as if it continued to hold the shares during the term of the share loan. The manufactured dividend payment is treated as if it were an exempt dividend on the underlying shares so that A Co has no net tax to pay under the arrangement (other than on the stock-lending fee).

3. Under Country B law, B Co is treated as deriving a taxable dividend on the borrowed shares and is entitled to a deduction for the manufactured dividend it pays to A Co. B Co is also taxable on the interest paid on the collateral and thus has a net return equal to its taxable income.

4. The net effect of this arrangement, both from a tax and economic standpoint, and after taking into account the tax treatment of the underlying dividend received by B Co, is that both parties are left in the same position as if the transaction had not been entered into (save that A Co derives a stock-lending fee).

Question

5. Whether the share lending arrangement falls within the scope of the hybrid financial instrument rule?

Answer

6. The share loan is a hybrid transfer and the payment of the manufactured dividend under the share loan gives rise to a D/NI outcome. Country B treats the manufactured dividend as a separate deductible expense while Country A treats the same payment as a return on the underlying shares (and, accordingly, as exempt from taxation). Therefore the mismatch in tax outcomes should be treated as a hybrid mismatch because it is attributable to differences in the way Country A and B characterise and treat the payments made under the hybrid transfer.

7. As with other types of financial instrument, the hybrid transfer rules do not take into account whether the funds obtained under the transfer have been invested in assets that generate a taxable or exempt return. The adjustment that the transferor is required to make in respect of payment under a repo or stock loan is not be affected by the fact that B Co is taxable on the underlying dividend.

8. No adjustment will be required, however, under the hybrid financial instrument rule in Country B, if B Co is a trader that acquires the shares as part of a share dealing business, provided B Co will be subject to tax on the net return from the acquisition, holding and disposal of that asset. Although the manufactured dividend is a substitute payment that gives rise to a D/NI outcome, no adjustment will be required under the substitute payment rule as B Co is taxable on the dividend it receives on the underlying shares and A Co would not ordinarily have been required to include that dividend in income.

9. In this case, the arrangement is unlikely to be a structured arrangement (as both parties are left in the same after-tax position as if the transaction had not been entered into). Therefore the hybrid financial instrument rule will generally only apply where A Co and B Co are related parties.

Analysis

The payment under the share loan gives rise to a hybrid mismatch

10. As discussed further in **Example 1.32**, the share lending arrangement is treated as a financial instrument under Country B law and a hybrid transfer under Country A law and the payment of a manufactured dividend gives rise to a D/NI outcome that is attributable to the terms of the instrument. Accordingly the analysis that applies to this arrangement is the same as set out in **Example 1.32** and the payment should be treated as subject to adjustment under the hybrid financial instrument rule.

11. Although, on the facts of this case, the transaction does not generate a tax advantage for either A Co or B Co, this is because B Co retained the borrowed shares and derived a taxable return on the underlying dividend. The underlying policy of Recommendation 1 is to align the tax treatment of the payments made under a financing or equity instrument so that amounts that are not fully taxed in the payee jurisdiction are not treated as a deductible expense in the payer jurisdiction. The operation of the hybrid financial instrument rule looks only to the expected tax treatment of the payments under the instrument and does not take into account whether the income funding the expenditure under the arrangement is subject to tax in the payer jurisdiction. B Co is no different position from what it would have been had it borrowed money from A Co under an ordinary hybrid financial instrument and invested the borrowed funds in an asset that generates a taxable return.

Tax treatment of B Co in the event payment of manufactured dividend gives rise to a trading loss

12. The adjustment that is required to be made under the hybrid financial instrument rule is, however, generally confined to adjusting those tax consequences that are attributable to the tax treatment of the instrument itself. The adjustment is not intended to impact on tax outcomes that are solely attributable to the status of the taxpayer or the context in which the instrument is held. Thus, as set out in further detail in **Example 1.34**, the denial of the deduction in Country B under the hybrid financial instrument rule should not generally impact on the position of a financial trader in relation to the taxation of any net gain or loss in respect of its share trading business

13. Furthermore the manufactured dividend is not a substitute payment that falls within the scope of Recommendation 1.2(e) as the dividend on the underlying shares is both taxable as ordinary income under Country B law and treated as exempt under Country A law. Therefore, if B Co is a trader that acquires the shares as part of its trade, it should be permitted to take the manufactured dividend into account as a deduction when calculating its net income.

Example 1.34

Share lending arrangement where manufactured dividend gives rise to a trading loss

Facts

1. This example has the same facts as **Example 1.33** except that B Co is a share trader that, under Country B law, is required to include the net return from its trading activities in income. B Co borrows shares from A Co (a member of the same control group) in order to sell them 'short'. During the term of the share loan B Co is required to make a manufactured dividend payment to A Co. B Co then acquires the same shares on the market and returns them to A Co to satisfy its obligations under the share lending arrangement.

2. As noted in **Example 1.32**, a common reason for undertaking a securities lending transaction is that the borrower has agreed to sell the shares 'short' (i.e. shares the borrower does not have) and needs to deliver these shares to the purchaser. The borrower anticipates that the shares will be able to be acquired back at a later date for a lower price and can then be transferred back to the lender realising a gain reflecting the difference between the sales proceeds and the subsequent market purchase price, as reduced by any cost of the share lending arrangement. In this example B Co may have expected the value of the shares to fall, first once the shares become "ex-dividend" and subsequently still further reflecting its "bearish" view on the shares, in the event the value of the shares does not fall and B Co ends up repurchasing the shares for an amount equal to the original proceeds from the short sale. A simplified illustration of the tax consequences of such an arrangement is set out below:

A Co			B Co		
	Tax	Book		Tax	Book
Income			Income		
Fee paid by B Co	5	5	Interest paid by A Co	25	25
Interest on collateral	25	25			
Exempt dividend	-	70			
Expenditure			Expenditure		
			Fee paid to A Co	(5)	(5)
Interest paid to B Co	(25)	(25)	Net expenditure under share loan	(70)	(70)
Net return		**75**	**Net return**		**65**
Taxable income	**5**		**Taxable income**	**(50)**	

3. In this case, B Co borrows the shares from A Co and sells them to an unrelated party for their market value of 1 000. B Co eventually acquires these shares back, in this case, at the same price (1 000) and returns them to A Co to close-out the transaction. B Co incorporates the cost of the manufactured dividend into the calculation of its overall taxable gain or loss on the share trade as follows:

	B Co
Proceeds from the on-market sale of borrowed shares	1 000
Additional amount paid to A Co in respect of manufactured dividend	(70)
Cost of re-acquiring shares on-market	(1 000)
Total return on trade	(70)

4. B Co has made a total loss on the share trade of 70 which, when added to the income derived on the posted collateral, gives B Co a loss for the period. A Co treats the manufactured dividend as an exempt return on the underlying share.

Question

5. Whether the share lending arrangement falls within the scope of the hybrid financial instrument rule?

Answer

6. Although the share loan is treated as a hybrid transfer, the adjustment to be made under the hybrid financial instrument rule should not affect B Co's deduction for the manufactured dividend to the extent Country B law requires that payment to be taken into account in calculating B Co's (taxable) return on the overall trade.

7. The manufactured dividend will, however, constitute a substitute payment subject to adjustment under Recommendation 1.2(e), if Country B law would not have treated B Co as subject to tax at the full rate on the underlying dividend.

Analysis

Manufactured dividend gives rise to a trading loss and is not treated as a deductible payment under a financial instrument

8. The hybrid financial instrument rule is not generally intended to impact on a country's domestic rules for taxing the gain or loss on the acquisition and disposal of property. Similarly, a trading entity should be entitled to take into account all the amounts paid or received in respect of the acquisition, holding or disposal of a trading asset for the purposes of calculating its net income from its trading activities even where such amounts are paid or received under a financial instrument such as a share loan.

9. The policy basis for the deduction claimed by B Co in this case is not the fact that the payment constitutes a financing expense but rather the fact that all the expenditure needs to be taken into account in order to calculate the overall return on the trade. The deduction is thus, not attributable to the terms of the instrument, but rather to the

taxpayer's particular tax treatment and the nature of the underlying asset that is the subject matter of the trade.

10. The hybrid financial instrument rule should not operate to restrict the ability of the trading entity to claim a deduction in respect of a payment under a financial instrument provided the payment is made as part of that trading activity and the taxpayer will be fully taxable on the net return from that trading activity. The precise mechanism by which the trader obtains the benefit of the deduction should not affect the trader's entitlement to claim such deduction provided the net return from the acquisition, holding and disposal of the shares will be subject to tax as ordinary income.

Manufactured dividend could be a substitute payment subject to adjustment under Recommendation 1

11. The manufactured dividend is a payment of an equity return under an asset transfer agreement that gives rise to a D/NI outcome and may therefore fall within the scope of the substitute payment rules. While, in this case, Recommendation 1.2(e)(ii) will not apply (as the example indicates that Country A law would treat the underlying dividend as exempt) the rule could still apply if the laws of Country B would otherwise have treated the dividend on the underlying shares as exempt or eligible for some other type of tax relief. The fact that B Co does not actually receive a dividend on the underlying shares does not impact on the application of the substitute payment rules which look to the expected tax outcome under the arrangement based on the character of the arrangement and the payments made under it rather than the actual outcome under the trade.

Example 1.35

Share lending arrangement where neither party treats the arrangement as a financial instrument

Facts

1. These facts are the same as in **Example 1.34** except that both jurisdictions respect the legal form of the transaction (as a sale and repurchase of securities) so that neither jurisdiction treats the share loan as a financial instrument for tax purposes. A simplified illustration of the tax consequences of such an arrangement is set out below:

A Co			B Co		
	Tax	Book		Tax	Book
Income			Income		
Fee paid by B Co	5	5	Interest paid by A Co	25	25
Interest on collateral	25	25			
Gain on share loan	0	70			
Expenditure			Expenditure		
			Fee paid to A Co	(5)	(5)
Interest paid to B Co	(25)	(25)	Loss on share loan	(70)	(70)
Net return		**75**	**Net return**		**65**
Taxable income	**5**		**Taxable income**	**(50)**	

2. As in **Example 1.34**, B Co borrows the shares from A Co and sells them 'short' to an unrelated party for their market value of 1 000. During the period of the share loan, B Co is required to pay a manufactured dividend to A Co. B Co eventually buys back the shares for the same price and returns them to A Co to close-out the transaction. During the terms of the loan A Co earns interest on the collateral. It pays both the collateral and the interest on that collateral back to B Co at the end of the transaction minus a fee.

3. Rather than treating the manufactured dividend as a separate deductible item, both A Co and B Co treat it as an adjustment to the cost of acquiring the shares. The total return from the share lending transaction for A Co and B Co can be calculated as follows:

	A Co	B Co
Market value of shares lent	1 000	(1 000)
Proceeds from the on market sale of borrowed shares		1 000
Additional amount paid to A Co in respect of manufactured dividend	70	(70)
Cost of re-acquiring shares on-market		(1 000)
Market value of shares returned	(1 000)	1 000
Total return on trade	70	(70)

4. B Co's loss on the share trade is deductible under Country B law while the gain on the share trade is treated as an excluded return under Country A law

Question

5. Does the hybrid financial instrument rule apply to neutralise the mismatch in tax outcomes under this arrangement?

Answer

6. Recommendation 1.2(e) will apply to neutralise the mismatch in tax outcomes if A Co would have been required to treat the dividend paid on the underlying shares as ordinary income or B Co would have been exempt on the underlying dividend.

Analysis

Manufactured payment is not treated as a payment under a financial instrument

7. Both Country A and B treat the share loan as a genuine sale so that the payment is not treated, under either Country A or Country B law, as a payment that is subject to the local law rules for taxing debt, equity or derivatives. Furthermore the asset transfer is not treated as a hybrid transfer subject to adjustment under the hybrid financial instrument rule. Accordingly, neither Country A nor Country B will apply the hybrid financial instrument rule to adjust the tax treatment of the payment.

Adjustment required to extent there is a mismatch in the tax treatment of the dividend and the manufactured dividend.

8. An asset transfer arrangement such as this will give rise to tax policy concerns where the transfer results in the parties obtaining a better tax outcome, in aggregate, than they would have obtained had the transferor received a direct payment of the underlying financing or equity return.

9. If the asset transfer agreement effectively allows A Co to substitute what would otherwise have been a taxable dividend on the shares for a non-taxable gain, or if B Co would have been entitled to an exemption on the underlying dividend then Recommendation 1.2(e) will apply to adjust the D/NI outcome between the parties to prevent these type of arrangements undermining the integrity of the hybrid financial instrument rule.

Example 1.36

Deduction for premium paid to acquire a bond with accrued interest

Facts

1. In the example illustrated in the figure below, A Co (a company resident in Country A) and B Co (a company resident in Country B) each own 50% of the ordinary shares in C Co (a company resident in Country C). C Co issues a bond to B Co. The bond is treated as a debt instrument under the laws of Country C, but as an equity instrument (i.e. a share) under the laws of Country B. Interest payments on the loan are deductible in Country C but treated as exempt dividends under Country B law. B Co subsequently transfers the bond to A Co.

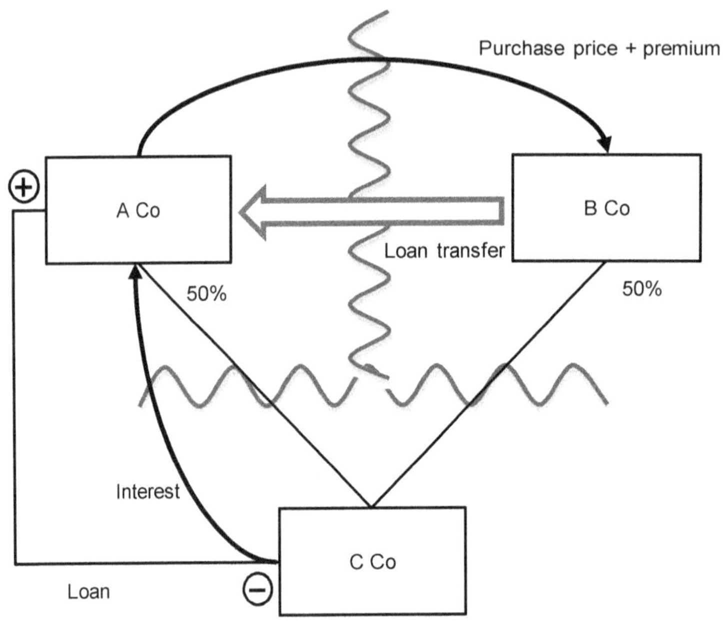

2. The bond is issued for its principal amount of 20 million and has an interest rate of 12% which is paid in two equal instalments throughout the year. A Co acquires the bond from B Co part-way through an interest period under an ordinary contract of sale. A Co pays a premium of 0.8 million to acquire the bond which represents the accrued but unpaid interest on the bond. Under Country A law the bond premium can be deducted against interest income whereas, under Country B law, the premium is treated as an excluded capital gain. A table setting out the tax treatment of A Co, B Co and C Co in respect of the sale and purchase of the bond is set out below:

	A Co		B Co		C Co	
	Interest coupon	1.2	Interest coupon	-	Interest coupon	(1.2)
	Bond premium	(0.8)	Bond premium	-		
Net taxable income		**0.4**		**0**		**(1.2)**

3. As illustrated in the table above, the interest payment of 1.2 million gives rise to a deduction for C Co and income for A Co. A Co is, however, entitled to a deduction of 0.8 million for the premium paid on the bond. B Co does not receive any interest on the bond and treats the premium paid for the bond by A Co as an (exempt) gain on the disposal of an asset. In aggregate the arrangement gives rise to a deduction (for C Co) of 1.2 million and net income (for A Co) of 0.4 million.

Question

4. Does the hybrid financial instrument rule operate to neutralise the mismatch in tax outcomes under this arrangement.

Answer

5. The premium paid for the bond is a substitute payment within the meaning of Recommendation 1.2(e). Accordingly, if the bond transfer agreement was entered into as part of a structured transaction, the hybrid financial instrument rule should apply to adjust the tax treatment of the consideration paid for the bond to the extent necessary to neutralise the mismatch in tax outcomes.

Analysis

The bond is a financial instrument but a payment of interest under the bond does not give rise to a hybrid mismatch.

6. While the payment of interest on the bond gives rise to a deduction within the scope of the hybrid financial instrument rule, the full amount of that payment is included in ordinary income under Country A law. Therefore the payment of interest under the bond does not give rise to a mismatch in tax outcomes.

7. While the purchase price premium is deductible under Country A law and not included in ordinary income under Country B law, this payment is not a payment under the bond but rather a payment to acquire the bond and such a payment will only give rise a mismatch in tax outcomes under the hybrid financial instrument rule if the contract to acquire the bond is treated as a financial instrument or a hybrid transfer.

The contract to acquire the bond is not a financial instrument

8. In this case, the asset transfer is described as an ordinary contract of sale so that neither Country A nor Country B law tax the premium paid for the bond as a separate financing return. The contract to acquire the bond is therefore not a financial instrument that falls within the language or intent of Recommendation 1.

The premium is a substitute payment

9. Although neither party to the arrangement treats the sale contract as a financial instrument, the consideration for the sale of the bond includes an amount representing a financing or equity return on the underlying financial instrument that falls within the Recommendation 1.2(e). In this case the premium represents the accrued financing return on the underlying instrument. If that financing return had been paid directly to the transferor it would have given rise to a hybrid mismatch under Recommendation 1. Accordingly the payment of the premium should be treated as giving rise to a mismatch that is subject to adjustment under the hybrid financial instrument rule.

Adjustment required if the arrangement is a structured arrangement

10. The hybrid financial instrument rule applies to arrangements entered into with a related person or where the payment is made under a structured arrangement and the taxpayer is party to that structured arrangement. In this case the fact that A Co and B Co both own shares in C Co does not make them related parties for the purposes of the Recommendation 10. The arrangement will be a structured arrangement, however, if the facts and circumstances, including the joint shareholding in C Co, indicate that the arrangement was designed to produce the mismatch in tax outcomes.

Example 1.37

Manufactured dividend on a failed share trade

Facts

1. The figure below illustrates a situation where a trading entity (A Co) has acquired or borrowed shares from an unrelated third party and on-sells these shares to B Co. The transferred shares carry an entitlement to a declared but unpaid dividend (i.e. the shares are sold to B Co cum-dividend). Because of a processing error, however, the shares are delivered after the dividend record date is set, so that the dividend is, in fact, paid to A Co. On the date the (non-deductible) dividend is actually paid A Co receives the dividend (even though it holds no shares) and pays the dividend across to B Co to whom it had agreed to sell the shares cum-dividend, but delivered the shares ex-dividend.

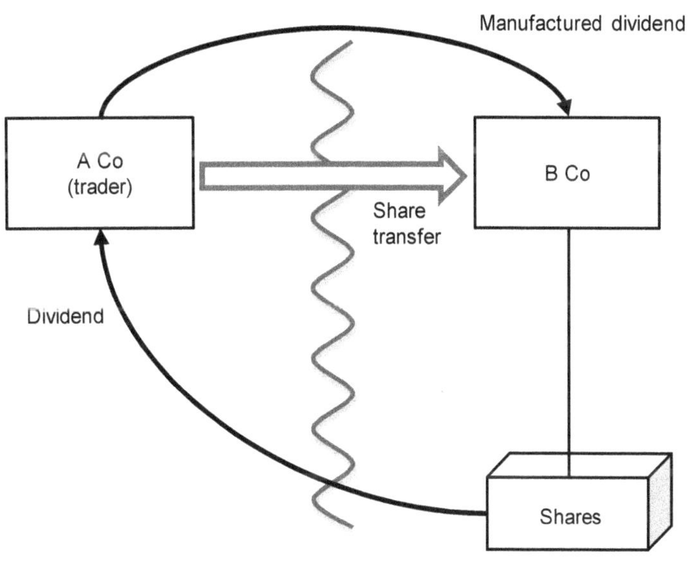

2. Under Country A law, A Co would be treated as the owner of the shares at the time the dividend is paid and, in the case of a taxpayer of normal status, a dividend exemption would apply. A Co is, however, a financial trader and accordingly the dividend is incorporated into the calculation of A Co's overall (taxable) return on the acquisition, holding and disposal of the shares. The dividend is therefore treated as ordinary income of A Co and the manufactured dividend is treated as a deductible trading expense. Under Country B law, B Co is also treated as the owner of the shares and treats the manufactured dividend as an exempt dividend on the underlying shares. The manufactured payment thus gives rise to a D/NI outcome.

Question

3. Does the payment of the manufactured dividend fall within the scope of the hybrid financial instrument rule?

Answer

4. Although the asset transfer agreement is a hybrid transfer, the manufactured dividend does not fall within the scope of the hybrid financial instrument rule because the D/NI outcome is solely attributable to the different tax status of the counterparties, in particular, because B Co is a financial trader, and all of its gains, receipts, expenses and losses are taken into account in computing profits taxable as ordinary income. Further the payment of the manufactured dividend is not a substitute payment that has the effect of avoiding a hybrid mismatch on the underlying instrument because the ordinary tax treatment of the payer and payee have been preserved under the arrangement and the dividend is not tax-deductible for the issuer.

5. Recommendation 2.2 will apply to the arrangement to limit the ability of A Co to benefit from any withholding tax credits on the underlying dividend.

Analysis

6. While both parties to this arrangement would ordinarily treat this arrangement as an asset transfer, and therefore outside the scope of the hybrid financial instrument rule, the arrangement is a hybrid transfer (which is deemed to be a financial instrument for the purposes of these rules) because it is an asset transfer agreement where:

(a) under the laws of Country A, A Co is the owner of the shares and B Co's rights in those shares are treated as A Co's obligation to transfer the dividend to B Co; and

(b) under the laws of Country B, B Co is the owner of the shares while A Co's rights in those shares are treated as arising under the asset transfer agreement with B Co.

Ownership in this context includes any rules that result in the taxpayer being taxed as the cash-flows from the underlying asset.

7. Although the arrangement is a hybrid transfer, the D/NI outcome that arises under the hybrid transfer is not attributable to the terms of the instrument (but to A Co's status as a trader) and will therefore not give rise to a hybrid mismatch. Because the underlying dividend is both taxable for A Co and exempt for B Co, the substitute payment rules also do not apply. If, however, the tax regime in Country A had unusual features, which meant that the dividend on the underlying shares was not taxable in Country A or if the arrangement had been deliberately structured as broken trade in order to allow B Co to receive an exempt return of purchase price rather than a taxable dividend on the underlying share, then the payment may be treated as a substitute payment caught by the hybrid financial instrument rule.

Example 2.1

Application of Recommendation 2.1 to franked dividends

Facts

1. In the example illustrated in the figure below, A Co is a company established and tax resident in Country A. A Co has a PE in Country B. Country A does not tax the net income of a foreign PE. A Co issues a bond to investors in Country A through the PE in Country B. The bond is issued for its principal amount and pays accrued interest every six months. The loan is subordinated to the ordinary creditors of A Co and payments of interest and principal can be suspended in the event A Co fails to meet certain solvency requirements. Some of the bonds issued by A Co are acquired by unrelated investors on the open market.

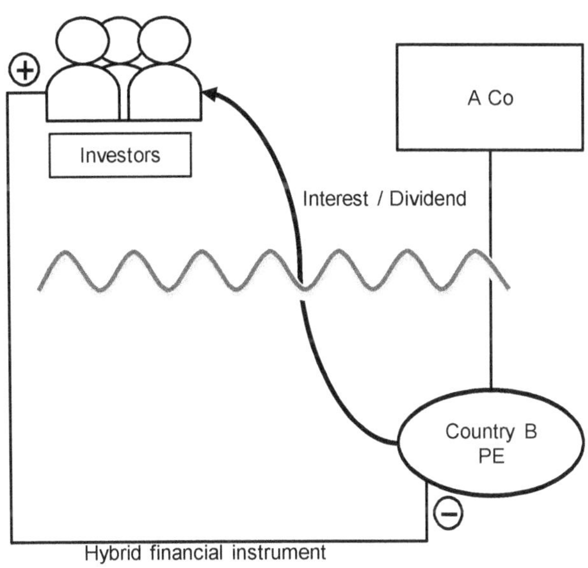

2. The bond is treated as a debt instrument under the laws of Country B and as an equity instrument under the laws of Country A. Country B grants a deduction to the PE for payments made under the bond. Country A treats the payments as a dividend paid by a resident company to a resident shareholder. Country A taxes dividends at the taxpayer's marginal rate but also permits the paying company to attach an "franking credit", which the shareholder can credit against the tax liability on the dividend.

Question

3. Whether an interest payment under the bond falls within the scope of the hybrid financial instrument rule and, if so, whether an adjustment is required to be made in accordance with that rule.

Answer

4. Under Recommendation 2.1, A Co should be prevented from attaching an imputation credit to the payment made under the bond.

5. If Country A does not apply Recommendation 2.1, Country B may be able to deny the PE of A Co a deduction for the interest payment if the investors are related parties or the loan was issued as part of a structured arrangement.

Analysis

Country A should apply Recommendation 2.1 to prevent A Co attaching an imputation credit to the payment on the bond

6. Recommendation 2.1 states that jurisdictions should not grant dividend relief for a deductible payment. Recommendation encourages countries to limit the availability of tax relief on dividends to prevent such tax relief being claimed where the profits out of which the distribution is made have not borne underlying tax. In the present case, the payment made under the bond has been paid out of such pre-tax income because:

(a) the payment was deductible under the laws of Country B; and

(b) while not deductible under Country A law, the profits out of which the payment is made were not subject to tax in Country A (due to the operation of the branch exemption).

The effect of Recommendation 2.1 is therefore that Country A, should prevent A Co from attaching an imputation credit to the payment made under the bond.

A payment made under the financial instrument will give rise to a hybrid mismatch

7. If Country A does not apply Recommendation 2.1 then there is still scope for Country B to apply Recommendation 1 on the grounds that the payment is deductible under the laws of Country B but sheltered from taxation as ordinary income in Country A.

8. As the investors are not related, the hybrid financial instrument rule will only apply if the payment is made under a structured arrangement. In this case the loan itself may not have any features indicating that it was designed to produce a mismatch in tax outcomes. It is possible, however, that the tax benefits of the mismatch were marketed to the original investors in Country A or that the bond was primarily marketed to investors who could take advantage of the mismatch in tax outcomes. If this is the case then the A Co and those investors are likely to be party to the structured arrangement as they can reasonably be expected to be aware of the mismatch and have shared in the value of the tax benefit (through a return on the instrument that was calculated by reference to the benefit of the imputation credit).

Example 2.2

Application of Recommendation 2.2 to a bond lending arrangement

Facts

1. The figure below illustrates a securities loan that is similar to the structure described in **Example 1.32** except that the instrument loaned under the arrangement is a bond rather than a share. B Co is the "borrower" under the arrangement with obligations that include the requirement for B Co to pay A Co the amount of any interest payments that are paid on the underlying bonds (net of any withholding taxes) during the period of the loan (the "manufactured interest payment"). The net economic effect of this arrangement is that A Co continues to be exposed to the full risk and return of holding the bonds, through the obligations owed by B Co under the arrangement.

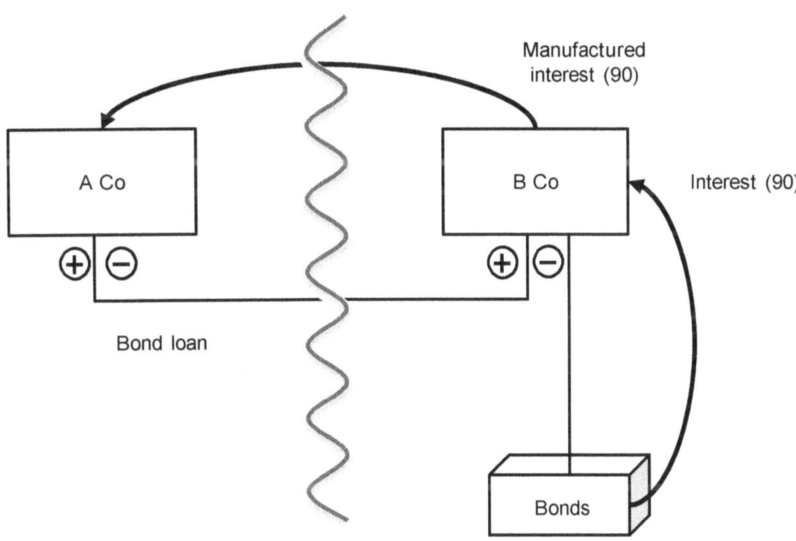

2. A simplified tax calculation showing the net effect of this arrangement is set out below. In this example it is assumed that the payment of 100 of interest on the bond is subject to 10% withholding tax and this tax is creditable against B Co's tax liability. B Co makes a manufactured payment of the interest payment (reduced by withholding tax) to A Co.

A Co	Tax	Book	B Co	Tax	Book
Income			Income		
Manufactured interest	90	90	Interest	90	90
Amounts withheld	10	0	Amounts withheld	10	0
			Expenditure		
			Manufactured interest	(90)	(90)
Net return		**90**	**Net return**		**0**
Taxable income	**100**		**Taxable income**	**10**	
Tax on income (30%)	(30)		Tax on income (30%)	(3)	
Tax credit	10		Tax credit	10	
Tax to pay		(20)	Tax benefit		7
After-tax return		**70**	**After-tax return**		**7**

3. Both A Co and B Co are treated as receiving an interest payment of 100 subject to foreign withholding taxes of 10%. B Co's taxable income (after the payment of the manufactured dividend payment) is 10. Despite taxing only the net income under the arrangement Country B still allows a credit for the whole of the withholding tax thus generating an excess credit that is eligible to bee set-off against Country B tax on other income (or certain other classes of income).

4. Ordinarily it would be expected that a payment of interest under the bond would generate a net taxation (in either Country A or B) of 20 (i.e. 30 of tax payable in the country of residence minus a credit for 10 of withholding tax). Because, however, in this example, both A Co and B Co have claimed tax credits in respect of the same payment the aggregate tax liability for both parties under the arrangement is 13 including a surplus 7 tax credit for B Co which (it is assumed) may be used against other income.

5. In this example the arrangement is not the product of a mismatch, as both Country A and B treat all amounts received under the arrangement as ordinary income, nevertheless the hybrid transfer permits A Co and B Co to double-dip on withholding tax credits to lower their effective tax under the instrument.

Question

6. Whether a securities lending arrangement falls within the scope of Recommendation 2.2 and, if so, to what extent an adjustment is required to be made in accordance with that rule.

Answer

7. The arrangement is a hybrid transfer that does not give rise to a D/NI outcome. Any jurisdiction that grants relief for tax withheld at source on a payment made under a hybrid transfer should restrict the benefit of the relief to the net taxable income of the taxpayer under the arrangement.

The arrangement is a hybrid transfer

8. The securities lending arrangement falls within the definition of a hybrid transfer because, under the laws of Country A, A Co is the owner of the bond and B Co's rights of in the bond are characterised as obligations owed to A Co, while, under the laws of Country B, B Co is the owner of the bond and A Co's ownership rights are treated as obligations of B Co.

Recommendation 2(2) applies to restrict the amount of foreign tax credits under a hybrid transfer

9. Recommendation 2.2 states that, "in order to prevent duplication of tax credits under a hybrid transfer, any jurisdiction that grants relief for tax withheld at source on a payment made under a hybrid transfer should restrict the benefit of such relief in proportion to the net taxable income of the taxpayer under the arrangement."

10. The credit should be allowed in each jurisdiction only up to amount of net income under the arrangement. A simplified tax calculation showing the net effect of these adjustments is set out below.

A Co			B Co		
	Tax	Book		Tax	Book
Income			Income		
Manufactured interest	90	90	Interest	90	90
Amounts withheld	10	0	Amounts withheld	10	0
			Expenditure		
			Manufactured interest	(90)	(90)
Net return		**90**	**Net return**		**0**
Taxable income	**100**		**Taxable income**	**10**	
Tax on income (30%)	(30)		Tax on income (30%)	(3)	
Tax credit	10		Tax credit	3	
Tax to pay		(20)	Tax to pay		0
After-tax return		**70**	**After-tax return**		**0**

11. Limiting the credit to the extent of the taxpayer's net income under the arrangement has no effect on A Co's tax position in this example as A Co's net income from the arrangement is equal to the gross amount of the payment. The calculation continues to allow for to a duplication of credits under the laws of Country B, but only to the extent necessary to shelter the income in respect of the payment that has been withheld at source.

Example 2.3

Co-ordination of hybrid financial instrument rule and Recommendation 2.1

Facts

1. In the example illustrated in the figure below, A Co (a company resident in Country A) owns all the shares in B Co (a company resident in Country B). A Co lends money to B Co under a loan that pays accrued interest every 12 months on 1 October each year. The loan is subordinated to the ordinary creditors of B Co and payments of interest and principal can be suspended in the event B Co fails to meet certain solvency requirements.

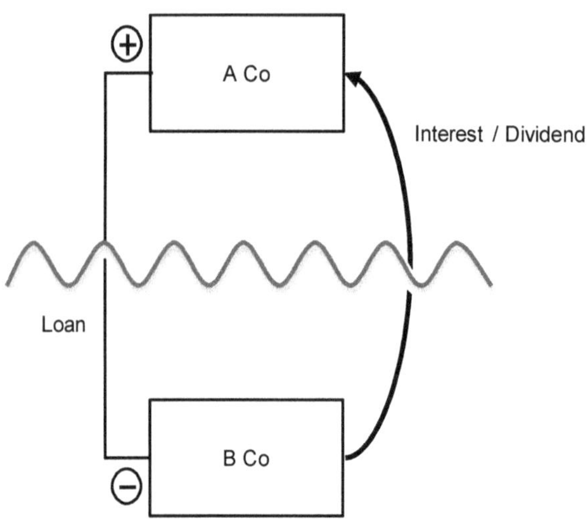

2. The bond is treated as a debt instrument under the laws of Country B but as an equity instrument (i.e. a share) under the laws of Country A. Accordingly interest payments on the loan are treated as dividends under Country A law. Under its domestic law Country A generally exempts foreign dividends.

3. In Year 2 Country B introduces hybrid mismatch rules so that the deduction for the interest payment is denied in that year. One year later Country A amends its domestic law in line with Recommendation 2.1 so that the benefit of a dividend exemption for a deductible payment is no longer available under Country A law.

Question

4. What proportion of the payment is required to be brought into account under the hybrid mismatch rule by A Co and B Co in Years 2 to 4 of the arrangement?

Answer

5. The payer jurisdiction applying the primary response under the hybrid financial instrument rule in a period when the payee jurisdiction introduces domestic changes in accordance with Recommendation 2.1 (the switch-over period), should cease to apply the primary response to the extent the mismatch is neutralised by the introduction of the domestic law changes in the payee jurisdiction. The payer jurisdiction should continue, however, to make the adjustment required under the hybrid financial instrument rule for periods prior to the switchover period. Accordingly:

(a) Country B should deny B Co a deduction for a payment to the extent it gives rise to a mismatch in an accounting period that ends on or before the effective date of the domestic law changes in Country A but should grant B Co relief for any payment made during the switch-over period to the extent the mismatch is neutralised due to the operation of the new rules in Country A.

(b) Country A will apply the domestic law changes to the payment at the time it is treated as received although Country A should take into account the effect of any adjustments that were made under the hybrid financial instrument rule in Country B for periods ending on or before the effective date of the domestic law changes in Country A.

Analysis

No application of the hybrid financial instrument rule where mismatch is neutralised consistent with Recommendation 2.1

6. A payment under a hybrid financial instrument will not be treated as giving rise to a D/NI outcome if the mismatch is neutralised in the counterparty jurisdiction by a specific rule designed to align the tax treatment of the payment with tax policy outcomes applicable to an instrument of that nature. Specific rules of this nature include any rules in the payee jurisdiction, consistent with Recommendation 2.1, that limit the availability of a dividend exemption or equivalent tax relief to payments that are not deductible for tax purposes. Accordingly, if and when Country A introduces rules that deny the benefit of an exemption for a deductible dividend payment, Country B should cease to apply the primary response under the hybrid financial instrument rule.

Co-ordination between the hybrid financial instrument rule and Recommendation 2.1

7. Complications in the application of the rule and a risk of double taxation could arise, however, in situations where the payee jurisdiction applies the rules under Recommendation 2.1 to a payment that has already been subject to adjustment under the hybrid financial instrument rule in the payer jurisdiction. While the hybrid financial instrument rule will not apply to a payment that is included in ordinary income under the laws of Country A, equally, in order to minimise disruption to the rules in Country B and to avoid the need to calculate split periods or re-open old tax returns, Country B should

continue to apply the hybrid financial instrument rule to any payment in a period prior to the switch-over period.

8. A table setting out the effect of these adjustments in Years 2 to 4 is set out below. The table shows the accrued interest under the loan in each calendar year and the income tax consequences applying to payments made under the loan. In this table it is assumed that the interest payment is 100 each year and that B Co and A Co have no other income or expenditure. Country B and Country A both calculate income and expenditure for tax purposes on a calendar year basis.

	Country A A Co			Country B B Co			Total
		Tax	Book		Tax	Book	
Year 2	Income			Income			
	Dividend	0	100	Operating income	100	100	
				Expenditure			
				Interest	0	(100)	
	Net return		100	Net return		0	100
	Taxable income	0		Taxable income	100		100

	Country A A Co			Country B B Co			Total
		Tax	Book		Tax	Book	
Year 3	Income			Income			
	Dividend	75	100	Operating income	100	100	
				Expenditure			
				Interest	(100)	(100)	
	Net return		100	Net return		0	100
	Taxable income	75		Taxable income	0		75

	Country A A Co			Country B B Co			Total
		Tax	Book		Tax	Book	
Year 4	Income			Income			
	Dividend	100	75	Operating income	100	100	
				Expenditure			
				Interest	0	(100)	
	Net return		**75**	**Net return**		**0**	**75**
	Taxable income	**100**		**Taxable income**	**0**		**100**

9. In Year 2, Recommendation 2.1 has not yet been introduced into Country A law so that a deduction for the entire amount of the interest payment is denied under Country B law.

10. In Year 3, Recommendation 2.1 is introduced into Country A law from the beginning of that year.

(a) Country B does not apply the hybrid financial instrument rule in Year 3 as the entire amount of the payment for that period will be subject to taxation as ordinary income in Country A;

(b) The amount of the income included under Recommendation 2.1 should not include a payment to the extent it has been already subject to adjustment under the hybrid financial instrument rule in a prior period. Because Country B allows for interest expenses to be claimed on an accrual basis, a deduction for 25% of the interest payment has already been denied by Country B in the prior year (Year 2), accordingly the amount Country A treats as a deductible dividend should be reduced by the same proportion.

11. In Year 4 the loan matures and the final payment of accrued interest on the loan is paid on 1 October of Year 4. The hybrid financial instrument rule does not apply in Country B as the interest payment will be caught by Recommendation 2.1. The exemption is denied for the full amount of the interest payment (100) in Country A, effectively triggering an additional 25 of taxable income in the hands of B Co and reversing out the timing advantage that arose in the previous year due to the differences in the timing of the recognition of payments.

Example 3.1

Disregarded hybrid payment structure using a disregarded entity and a hybrid loan

Facts

1. In the example illustrated in the figure below, A Co establishes B Co 1 as the holding company for its operating subsidiary (B Co 2). B Co 1 is a hybrid entity (i.e. an entity that is treated as a separate entity for tax purposes in Country B but as a disregarded entity under Country A law). B Co 2 is treated as a separate taxable entity under Country A and B laws.

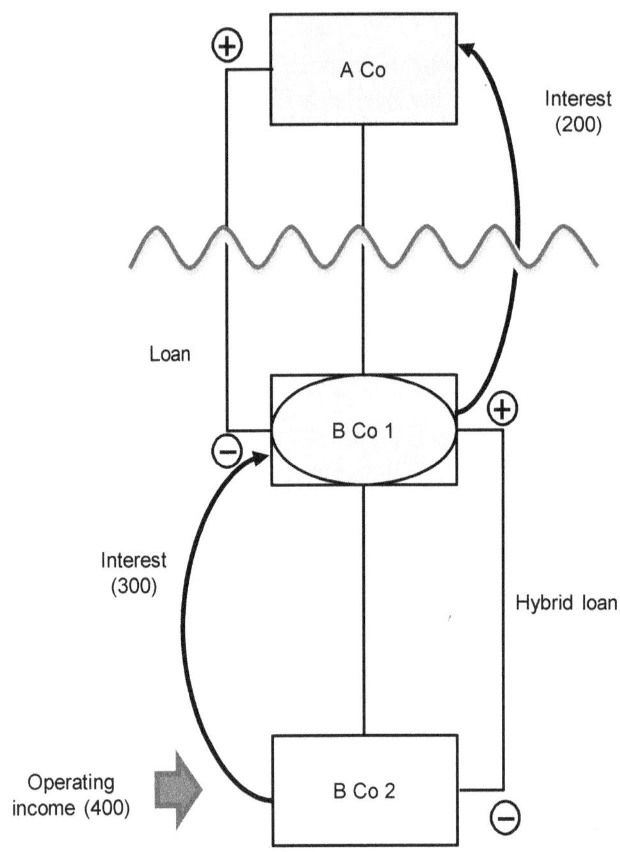

2. B Co 1 borrows money from A Co. B Co 1 on-lends that money under a hybrid loan. Interest payments on the loan are treated as ordinary income under Country B law but treated as exempt dividends under Country A law. A table setting out the combined net income position for A Co and the Country B Group is set out below.

Country A A Co			Country B B Co 1		
	Tax	Book		Tax	Book
Income			Income		
Interest paid by B Co 1	0	200	Interest paid by B Co 2	300	300
			Expenditure		
			Interest paid to A Co	(200)	(200)
			Net return		100
			Taxable income	100	
			B Co 2		
			Income		
			Operating Income	400	400
			Expenditure		
			Interest under hybrid loan	(300)	(300)
Net return		200	Net return		100
Taxable income	0		Taxable income	100	

3. Because B Co 1 is a disregarded entity under Country A law, the interest on the loan between A Co and B Co 1 is disregarded for tax purposes and does not give rise to taxable income in Country A. Although the payment of interest on the hybrid loan is recognised under Country A law it is treated as an exempt dividend for tax purposes and is not taken into account in calculating A Co's taxable income for the period. Accordingly A Co recognises no taxable income under this structure.

4. Under Country B law B Co 2 has 400 of operating income and is entitled to a deduction of 300 on the hybrid loan. B Co 1 recognises the interest payment on the hybrid loan but is further entitled to a deduction of 200 on the disregarded interest payment to A Co. Accordingly, in aggregate, the Country B Group recognises 200 of taxable income under this structure on a net return of 400.

Question

5. Are the tax outcomes described above subject to adjustment under the hybrid mismatch rules?

Answer

6. For both Country A and Country B, the hybrid financial instrument rule will not apply to the interest payment on the hybrid loan because the interest payment does not give rise to a D/NI outcome (as it is included in income under the laws of Country B).

However, the fact that B Co 1 is disregarded as a separate entity under the laws of Country B means that the deductible interest payment that B Co 1 makes to A Co is disregarded under Country A law and, accordingly, will be caught by the disregarded hybrid payments rule in Recommendation 3.

7. In the event that Country B does not apply the primary rule under Recommendation 3.1 to the interest payment made by B Co 1, then Country A should include the full amount of that interest payment in ordinary income under the defensive rule set out at Recommendation 3.2.

Analysis

Interest payment on the hybrid loan is not subject to adjustment under the hybrid financial instrument rule

8. Although the loan can be described as *hybrid* in the sense that payments on the loan are treated as deductible interest under the laws of Country B and exempt dividends under the laws of Country A, the loan does not give rise to a mismatch falling within the hybrid financial instrument rule because the interest is included in income under the laws of Country B.

The disregarded hybrid payments rule will apply to deny B Co 1 a deduction for the disregarded interest payment

9. In this case B Co 1 is a hybrid payer because both the payer and the payment are disregarded under the laws of Country A. Accordingly Country B should apply the primary recommendation to deny B Co 1 a deduction for the interest payment to the extent that payment exceeds dual inclusion income. The payment of interest on the hybrid loan does not constitute dual inclusion income because it is not included in ordinary income under the laws of Country A. Therefore the full amount of the interest deduction should be denied under Country B law. The table below illustrates the net effect of this adjustment.

Country A A Co	Tax	Book	Country B B Co 1	Tax	Book
Income			Income		
Interest paid by B Co 1	0	200	Interest paid by B Co 2	300	300
			Expenditure		
			Interest paid to A Co	0	(200)
			Net return		**100**
			Taxable income	**300**	
			B Co 2		
			Income		
			Operating Income	400	400
			Expenditure		
			Interest under hybrid loan	(300)	(300)
Net return		**200**	**Net return**		**100**
Taxable income	**0**		**Taxable income**	**100**	

10. B Co 1 is denied a deduction for the entire amount of the disregarded interest payment. The net effect of the adjustment is that the entire return under the arrangement is brought into account under Country B law.

In the event Country B does not make any adjustment A Co will treat the interest payment as ordinary income

11. If the disregarded hybrid payments rule is not applied to the payment in Country B then Country A should apply the rule to require the interest payment to be included in ordinary income. The table below illustrates the net effect of Country A making an adjustment under the disregarded hybrid payments rule.

Country A A Co	Tax	Book	Country B B Co 1	Tax	Book
Income			Income		
Interest paid by B Co 2	200	200	Interest paid by B Co 2	300	300
			Expenditure		
			Interest paid to A Co	(200)	(200)
			Net return		100
			Taxable income	100	
			B Co 2		
			Income		
			Operating Income	400	400
			Expenditure		
			Interest under hybrid loan	(300)	(300)
Net return		200	**Net return**		100
Taxable income	200		**Taxable income**	100	

12. A Co is required to bring into account, as ordinary income, the full amount of the interest payment so that the taxable income of A Co and B Co under the arrangement is equal to their net return under the arrangement.

Implementation solutions

13. B Co 1 is likely to prepare separate accounts showing all the amounts of income and expenditure that are subject to tax under Country B law. Country B could require B Co 1 to maintain a cumulative total of all the items of income that were dual inclusion income and prohibit B Co 1 from claiming deductions for a disregarded payment to the extent they exceeded this cumulative amount.

14. A Co will have information (obtained under Country B law) on the deductions that B Co 1 has claimed in Country B for intra-group payments and information (under Country A law) of the amount of B Co 1's net income that is attributed to A Co. Country A could require A Co to recognise ordinary income to the extent the former amount (the amount of deductions claimed by B Co 1 for disregarded payments) exceeds the latter (the amount of B Co 1's net income that is attributed to A Co under Country A law).

Example 3.2

Disregarded hybrid payment using consolidation regime and tax grouping

Facts

1. In the example set out in the figure below, A Co 1 forms a consolidated group with its wholly-owned subsidiary A Co 2. The effect of tax consolidation under Country law is that all transactions and payments between group members are disregarded for tax purposes. A Co 2 establishes a PE in Country B. The PE holds all of the shares in B Co. The PE is consolidated with B Co for tax purposes under Country B law.

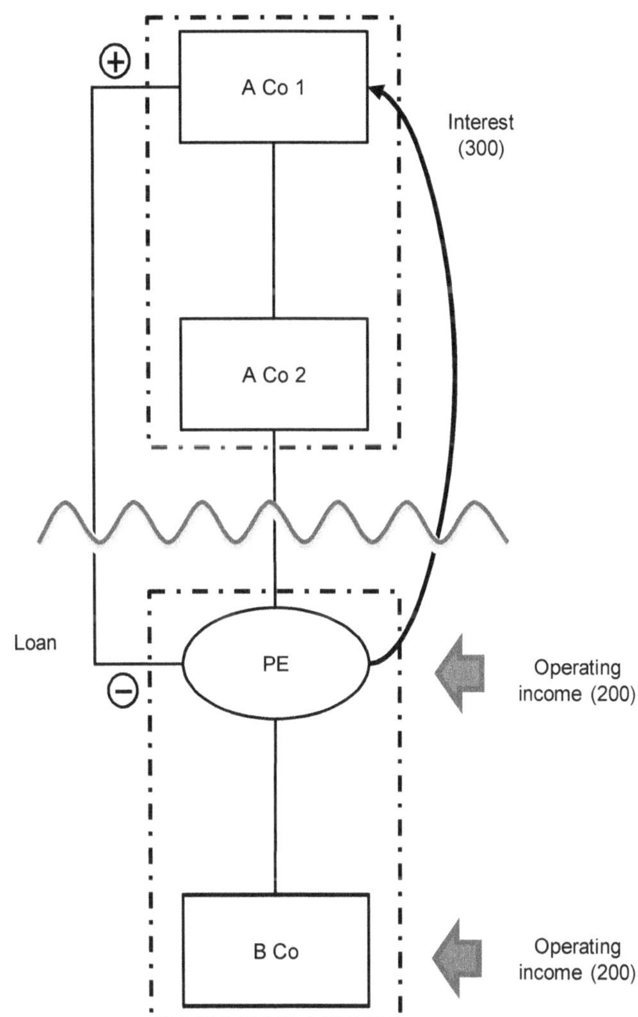

2. A Co 2 borrows money from A Co 1. This loan is attributed to A Co 2's PE in Country B. The payment of interest on the loan is deductible under Country B law but is not recognised by A Co 1. A table setting out the combined net income position for Country A Group and Country B Group is set out below.

Country A A Co 1			Country B A Co 2 and B Co combined		
	Tax	Book		Tax	Book
Income			Income		
Interest paid by A Co 2	0	300	Operating income of A Co 2 and B Co	400	400
Operating income of A Co 2	200	0			
			Expenditure		
			Interest paid by A Co 2 to A Co 1 under loan	(300)	(300)
Net return		**300**	**Net return**		**100**
Taxable income	**200**		**Taxable income**	**100**	
Tax on income (30%)	(60)		Tax on income (30%)	(30)	
Tax to pay		(60)	Tax to pay		(30)
After-tax return		**240**	**After-tax return**		**70**

3. The only item of income recognised for tax purposes under Country A law is the operating income of the A Co 2's PE. This income is subject to tax at a 30% rate under Country A law. Under Country B law the 300 of interest paid by A Co 2 to A Co 1 is treated as deductible against the income of the Country B Group leaving the group with net taxable income of $100 which is subject to Country B tax at a 30% rate. The net effect of this structure is, therefore, that the entities in the AB Group derive a total net return of 400 but have taxable income of 300.

Question

4. Are the tax outcomes described above subject to adjustment under the hybrid mismatch rules?

Answer

5. Country B should apply the hybrid financial instrument rule to deny a deduction for the interest paid by A Co 2 to A Co 1 if the mismatch in the tax treatment of the interest payment can be attributed to the terms of the instrument between the parties. If the interest payment is not treated, under Country B law, as subject to adjustment under the hybrid financial instrument rule then Country B will apply the disregarded hybrid payments rule to deny A Co 2 a deduction for the interest payment to the extent the interest expense exceeds dual inclusion income.

6. In the event the deduction for the interest payment is not subject to adjustment under Country B law then Country A should treat the interest payment as included in income to the extent it exceeds dual inclusion income.

Analysis

Interest payment is potentially subject to adjustment under the hybrid financial instrument rule

7. Under Country B law, the interest payment is a deductible payment to a related party that gives rise to a mismatch in tax outcomes and will fall within the scope of the hybrid financial instrument rule if the mismatch can be attributed to differences in the tax treatment of the loan under the laws of Country A and B.

8. The fact that the loan and the interest payment itself may not be recognised under County A law, due to the operation of the tax consolidation regime in Country A, does not impact on whether the interest payment can be subject to adjustment under the hybrid financial instrument rule in Country B. The identification of a mismatch as a hybrid mismatch under a financial instrument is primarily a legal question that requires an analysis of the general rules for determining the character, amount and timing of payments under a financial instrument in the payer and payee jurisdictions. The hybrid financial instrument rule is designed so that it is not necessary for the taxpayer or tax administration to know precisely how the payments under a financial instrument have actually been taken into account in the calculation of the counterparty's taxable income in order to apply the rule.

9. The table below illustrates the net effect on the Country A Group and Country B Group of denying a deduction for the interest payment under the hybrid financial instrument rule.

Country A A Co 1			Country B A Co 2 and B Co combined		
	Tax	Book		Tax	Book
Income			Income		
Interest paid by A Co 2	0	300	Operating income of A Co 2 and B Co	400	400
Operating income of A Co 2	200	0			
			Expenditure		
			Interest paid by A Co 2 to A Co 1 under loan	0	(300)
Net return		**300**	**Net return**		**100**
Taxable income	**200**		**Taxable income**	**400**	
Tax on income (30%)	(60)		Tax on income (30%)	(120)	
Credit for taxes paid by A Co 2 in Country B	60				
Tax to pay		(0)	Tax to pay		(120)
After-tax return		**300**	**After-tax return**		**(20)**

10. The effect of Country B denying a deduction for the full amount of the interest payment made by A Co 2 is that all the income arising under the arrangement will be subjcct to tax under Country B law. The tax charge triggered in Country B by the

adjustment under the hybrid financial instrument rule means that A Co 1 benefits from a credit for taxes paid by A Co 2.

The disregarded hybrid payments rule will apply to deny the Country B Group a deduction for the interest payment

11. If the interest payment is not treated, under the laws of Country B as subject to adjustment under the hybrid financial instrument rule then Country B should apply the disregarded hybrid payments rule to deny the deduction for the interest payment if the payment falls within the description of a disregarded payment made by a hybrid payer.

12. In this case A Co 2 is a hybrid payer making a disregarded payment because it is a member of the same group under the tax consolidation regime in Country A and that regime treats all transactions and payments between consolidated group members as disregarded for tax purposes. Accordingly Country B should apply the primary recommendation to deny a deduction for the interest payment made by A Co 2 to A Co 1 to the extent that payment exceeds dual inclusion income. The table below illustrates the net effect of Country B making an adjustment under the disregarded hybrid payments rule for both groups.

Country A A Co 1			Country B A Co 2 and B Co combined		
	Tax	**Book**		**Tax**	**Book**
Income			Income		
Interest paid by A Co 2	0	300	Operating income of A Co 2 and B Co	400	400
Operating income of A Co 2	200	0			
			Expenditure		
			Interest paid by A Co 2 to A Co 1 under loan	(200)	(300)
Net return		**300**	**Net return**		**100**
Taxable income	**200**		**Taxable income**	**200**	
Tax on income (30%)	(60)		Tax on income (30%)	(60)	
Credit for taxes paid by A Co 1 in Country B	0				
Tax to pay		(60)	Tax to pay		(60)
After-tax return		**240**	**After-tax return**		**40**

13. A Co 2 is denied a deduction for the disregarded interest payment (300) to the extent the payment exceeds dual inclusion income (200). The net effect of the adjustment is that the full amount of the income under the arrangement is brought into account under Country A and B laws.

In the event Country B does not make any adjustment A Co 1 will treat the amount that gives rise to a DD outcome as included in income under Country A law

14. If the disregarded hybrid payments rule is not applied to the payment in Country B then Country A should apply the rule to require the payment to be included in ordinary income to the extent of the mismatch. The table below illustrates the net effect of Country A making an adjustment under the disregarded hybrid payments rule.

Country A A Co 1			Country B A Co 2 and B Co combined		
	Tax	Book		Tax	Book
Income			Income		
Interest paid by A Co 2	100	300	Operating income of A Co 2 and B Co	400	400
Operating income of A Co 2	200	0			
			Expenditure		
			Interest paid by A Co 2 to A Co 1 under loan	(300)	(300)
Net return		**300**	**Net return**		**100**
Taxable income	**300**		**Taxable income**	**100**	
Tax on income (30%)	(90)		Tax on income (30%)	(30)	
Credit for taxes paid by A Co 1 in Country B	0				
Tax to pay		(90)	Tax to pay		(30)
After-tax return		**210**	**After-tax return**		**70**

15. A Co 1 is required to bring into account, as ordinary income, the amount by which the interest deduction (300) exceeds A Co 2's dual inclusion income (200). The net effect of the adjustment is that the full amount of the income under the arrangement is brought into account under Country A and B laws.

Implementation solutions

16. Country B is likely to require A Co 2 to prepare separate accounts for the PE showing all the amounts of income and expenditure that are subject to tax under Country B law. Country B could prohibit an entity in the position of A Co 2 from utilising the benefit of the PE loss to the extent the PE has made deductible payments that were disregarded under Country A law. This solution may require further transaction specific rules that prevent A Co 2 entering into arrangements to stream non-dual inclusion income to the PE to soak-up unused losses.

17. The Country A Group will have information on the deductions that A Co 2 has claimed in Country B for intra-group payments and the amount of the PE's loss as calculated under Country B law. Country A could require a taxpayer in the position of A Co 1 to recognise as ordinary income in each accounting period, A Co 2's deductible intra-group payments to the extent they gave rise to a net loss for Country B tax purposes. This solution may require further transaction specific adjustments to the calculation of the

PE's net loss under Country B law which are designed to back-out material items that were treated as income under Country B law but would not be included under Country A law.

Example 4.1

Use of reverse hybrid by a tax exempt entity

Facts

1. In the example illustrated in the figure below, B Co is an entity incorporated in Country B that is treated as transparent for Country B tax purposes. Entities such as B Co are required under Country B law to maintain a shareholder register which must be made available to members of the public on request. In this case, B Co is wholly-owned by A Co, which treats B Co as a separate taxable person. A Co is exempt from tax under Country A law.

2. Borrower Co (a company resident in Country B) borrows money from B Co on arm's length and standard commercial terms and at a market interest rate. The arrangement is not marketed to Borrower Co as a tax-advantaged financing arrangement and Borrower Co is not provided with any information about the owners of B Co. The interest payments on the loan are deductible for the purposes of Country B law but not included in income by either B Co or A Co.

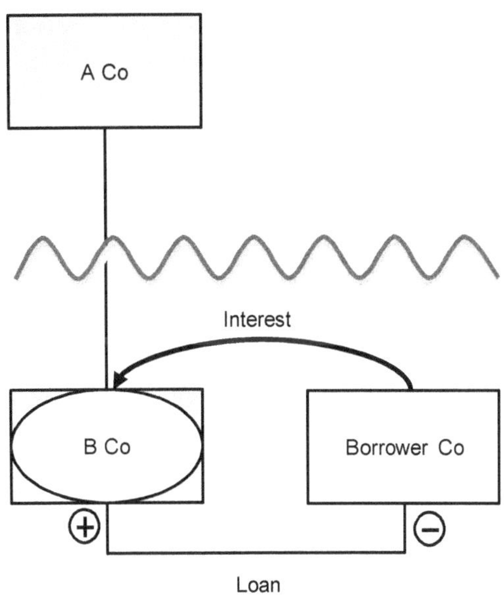

Question

3. Are the interest payments made by Borrower Co to B Co caught by the reverse hybrid rule?

Answer

4. The payments are not caught by the reverse hybrid rule because the mismatch in tax outcomes is not a hybrid mismatch. Furthermore the arrangement is not within the scope of the reverse hybrid rule because Borrower Co, A Co and B Co are not part of the same control group and Borrower Co is not party to a structured arrangement.

Analysis

Mismatch is not a hybrid mismatch

5. In this case the receipt of the interest payment is not recognised under the laws of either Country A or B and therefore the payment gives rise to a D/NI outcome, however the mismatch will not be treated as a hybrid mismatch unless the payment would have been included in ordinary income if it had been made directly to the investor.

6. Unlike in the hybrid financial instrument rule, which applies whenever the terms of the instrument were sufficient to bring about a mismatch in tax outcomes, the reverse hybrid rule will not apply unless the payment attributed to the investor would have been included as ordinary income if it had been paid directly to the investor (i.e. the interposition of the reverse hybrid must have been necessary to bring about the mismatch in tax outcomes). In this case, where income is allocated by a reverse hybrid to a tax exempt entity, the payment would not have been taxable even if it had been made directly to the investor and the reverse hybrid rule should therefore not apply to deny the deduction.

Arrangement is not in scope

7. If A Co were not a tax exempt entity under the laws of Country A, so that the interest payment *would* have been included in ordinary income if it had been made directly to A Co, then mismatch in tax outcomes would be treated as giving rise to a hybrid mismatch. As Borrower Co is not part of the same control group as A Co and B Co, the hybrid mismatch would only fall within the scope of the reverse hybrid rule under Country B law if it was made under a structured arrangement and Borrower Co was a party to that structured arrangement.

8. The facts and circumstances of this case would *prima facie* indicate a structured arrangement between A Co and B Co. In particular, the use of B Co as single purpose entity to make this loan appears to be an additional step inserted into the lending arrangement to produce the mismatch in tax outcomes. Borrower Co, however, should not be treated as a party to that structured arrangement, unless it (or any member of Borrower Co's control group) obtained a benefit under the hybrid mismatch or had sufficient information about the arrangement to be aware of the fact that it gave rise to a mismatch.

9. In this case, the loan is on arm's length and standard commercial terms and Borrower Co pays a market rate of interest. While Borrower Co might be aware (or in certain cases should be aware) of B Co's tax transparency, Borrower Co would not be expected, as part of its ordinary commercial due diligence, to take into account the tax treatment of A Co or whether the interest payment will be treated as ordinary income under the laws of Country A when borrowing money on standard terms from an unrelated party. In this case, in particular, Borrower Co derives no benefit from the mismatch and is not provided with information that would make it aware of the fact that the payment gives

rise to a mismatch in tax outcomes. Importantly, the test for whether a person is a party to structured arrangement is not intended to impose an obligation on that person to undertake additional due diligence on a commercial transaction over and above what would be expected of a reasonable and prudent person. Accordingly, even if A Co were not treated as an exempt entity under the laws of Country A, Borrower Co should not be treated as party to any structured arrangement between B Co and A Co.

10. In contrast, however, and consistent with the analysis in, **Example 10.5**, if Borrower Co was originally approached by A Co for a loan and A Co proposed structuring the loan through a reverse hybrid in order to secure an improved tax outcome, the entire financing arrangement, including the loan to Borrower Co, would be treated as part of a single structured arrangement and Borrower Co will be treated as a party to that arrangement provided it had sufficient involvement in the design of the arrangement to understand how it had been structured and to anticipate what its tax effects would be.

Example 4.2

Application of Recommendation 4 to payments that are partially excluded from income

Facts

1. In the example illustrated in the figure below, two individuals, one resident in Country A (Individual A) and one in Country B (Individual B) intend to make a loan to A Co, a company wholly owned by Individual A. Rather than make the loan directly, A and B contribute equity to B Co, an entity incorporated in Country B. B Co loans money to A Co and A Co makes a deductible interest payment on the loan.

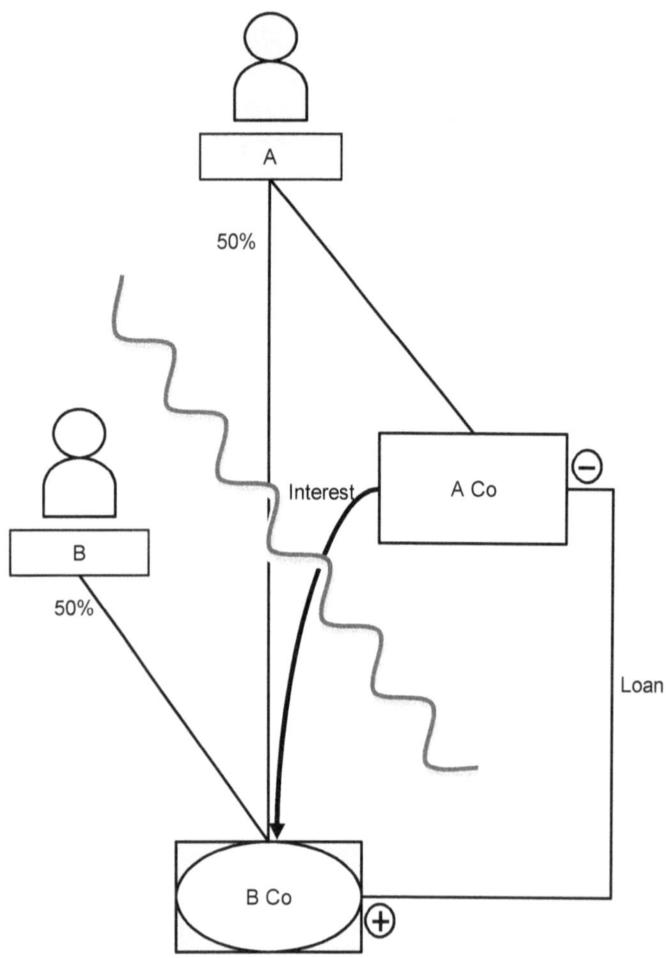

2. Under Country B law half the payment is attributed to Individual A and is exempt from tax as foreign source income of a non-resident. The other half of the payment is attributed to Individual B and is subject to tax at the full marginal rate applicable to interest income. Country A has implemented the hybrid financial instrument rules.

Question

3. To what extent is the interest payment made by A Co to B Co caught by the reverse hybrid rule in Country A.

Answer

4. The interest payment is made to a reverse hybrid. The payment of interest is deductible under the laws of the payer jurisdiction but the allocation of half the interest payment to a non-resident means that the payment is not fully included in ordinary income under the laws of Country B.

5. Provided the interest payment allocated to A would have been taxable if it had been made directly, then Country A should apply Recommendation 4 to the interest payment to deny A Co a deduction for half the interest payment.

Analysis

B Co is a reverse hybrid

6. A reverse hybrid is any person that is treated as transparent under the laws of the jurisdiction where it is established but as a separate entity by its investor. In this case the establishment jurisdiction is Country B (the country where B Co is incorporated). B Co is a resident taxpayer for Country B purposes and is treated as an ordinary company under the laws of Country A. However, under the laws of the jurisdiction where it is established, B Co is entitled to claim the benefit of an exemption from foreign source interest if that interest is allocated or attributed to a non-resident investor. This type of regime falls within the definition of a transparent regime because the laws of Country B permit or require B Co to allocate or attribute ordinary income to an investor (Individual A) and that allocation or attribution has the effect that the payment is subject to tax under the laws of the establishment jurisdiction at the investor's marginal rate. The allocation of the payment to individual A has no impact on A's tax treatment in Country A.

Payment gives rise to a partial D/NI outcome

7. A D/NI outcome will arise in respect of a payment to a reverse hybrid to the extent that the payment is deductible under the laws of one jurisdiction (the payer jurisdiction) and not included in ordinary income by a taxpayer under the laws of any other jurisdiction where the payment is treated as being received (the payee jurisdiction). In this case only half the payment is included in ordinary income under Country B law (and no amount of the payment is included in income under Country A law).

8. The adjustment under the reverse hybrid rule should result in an outcome that is proportionate and that does not lead to double taxation. In this case the payer jurisdiction should only deny a deduction for that part of the payment that is exempt from taxation under the laws of the establishment jurisdiction.

Arrangement is in scope

9. In this case the payer (A Co), the reverse hybrid (B Co) and the investor (A) are all part of the same control group because A holds at least 50% of them both. Even if A's holding in B Co was lower than 50%, the example suggests that B Co was inserted into the structure in order to produce the mismatch in tax outcomes. A Co would generally be considered a party to this structured arrangement as it is wholly-owned by one of the people responsible for the design of the arrangement.

Example 4.3

Recommendation 4 and payments that are included under a CFC regime

Facts

1. In the example illustrated in the figure below, A Co is a company resident in Country A which owns all of the shares in B Co (a company resident in Country B). B Co has established a reverse hybrid under the laws of Country D (D Co). D Co receives a services payment from C Co (a company resident in Country C and member of the same group).

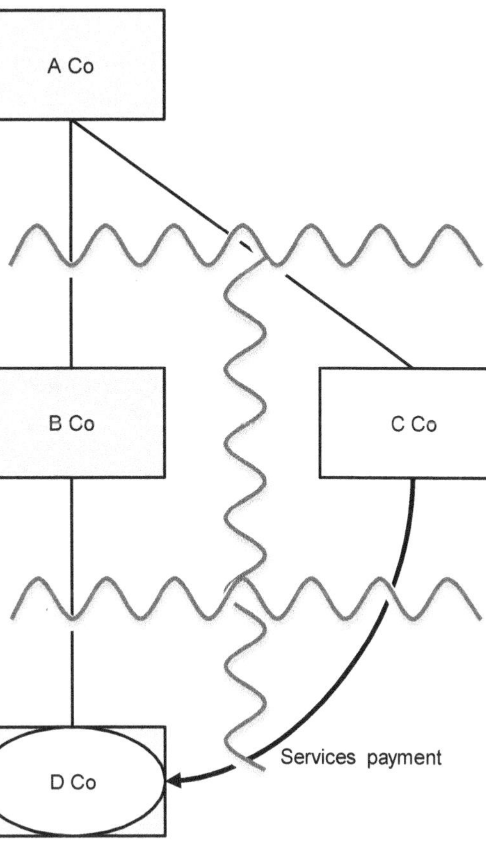

2. Country A's CFC regime treats services income paid by a related party as attributable income and subjects such income to taxation at the full marginal rate applicable to income of that nature. D Co has no other items of income or expenditure.

Question

3. Does Recommendation 4 apply in Country C to deny the deduction for the services payment made by C Co to D Co?

Answer

4. The services payment does not give rise to a D/NI outcome as the payment is included in income under laws of Country A. Provided C Co can demonstrate to the tax authorities in Country C that such a payment has been attributed to A Co under the Country A CFC regime and will be subject to tax as ordinary income without the benefit of any deduction, credit or other tax relief then the services payment should not be treated as giving rise to a D/NI outcome under Recommendation 4.

Analysis

D/NI outcome in respect of a payment to a reverse hybrid

5. A D/NI outcome will arise in respect of a payment to a reverse hybrid to the extent that the payment is deductible under the laws of one jurisdiction (the payer jurisdiction) and not included in ordinary income by a taxpayer under the laws of any other jurisdiction where the payment is treated as being received (the payee jurisdiction). Accordingly if the services payment is brought into account as ordinary income in at least one jurisdiction then there will be no mismatch for the rule to apply to.

6. A payment that has been fully attributed to the ultimate parent of the group under a CFC regime and has been subject to tax at the full rate should be treated as having been included in ordinary income for the purposes of the reverse hybrid rule. In this case A Co includes the full amount of the intra-group services fee as ordinary income under its CFC rules. D Co has no other income so no question arises as to whether the full amount of such income has been attributed under A Co's CFC rules. The reverse hybrid rule therefore does not apply in such a case because the payment has not given rise to a mismatch in tax outcomes.

Example 4.4

Interaction between Recommendation 4 and Recommendation 6

Facts

1. In the example illustrated in the figure below, A Co 1 and A Co 2 are companies resident in Country A. A Co 1 owns all the shares in A Co 2 and in B Co (a company resident in Country B).

2. A Co 2 has established C Co in Country C. C Co is treated as a disregarded entity for the purposes of Country C law but as a separate company for Country A purposes. Country A does not have any CFC or equivalent rules that would treat interest derived by a foreign controlled entity as attributable to its shareholder for tax purposes.

3. B Co has established a hybrid subsidiary in Country D (D Co 1). D Co 1 is consolidated for tax purposes with D Co 2 (another subsidiary of B Co.). C Co makes a loan to D Co 1. Country B and Country D have both introduced hybrid mismatch rules.

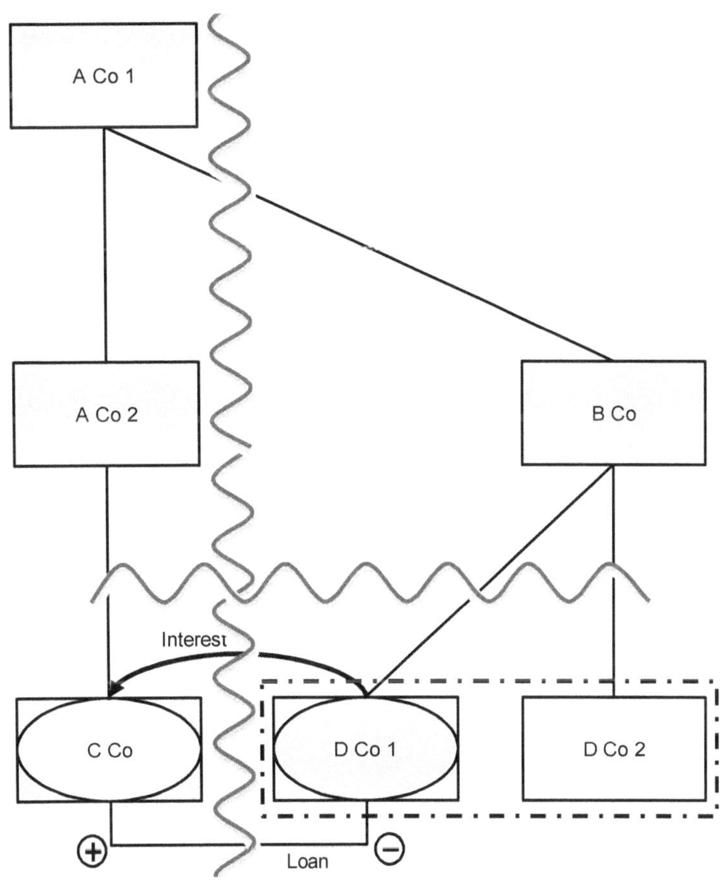

Question

4. Does Recommendation 4 (reverse hybrid rule) or Recommendation 6 (deductible hybrid payments rule) apply in Country B or D to deny the deduction for the interest payment under the loan?

Answer

5. The interest payment is made to a reverse hybrid and will give rise to a hybrid mismatch under Recommendation 4. Both B Co and D Co 1 are treated as payers under the hybrid mismatch rule and therefore both should deny a deduction for the interest payment under Recommendation 4.

6. As Recommendation 4 operates to deny the deduction in both Country B and D there is no scope for the application of the deductible hybrid payments rule under Recommendation 6.

Analysis

C Co is a reverse hybrid

7. A reverse hybrid is any person that is treated as transparent under the laws of the jurisdiction where it is established but as a separate entity by its investor (A Co 2). In this case the establishment jurisdiction is Country C (the country where C Co is incorporated). C Co is disregarded for Country C tax purposes, which means that all the income of C Co is treated as being derived directly by A Co 2 (its immediate parent). C Co is treated as a separate entity for tax purposes under Country A law so that the income allocated to A Co 2 under Country C law is not taken into account as ordinary income in Country A.

Payment gives rise to a D/NI outcome in Country D and Country B

8. A D/NI outcome will arise in respect of a payment to a reverse hybrid to the extent that the payment is deductible under the laws of one jurisdiction (the payer jurisdiction) and is not included in ordinary income by a taxpayer under the laws of any other jurisdiction where the payment is treated as being received (the payee jurisdiction).

9. As the payment is treated as made in both Country D and Country B both jurisdictions should apply the reverse hybrid rule. The tax treatment of the payment in the other payer jurisdiction is not relevant to the question of whether the payment gives rise to a D/NI outcome under the laws of the jurisdiction that is applying the rules.

Mismatch is a hybrid mismatch

10. A payment made to a reverse hybrid that gives rise to a D/NI outcome will be subject to adjustment under the reverse hybrid rule if that D/NI outcome would not have arisen had the payment been made directly to the investor. The identification of a mismatch as a hybrid mismatch under a reverse hybrid structure requires an analysis of how the payment would have been taxed under the laws of the investor jurisdiction. A payment of interest to C Co will be treated as giving rise to a mismatch if that payment would ordinarily have been taxable under Country A law.

11. Furthermore, in order to prevent a reverse hybrid being used to circumvent the operation of the hybrid financial instrument rule, the reverse hybrid rule will apply if an

interest payment made to A Co 2 would have been subject to adjustment under the primary rule in Recommendation 1. If, for example, the loan would have been treated as an equity instrument (i.e. a share) under Country A law and payments of interest treated as exempt dividends then D Co 1 and B Co will continue to deny the deduction for the payment.

No scope for the application of Recommendation 6

12. Because the effect of Recommendation 4 is to deny a deduction for the interest payment, the arrangement does not give rise to a DD outcome that falls within Recommendation 6.

Example 6.1

Accounting for timing and valuation differences

Facts

1. In the example illustrated in the figure below, A Co owns all of the shares in a hybrid subsidiary in Country B (B Co 1). B Co 1 has borrowed money from a local bank and holds depreciable property. B Co 1 also owns all of the shares in B Co 2.

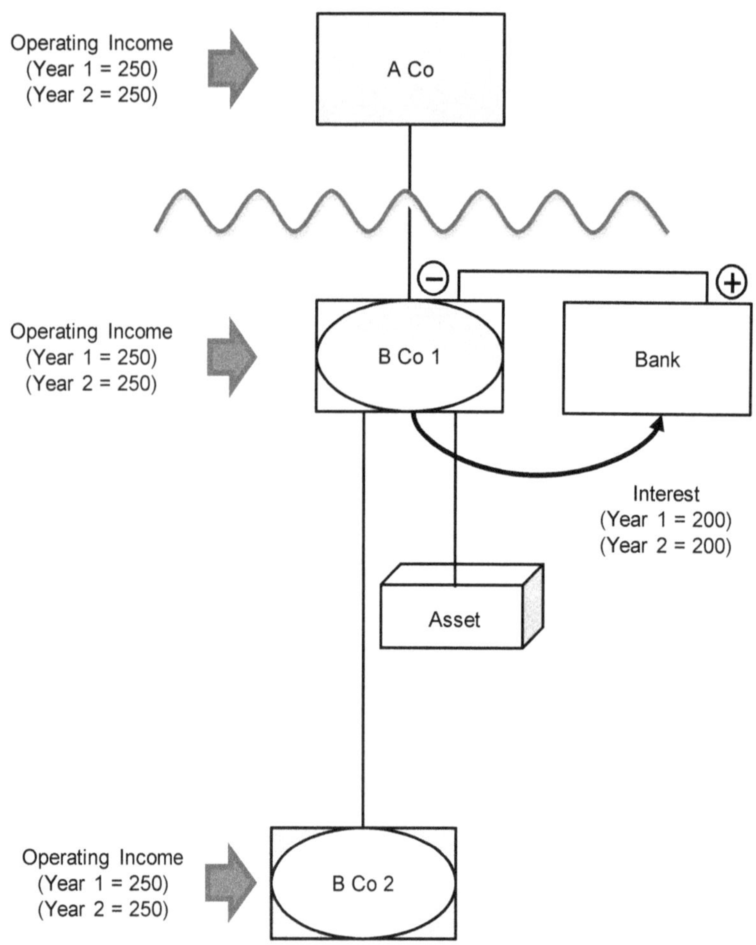

2. B Co 1 is treated as a disregarded entity under Country A law but as a resident taxpayer in Country B so that all of B Co 1's income and expenditure are fully taxable in both countries. B Co 2 is a reverse hybrid that is treated as a separate entity, for the purposes of Country A law, but disregarded under Country B law. Because of the

differences between Country A and Country B law in the characterisation of B Co 2, all of B Co 2's income is treated as derived by B Co 1 (and is subject to tax under Country B law) but none of this income is brought into account under Country A law.

3. B Co 1 and B Co 2 each derive 500 of operating income over a two year period. Due to the way the arrangement has been structured, B Co 1's income and expenses (including depreciation allowances) are treated as taxable income and deductible expenditure under Country A and Country B laws. However differences in the way Country A and Country B recognise the amount and the timing of such income and expenditure mean that these items are recognised in different amounts and in different periods. In particular:

(a) Under the laws of Country A, 20% of B Co 1's operating income for the two year period is treated as derived in Year 1 (100) and 80% in Year 2 (400). Country A law also requires 50% of the interest expense accrued by B Co 1 in Year 1 (100) to be recognised in Year 2. Tax incentives in Country A also allow A Co to claim a larger depreciation allowance for the property held by B Co 1.

(b) Under Country B law, 60% of the income of B Co 1 (300) is treated as derived in Year 1 and 40% (200) in Year 2. The interest expense and depreciation deductions are, however, spread evenly over the two accounting periods.

4. Tables setting out the combined net income position for the AB Group for Years 1 and 2 are set out below.

	Country A A Co			Country B B Co 1 and B Co 2 Combined		
		Tax	**Book**		**Tax**	**Book**
Year 1	Income			Income		
	Operating income of A Co	250	250			
	Operating income of B Co 1	100	0	Operating income of B Co 1	300	250
				Operating income of B Co 2	250	250
	Expenditure			Expenditure		
	Interest paid by B Co 1	(100)	0	Interest paid by B Co 1	(200)	(200)
	Depreciation	(180)	0	Depreciation	(120)	(120)
	Net return		**250**	**Net return**		**180**
	Taxable income	**70**		**Taxable income**	**230**	

Year 2	Country A A Co			Country B B Co 1 and B Co 2 Combined		
		Tax	Book		Tax	Book
	Income			Income		
	Operating income of A Co	250	250			
	Operating income of B Co 1	400	0	Operating income of B Co 1	200	250
				Operating income of B Co 2	250	250
	Expenditure			Expenditure		
	Interest paid by B Co 1	(300)	0	Interest paid by B Co 1	(200)	(200)
	Depreciation	(180)	0	Depreciation	(120)	(120)
	Net return		**250**	**Net return**		**180**
	Taxable income	**170**		**Taxable income**	**130**	

Net return for Years 1 & 2		**500**		**360**
Taxable income for Years 1 & 2	**240**		**360**	

Country B law

5. In Year 1 B Co 1 and B Co 2 are treated, on a combined basis, as deriving a total of 550 of income and incurring 320 of deductions for tax purposes resulting in net taxable income of 230. In the following year, the Country B group recognises 100 less of operating income than in the previous year but has the same amount of deductions resulting in net taxable income of 130 for that year.

Country A law

6. Differences under Country A law in the recognition of timing of payments mean that Country A treats B Co 1 as only having derived 100 of operating income in Year 1 and having incurred 100 of interest expense. A Co is, however, entitled to a higher amount of depreciation than is available under Country B law. The net effect of these differences is that A Co is treated as deriving 70 of net taxable income in Year 1. In Year 2 Country A law requires A Co to recognise the additional income and expenses, effectively reversing out the timing differences that arose in Year 1. A Co continues to claim depreciation deductions at the higher rate leaving it with net taxable income for the period of 170.

7. The entities in this structure have an aggregate net return of 860 over the two year period while the net taxable income recognised under the arrangement is only 600. This indicates that up to 260 of double deductions are being set-off against non-dual inclusion income.

Question

8. How should the deductible hybrid payments rule be applied to neutralise the effect of the hybrid mismatch under this structure?

Answer

9. The laws of both Country A and B grant a deduction for the same payment (and for depreciation on the same asset) and accordingly these deductions give rise to a DD outcome. Similarly the income of B Co 1 should be treated as dual inclusion income under the laws of both jurisdictions as the item is included in ordinary income under the laws of the other jurisdiction.

10. The recommended response under the deductible hybrid payments rule is that the parent jurisdiction should deny the duplicate deduction to the extent it gives rise to a hybrid mismatch. In this case the application of the rule would result in Country A denying a deduction for 180 in Year 1 (being the amount by which A Co's interest and depreciation deductions exceed the amount of A Co's dual inclusion income) but Country A may allow that excess deduction to be carried-forward into Year 2 to be set-off against dual inclusion income that arises in the following year.

11. In the event Country A does not apply the primary response, Country B would deny a deduction to the extent it gives rise to a hybrid mismatch. In this case, the rule would result in Country B denying 20 of deductions in Year 1 (being the amount by which B Co 1's interest and depreciation deductions exceed the amount of B Co 1's dual inclusion income). Country B may allow that excess deduction to be carried-forward into subsequent years to be set-off against future dual inclusion income.

12. While it may be possible in straightforward cases to undertake a line by line comparison of each item of income and expenditure, tax administrations may choose to adopt an implementation solution for the deductible hybrid payments rule that preserves the policy objectives of the rule and arrives at a substantially similar result but is based, as much as possible, on existing domestic rules and tax calculations.

Analysis

The interest deduction and depreciation allowance give rise to a DD outcome

13. B Co 1 is a hybrid payer because; although it is resident in Country B (the payer jurisdiction), the interest payments and depreciation allowances trigger a duplicate deduction for A Co (an investor in B Co 1). These payments will be treated as giving rise to a double deduction to the extent they exceed dual inclusion income.

Determination of DD outcomes under Country A law and application of the primary response

14. The primary response under Recommendation 6 is that the parent jurisdiction (in this case Country A) should deny the duplicate deduction that is available under local law to the extent it exceeds dual inclusion income. The only item of income recognised under Country A law that is also treated as ordinary income under Country B law is the operating income of B Co 1. Accordingly, the amount of the deduction denied under the primary response in Year 1 is 180. Denying a deduction for this amount will cause A Co to recognise net income in Year 1 of 250.

15. Country A may permit A Co to carry-forward the excess deduction into the subsequent year so that it can be set-off against surplus dual inclusion income in the subsequent year. The calculation of these adjustments is illustrated in the table below. Example 6.1 – Table 2

Year 1	Country A A Co	Tax	Book	Calculation of adjustment under Country A law	Tax	Book	Carry forward
	Income			Dual inclusion income			
	Operating income of A Co	250	250				
	Operating income of B Co 1	100	0	Operating income of B Co 1		(100)	
	Adjustment	180					
	Expenditure			Double deductions			
	Interest paid by B Co 1	(100)	0	Interest paid by B Co 1		100	
	Depreciation	(180)	0	Depreciation		180	
	Net return		**250**				
	Taxable income	**250**		**Adjustment**		**180**	**(180)**

Year 2	Country A A Co	Tax	Book	Calculation of adjustment under Country A law	Tax	Book	Carry forward
	Income			Dual inclusion income			
	Operating income of A Co	250	250				
	Operating income of B Co 1	100	0	Operating income of B Co 1		(400)	
	Adjustment	80					
	Expenditure			Double deductions			
	Interest paid by B Co 1	(100)	0	Interest paid by B Co 1		300	
	Depreciation	(180)	0	Depreciation		180	
	Net return		**250**				
	Taxable income	**250**		**Adjustment**		**80**	**(260)**

16. A Co is denied a deduction for 180 in Year 1 and 80 in Year 2. The net effect of applying the deductible hybrid payments rule over the two year period is that A Co will be fully taxable on its non-dual inclusion income from its own activities over the two year period and will have an excess deduction to carry-forward that effectively represents the net loss (for tax purposes) arising from B Co 1's operations.

Defensive rule

17. The defensive rule under Recommendation 6 is that the payer jurisdiction (in this case Country B) should deny the duplicate deduction that is available under local law to the extent it exceeds dual inclusion income. In this example, the only item of income that is recognised under Country B law that will also be treated as ordinary income under Country A law is the operating income of B Co 1. Accordingly the amount of the deduction denied under the primary response in Year 1 is 20. Denying a deduction for this amount will cause B Co 1 to recognise net income in Year 1 of 250.

18. Country B may permit B Co 1 to carry-forward the excess deduction into the subsequent year so that it can be set-off against surplus dual inclusion income in the subsequent year. The effect of these adjustments is illustrated in the table below.

	Country B B Co 1 and B Co 2 Combined			Calculation of adjustment under Country B law			Carry forward
		Tax	Book		Tax	Book	
Year 1	Income			Dual inclusion income			
	Operating income of B Co 1	300	250				
	Operating income of B Co 2	250	250	Operating income of B Co 1		(300)	
	Adjustment	20					
	Expenditure			Double deductions			
	Interest paid by B Co 1	(200)	(200)	Interest paid by B Co 1		200	
	Depreciation	(120)	(120)	Depreciation		120	
	Net return		**180**				
	Taxable income	**250**		**Adjustment**		**20**	**(20)**

	Country B B Co 1 and B Co 2 Combined			Calculation of adjustment under Country B law			Carry forward
		Tax	Book		Tax	Book	
Year 2	Income			Dual inclusion income			
	Operating income of B Co 1	200	250				
	Operating income of B Co 2	250	250	Operating income of B Co 1		(200)	
	Adjustment	120					
	Expenditure			Double deductions			
	Interest paid by B Co 1	(200)	(200)	Interest paid by B Co 1		200	
	Depreciation	(120)	(120)	Depreciation		120	
	Net return		**180**				
	Taxable income	**250**		**Adjustment**		**120**	**(140)**

19. The net effect of applying the deductible hybrid payments rule over the two year period is that B Co 1 will be taxable on its non-dual inclusion income from B Co 2 (500) over the two year period and will have an excess deduction to carry-forward that effectively represents the net loss (for tax purposes) arising from B Co 1's operations.

Implementation solutions

20. In structures such as this it will generally be the case that tax returns have been prepared under the laws of both jurisdictions which will show the income and expenditure as determined under local law using domestic tax concepts. Tax administrations may use

these existing sources of information and tax calculations as a starting point for identifying duplicate deductions and dual inclusion income.

21. For example, Country A could require A Co to separately identify the items of income and deduction that are derived and incurred through B Co 1 and deny A Co a deduction to the extent of any adjusted net loss under such calculation. When applying the defensive rule, Country B could require the losses of B Co 1 to be applied only against income of B Co 1 and apply a loss-continuity rule that prevents B Co 1 from carrying any such losses forward in the event of a change of control.

Example 6.2

Whether DD may be set off against dual inclusion income

Facts

1. In the example illustrated in the figure below, A Co establishes a PE in Country B. The PE borrows money from a local bank. Interest on the loan is deductible in both Country A and Country B. The PE has no other income.

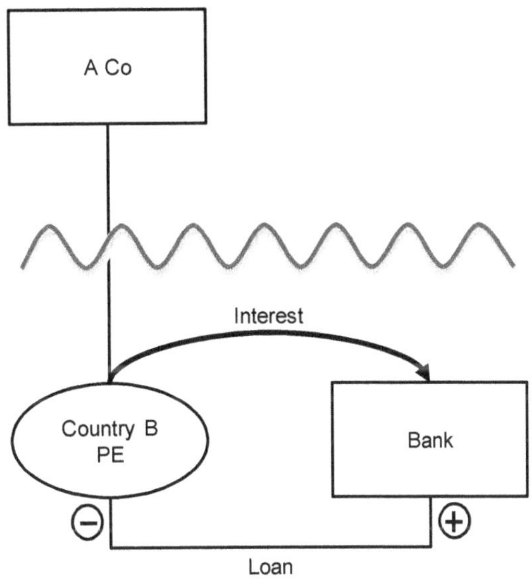

Question

2. Does the deductible hybrid payments rule apply to the interest payment by the PE?

Answer

3. The interest payment will be subject to the deductible hybrid payments rule unless:

(a) the rules in Country B prevent the payment from being set-off against income that is not dual inclusion income; or

(b) the taxpayer can establish, to the satisfaction of the tax administration, that the deduction has given rise to a stranded loss (i.e. the deduction cannot be set-off against the income of any person under the laws of the other jurisdiction).

Analysis

A Co is a hybrid payer making a payment that gives rise to a DD outcome

4. A Co falls within the definition of a "hybrid payer" as A Co is a non-resident making a payment of interest, which is deductible under the laws of Country B (the payer jurisdiction) and which triggers a duplicate deduction for A Co under the laws of Country A (the parent jurisdiction).

5. While income of the PE would presumably be taxable under the laws of both Country A and B, on the facts of this example, the payment will give rise to a DD outcome because the PE has no other income against which the deduction can be off-set.

DD outcome will give rise to a hybrid mismatch if deduction is capable of being set-off against non-dual inclusion income under Country B law

6. A payment results in a hybrid mismatch under the deductible hybrid payments rule where the deduction for that payment may be set-off against income that is not dual inclusion income. It is not necessary for a tax administration to know how the deduction has been used in the other jurisdiction before it applies the rule.

7. Under Country A law the interest deduction will automatically be eligible to be set-off against income of A Co, which may not have a source in Country B. Therefore, unless Country A applies the primary response under the deductible hybrid payments rule, the interest deduction may be set-off against non-dual inclusion income in that jurisdiction. Under Country B law the interest payment will give rise to a net loss. Whether this loss "may" be set-off in the future against non-dual inclusion income under Country B law will depend on the Country B rules governing the utilisation of losses and other interactions between Country A and B laws.

8. The PE may, for example, be able to join a tax grouping regime that would allow the benefit of the loss to be used against the income of another group member. Alternatively the PE may be able to structure an investment through a reverse hybrid in order to derive income that is only brought into account under the laws of the payer jurisdiction or it may be able to enter into a financial instrument or other arrangement where payments on the instrument will not be included in ordinary income in the parent jurisdiction. Unless the taxpayer can show that the interaction between Country A and B laws makes it practically impossible to utilise the deduction against anything other than dual inclusion income, the deduction should be treated as giving rise to a hybrid mismatch under Recommendation 6.3.

Application of the primary response

9. In this case the jurisdiction that should apply the primary response under the deductible hybrid payments rule is Country A. Country A should prevent A Co from offsetting the deduction against A Co's other income and require A Co to apply the excess deduction against dual inclusion income in another period in accordance with Country A law.

Application of the defensive rule

10. In the event Country A does not apply the primary response, Country B should prevent the PE from taking advantage of any structuring opportunities that would allow

the deduction for the payment to be set-off against income that is not dual inclusion income.

Treatment of stranded losses

11. Because the primary rule operates to restrict a deduction in the parent jurisdiction, even in circumstances where the deduction has not been utilised in the payer jurisdiction, the deductible hybrid payments rule has the potential to generate "stranded losses". This could occur, for example where A Co abandons its operations in Country B and winds up the PE in Country B at a time when it still has unused carry-forward losses from a prior period. In this case, Recommendation 6.1(d)(ii) provides that Country A's tax administration may permit those excess deductions to be set-off against non-dual inclusion income under the laws of Country A at that time provided the taxpayer can establish that the winding up of the PE in Country B will prevent A Co from using those losses in Country B.

Implementation solutions

12. If Country A requires A Co to prepare separate accounts for the PE showing the items of income and expenditure that are brought into account under Country A law then Country A could restrict the taxpayer's ability to deduct any net loss of the PE from the income of any member of the parent group. If, on the other hand, A Co is not required to prepare separate accounts for the branch, it could use the tax return and filing information in Country B to determine the net loss of the branch for Country B purposes, and after making adjustments for material items or amounts of income and expenditure that are not recognised under the law of the parent jurisdiction, deny A Co a deduction to the extent of any net loss as calculated under the rules of the parent jurisdiction.

13. Country B will likely require the branch to prepare separate accounts showing all the amounts of income and expenditure that are subject to tax under Country B law. Country B could prohibit the branch from surrendering the benefit of any deductions to any other group member and implement other transaction specific rules designed to prevent taxable income from being shifted into the branch to soak up any net losses. Loss continuity rules may prevent the economic benefit of the carry-forward losses being used against dual inclusion income of another taxpayer.

Example 6.3

Double deduction outcome from the grant of share options

Facts

1. In the example illustrated in the figure below, A Co establishes B Co 1 as the holding company for its operating subsidiary (B Co 2). B Co 1 is a hybrid entity (i.e. an entity that is treated as a separate entity for tax purposes in Country B but as a disregarded entity under Country A law). B Co 1 and B Co 2 are members of the same tax group under Country B law which means that the net loss of B Co 1 can be set-off against the net income of B Co 2.

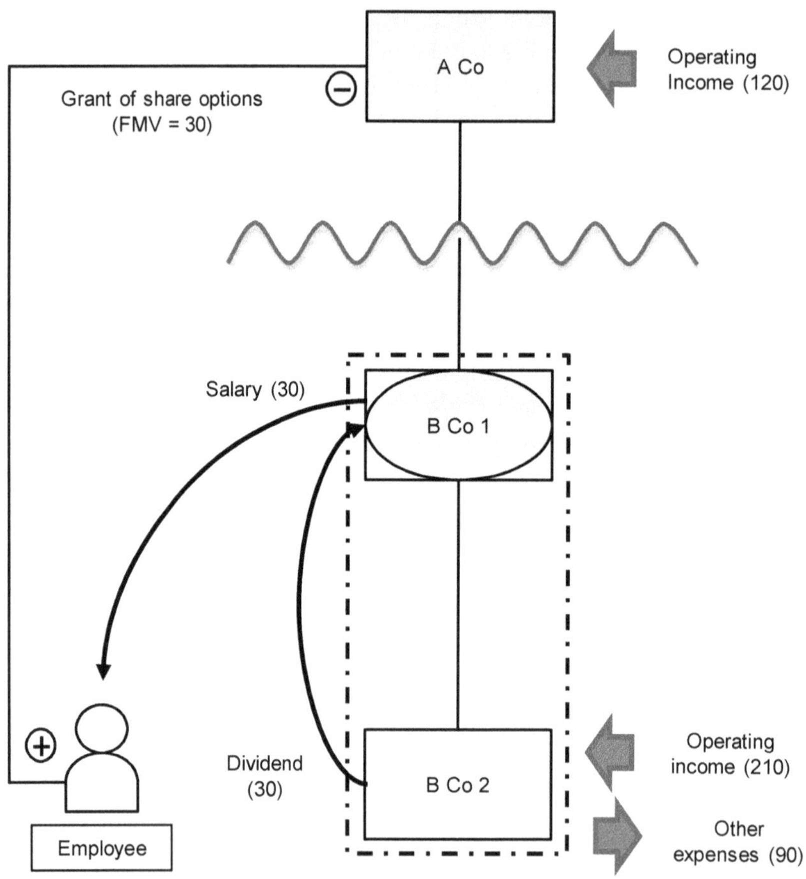

2. B Co 1 has a single employee. The employee is entitled to an annual salary (paid by B Co 1) The salary cost is funded by a dividend payment from B Co 2 that is excluded from taxation under Country B law. The employee also participates in a share incentive

scheme which provides the employee with an option to acquire shares in A Co at a discount to their market value. The market value of the share options is treated as a deductible employment expense. Below is a table setting out the tax position in respect of A Co, B Co 1 and B Co 2 under this structure.

Country A **A Co**			**Country B** **B Co 1**		
	Tax	**Book**		**Tax**	**Book**
Income			Income		
Operating income (A Co)	120	120			
Dividend from B Co 2	30		Dividend from B Co 2		30
Expenditure			Expenditure		
Salary and wages	(30)	-	Salary and wages	(30)	(30)
Share option grant	(30)	(30)	Share option grant	(15)	-
			Net return		**0**
			Taxable income (loss)	(45)	
			Loss surrender to B Co 2	45	
			Loss carry forward	**0**	
			B Co 2		
			Income		
			Operating Income	210	210
			Expenditure		
			Operating expenses	(90)	(90)
			Dividend paid to B Co 1	-	(30)
			Loss surrender	(45)	-
Net return		**90**	**Net return**		**90**
Taxable income	**90**		**Taxable income**	**75**	

Result under Country B law

3. B Co 1 is treated as incurring 45 of employment expenses. The cash portion of these expenses (i.e. the salary and wages) is funded by an exempt dividend from B Co 2. B Co 1's net loss is surrendered to B Co 2 under the tax grouping regime of Country B and is applied against that company's net income. B Co 2 has 75 of taxable income after taking into account expenses and the benefit of the loss surrendered by B Co 1.

Result under Country A law

4. A Co earns 120 of operating income from its activities in Country A. A Co also treats the dividend paid by B Co 2, to fund B Co 1's employment expenses, as ordinary income for tax purposes. Country A grants a deduction for the salary and wages and the value of the share options but uses a different valuation methodology for calculating the share option expense that results in a higher deduction.

5. The entities in this structure have a total net return of 180 under the arrangement but the aggregate taxable income under the arrangement is 165. This indicates that at least 15 of double deductions are being set-off against non-dual inclusion income.

Question

6. What adjustments should be made to tax returns of the AB group under the deductible hybrid payments rule?

Answer

7. In this case Country A should apply the primary response under the deductible hybrid payments rule and require A Co to carry-forward 30 of deductions into another period to be set-off against future dual inclusion income. In the event Country A does not apply the primary response, Country B should deny B Co a deduction of 15.

Analysis

The payment of the salary gives rise to a DD outcome

8. The question of whether a payment has given rise to a "DD outcome" is primarily a legal question that should be determined by an analysis of the character and tax treatment of the payment under the laws of both jurisdictions. This requires an assessment of the legal basis for the deduction in one jurisdiction and a comparison with the tax outcomes in the other jurisdiction to determine whether a deduction has been granted in respect of the same circumstances and on the same basis. If both jurisdictions grant a deduction for the same expenditure item, then that deduction should be treated as giving rise to a DD outcome. The labels that are ascribed to each category of payment (e.g. travel subsidy, meal allowance, or wages) are less significant than identifying what the deduction is for (i.e. employment expenses). If one jurisdiction treats a travel subsidy as a separate deductible allowance, while the other simply treats it as part of the taxpayer's salary or wages, then the payment will still be treated as giving rise to a DD outcome notwithstanding the different ways in which the payment is described under the laws of each jurisdiction.

9. In this case, both Country A and B treat salary or wages as deductible and accordingly such a payment will generally give rise to a DD outcome. Under the deductible hybrid payments rule the breakdown of salary and wages into its specific components (e.g. meal allowances, wages) is not important provided both jurisdictions are granting a deduction for the same expense. The final conclusion that a payment has given rise to a DD outcome should only be made, however after the application of any transaction or entity specific rules that prevent the deduction being claimed under the laws of either jurisdiction. No DD outcome would arise, for example, if A Co was a tax exempt entity that was not entitled to claim deductions for any type of expenditure.

The grant of the share options will give rise to a DD outcome

10. If the laws of both Country A and B treat the granting of the share options as a deductible expense then the grant of the shares will be treated as giving rise to a DD outcome to the extent of the deduction in each jurisdiction. Although there are differences between Country A and B in how the share options are valued this will generally not impact on the extent to which a payment has given rise to a mismatch in tax outcomes.

The payment of the dividend gives rise to dual inclusion income

11. While a payment must generally be recognised as ordinary income under the laws of both jurisdictions before it can be treated as dual inclusion income, a payment that is treated as ordinary income in the parent jurisdiction should still qualify as dual inclusion income if the payment is subject to taxation relief in the payer jurisdiction in order to relieve the payment from economic double taxation. In this case, the dividend paid by B Co 2 to B Co 1 is treated as an exempt intra-group dividend. The dividend is not deductible for B Co 2 and therefore does not trigger any further deductible expense under the laws of the payer jurisdiction and cannot be used to erode the tax base of Country B. Allowing the dividend recipient a deduction against this type of exempt or excluded equity return preserves the intended tax policy outcomes in both Country A and Country B and accordingly the dividend should be treated as dual inclusion income for the purposes of the deductible hybrid payments rule even where such dividend carries an entitlement to an underlying foreign tax credit in the parent jurisdiction. Such double taxation relief may give rise to tax policy concerns, however, if it has the same net effect as allowing for a DD outcome. In determining whether to treat an item of income, which benefits from such double-taxation relief, as dual-inclusion income, countries should seek to strike a balance between rules that minimise compliance costs, preserve the intended effect of such double taxation relief and prevent taxpayers from entering into structures that undermine the integrity of the rules.

Application of the primary response

12. In this case the jurisdiction that should apply the primary response under the deductible hybrid payments rule is Country A. Country A should deny A Co's duplicate deductions to the extent it gives rise to a mismatch in tax outcomes. The duplicate deduction will not give rise to a mismatch to the extent it does not exceed dual inclusion income as determined under the laws of the parent jurisdiction. In this case, the total amount of duplicate deduction incurred by A Co is 60 and A Co's dual inclusion income is 30. The total amount of adjustment that should be made under the deductible hybrid payments rule is therefore 30.

Country A A Co	Tax	Book
Income		
Operating income (A Co)	120	120
Dividend from B Co 2	30	
Adjustment	30	
Expenditure		
Salary and wages	(30)	
Share option grant	(30)	(30)
Income		
Net return		**90**
Taxable income	**120**	

Calculation of adjustment under Country A law	Tax	Book	Carry forward
Dual inclusion income			
Dividend from B Co 2		(30)	
Double deductions			
Salary and wages		30	
Share option grant		30	
Adjustment		**30**	**(30)**

Application of the defensive rule

13. In the event Country A does not apply the primary response, Country B should deny B Co a deduction for the payment to the extent necessary to prevent the deduction from being set-off against income that is not dual inclusion income. While the dividend paid by B Co 2 to B Co 1 is treated as exempt income under Country B law, this payment should be included in the calculation of dual inclusion income as it is included in income under the laws of Country A. In this case, the total amount of duplicate deduction incurred by B Co is (45) and A Co's dual inclusion income is 30. The total amount of adjustment required under the deductible hybrid payments rule under Country B law is 15.

Country B B Co 1	Tax	Book
Income		
Dividend from B Co 2		30
Adjustment	15	
Expenditure		
Salary and wages	(30)	
Share option grant	(15)	(30)
Income		
Net return		**0**
Taxable income (loss)	**(30)**	

Calculation of adjustment under Country B law	Tax	Book	Carry forward
Dual inclusion income			
Dividend from B Co 2		(30)	
Double deductions			
Salary and wages		30	
Share option grant		15	
Adjustment		**15**	**(15)**

Implementation solutions

14. In this case, given that B Co has no income and incurs a limited amount of expenses, it may be possible for both Country A and B to make a direct comparison between the tax treatment of the employment expenses in both countries to determine whether and to what extent they give rise to a DD outcome. When applying the deductible hybrid payments rule, the tax administration in Country B should take into account, as dual inclusion income, any payment that is eligible for exclusion, exemption other forms of tax relief in order to avoid economic double taxation provided such payment is included in income under Country A law.

Example 6.4

Calculating dual inclusion income under a CFC regime

Facts

1. In the example illustrated in the figure below, A Co establishes B Co 1 as the holding company for its operating subsidiary (B Co 2).

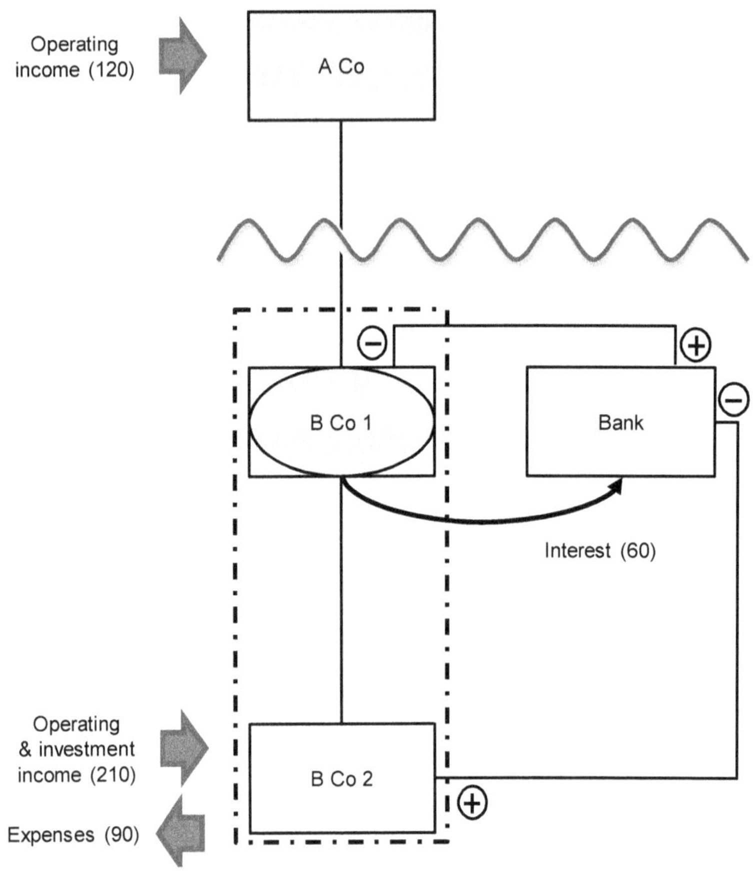

2. B Co 1 is a hybrid entity (i.e. an entity that is treated as a separate entity for tax purposes in Country B but as a disregarded entity under Country A law). B Co 1 and B Co 2 are members of the same tax group under Country B law so that any net loss of B Co 1 can be surrendered under the grouping regime to be set-off against the income of B Co 2. B Co 1 borrows money from a local bank. The interest on the loan is treated as a deductible expense under both Country A and B laws.

3. B Co 2 is treated as a separate taxable entity by both A Co and B Co 1. Certain items of income derived by B Co 2 are, however, attributed to A Co under Country A's CFC regime. B Co 2 has funds on deposit with the same bank and earns interest income which is subject to tax in the hands of B Co 2. Below is a table setting out the tax position in respect of the AB Group under this structure.

Country A A Co	Tax	Book	Country B B Co 1	Tax	Book
Income			Income		
Operating income (A Co)	120	120			
Attributed CFC Income from B Co 2	30	-			
Tax credit on attributed CFC Income	6	-			
Expenditure			Expenditure		
Interest paid by B Co 1	(60)	-	Interest paid	(60)	(60)
Net return		**120**	**Net return**		**(60)**
Taxable income	**96**		Taxable income (loss)	(60)	
Tax on income (30%)	(28.8)				
Credit for underlying foreign taxes	6		Loss surrender to B Co 2	60	
Tax to pay		(22.8)	**Loss carry forward**	**0**	
After-tax return		**97.2**			

B Co 2	Tax	Book
Income		
Operating Income	180	180
Interest Income	30	30
Expenditure		
Operating expenses	(90)	(90)
Loss surrender	(60)	-
Net return		**120**
Taxable income	**60**	
Tax on income (20%)	(12)	
Tax to pay		(12)
After-tax return		**108**

Result under Country B law

4. B Co 1 incurs 60 of interest expenses. The net loss resulting from this interest expense is surrendered under the tax grouping regime of Country B and applied against

the income of B Co 2. B Co 2 has 60 of taxable income after taking into account expenses and the benefit of the loss surrendered by B Co 1.

Result under Country A law

5. A Co earns 120 of net operating income from its activities in Country A and is entitled to claim the 60 of interest expenses incurred by B Co 1. A Co is also attributed, under the Country A's CFC regime, a gross amount of 30 interest derived by B Co 2 together with tax on that income of 6. This attributed income is brought into account as ordinary income and subject to tax at the full corporate rate after taking into account a credit for underlying taxes paid in Country B.

6. The total net return for the group is 180 while the net income for the group is 156 (including 6 of foreign tax credits).

Question

7. What adjustments should be made to tax returns of A Co and B Co 1 under the deductible hybrid payments rule?

Answer

8. A tax administration may treat the net income of a controlled foreign company (CFC) that is attributed to a shareholder of that company under a CFC or other offshore inclusion regime as dual inclusion income if the taxpayer can satisfy the tax administration that such income has been calculated on the same basis and is treated as ordinary income that is subject to tax at the full rate under the laws of both jurisdictions. Such income will be eligible to be treated as dual inclusion income even if it carries with it an entitlement to credit for underlying foreign taxes that shelters a liability to tax in the parent jurisdiction.

Analysis

Attributed income under a CFC regime can give rise to dual inclusion income.

9. In this simplified example, where there is a single item of interest income that is brought into account under the laws of both jurisdictions, the amount of attributed CFC income that may be treated as dual inclusion income is the amount recognised as ordinary income under the laws of Country A (including the benefit of any tax credits). The table below shows the effect of an adjustment under the deductible hybrids payment rule taking into account the operation of the CFC regime under Country A law.

Country A A Co	Tax	Book
Income		
Operating income (A Co)	120	120
Attributed CFC Income from B Co 2	30	-
Tax credit on attributed CFC Income	6	-
Expenditure		
Interest paid by B Co 1	(36)	-
Net return		**120**
Taxable income	**120**	
Tax on income (30%)	(36)	
Credit for underlying foreign taxes	6	
Tax to pay		(30)
After-tax return		**90**

10. The effect of this adjustment is that Country A permits A Co 1 to deduct the interest expense to the extent that interest is set-off against amounts that are included in income under Country A's CFC regime. The total amount of income brought into account under Country A and B laws is equal to 180. The reduced final level of tax in Country A (25%) is the result of Country A continuing to provide the benefit of a tax credit on dual inclusion income, despite the fact that the net dual inclusion income under Country A law is nil (after that income has been set-off against a duplicate deduction).

11. Under Country B law, the amount of income that is considered to be dual inclusion income is the 30 of interest income derived by B Co 2. Accordingly, this amount of loss should be treated as eligible for surrender under Country B law. The table below shows the effect of the adjustment on the tax position of B Co 2.

Country B B Co 2	Tax	Book
Income		
Adjustment	30	
Expenditure		
Interest paid by B Co 1	(60)	(60)
Net return		**(60)**
Taxable income	(30)	
Loss surrender to B Co 2	30	
Loss carry forward	**0**	

Calculation of adjustment under Country B law	Tax	Book	Carry forward
Dual inclusion income			
Interest income		(30)	
Double deductions			
Interest paid by B Co 1		60	
Adjustment		**30**	**(30)**

B Co 2	Tax	Book
Income		
Operating Income	180	180
Interest Income	30	30
Expenditure		
Operating expenses	(90)	(90)
Loss surrender	(30)	-
Net return		**120**
Taxable income	**90**	
Tax on income (20%)	(18)	
Tax to pay		(18)
After-tax return		**102**

12. Country B permits B Co 1 to surrender 30 of losses to B Co 2 (i.e. the amount that is included in ordinary income under Country A's CFC regime, ignoring the effect of any credits). The effect of this adjustment is that Country A and B will include an aggregate of 180 of income under the arrangement in addition to the foreign tax credit.

Implementation solutions

13. In cases where dual inclusion income carries a right to a tax credit for an underlying foreign taxes the parent jurisdiction could further choose to restrict the amount of the foreign tax credit to the tax liability of the net dual inclusion income under the arrangement. An illustration of the effect of these CFC changes is set out below:

Country A A Co		
	Tax	**Book**
Income		
Operating income (A Co)	120	120
Attributed CFC Income from B Co 2	30	-
Tax credit on attributed CFC Income	6	-
Expenditure		
Interest paid by B Co 1	(36)	-
Net return		**120**
Taxable income	**120**	
Tax on income (30%)	(36)	
Credit for underlying foreign taxes	0	
Tax to pay		(36)
After-tax return		**84**

14. Adjusting the entitlement to foreign tax credits in this way would protect Country A from using double deduction structures to bring up tax credits without a corresponding income item. Denying the foreign tax credit in these cases would make it easier for a taxpayer to establish that the income attributed under the CFC regime is, in fact, dual inclusion that has been calculated on the same basis in both jurisdictions and is subject to tax in both jurisdictions at the full rate.

Example 6.5

DD outcome under a loan to a partnership

Facts

1. In the example illustrated in the figure below, B Partnership is a hybrid entity that is 25% owned by A Co (a company resident in Country A). The partnership has no income. A Co lends money to B Partnership.

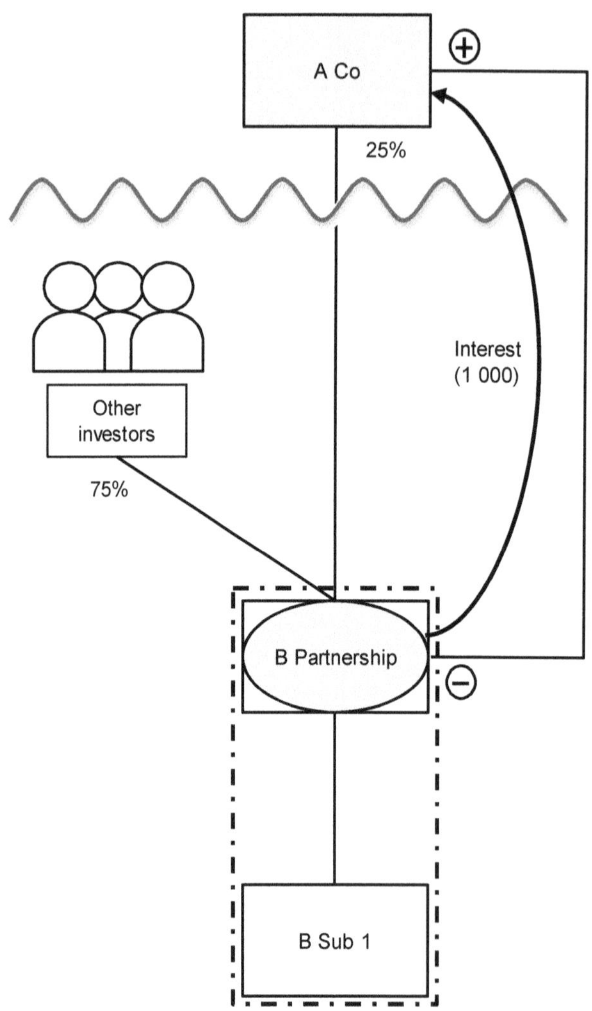

2. The tax laws of Country A treat B Partnership as a transparent entity so that a proportionate share of the items of income, gain and expenditure derived and incurred by B Partnership are allocated (under Country A law only) through the partnership to A Co in accordance with A Co's interest in the partnership. B Partnership is consolidated with B Sub 1, which is treated as a separate taxable entity under Country B law.

3. The interest payment is treated as a deductible expense under Country B law and can be surrendered against income of B Sub 1 under Country B's tax grouping regime. Under Country A law, however, both the income from interest payment and the deduction from the interest expense are set-off against each other on the same tax return so that only net 75% of the interest payment (effectively the portion of the interest cost economically borne by the other investors) is included in A Co's income. If the interest payment under the loan is 1 000 and the partnership has no other income then a simplified tax calculation for A Co (assuming a corporate tax rate of 30%) can be illustrated as follows:

Country A A Co		
	Tax	**Book**
Income		
Interest	1 000	1 000
Expenditure		
Interest	(250)	-
Net return		**1000**
Taxable income	**750**	
Tax to pay (33%)		(250)
After-tax return		**750**

4. While A Co receives a net return of 1 000, its taxable income under the arrangement is reduced by the portion of the interest expense on the loan that is allocated to A Co under Country A law. The net effect of this allocation is that A Co is taxable on the net return under the arrangement at a rate of 25% rather than the statutory rate of 33%.

Question

5. Does Recommendation 6 apply to deny the deduction for any portion of the interest payment under the loan?

Answer

6. The interest payment falls within the deductible hybrid payments rule because the interest payment by the B Partnership gives rise to a deduction in Country B that may be set-off against income of B Sub 1 (under the tax grouping regime of Country B) and a duplicate deduction for A Co (an investor in B Partnership). Accordingly, under the primary rule, the duplicate deduction in Country A should be denied to the extent that exceeds the investor's dual inclusion income. A Co's dual inclusion income in this example is *nil* as the interest paid on the loan is not subject to tax in Country A.

Accordingly, Country A should deny a deduction for the full amount of the interest expense.

7. In the event that Country A does not apply the primary response under Recommendation 6, Country B should apply the defensive rule to restrict a deduction for the interest payment to the extent it gives rise to a duplicate deduction under Country A law and to the extent the interest payment is not set-off against dual inclusion income. Because B Partnership and A Co are not members of the same control group, the defensive rule will only apply, however, to the extent the mismatch arises under a structured arrangement and B Partnership is a party to that arrangement. The amount of the deduction denied under the defensive rule is the entire amount of the interest payment (i.e. 1 000) as that is the amount necessary to eliminate the mismatch in tax outcomes.

Analysis

B Partnership is a hybrid payer making a payment that gives rise to a DD outcome

8. The partnership falls within the definition of a "hybrid payer" as it is tax resident in Country B and makes a deductible payment in that jurisdiction that triggers a duplicate deduction for an investor in the partnership (A Co) under the laws of another jurisdiction (Country A). If the partnership had other income this would likely be dual inclusion income that could be offset against the deduction under the laws of both jurisdictions. In this case, however, the partnership derives no other income and, accordingly, the entire amount of the interest payment gives rise to a DD outcome.

If mismatch is not neutralised under Country A law then Country B should deny a deduction for the interest payment under the secondary rule

9. In the case of hybrid entities such as partnerships, the parent jurisdiction is the jurisdiction where the partner is resident (Country A), Country A should therefore deny the full amount of the deduction (250) in order to neutralise the mismatch in tax outcomes.

10. In the event Country A does not apply the primary rule, Country B should deny the deduction to the extent necessary to neutralise the mismatch. This will result in a deduction being denied for the full amount of the interest payment (1 000), because any deduction incurred by the partnership in these circumstances, that is in excess of dual inclusion income, will give rise to a mismatch in tax outcomes due to the tax transparency of the partnership under Country A law.

Secondary rule will not apply unless B Partnership is a party to structured arrangement

11. The secondary rule will not apply unless the mismatch arises within the confines of a control group or under a structured arrangement and the payer is a party to that structured arrangement. A payer will not be a party to a structured arrangement if it could not reasonably have been expected to be aware of the hybrid mismatch and did not share in the value of the tax benefit arising from it. In this case the partnership would not necessarily be expected to be aware of the tax treatment adopted by A Co (because B Partnership is not treated as transparent under the law of County B) and unless the pricing

of the loan reflects the benefit of the resulting mismatch the partnership will not be treated as sharing in the value of the tax benefit.

Implementation solutions

12. In this case, the easiest way of preventing a double deduction being set-off against non-dual inclusion income under Country A law would be for Country A to prevent A Co from claiming any net loss from the partnership. Country B could restrict the ability of the partnership to surrender the benefit of any resulting net loss under Country B's tax grouping regime and impose further transaction specific rules that prevent B Partnership from entering into transactions designed to stream non-dual inclusion income to the partnership in order to soak-up unused losses.

Example 7.1

DD outcome using a dual resident entity

Facts

1. In the example illustrated in the figure below A Co 1 owns all of the shares in A Co 2. A Co 2 is resident for tax purposes in both Country A and Country B. A Co 1 is consolidated with A Co 2 under Country A law. A Co 2 acquires all the shares in B Co. B Co is a reverse hybrid that is treated as a separate entity, for the purposes of Country A law, but disregarded under Country B law.

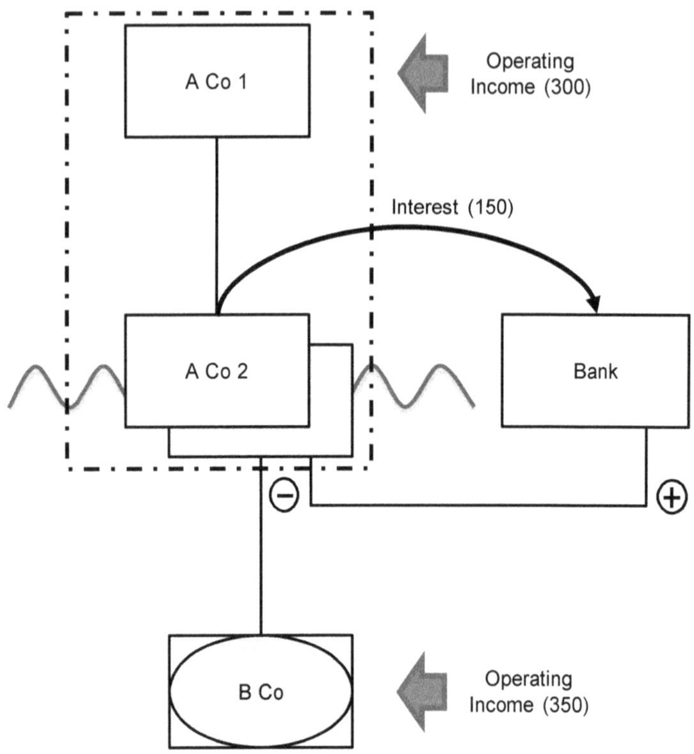

2. A Co 2 borrows money from a bank. Interest on the loan is deductible in both Country A and Country B. A Co 2 has no other income or expenditure. A table setting out the combined net income position for the AB Group is set out below.

Country A A Co 1	Tax	Book	Country B A Co 1 and B Co Combined	Tax	Book
Income			Income		
Operating income of A Co 1	300	300	Operating income of B Co	350	350
Expenditure			Expenditure		
Interest paid by A Co 2 to bank	(150)	-	Interest paid by A Co 2 to bank	(150)	(150)
Net return		300	**Net return**		200
Taxable income	150		**Taxable income**	200	

3. Country A's tax consolidation regime permits A Co 2's interest payment (150) to be directly set-off against the operating income of A Co 1 leaving A Co 1 with 150 of taxable income. Under Country B law, the taxable income of B Co is treated as derived by A Co 2 and is set-off against A Co 2's interest deduction, leaving the Country B Group with taxable income of 200. The net effect of this structure is, therefore, that the entities in the AB Group derive a net return of 500 of net income but only have taxable income of 350.

Question

4. Are the tax outcomes described above subject to adjustment under the dual resident payer rule?

Answer

5. Both Country A and B should apply the dual resident payer rule to deny the benefit of the interest deduction. While having both countries apply the same rule to the same payment raises the risk of double taxation there is no reliable way of ordering the application of the rules and structuring alternatives are available which can prevent double taxation from arising.

6. If the dual resident ceases to be a dual resident excess deductions may be able to be applied against non-dual inclusion income under the rule in Recommendation 7.1 (c) dealing with stranded losses.

Analysis

Application of the dual resident payer rule

7. A Co 2 is a dual resident entity and the interest payment triggers deductions under the laws of both jurisdictions where A Co 2 is resident. A person should be treated as a resident of a jurisdiction for tax purposes if they qualify as tax resident in that jurisdiction or they are taxable in that jurisdiction on their worldwide net income. A person will be treated as a resident of a jurisdiction even if that person forms part of a tax consolidation group which treats that person as a disregarded entity for local law purposes. Thus, if the tax consolidation regime in Country A was to treat all the taxpayers in the same

consolidated group as a single taxpayer and to disregard the transactions between them, A Co 2 would still be treated as a resident of Country A for the purposes of the rule.

8. A Co 2 has no other income so that the deduction gives rise to a DD outcome under the laws of both Country A and B. The tax consolidation regime in Country A and the ability of A Co 2 to invest in a reverse hybrid under Country B law mean that, in each case, the DD outcome gives rise to a hybrid mismatch. Accordingly, both Country A and B, should deny the interest deduction under the dual resident payer rule. A table setting out the combined effect of these adjustments is set out below.

Country A A Co 1		
	Tax	**Book**
Income		
Operating income of A Co 1	300	300
Adjustment	150	
Expenditure		
Interest paid by A Co 2 to bank	(150)	-
Net return		**300**
Taxable income	**300**	

Calculation of adjustment under Country A law			Carry forward
	Tax	**Book**	
Dual inclusion income			
Double deductions			
Interest paid by A Co 2 to bank		150	
Adjustment		**150**	**(150)**

Country B A Co 1 and B Co		
	Tax	**Book**
Income		
Operating income of B Co	350	350
Adjustment	150	
Expenditure		
Interest paid by A Co 2	(150)	(150)
Net return		**200**
Taxable income	**350**	

Calculation of adjustment under Country B law			Carry forward
	Tax	**Book**	
Dual inclusion income			
Double deductions			
Interest paid by A Co 2 to bank		150	
Adjustment		**150**	**(150)**

9. As can be seen from the above table, the net effect of applying the dual resident payer rules in both jurisdictions is to increase the aggregate amount of taxable income to 650. This is in excess of the actual net income under the arrangement. Structuring opportunities are available to A Co 2, however, that will eliminate the net tax burden. A Co 2 could, for example, loan the borrowed money to A Co 1 at an equivalent rate of interest. As illustrated in the table below, the effect of on-lending the money will be to create dual inclusion income that will eliminate the mismatch in tax outcomes.

Country A A Co 1			Country B A Co 2 and B Co Combined		
	Tax	Book		Tax	Book
Income			Income		
Operating income of A Co 1	300	300	Operating income of B Co	350	350
			Interest paid by A Co 1	150	150
Expenditure			Expenditure		
Interest paid by A Co 2 to bank	(150)	-	Interest paid by A Co 2 to bank	(150)	(150)
Interest paid by A Co 1 to A Co 2	-	(150)			
Net return		**150**	**Net return**		**300**
Taxable income	**150**		**Taxable income**	**300**	

10. The net effect of on-lending the money to A Co 1 is to create an amount of dual inclusion income that is equal to the double deduction thus eliminating any mismatch in tax outcomes under the laws of both jurisdictions and ensuring the aggregate net income under the arrangement is subject to tax under the laws of both jurisdictions. Although this interest payment is not taxable under Country A law (because it would be a payment made between members of a consolidated group) it would meet the definition of dual inclusion income because, in this case, the effect of consolidation is to relieve the payee from the economic double taxation on the same income.

11. An alternative way of escaping the effect of the over-taxation under the rule would be to pay a dividend from B Co that was taxable under the laws of Country A. Although this dividend would not be taxable under Country B law (because it would be a payment made by a disregarded entity) it would meet the definition of dual inclusion income because it is excluded from taxation under the laws of Country B in order to relieve the payee from the effects of double taxation. This will be the case even where the parent jurisdiction recognises a tax credit for underlying foreign taxes paid on the distribution. The effect of paying a dividend to A Co 2 is illustrated in the table below.

Country A A Co 1			Country B A Co 2 and B Co Combined		
	Tax	Book		Tax	Book
Income			Income		
Operating income of A Co 1	300	300	Operating income of B Co	350	350
				-	-
Expenditure			Expenditure		
Interest paid by A Co 2 to bank	(150)	-	Interest paid by A Co 2 to bank	(150)	(150)
Dividend paid by B Co	150				
Net return		**300**	**Net return**		**200**
Taxable income	**300**		**Taxable income**	**200**	

12. The effect of dividend is to create an additional amount of dual inclusion income under Country A law that is equal to the interest deduction thus eliminating any mismatch in tax outcomes under the laws of Country A. Although the dividend is not taken into account under Country B law the dividend is still considered to be dual inclusion income because the exclusion granted under Country B law simply protects the taxpayer in Country B from double taxation on the same economic income.

Treatment of stranded losses

13. As with the deductible hybrid payments rule, the dual resident payer rule has the potential to generate "stranded losses" in circumstances where it restricts the deduction in both jurisdictions or where the deduction that arises in the other jurisdiction is unable to be utilised for commercial reasons. Stranded losses could arise, for example under the laws of Country A if the operating income of B Co was insufficient to cover the interest obligations on the bank loan. If a dual resident entity with excess deductions under the dual resident payer rule abandons its dual resident status, the residence jurisdiction may release those excess losses and allow them to be set-off against non-dual inclusion income if the residence jurisdiction is satisfied that the taxpayer can no longer take advantage of any carry-forward losses in the other jurisdiction.

Implementation solutions

14. Countries may choose to prevent dual resident entities joining any tax consolidation or other grouping regime and may introduce transaction specific rules designed to prevent such entities from streaming non-dual inclusion income to a dual resident entity to soak-up unused losses.

Example 8.1

Structured imported mismatch rule

Facts

1. In the example illustrated in the figure below, A Co (a company resident in Country A) is the parent of the ABCDE Group. A Co provides financing to B Co (a wholly-owned subsidiary of A Co resident in Country B) under a hybrid financial instrument. Interest payments on the loan are deductible under Country B law but not included in ordinary income under Country A law. B Co on-lends the money provided under the hybrid financial instrument to C Co and D Co (companies that are resident in Country C and D respectively). C Co on-lends money to E Co (a wholly-owned subsidiary of C Co resident in Country E).

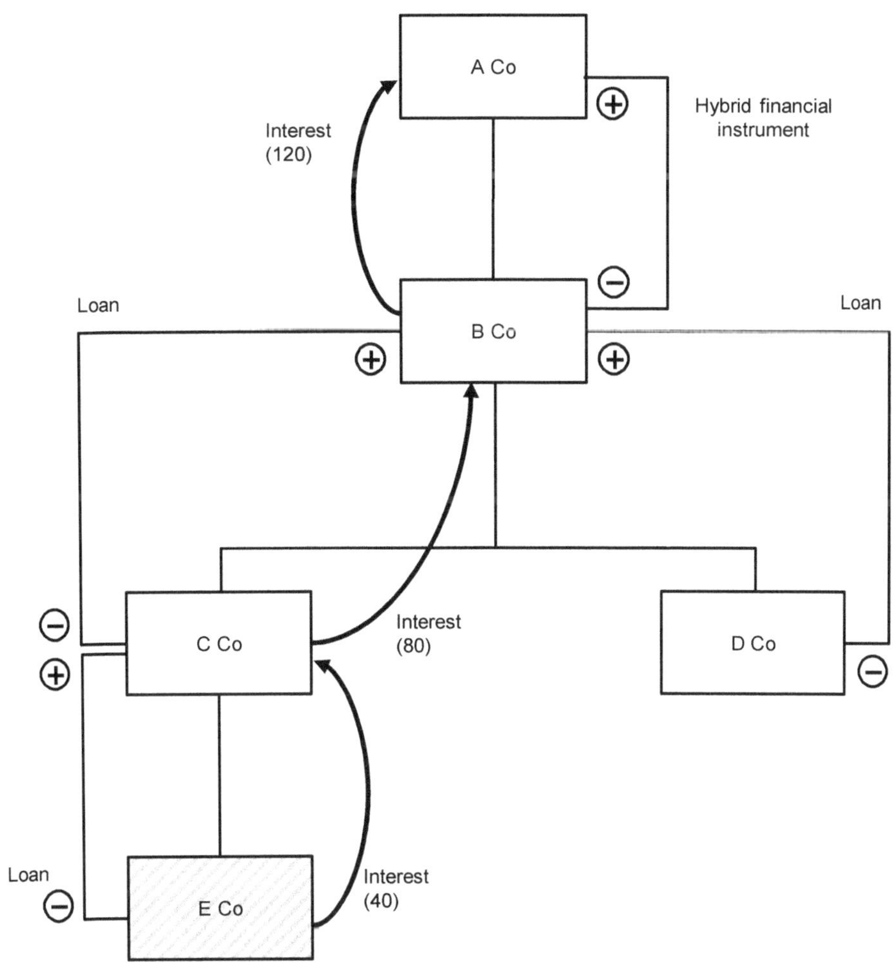

2. All loans are made as part of the same intra-group financing arrangement. The figure above illustrates the group financing structure and the total gross amount of interest payments made in each accounting period under this structure. E Co (the shaded entity) is the only group entity resident in a country that has implemented the recommendations set out in the report.

Question

3. Whether the interest payments made by E Co to C Co are subject to adjustment under the imported mismatch rule and, if so, the amount of the adjustment required under that rule.

Answer

4. E Co's imported mismatch payment and the payment under the hybrid financial instrument that gives rise to a hybrid deduction are payments made under the same structured imported mismatch arrangement. Country E should, therefore, deny the full amount of the interest deduction under the structured imported mismatch rule. See the flow diagram at the end of this example which outlines of the steps to be taken in applying the structured imported mismatch rule.

Analysis

The interest payment made by E Co and the payment giving rise to the hybrid deduction are part of the same structured arrangement

5. In this case the money raised under the hybrid financing instrument has been on-lent to other group companies as part of the same financing arrangement. All the lending transactions and associated payments made under the group financing arrangement (including the loan to E Co) should be treated as part of the same structured arrangement. Accordingly, the payment made by B Co under the hybrid financial instrument, which gives rise to the hybrid deduction, and the imported mismatch payment made by E Co, which is subject to adjustment under the imported mismatch rules in Country E, should be treated as made under the same structured arrangement.

Country E should deny the full amount of the interest deduction under the structured imported mismatch rule

Step 1 –B Co's payment under the hybrid financial instrument gives rise to a direct hybrid deduction

6. A Co has provided financing to B Co under a hybrid financial instrument. Interest payments on that financial instrument are deductible under Country B law but not included in ordinary income under Country A law. The interest payments therefore give rise to a direct hybrid deduction for B Co of 120.

Step 2 –the imported mismatch payment and the hybrid deduction are part of the same structured arrangement

7. The payment made by B Co under the hybrid financial instrument and the imported mismatch payment made by E Co are treated as part of the same structured

arrangement (see analysis above). The structured imported mismatch rule requires the payer jurisdiction to deny a deduction under an imported mismatch payment to the extent the income from such payment is offset (directly or indirectly) against a hybrid deduction under the same structured arrangement.

8. The taxpayer should apply a tracing approach to determine the extent to which the imported mismatch payment has been indirectly offset against that hybrid deduction. The tracing approach requires E Co to trace the chain of payments that give rise to offsetting income and expenditure under the structured arrangement through tiers of intermediate entities to determine the extent to which the payment has directly or indirectly funded the hybrid deduction. The mechanical steps involved in tracing the payment flows are described below:

(a) B Co's payment to A Co under the hybrid financial instrument gives rise to a hybrid deduction of (120). C Co has made a cross-border payment to B Co under the same arrangement of (80). The lower of these two numbers (i.e. 80) is treated as the amount of C Co's indirect hybrid deduction under an imported mismatch arrangement.

(b) C Co's indirect hybrid deduction under the imported mismatch arrangement is 80, E Co's cross-border payment to C Co under the same arrangement is 40. The lower of these two numbers (i.e. 40) is treated as the amount of E Co's indirect hybrid deduction under the imported mismatch arrangement. Country E should therefore deny 40 of deduction under the imported mismatch rule.

Flow Diagram 1 (Example 8.1)

Neutralising hybrid deduction under the structured and direct imported mismatch rule

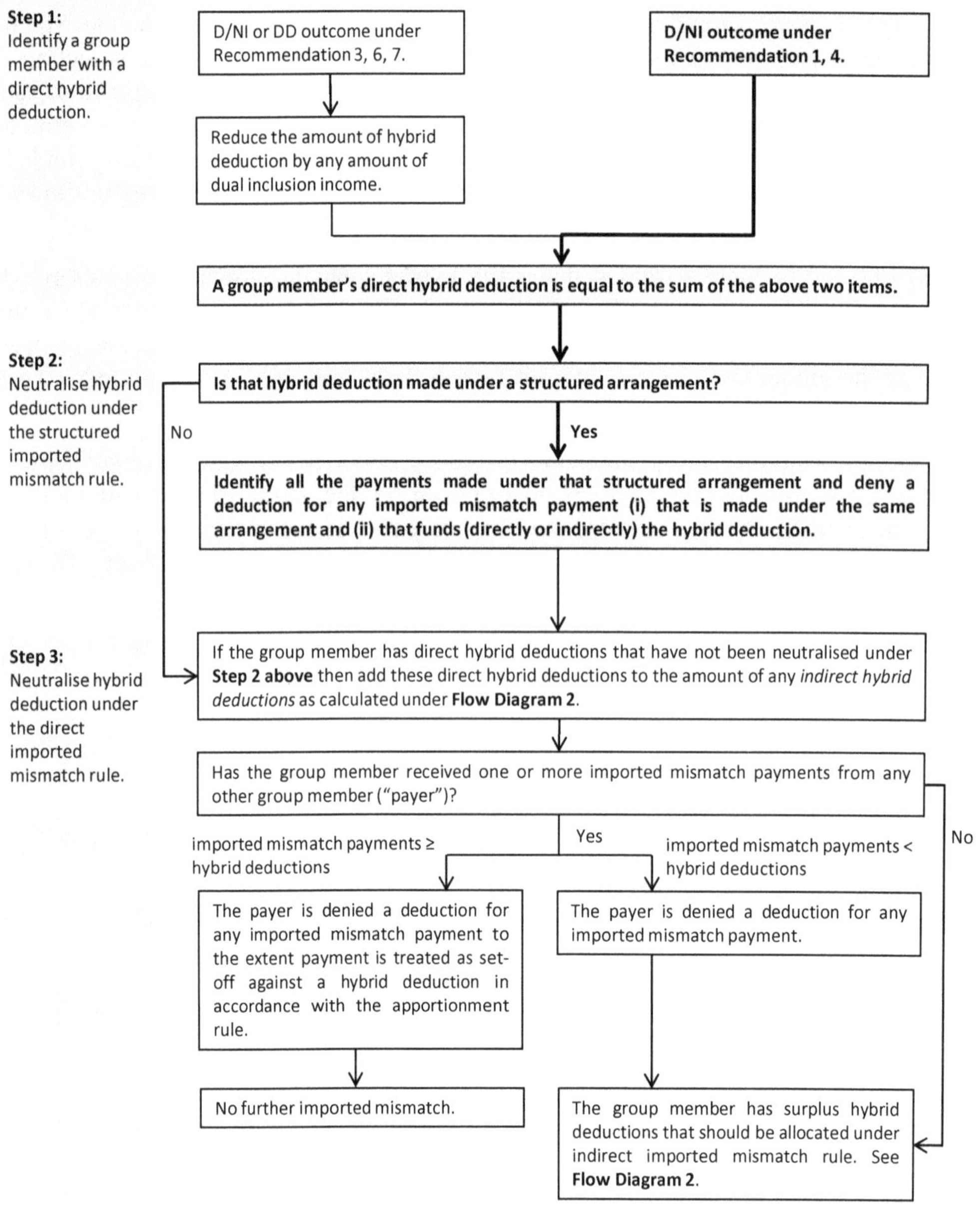

Example 8.2

Structured imported mismatch rule and direct imported mismatch rule

Facts

1. The facts are the same as in **Example 8.1** except that B Co already has an existing funding arrangement in place with D Co that is unconnected with the group financing structure and that C Co, D Co and E Co (the shaded entities) are all resident in jurisdictions that have implemented the recommendations set out in the report. The figure below illustrates the total gross interest payments made in each accounting period under the group's financing structure.

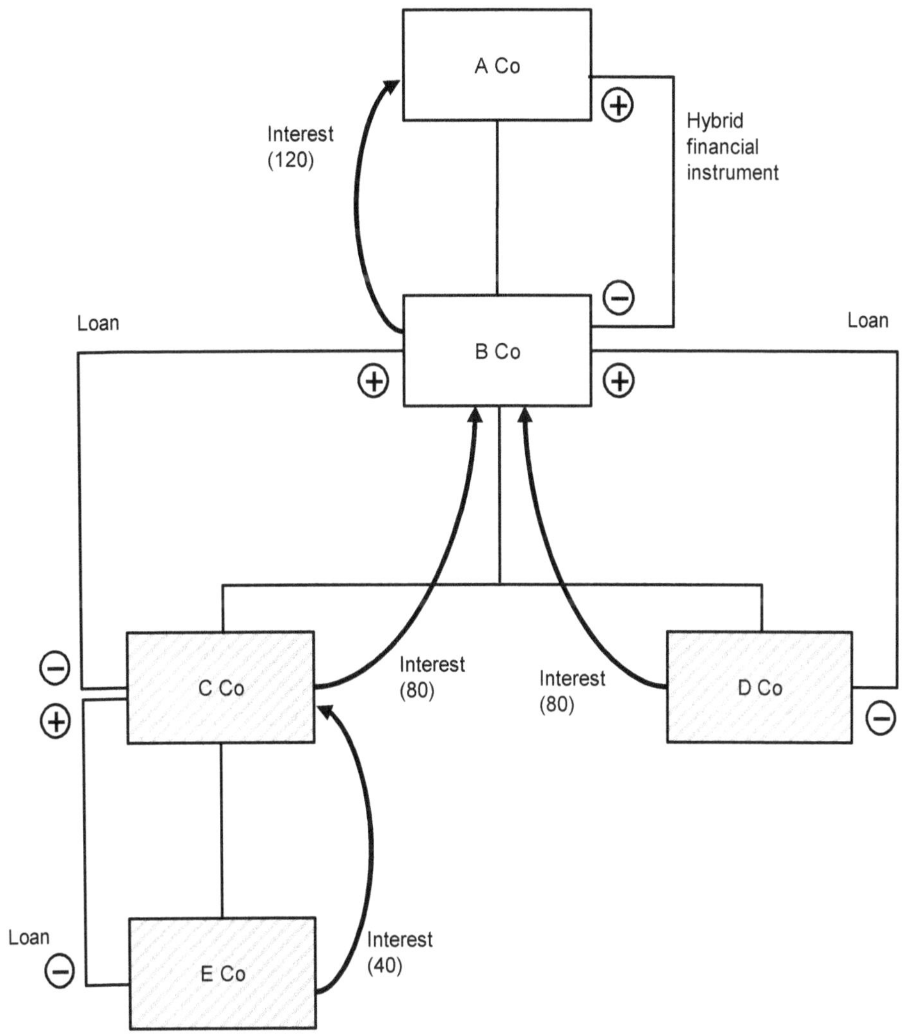

Question

2. Whether the interest payments made by C Co, D Co or E Co are subject to adjustment under the imported mismatch rule and, if so, the amount of the adjustment required under the rule.

Answer

3. The structured imported mismatch rule will apply in Country C to deny the full amount of C Co's interest deduction.

4. The interest payment made by D Co should not be treated as made under a structured arrangement unless the D Co loan and the other group financing arrangements were entered into as part of the same overall scheme, plan or understanding. Country D should, however, apply the direct imported mismatch rule to deny half of the interest payment paid to B Co (i.e. 40 of deductions should be denied under Country D law).

5. The interest payment made by E Co is made to a payee that is subject to the hybrid mismatch rules. The payment is therefore not an imported mismatch payment and is not subject to adjustment under Recommendation 8.

6. See the flow diagram at the end of this example which outlines of the steps to be taken in applying the imported mismatch rule.

Analysis

No application of the imported mismatch rule in Country E

7. The imported mismatch rule will not apply to any payment made to a payee that is a taxpayer in a jurisdiction that has implemented the full set of recommendations set out in the report. The hybrid mismatch rules in Country C will neutralise the effect of any hybrid mismatch arrangements entered into by C Co (including the effect of any imported mismatch arrangements) so that the income from any payment made by E Co to C Co will not be offset against a hybrid deduction.

D Co's interest payment is not made under a structured imported mismatch arrangement

8. The interest payments made by C Co are treated as paid under a structured imported mismatch arrangement because the hybrid financial instrument and the loan between C Co and B Co are part of the same group financing arrangement. The loan between C Co and D Co was in place before the hybrid financial arrangement was entered into and, unless that loan could be shown to be part of the same scheme plan or understanding as the financing arrangements put in place for the rest of the group, then the interest payment made by D Co should be treated as outside the scope of the structured imported mismatch rules.

The interest payments made by C Co and D Co should be subject to adjustment under the structured and direct imported mismatch rule

Step 1 – B Co's payment under the hybrid financial instrument gives rise to a direct hybrid deduction

9. The interest payments under the hybrid financial instrument give rise to a direct hybrid deduction for B Co of 120.

Step 2 –B Co's hybrid deduction and C Co's imported mismatch payment are part of the same structured arrangement

10. The payment made by B Co under the hybrid financial instrument and the imported mismatch payment made by C Co should be treated as part of the same structured arrangement (see the analysis in **Example 8.1** above).

11. The structured imported mismatch rule requires the payer jurisdiction to deny a deduction for an imported mismatch payment to the extent the income from such payment is offset (directly or indirectly) against a hybrid deduction under the same structured arrangement. In this case B Co has a hybrid deduction of 120 and C Co has made a cross-border payment to B Co under the same arrangement of 80. Accordingly the full amount of the imported mismatch payment is treated as set-off against the hybrid deduction under the structured imported mismatch rule.

Step 3 – B Co's remaining hybrid deductions should be treated as set-off against the imported mismatch payment made by D Co

12. The direct imported mismatch rule should be applied in Country D to deny D Co a deduction for the interest payment made to B Co to the extent that the income from that payment is off-set against any remaining hybrid deductions.

13. The guidance to the imported mismatch rule sets out an apportionment formula which can be used to determine the extent to which an imported mismatch payment has been directly set-off against any remaining hybrid deductions. The formula is as follows:

$$\text{Imported mismatch payment made by payer} \times \frac{\text{Total amount of remaining hybrid deductions incurred}}{\text{Total amount of imported mismatch payments received}}$$

14. On the facts of this example the ratio of remaining hybrid deductions to imported mismatch payments is 40/80 so that half the imported mismatch payments made by D Co to B Co are subject to adjustment under the direct imported mismatch rule.

Flow Diagram 1 (Example 8.2)

Neutralising hybrid deduction under the structured and direct imported mismatch rule

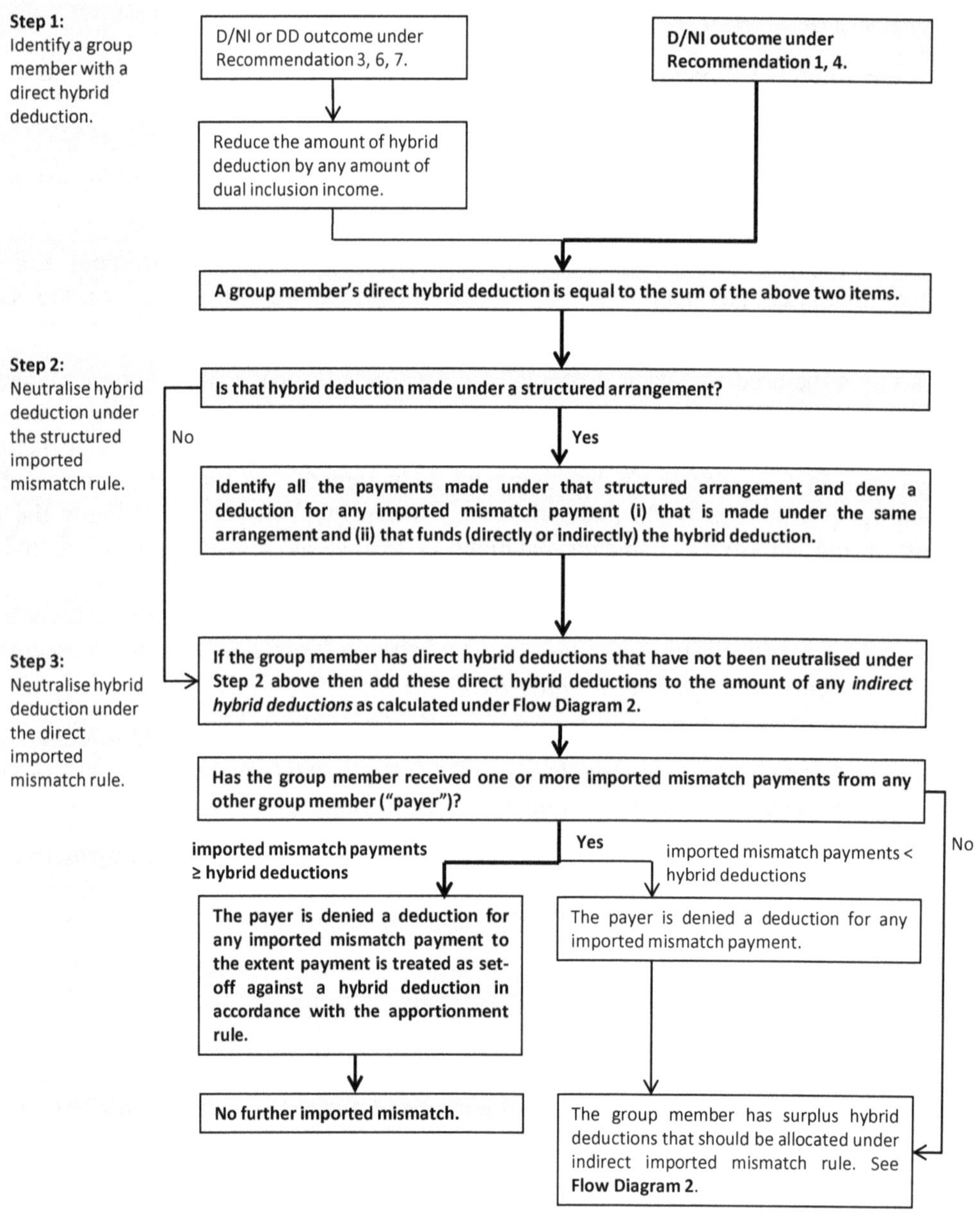

Example 8.3

Application of the direct imported mismatch rule

1. The figure below sets out the financing arrangements for companies that are members of the same group. In this case A Co has lent money to C Co. C Co has lent money to B Co and D Co and B Co and D Co have lent money to their subsidiaries. Each company is tax resident in different jurisdiction.

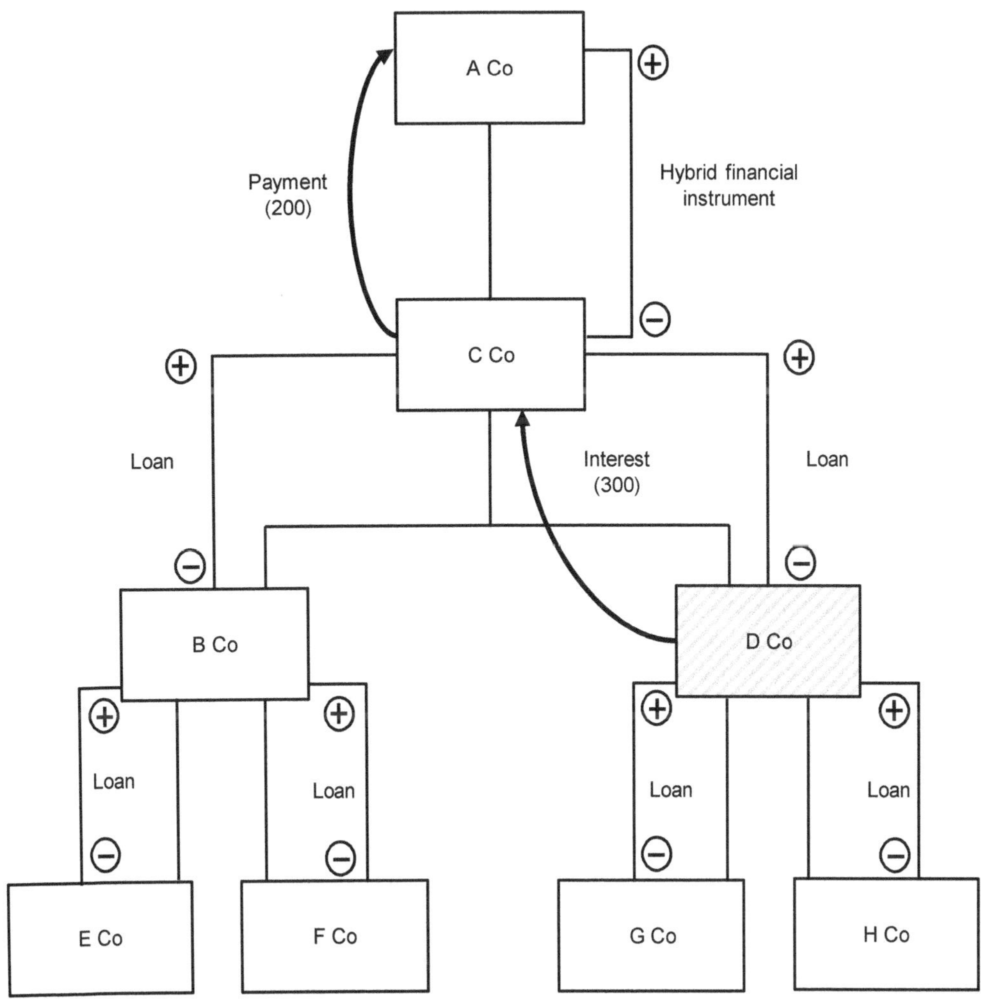

2. As illustrated in the diagram, the loan between A Co and C Co is a hybrid financial instrument. The hybrid financial instrument is not, however, entered into as part of a wider structured arrangement. The hybrid deduction arising under the hybrid financial instrument is 200. D Co (the shaded entity) is the only entity in the group that is

resident in a country that has implemented the recommendations set out in the report. D Co makes a deductible intra-group interest payment to C Co of 300.

Question

3. Whether the interest payment made by D Co is subject to adjustment under the imported mismatch rule and, if so, the amount of the adjustment required under the rule.

Answer

4. Country D should deny D Co a deduction for two-thirds (i.e. 200) of the interest paid to C Co. See the flow diagram at the end of this example which outlines of the steps to be taken in applying the imported mismatch rule.

Analysis

D Co's interest payments should be subject to adjustment under the direct imported mismatch rule

Step 1 – C Co's payment under the hybrid financial instrument gives rise to a direct hybrid deduction

5. The interest payments under the hybrid financial instrument give rise to a direct hybrid deduction for C Co of 200.

Step 2 – the structured imported mismatch rule does not apply

6. The facts of this example assume that the hybrid financial instrument is not entered into as part of a wider structured arrangement. Therefore the structured imported mismatch rule does not apply.

Step 3 – The imported mismatch payment made by D Co is treated as set-off against C Co's hybrid deduction under the direct imported mismatch rule

7. The direct imported mismatch rule should be applied in Country D to deny D Co a deduction for the interest payment to the extent C Co offsets the income from that payment against any hybrid deductions. The guidance to the imported mismatch rule sets out an apportionment formula which can be used to determine the extent to which an imported mismatch payment has been directly set-off against the hybrid deduction of a counterparty. The formula is as follows:

$$\text{Imported mismatch payment made by payer} \times \frac{\text{Total amount of remaining hybrid deductions incurred}}{\text{Total amount of imported mismatch payments received}}$$

8. In this case C Co receives only one imported mismatch payment (from D Co). Accordingly the amount of D Co's imported mismatch payment that should be treated as set-off against the hybrid deduction (and therefore the amount of deduction disallowed under Country D law) is calculated as follows:

$$\text{Imported mismatch payments made by D Co} \times \frac{\text{C Co's hybrid deduction}}{\text{Imported mismatch payments received by C Co}} = 300 \times \frac{200}{300} = 200$$

Flow Diagram 1 (Example 8.3)

Neutralising hybrid deduction under the structured and direct imported mismatch rule

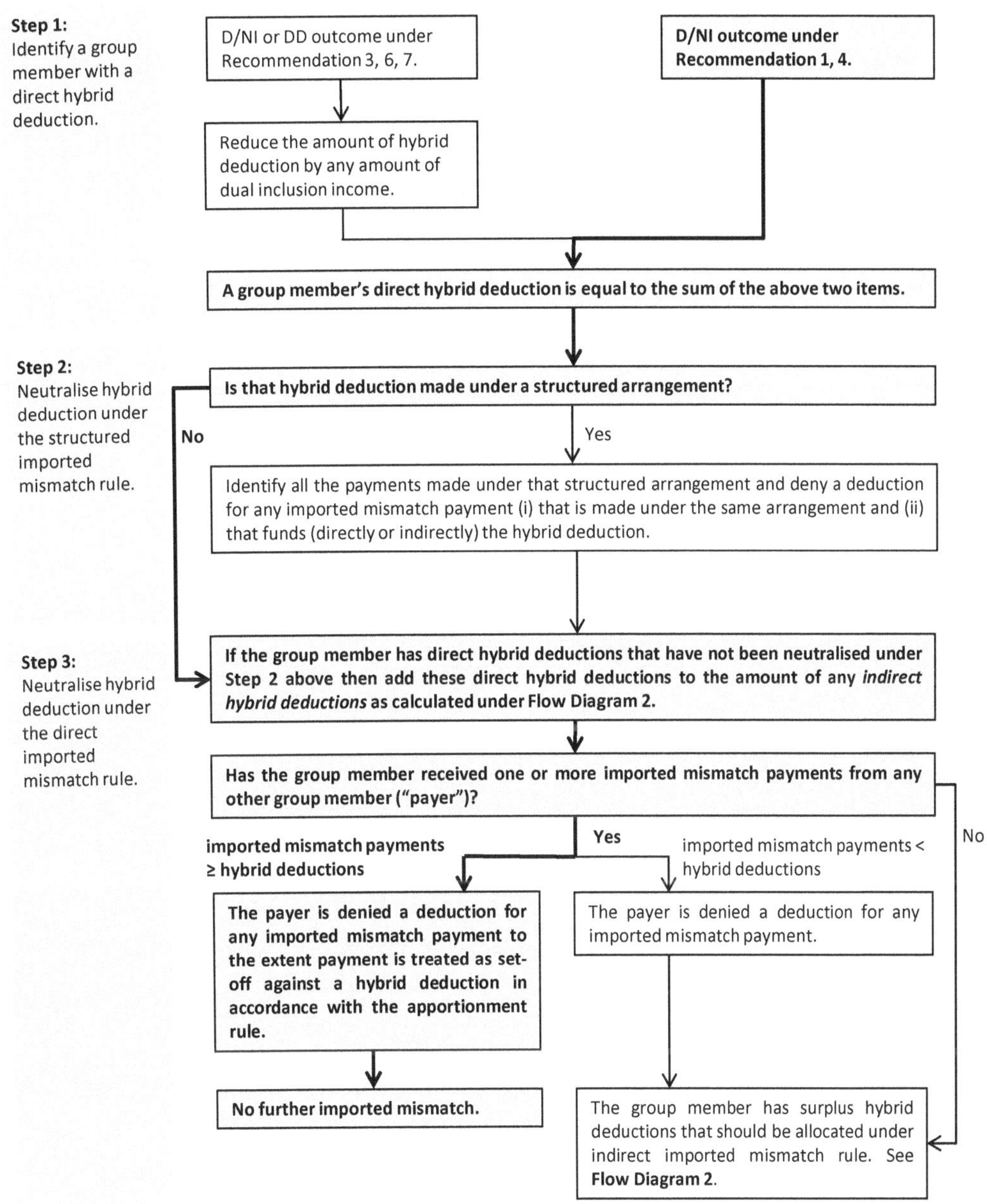

Example 8.4

Apportionment under direct imported mismatch rule

1. The facts as set out in the diagram below are the same as in **Example 8.3**, except that both B Co and D Co (the shaded entities) are resident in a country that has implemented the recommendations set out in the report. B Co makes a deductible intra-group interest payment to C Co of 100 and D Co makes a deductible intra-group interest payment to C Co of 300.

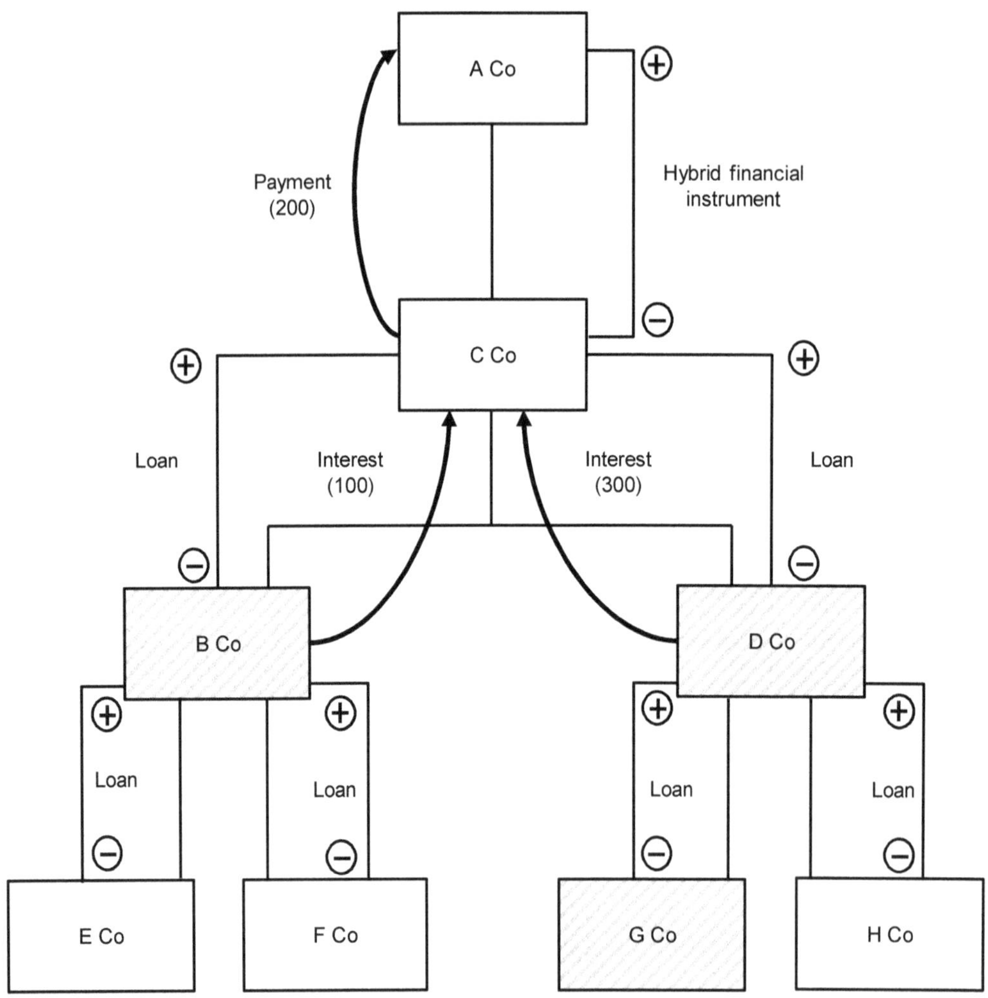

Question

2. Whether the interest payments made by B Co or D Co are subject to adjustment under the imported mismatch rule and, if so, the amount of the adjustment required under the rule.

Answer

Country B and Country D should deny their taxpayers a deduction for half (i.e. 50 and 150 respectively) of the interest paid to C Co. See the flow diagram at the end of this example which outlines of the steps to be taken in applying the imported mismatch rule.

Analysis

The interest payments made by B Co and D Co should be subject to adjustment under the direct imported mismatch rule

Step 1 – C Co's payment under the hybrid financial instrument gives rise to a direct hybrid deduction

3. The interest payments under the hybrid financial instrument give rise to a direct hybrid deduction for C Co of 200.

Step 2 – the structured imported mismatch rule does not apply

4. The facts of this example assume that the hybrid financial instrument is not entered into as part of a wider structured arrangement. Therefore the structured imported mismatch rule does not apply.

Step 3 – the imported mismatch payments made by B Co and D Co are treated as set-off against C Co's hybrid deduction under the direct imported mismatch rule

5. The direct imported mismatch rule should be applied, in both Country B and Country D, to deny B Co and D Co (respectively) deductions for the interest payments made to C Co to the extent these payments are offset against any hybrid deductions. The guidance to the imported mismatch rule sets out an apportionment formula which can be used to determine the extent to which an imported mismatch payment has been directly set-off against a counterparty's hybrid deductions. The formula is as follows:

$$\text{Imported mismatch payment made by payer} \times \frac{\text{Total amount of remaining hybrid deductions incurred}}{\text{Total amount of imported mismatch payments received}}$$

6. In this case the proportion of each imported mismatch payment that should be treated as set-off against a hybrid deduction (and therefore subject to adjustment under the laws imported mismatch rules in the payer jurisdiction) is calculated as follows:

$$\frac{\text{C Co's hybrid deduction}}{\text{Imported mismatch payments received by C Co}} = \frac{200}{100+300} = \frac{200}{400} = \frac{1}{2}$$

7. Applying this ratio under the direct imported mismatch rules of Country B and Country D, the amount of interest deduction denied under Country B law will be 50

(i.e. 1/2 x 100) and the amount of interest deduction denied under Country D law will be 150 (i.e. 1/2 x 300).

Flow Diagram 1 (Example 8.4)

Neutralising hybrid deduction under the structured and direct imported mismatch rule

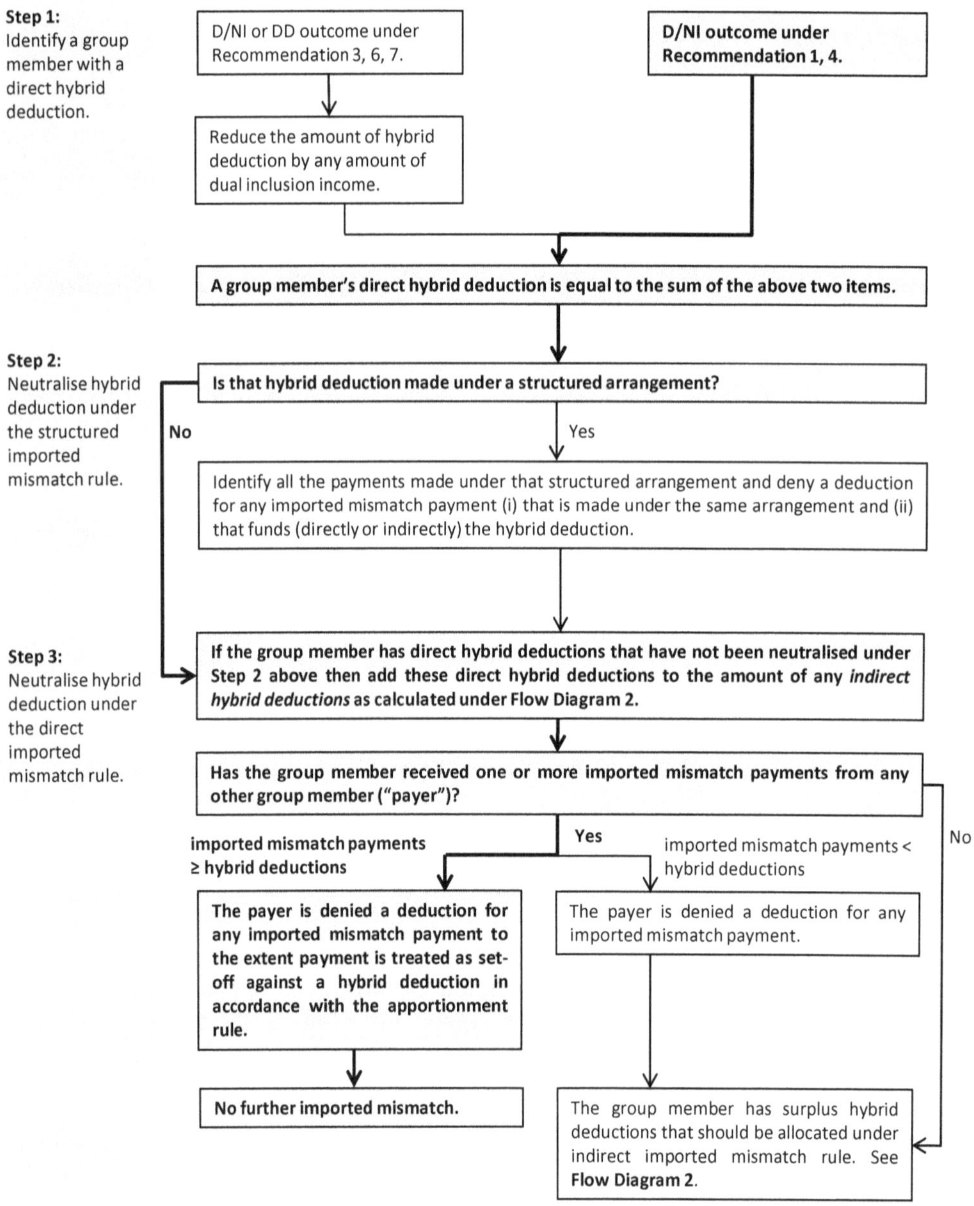

Example 8.5

Application of the indirect imported mismatch rule

1. The facts illustrated in the figure below are the same as in **Example 8.3**, except that G Co (the shaded entity) is the only group entity resident in a jurisdiction that has implemented the recommendations set out in the report. G Co makes a deductible intra-group interest payment to D Co of 200 and D Co makes a deductible intra-group interest payment to C Co of 300

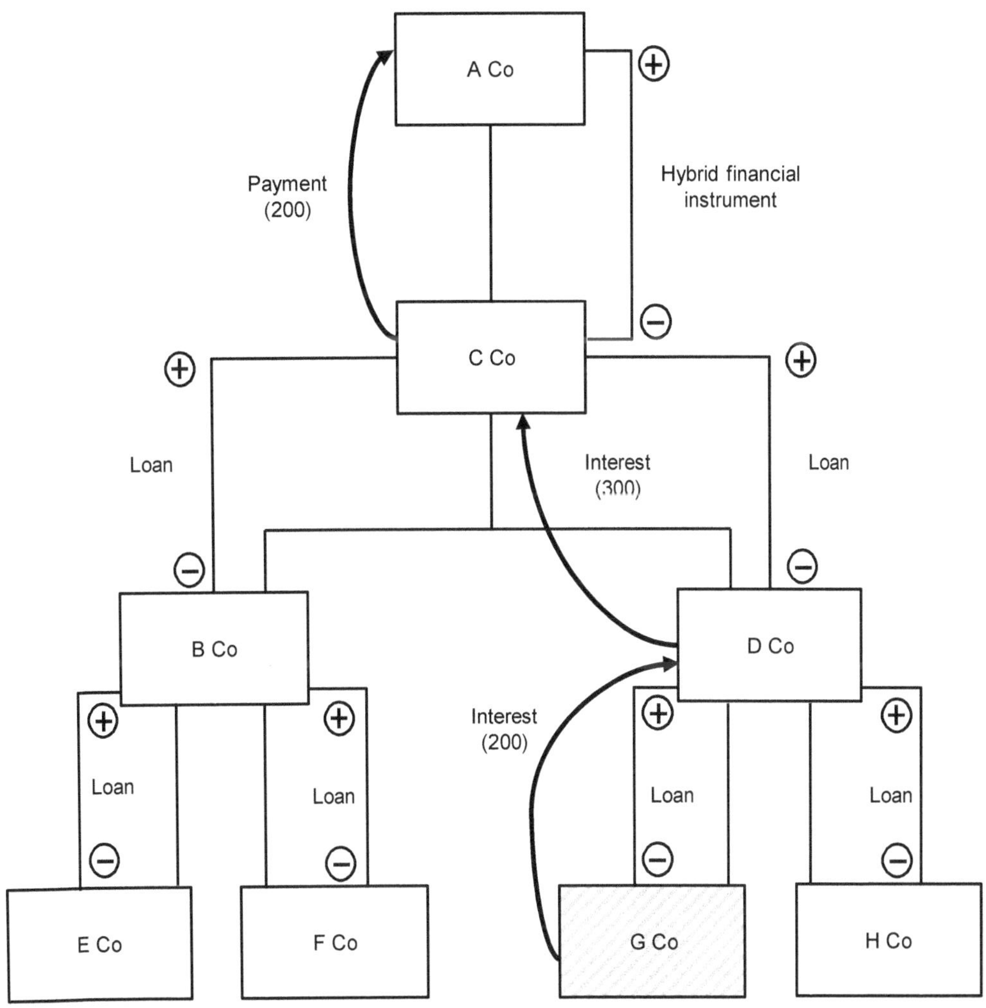

Question

2. Whether the interest payment made by G Co is subject to adjustment under the imported mismatch rule and, if so, the amount of the adjustment required under the rule.

Answer

3. Country G should deny G Co a deduction for all (i.e. 200) of the interest paid to D Co. See the flow diagrams at the end of this example which outline the steps to be taken in applying the imported mismatch rule.

Analysis

C Co's hybrid deduction is not set-off against an imported mismatch payment under the structured or direct imported mismatch rule

Step 1 – C Co's payment under the hybrid financial instrument gives rise to a direct hybrid deduction

4. The interest payments under the hybrid financial instrument give rise to a direct hybrid deduction for C Co of 200.

Step 2 – the structured imported mismatch rule does not apply

5. The facts of this example assume that the hybrid financial instrument is not entered into as part of a wider structured arrangement. Therefore the structured imported mismatch rule does not apply.

Step 3 – the direct imported mismatch rules does not apply

6. In this case the *direct imported mismatch rule* does not apply as the group entities that are *directly* funding the hybrid deduction (i.e. B Co and D Co) are resident in jurisdictions that have not implemented the imported mismatch rules.

The interest payments made by G Co should be subject to adjustment under the indirect imported mismatch rule

7. As C Co's hybrid deduction has not been neutralised under the structured or direct imported mismatch rule, the indirect imported mismatch rule applies to determine the extent to which C Co's surplus hybrid deduction should be treated as giving rise to an indirect hybrid deduction for another group member.

Step 1 – C Co has surplus hybrid deductions of 200

8. In this case the total amount of C Co's surplus hybrid deduction will be the amount of the direct hybrid deduction that is attributable to payments under the hybrid financial instrument (200) minus any amount of hybrid deduction that has been neutralised under either the structured or direct imported mismatch rules (0).

Step 2 – C Co's surplus hybrid deduction are fully set-off against funded taxable payments

9. C Co must first treat that surplus hybrid deduction as being offset against funded taxable payments received from group entities. A taxable payment will be treated as a funded taxable payment to the extent the payment is directly funded out of imported mismatch payments made by other group entities. In this case G Co makes an imported mismatch payment of 200 to D Co and, accordingly, two-thirds (i.e. 200/300) of the taxable payments that D Co makes to C Co should be treated as funded taxable payments.

10. In this case the funded taxable payment by D Co (200) is equal to the total amount of C Co's surplus hybrid deduction (200). C Co is therefore treated as setting-off all of its surplus hybrid deduction against funded taxable payments which results in D Co having an indirect hybrid deduction of 200.

Step 3 – C Co has no remaining surplus hybrid deduction

11. C Co's surplus hybrid deduction is fully set-off against funded taxable payments and C Co therefore has no remaining surplus hybrid deduction to be set-off against other taxable payments.

Step 4 – D Co's indirect hybrid deduction is neutralised in accordance with the direct imported mismatch rule

12. The indirect hybrid deduction incurred by D Co under Step 2 above is treated as being set-off against imported mismatch payments made by G Co. The amount of deduction that is treated as set-off against G Co's imported mismatch payment is calculated on the same basis as under the direct imported mismatch rule:

$$\text{Imported mismatch payments made by G Co} \times \frac{\text{D Co's hybrid deduction}}{\text{Imported mismatch payments received by D Co}} = 200 \times \frac{200}{200} = 200$$

Flow Diagram 1 (Example 8.5)

Neutralising hybrid deduction under the structured and direct imported mismatch rule

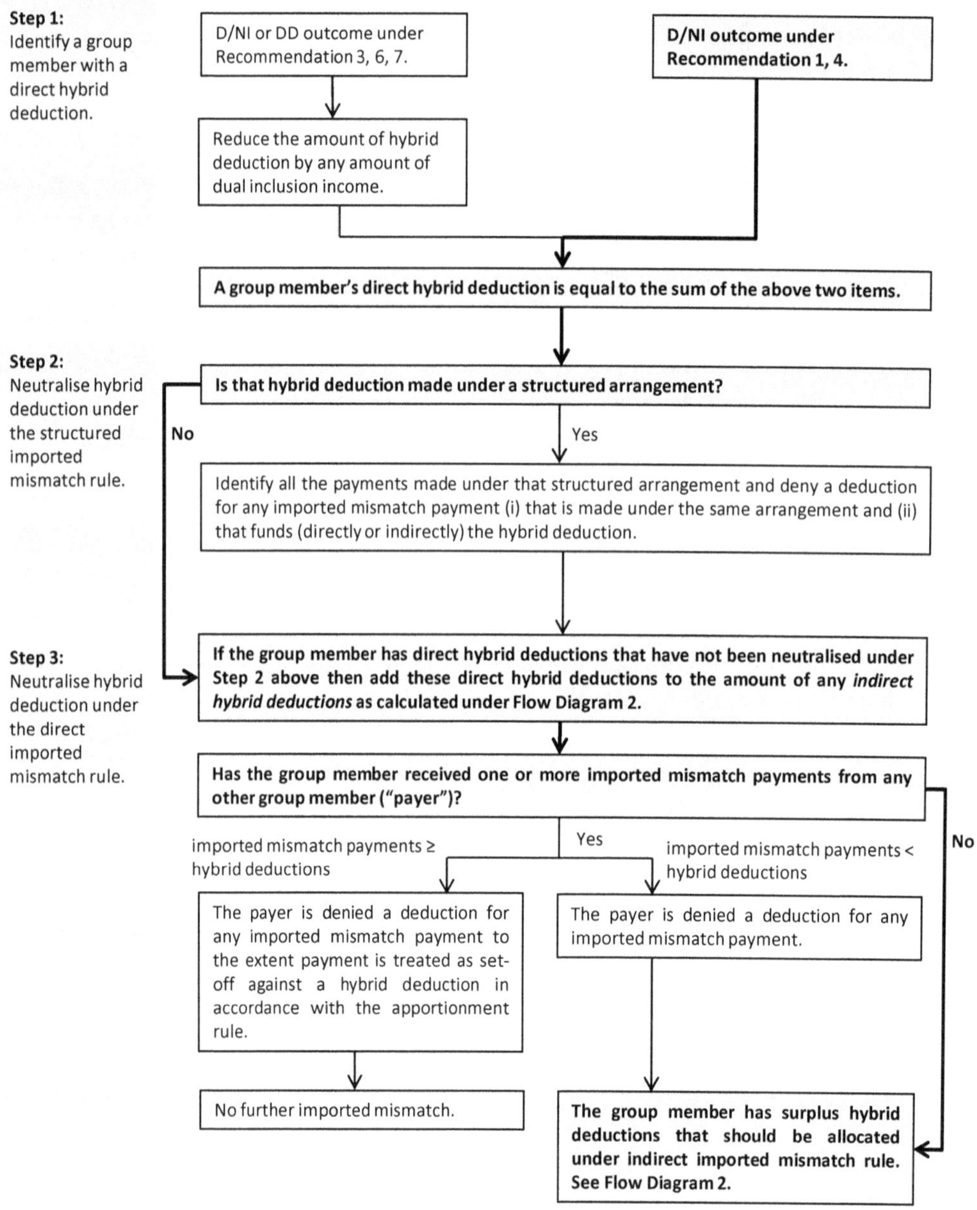

Flow Diagram 2 (Example 8.5)

Allocating surplus hybrid deduction under the indirect imported mismatch rule

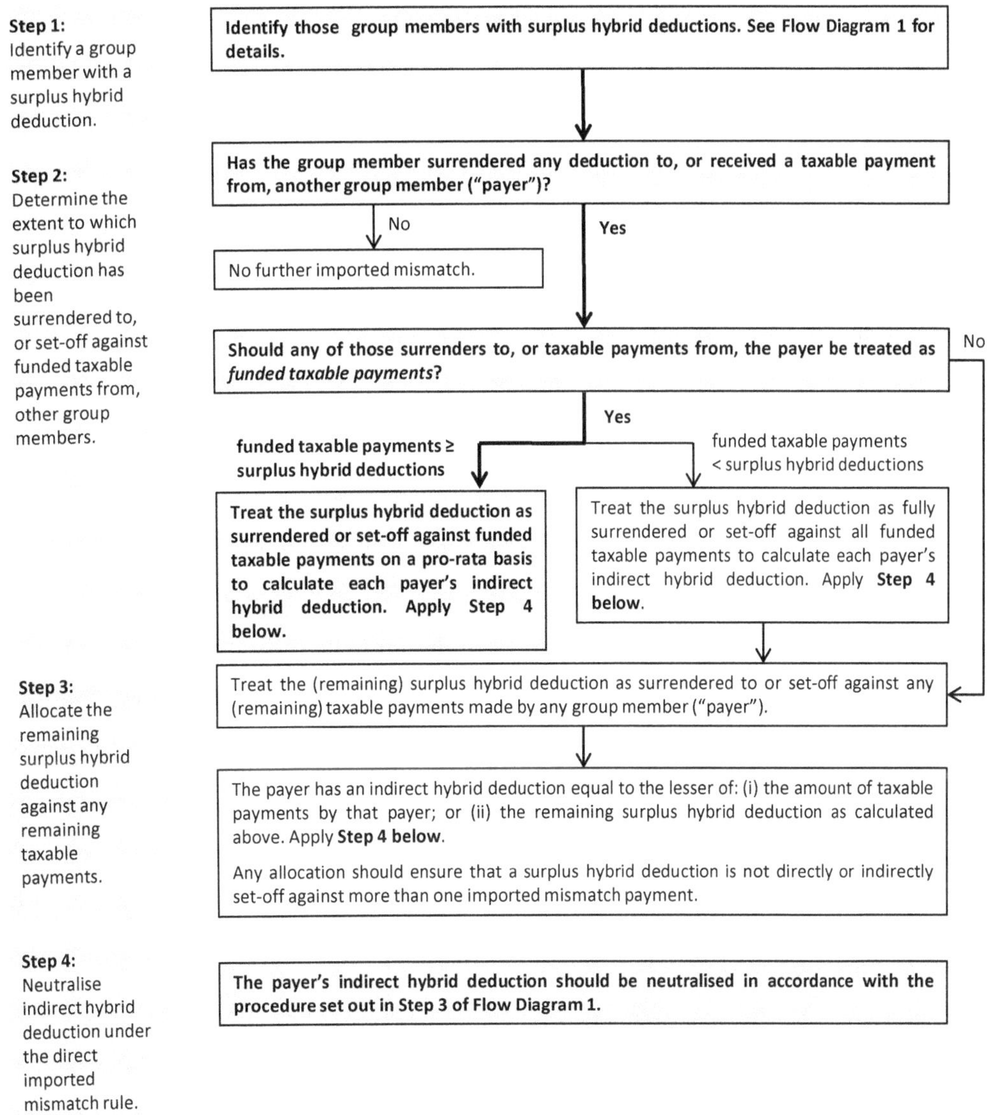

Example 8.6

Payments to a group member that is subject to the imported mismatch rules

1. The facts illustrated in the figure below are the same as in **Example 8.3**, except that D Co, G Co and H Co (the shaded entities) are all resident in jurisdictions that have implemented the recommendations set out in the report. G Co and H Co each make a deductible intra-group interest payment to D Co of 400 and D Co makes a deductible intra-group interest payment to C Co of 300. C Co's hybrid deduction is 400.

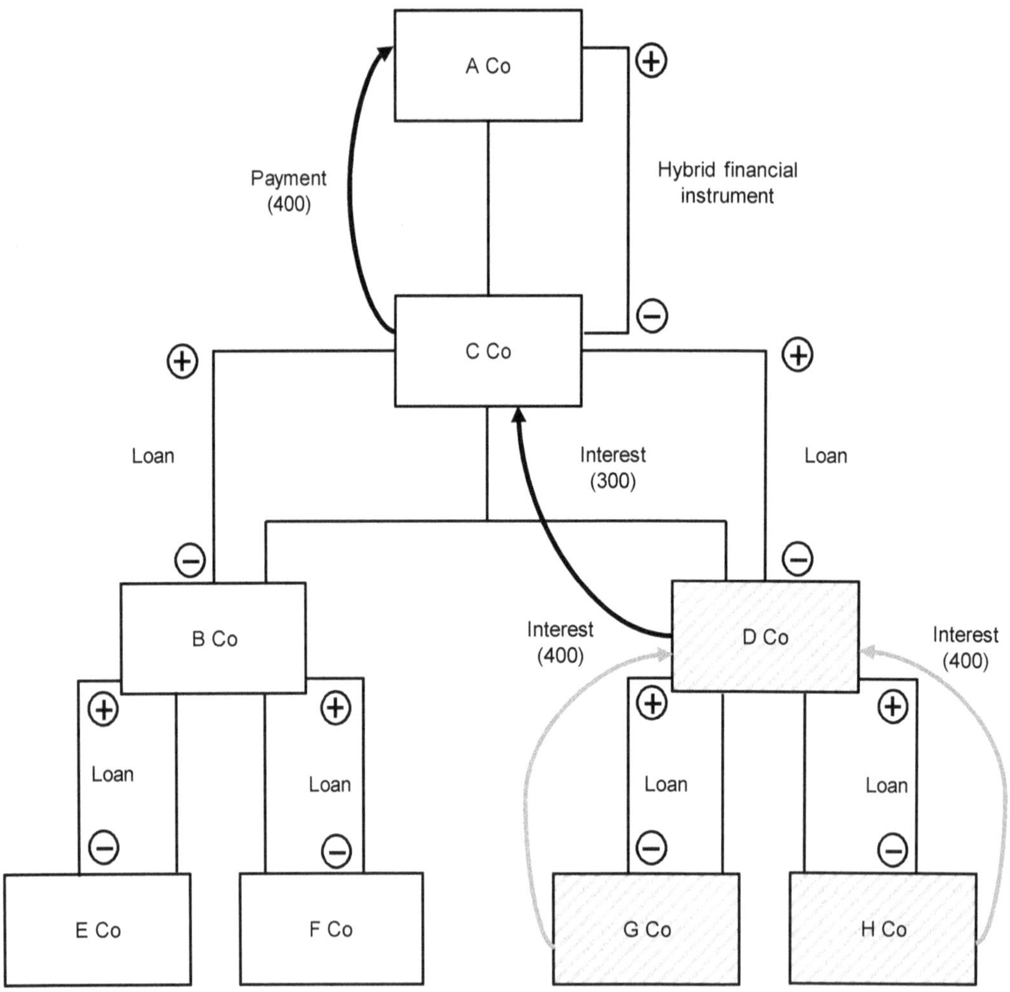

Question

2. Whether the interest payments made by G Co, H Co or D Co are subject to adjustment under the imported mismatch rule and, if so, the amount of the adjustment required under the rule.

Answer

3. Country D should deny D Co a deduction for all (i.e. 300) of the interest paid to C Co. No adjustment is required under the imported mismatch payments made by G Co and H Co as these payments are made to a taxpayer that is subject to the imported mismatch rule under the laws of its own jurisdiction. See the flow diagrams at the end of this example which outline the steps to be taken in applying the imported mismatch rule.

Analysis

No application of the imported mismatch rule in Country G or H

4. The imported mismatch rule will not apply to any payment made to a payee that is a taxpayer in a jurisdiction that has implemented the full set of recommendations set out in the report. The ability of D Co to generate direct or indirect hybrid deductions is eliminated through the hybrid mismatch rules in Country D, so that the income from any imported mismatch payment made by G Co or H Co cannot be offset against an indirect hybrid deduction incurred by D Co.

D Co's interest payments should be subject to adjustment under the imported mismatch rule

Step 1 – C Co's payment under the hybrid financial instrument gives rise to a direct hybrid deduction

5. The interest payments under the hybrid financial instrument give rise to a direct hybrid deduction for C Co of 400.

Step 2 – the structured imported mismatch rule does not apply

6. The facts of this example assume that the hybrid financial instrument is not entered into as part of a wider structured arrangement. Therefore the structured imported mismatch rule does not apply.

Step 3 – the imported mismatch payment made by D Co is treated as set-off against C Co's hybrid deduction under the direct imported mismatch rule

7. The direct imported mismatch rule should be applied in Country D to deny D Co a deduction for the interest payment to the extent C Co offsets the income from that payment against any hybrid deductions. In this case C Co receives only one imported mismatch payment (from D Co) which is less than the amount of C Co's hybrid deductions. D Co should therefore be denied a deduction for the full amount of the imported mismatch payment and C Co will have surplus hybrid deductions that would be eligible to be allocated in accordance with the indirect imported mismatch rule.

Flow Diagram 1 (Example 8.6)
Neutralising hybrid deduction under the structured and direct imported mismatch rule

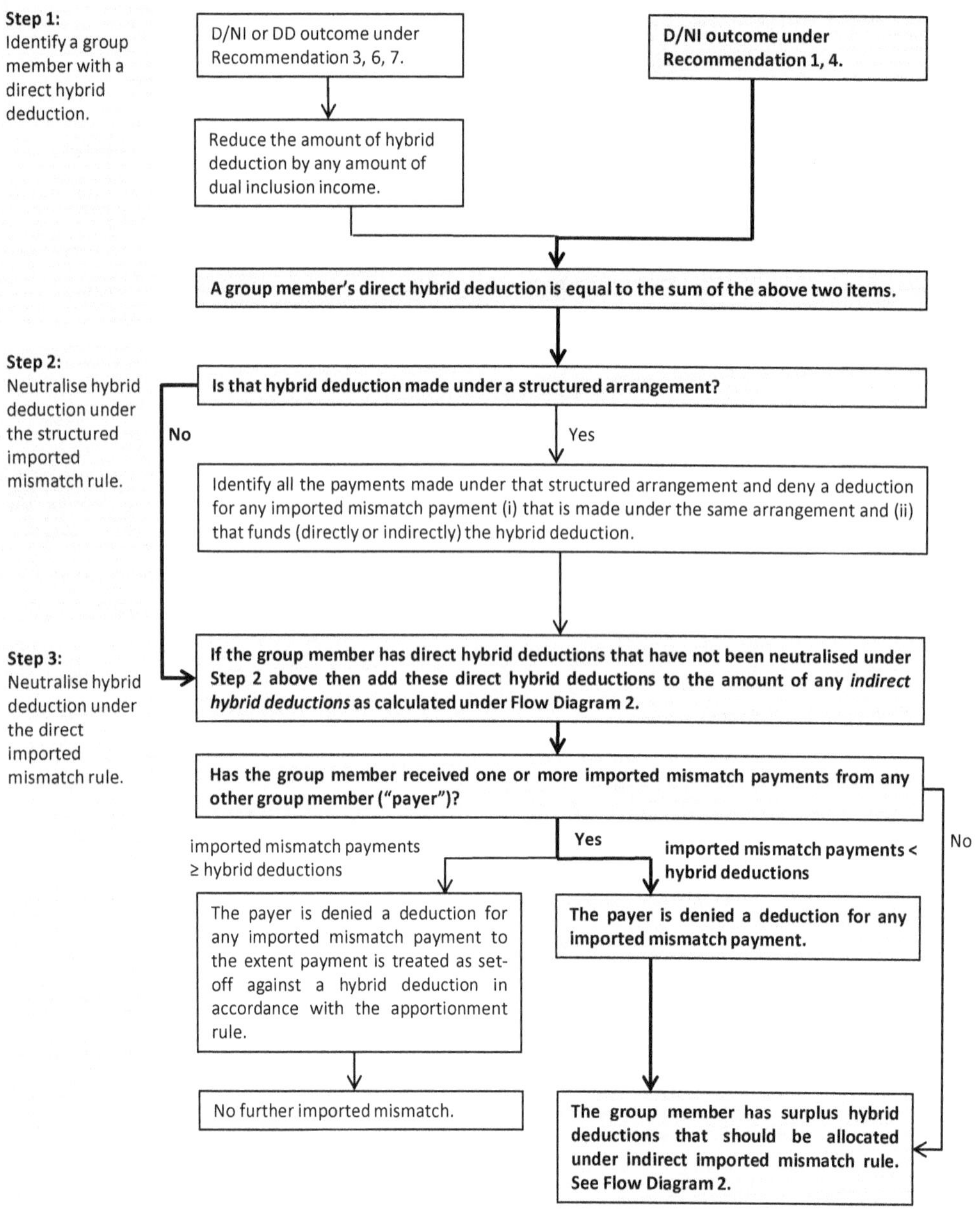

Example 8.7

Direct imported mismatch rule applies in priority to indirect imported mismatch rule

1. The facts illustrated in the figure below are the same as in **Example 8.3**, except that D Co, E Co and F Co (the shaded entities) are all resident in jurisdictions that have implemented the recommendations set out in the report. E Co and F Co each make a deductible intra-group interest payment to B Co of 100 and D Co makes a deductible intra-group interest payment to C Co of 200. C Co's hybrid deduction is 200.

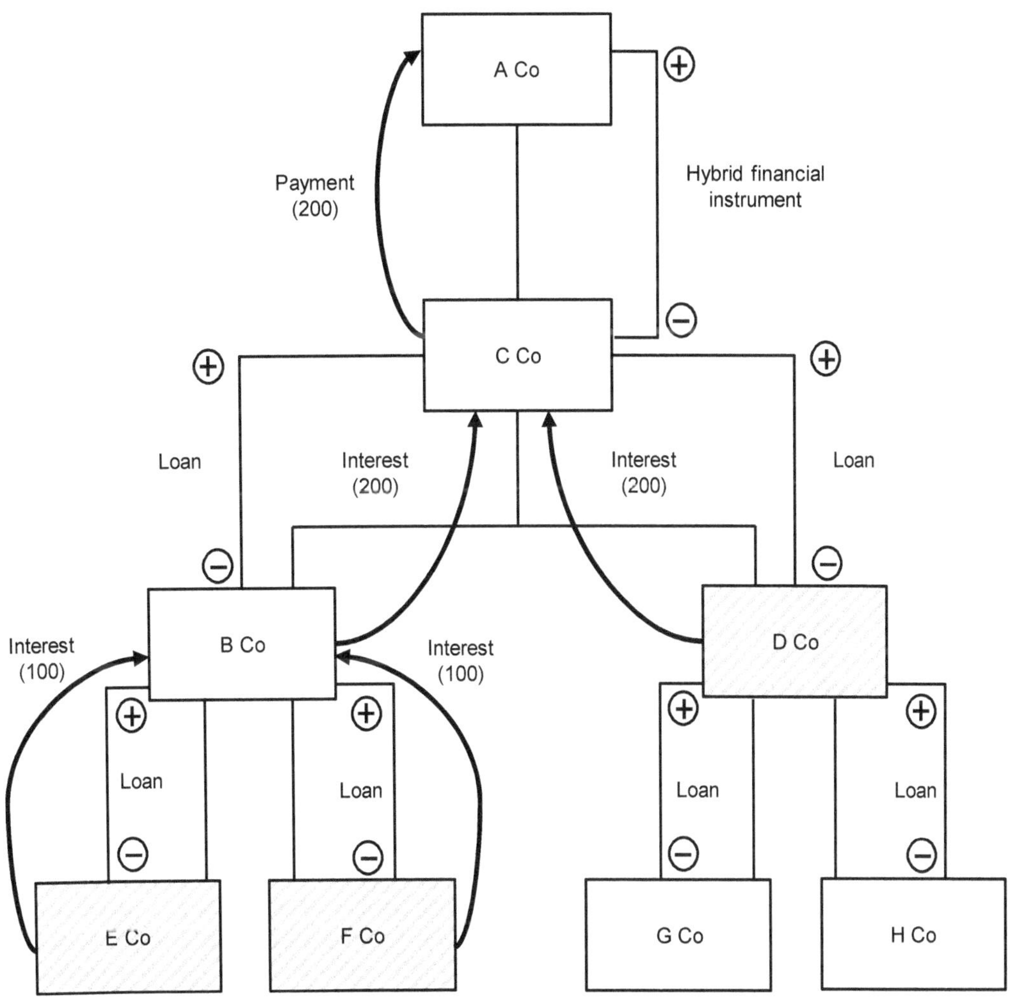

Question

2. Whether the interest payment made by E Co, F Co or D Co is subject to adjustment under the imported mismatch rule and, if so, the amount of the adjustment required under the rule.

Answer

3. Country D should deny D Co a deduction for all (i.e. 200) of the interest paid to C Co. C Co has no surplus hybrid deduction so that the application of the indirect imported mismatch rule in Country E and Country F does not result in any denial of a deduction for E Co or F Co. See the flow diagram at the end of this example which outlines of the steps to be taken in applying the imported mismatch rule.

Analysis

D Co's interest payments should be subject to adjustment under the imported mismatch rule

Step 1 – C Co's payment under the hybrid financial instrument gives rise to a direct hybrid deduction

4. The interest payments under the hybrid financial instrument give rise to a direct hybrid deduction for B Co of 200.

Step 2 – the structured imported mismatch rule does not apply

5. The facts of this example assume that the hybrid financial instrument is not entered into as part of a wider structured arrangement. Therefore the structured imported mismatch rule does not apply.

Step 3 – the imported mismatch payment made by D Co is treated as set-off against C Co's hybrid deduction under the direct imported mismatch rule

6. The direct imported mismatch rule should be applied in Country D to deny D Co a deduction for the interest payment to the extent C Co offsets the income from that payment against any hybrid deductions. The guidance to the imported mismatch rule sets out an apportionment formula which can be used to determine the extent to which an imported mismatch payment has been directly set-off against a counterparty's hybrid deductions. The formula is as follows:

$$\text{Imported mismatch payment made by payer} \times \frac{\text{Total amount of remaining hybrid deductions incurred}}{\text{Total amount of imported mismatch payments received}}$$

7. In this case C Co receives only one imported mismatch payment (from D Co). Accordingly the amount of D Co's imported mismatch payment that should be treated as set-off against the hybrid deduction (and therefore the amount of deduction disallowed under Country D law) is calculated as follows:

$$\text{Imported mismatch payments made by D Co} \times \frac{\text{C Co's hybrid deduction}}{\text{Imported mismatch payments received by C Co}} = 200 \times \frac{200}{200} = 200$$

8. Under this formula, all of C Co's hybrid deductions are treated as set-off against imported mismatch payments. C Co therefore has no surplus hybrid deductions and there is no scope to apply the indirect imported mismatch rule.

Flow Diagram 1 (Example 8.7)

Neutralising hybrid deduction under the structured and direct imported mismatch rule

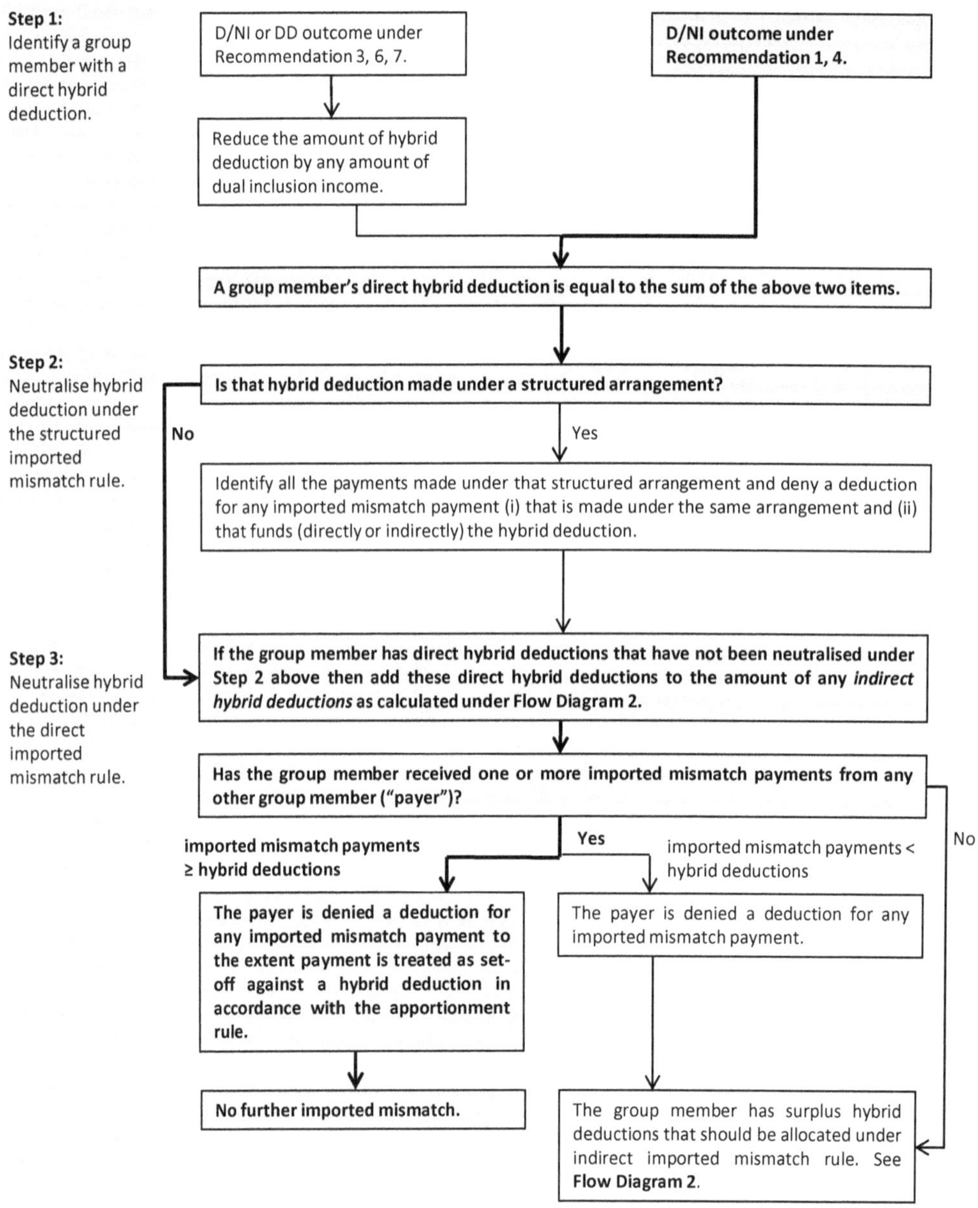

Example 8.8

Surplus hybrid deduction exceeds funded taxable payments

1. The facts illustrated in the figure below are the same as in **Example 8.3**, except that D Co, E Co and F Co (the shaded entities) are all resident in jurisdictions that have implemented the recommendations set out in the report. E Co makes a deductible intra-group interest payment to B Co of 50 while F Co makes a deductible intra-group interest payment to B Co of 150. D Co makes a deductible intra-group interest payment to C Co of 200 and B Co makes a payment of 500. C Co's hybrid deduction is 500.

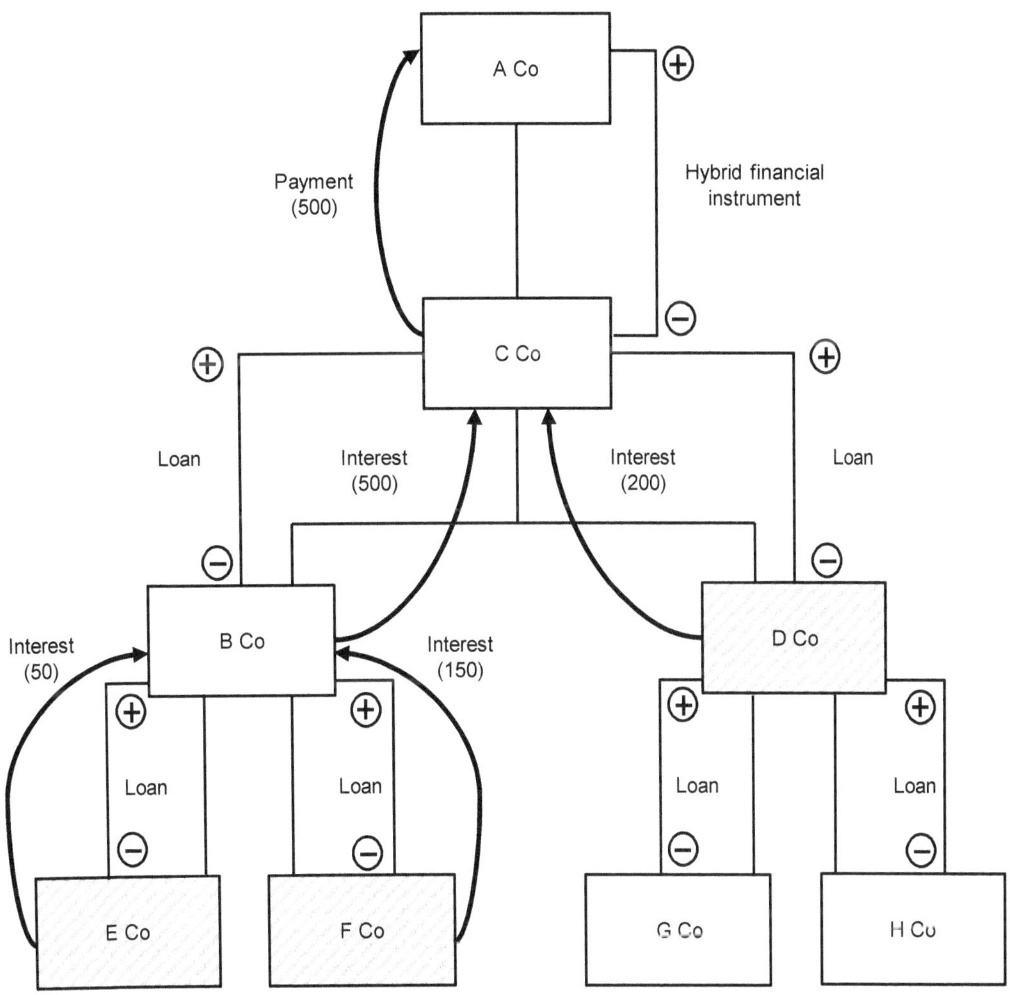

Question

2. Whether the interest payment made by D Co, E Co, or F Co is subject to adjustment under the imported mismatch rule and, if so, the amount of the adjustment required under the rule.

Answer

3. Countries D, E and F should deny D Co, E Co and F Co (respectively) a deduction for all the imported mismatch payments made by those taxpayers. C Co and B Co each are treated as having a remaining hybrid deduction of 100. See the flow diagrams at the end of this example which outline the steps to be taken in applying the imported mismatch rule.

Analysis

D Co's interest payments should be subject to adjustment under the imported mismatch rule

Step 1 – C Co's payment under the hybrid financial instrument gives rise to a direct hybrid deduction

4. The interest payments under the hybrid financial instrument give rise to a direct hybrid deduction for C Co of 500.

Step 2 – the structured imported mismatch rule does not apply

5. The facts of this example assume that the hybrid financial instrument is not entered into as part of a wider structured arrangement. Therefore the structured imported mismatch rule does not apply.

Step 3 – the imported mismatch payment made by D Co is treated as set-off against C Co's hybrid deduction under the direct imported mismatch rule

6. The direct imported mismatch rule should be applied in Country D to deny D Co a deduction for the interest payment to the extent C Co offsets the income from that payment against any hybrid deductions. In this case C Co receives only one imported mismatch payment (from D Co) which is less than the amount of C Co's hybrid deductions. D Co should therefore be denied a deduction for the full amount of the imported mismatch payment.

The interest payments made by E Co and F Co should be subject to adjustment under the indirect imported mismatch rule

7. As C Co's hybrid deduction has not been fully neutralised under the structured or direct imported mismatch rule, the indirect imported mismatch rule applies to determine the extent to which C Co's surplus hybrid deduction should be treated as giving rise to an indirect hybrid deduction for another group member.

Step 1 –C Co has surplus hybrid deductions of 300

8. In this case C Co's surplus hybrid deduction will be the amount of hybrid deduction that is attributable to payments under the hybrid financial instrument (500) minus any amount of hybrid deduction that has been neutralised under either the structured or direct imported mismatch rules (200).

Step 2 –C Co's surplus hybrid deduction are set-off against funded taxable payments

9. C Co must first treat that surplus hybrid deduction as being offset against funded taxable payments received from group entities. A taxable payment will be treated as a funded taxable payment to the extent the payment is directly funded out of imported mismatch payments made by other group entities. In this case B Co receives an imported mismatch payment of 50 from E Co and 150 from F Co and, accordingly, two fifths (i.e. 200/500 of the taxable payments that B Co makes to C Co should be treated as funded taxable payments.

10. In this case the funded taxable payment by B Co (200) is less than the total amount of C Co's surplus hybrid deduction (300). C Co therefore treats its surplus hybrid deduction as fully set-off against the funded taxable payment made by B Co which results in B Co having an indirect hybrid deduction of 200.

Step 3 – C Co's remaining surplus hybrid deductions are treated as set-off against any remaining taxable payments

11. C Co has a remaining surplus hybrid deduction of 100. This remaining surplus hybrid deduction should be treated as fully set-off against the remaining taxable payments made by B Co. This deemed offset will generate a further indirect hybrid deduction of 100 for B Co. Care should be taken, however, when applying the imported mismatch rule to ensure that the attribution of hybrid deductions under this step does not result in the same hybrid deduction being treated as offset against more than one imported mismatch payment. Any reduction in C Co's remaining surplus hybrid deduction (for example, as a consequence of the receiving an additional imported mismatch payment) should therefore be reflected in a corresponding adjustment to the amount of B Co's indirect hybrid deduction.

Step 4 – B Co's indirect hybrid deduction is neutralised in accordance with the direct imported mismatch rule

12. B Co treats indirect hybrid deduction as being set-off against imported mismatch payments made by E Co and F Co. The calculation is the same as under the direct imported mismatch rule. The proportion of deduction that E Co and F Co should be denied on their respective imported mismatch payments is 100% because B Co's indirect hybrid deductions are at least equal to the amount of imported mismatch payments it receives from E Co and F Co.

Flow Diagram 1 (Example 8.8)

Neutralising hybrid deduction under the structured and direct imported mismatch rule

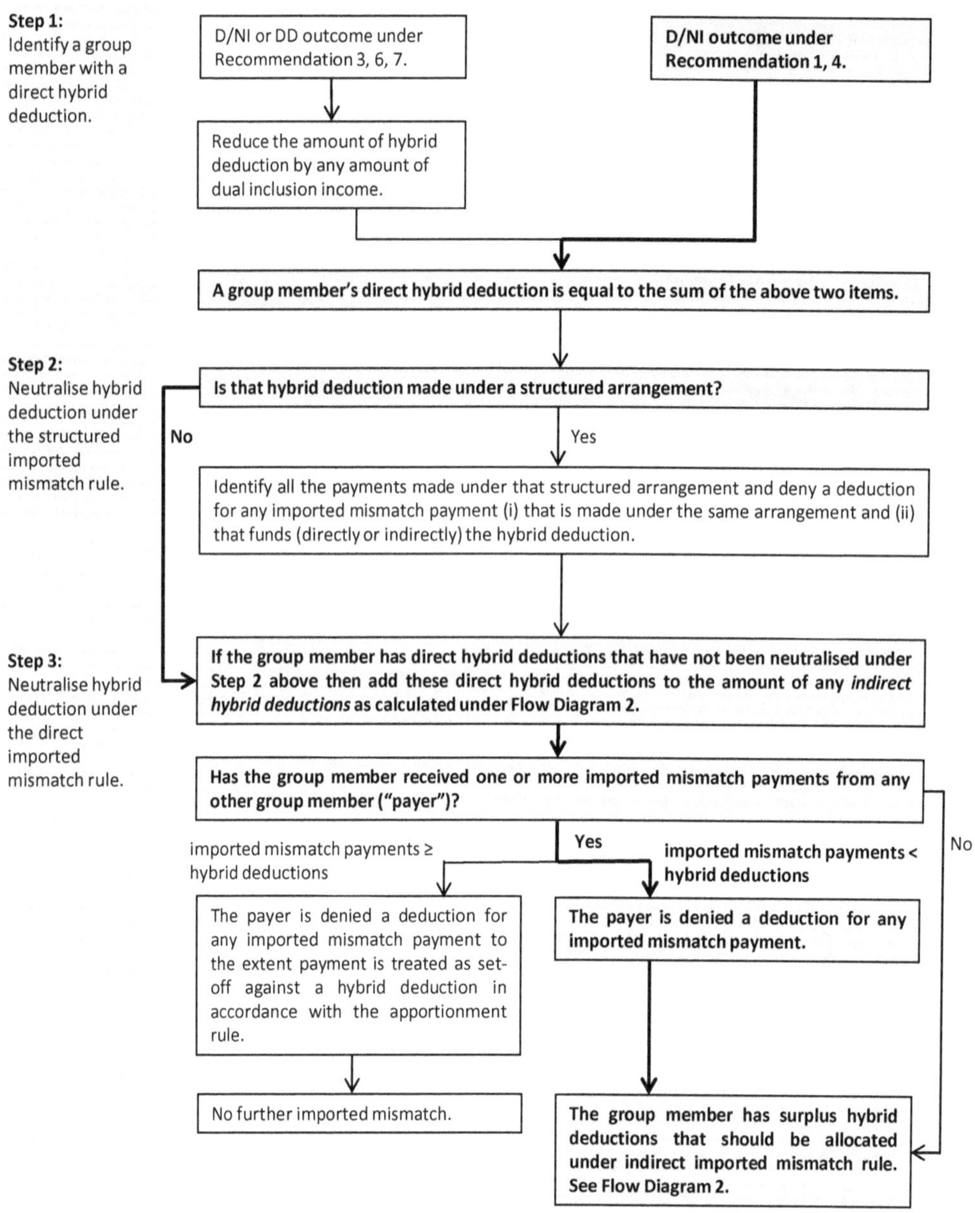

Flow Diagram 2 (Example 8.8)

Allocating surplus hybrid deduction under the indirect imported mismatch rule

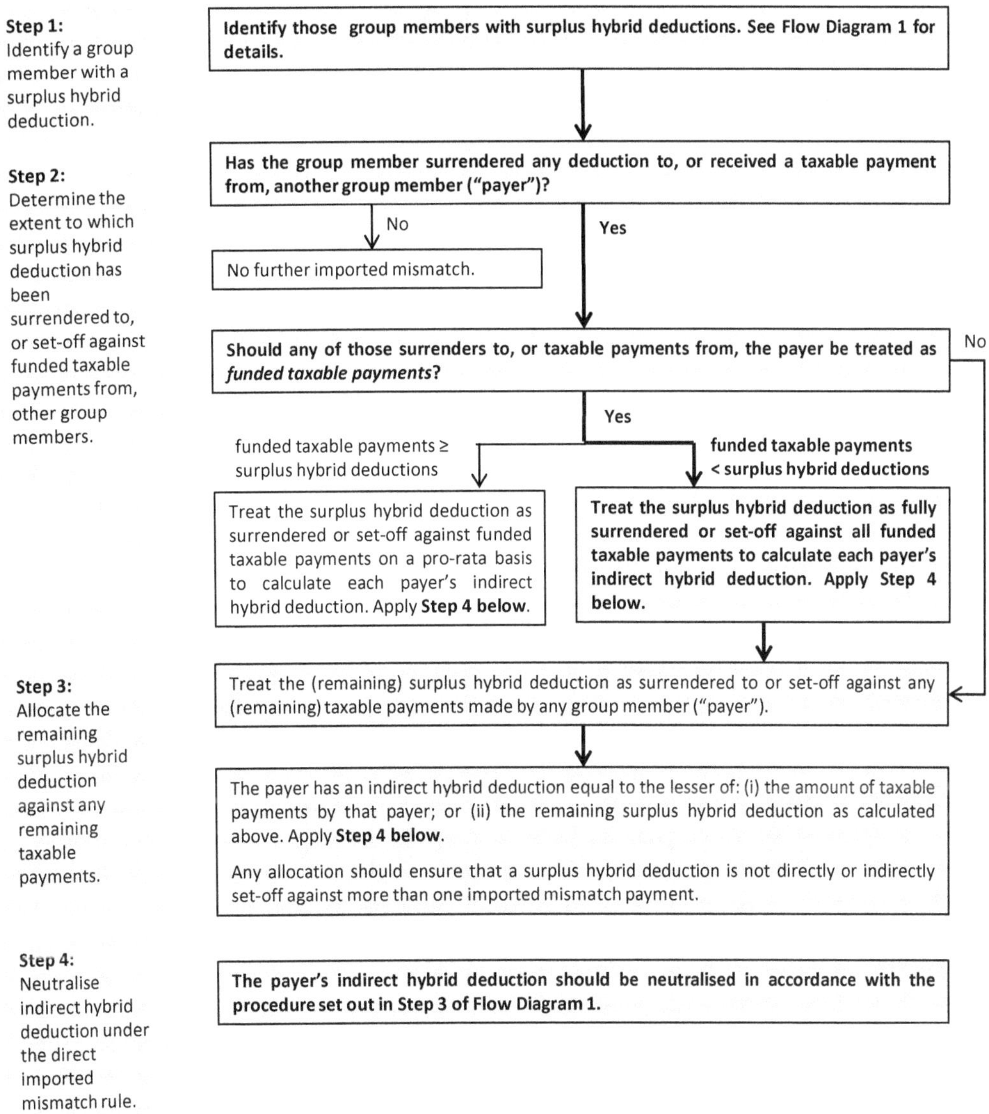

Example 8.9

Surplus hybrid deduction does not exceed funded taxable payments

1. The facts illustrated in the figure below are the same as in **Example 8.3**, except that E Co, F Co and G Co (the shaded entities) are all resident in jurisdictions that have implemented the recommendations set out in the report. E Co and F Co make deductible intra-group interest payment to B Co of 200 and B Co makes a deductible intra-group interest payment to C Co of 500. G Co makes a deductible intra-group interest payment to D Co of 200 and D Co makes a deductible intra-group interest payment to C Co of 200. C Co's hybrid deduction is 400.

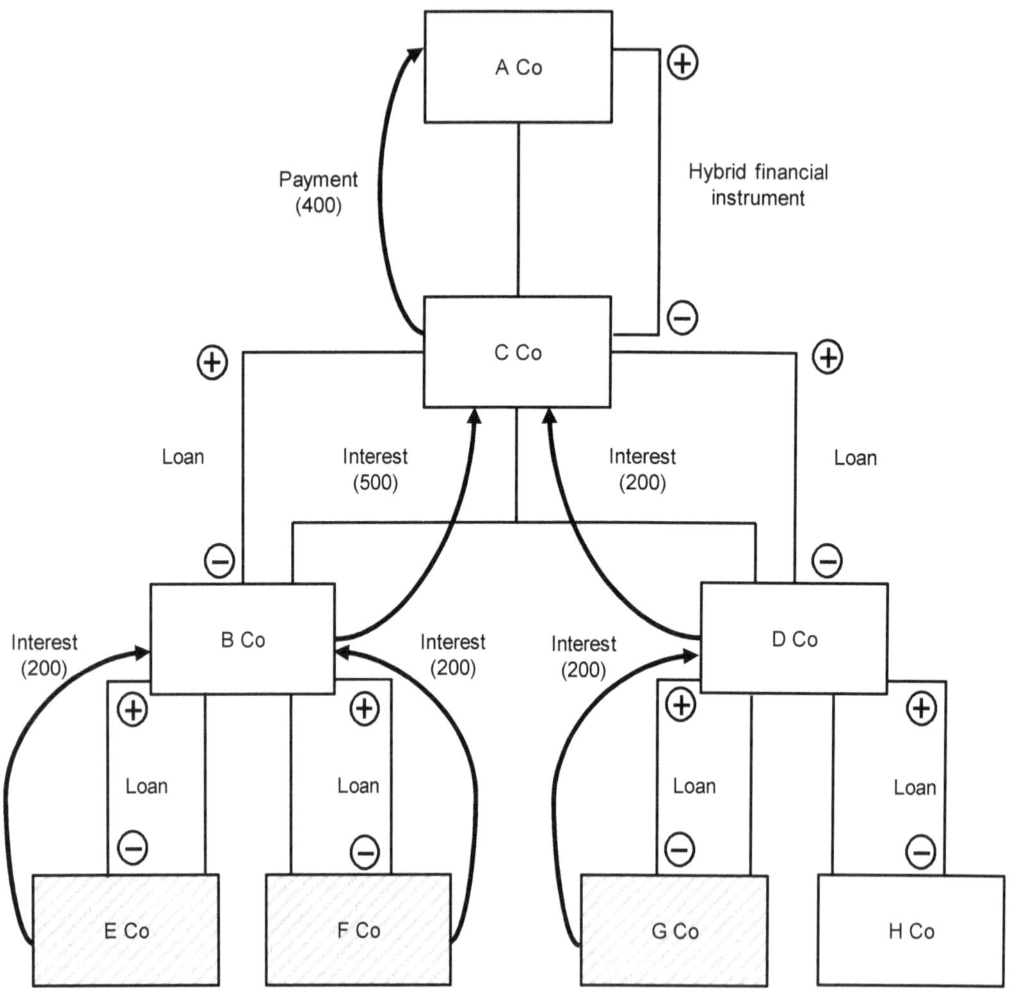

Question

2. Whether the interest payment made by E Co, F Co or G Co is subject to adjustment under the imported mismatch rule and, if so, the amount of the adjustment required under the rule.

Answer

3. Countries E, F and G should deny their taxpayers a deduction for two-thirds (133) of the interest payments. See the flow diagrams at the end of this example which outline the steps to be taken in applying the imported mismatch rule.

Analysis

C Co's hybrid deduction is not set-off against an imported mismatch payment under the structured or direct imported mismatch rule

Step 1 – C Co's payment under the hybrid financial instrument gives rise to a direct hybrid deduction

4. The interest payments under the hybrid financial instrument give rise to a direct hybrid deduction for C Co of 400.

Step 2 – the structured imported mismatch rule does not apply

5. The facts of this example assume that the hybrid financial instrument is not entered into as part of a wider structured arrangement. Therefore the structured imported mismatch rule does not apply.

Step 3 – the direct imported mismatch rules does not apply

6. In this case the *direct imported mismatch rule* does not apply as the group entities that are *directly* funding the hybrid deduction (i.e. B Co and D Co) are resident in jurisdictions that have not implemented the imported mismatch rules.

The interest payments made by E Co, F Co and G Co should be subject to adjustment under the indirect imported mismatch rule

7. As C Co's hybrid deduction has not been neutralised under the structured or direct imported mismatch rule, the indirect imported mismatch rule applies to determine the extent to which C Co's surplus hybrid deduction should be treated as giving rise to an indirect hybrid deduction for another group member.

Step 1 – C Co has surplus hybrid deductions of 400

8. In this case C Co's surplus hybrid deduction will be the amount of hybrid deduction that is attributable to payments under the hybrid financial instrument (400) minus any amount of hybrid deduction that has been neutralised under either the structured or direct imported mismatch rules (0).

Step 2 – C Co's surplus hybrid deduction are set-off against funded taxable payments

9. C Co must first treat that surplus hybrid deduction as being offset against funded taxable payments received from group entities. A taxable payment will be treated as a funded taxable payment to the extent the payment is directly funded out of imported mismatch payments made by other group entities. In this case the interest payments of 200 that B Co receives from E Co and F Co, and the payment of 200 that D Co receives from G Co, are imported mismatch payments and, accordingly, four fifths (i.e. 400/500 of the taxable payments that B Co makes to C Co and all (i.e. 200/200) of the interest payments C Co receives from D Co should be treated as funded taxable payments.

10. In this case the funded taxable payment received by C Co (600) exceeds C Co's surplus hybrid deduction (400). C Co therefore treats its surplus hybrid deduction as set-off against the funded taxable payments on a pro-rata basis. C Co's hybrid deduction must be apportioned between the taxable payments made by B Co and D Co so that B Co has an indirect hybrid deduction of 267 and D Co has an indirect hybrid deduction of 133, calculated as follows:

$$\frac{\text{Funded taxable payments made by payer}}{\text{Funded taxable payments received by C Co}} \times \text{C Co's surplus hybrid deduction}$$

Step 3 – C Co has no remaining surplus hybrid deduction

11. C Co's surplus hybrid deduction is fully set-off against funded taxable payments and C Co therefore has no remaining surplus hybrid deduction to be set-off against other taxable payments.

Step 4 – B Co and D Co's indirect hybrid deduction is neutralised in accordance with the direct imported mismatch rule

12. B Co's indirect hybrid deduction should be treated as set-off against the imported mismatch payments made by E Co and F Co. The calculation is the same as under the direct imported mismatch rule. The guidance to the direct imported mismatch rule sets out an apportionment formula which can be used to determine the extent to which an imported mismatch payment has been directly set-off against a counterparty's indirect hybrid deduction. The formula is as follows:

$$\frac{\text{B Co's hybrid deductions}}{\text{Imported mismatch payments received by B Co}} = \frac{267}{200 + 200} = \frac{267}{400} = \frac{2}{3}$$

Therefore two-thirds of the imported mismatch payments made by E Co and F Co are subject to adjustment under the imported mismatch rule.

13. The calculation with respect to G Co's imported mismatch payment is the same. D Co's indirect hybrid deduction should be treated as set-off against that imported mismatch payments using the same apportionment formula. The proportion of deduction that G Co should be denied on its imported mismatch payment is calculated as follows:

$$\frac{\text{D Co's hybrid deductions}}{\text{Imported mismatch payments received by D Co}} = \frac{133}{200} = \frac{2}{3}$$

14. Applying these ratios under the direct imported mismatch rules of Country E, F and G the amount of interest deduction denied under the laws of each Country will be 150 (i. e. 2/3 x 200).

Flow Diagram 1 (Example 8.9)

Neutralising hybrid deduction under the structured and direct imported mismatch rule

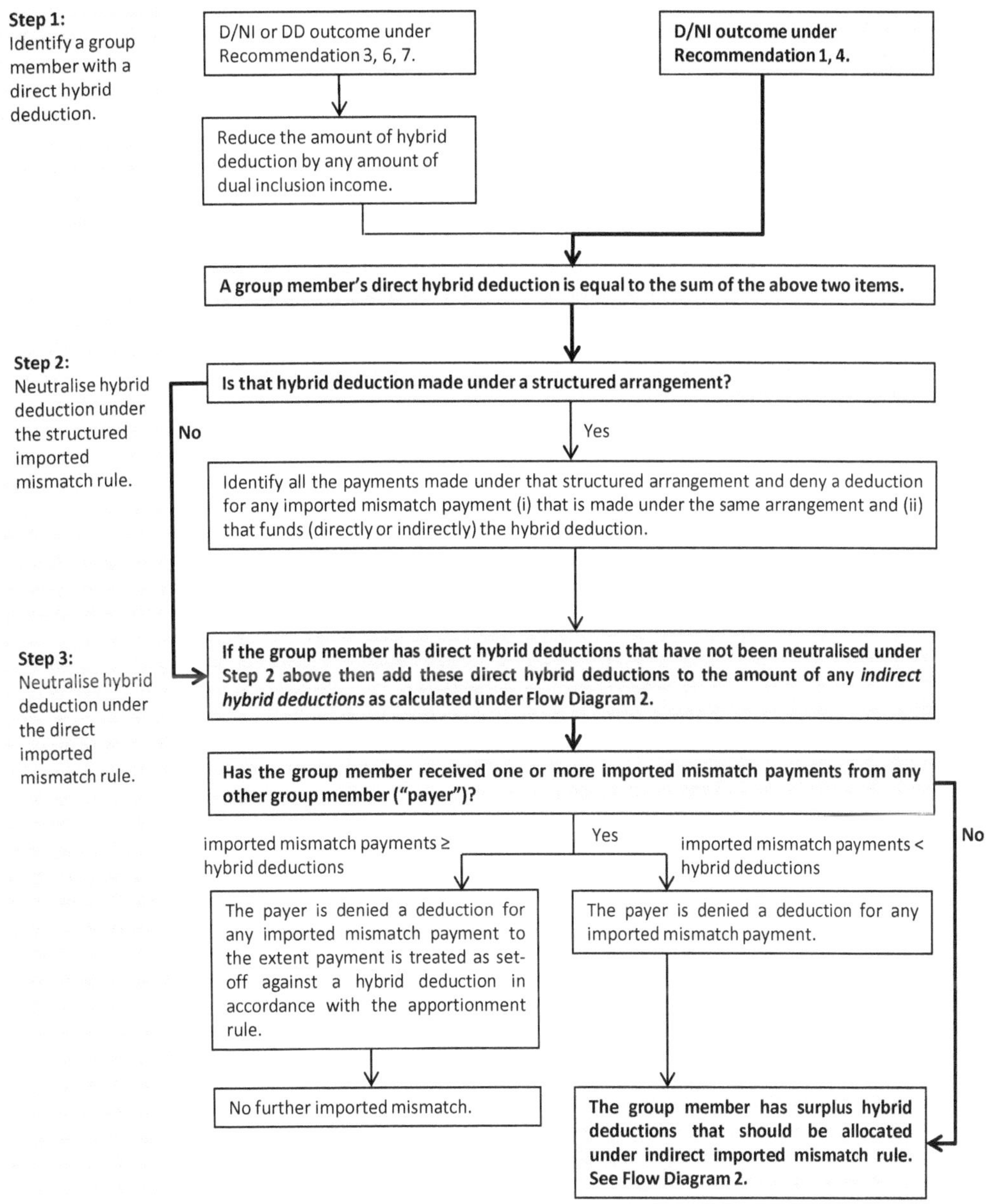

Flow Diagram 2 (Example 8.9)

Allocating surplus hybrid deduction under the indirect imported mismatch rule

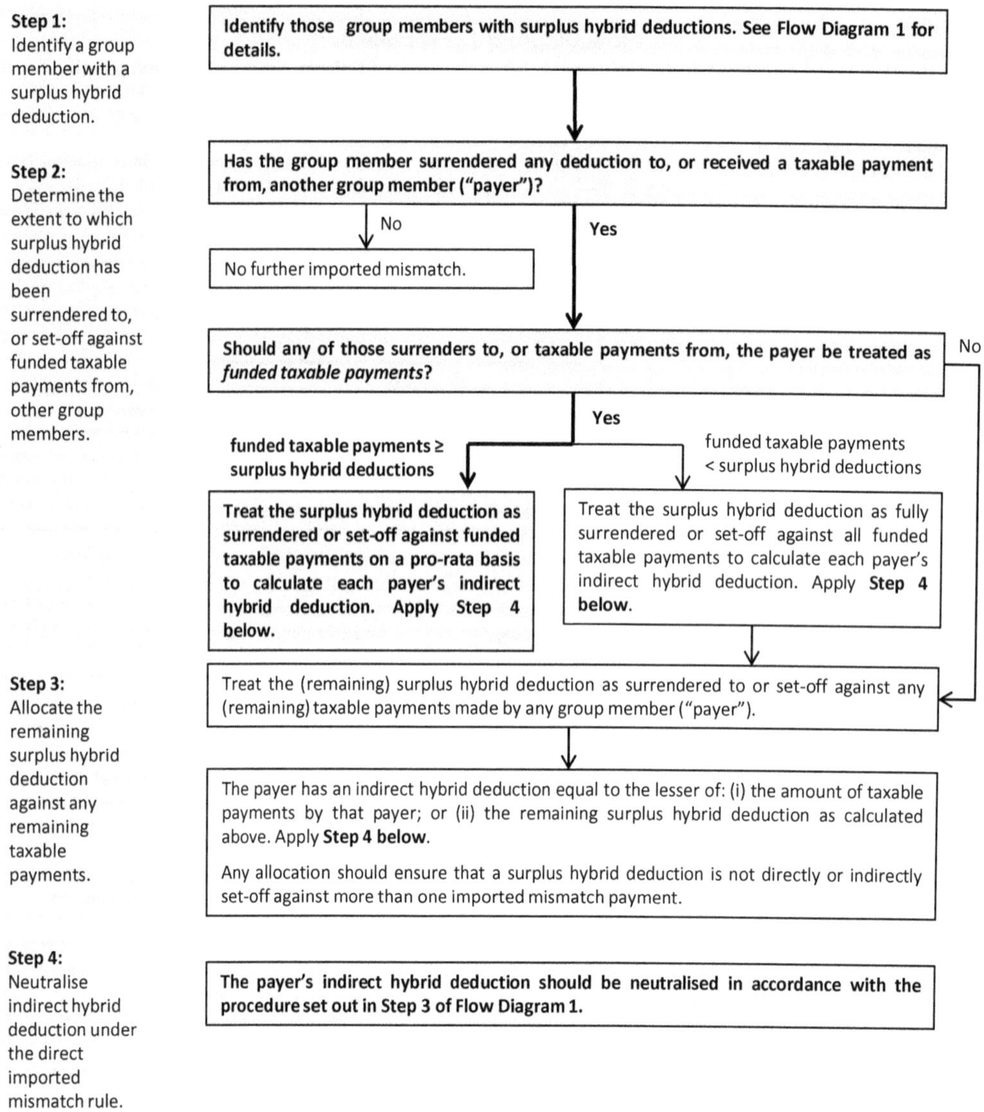

Example 8.10

Application of the imported mismatch rule to loss surrender under a tax grouping arrangement

Facts

1. In the example illustrated in the figure below, A Co (a company resident in Country A), B Co 1 and B Co 2 (companies resident in Country B) and C Co (a company resident in Country C) are all members of the ABC group. Companies B Co 1 and B Co 2 are members of the same tax group for the purposes of Country B law. These tax grouping rules allow one company to surrender a loss to another group member.

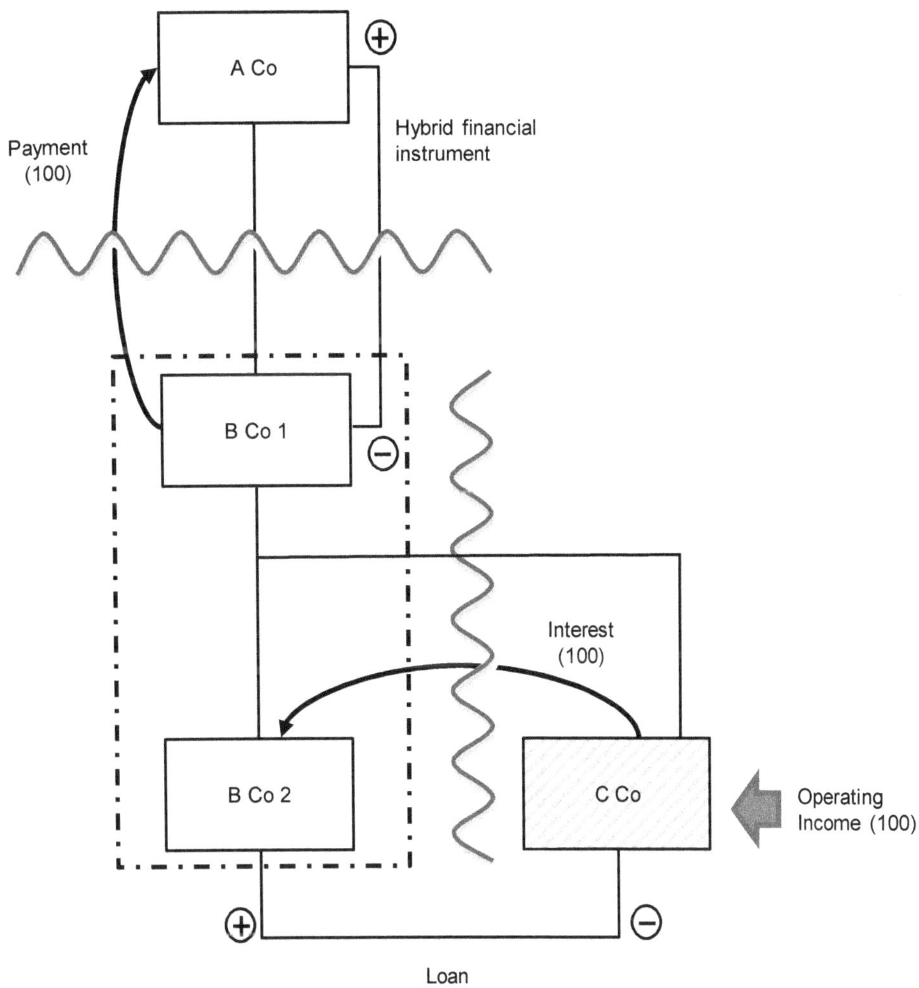

2. C Co receives operating income of 100 and makes an interest payment of 100 to B Co 2. B Co 1 makes interest payment of 100 to A Co under a hybrid financial

instrument. The payments of interest under the hybrid financial instrument are treated as deductible interest payments under Country B law but as exempt dividends under Country A law. The hybrid financial instrument is not, however, entered into as part of a wider structured arrangement.

3. Country B treats the hybrid financial instrument as an ordinary debt instrument and grants B Co 1 a deduction for interest paid on the loan. This interest payment is not included in A Co's ordinary income. This discrepancy in tax treatment results in a hybrid mismatch giving rise to a D/NI outcome and a net loss for B Co 1. That loss is surrendered by B Co 1 to B Co 2 under the tax grouping rule and set-off against the income from the interest payment received from C Co. The table below illustrates the effect of this transaction for the members of the ABC group.

Country A Law A Co			Country B Law B Co 1		
	Tax	Book		Tax	Book
Income			Income		
Dividend	0	100			
			Expenditure		
			Interest paid	(100)	(100)
Net return		**100**	**Net return**		**(100)**
Taxable income	**0**		Taxable income (loss)	(100)	
			Loss surrender to B Co 2	100	
			Loss carry-forward	**0**	
Country C Law C Co			**B Co 2**		
	Tax	Book		Tax	Book
Income			Income		
Ordinary income	100	100	Interest	100	100
Expenditure			Expenditure		
Interest	(100)	(100)	Loss surrender from B Co 1	(100)	
Net return		**0**	**Net return**		**100**
Taxable income	**0**		**Taxable income**	**0**	

4. C Co (the shaded entity) is the only group entity resident in a Country that has implemented the recommendations set out in the report.

Question

5. Whether the interest payments made by C Co are subject to adjustment under the imported mismatch rule, and, if so, the amount of the adjustment required under the rule?

Answer

6. The payment of interest by C Co is subject to adjustment under the imported mismatch rule because B Co 1's hybrid deduction is indirectly set-off against the interest income paid by C Co to B Co 2. Country C should therefore deny C Co a deduction for all the interest paid to B Co 2. See the flow diagrams at the end of this example which outline the steps to be taken in applying the imported mismatch rule.

Analysis

B Co 1's hybrid deduction is not set-off against an imported mismatch payment under the structured or direct imported mismatch rule

Step 1 – B Co 1's payment under the hybrid financial instrument gives rise to a direct hybrid deduction

7. The interest payments under the hybrid financial instrument give rise to a direct hybrid deduction for B Co 1 of 100.

Step 2 – the structured imported mismatch rule does not apply

8. The facts of this example assume that the hybrid financial instrument is not entered into as part of a wider structured arrangement. Therefore the structured imported mismatch rule does not apply.

Step 3 – the direct imported mismatch rule does not apply

9. In this case the *direct imported mismatch rule* does not apply as B Co 1 does not directly receive any imported mismatch payments from another group member.

The interest payments made by C Co should be subject to adjustment under the indirect imported mismatch rule

10. As B Co 1's hybrid deduction has not been neutralised under the structured or direct imported mismatch rule, the indirect imported mismatch rule applies to determine the extent to which B Co 1's surplus hybrid deduction should be treated as giving rise to an indirect hybrid deduction for another group member.

Step 1 –B Co 1 has surplus hybrid deductions of 100

11. In this case B Co 1's surplus hybrid deduction will be the amount of hybrid deduction that is attributable to payments under the hybrid financial instrument (100) minus any amount of hybrid deduction that has been neutralised under either the structured or direct imported mismatch rules (0).

Step 2 –B Co 1's surplus hybrid deduction are treated as fully set-off against funded taxable payments

12. B Co 1 has surrendered a loss of 100 to B Co 2. This loss surrender is treated in the same way as a funded taxable payment because it is treated as set-off against an imported mismatch payment. In this case the amount of the loss surrender is equal to the income from the imported mismatch payment and so 100% of the amount surrendered should be treated as set-off against a funded taxable payment under the indirect imported mismatch rule.

Step 3 – B Co 1 has no remaining surplus hybrid deduction

13. B Co 1's surplus hybrid deduction is fully set-off against funded taxable payments and B Co 1 therefore has no remaining surplus hybrid deduction to be set-off against other taxable payments.

Step 4 – B Co 2's indirect hybrid deduction is neutralised in accordance with the direct imported mismatch rule

14. B Co 2 treats indirect hybrid deduction as being set-off against imported mismatch payments made by C Co. The amount of deduction that is treated as set-off against C Co's imported mismatch payment is calculated on the same basis as under the direct imported mismatch rule:

$$\text{Imported mismatch payments made by C Co} \times \frac{\text{B Co 2's hybrid deduction}}{\text{Imported mismatch payments received by B Co 2}} = 100 \times \frac{100}{100} = 100$$

C Co should therefore be denied a deduction of 100.

Flow Diagram 1 (Example 8.10)

Neutralising hybrid deduction under the structured and direct imported mismatch rule

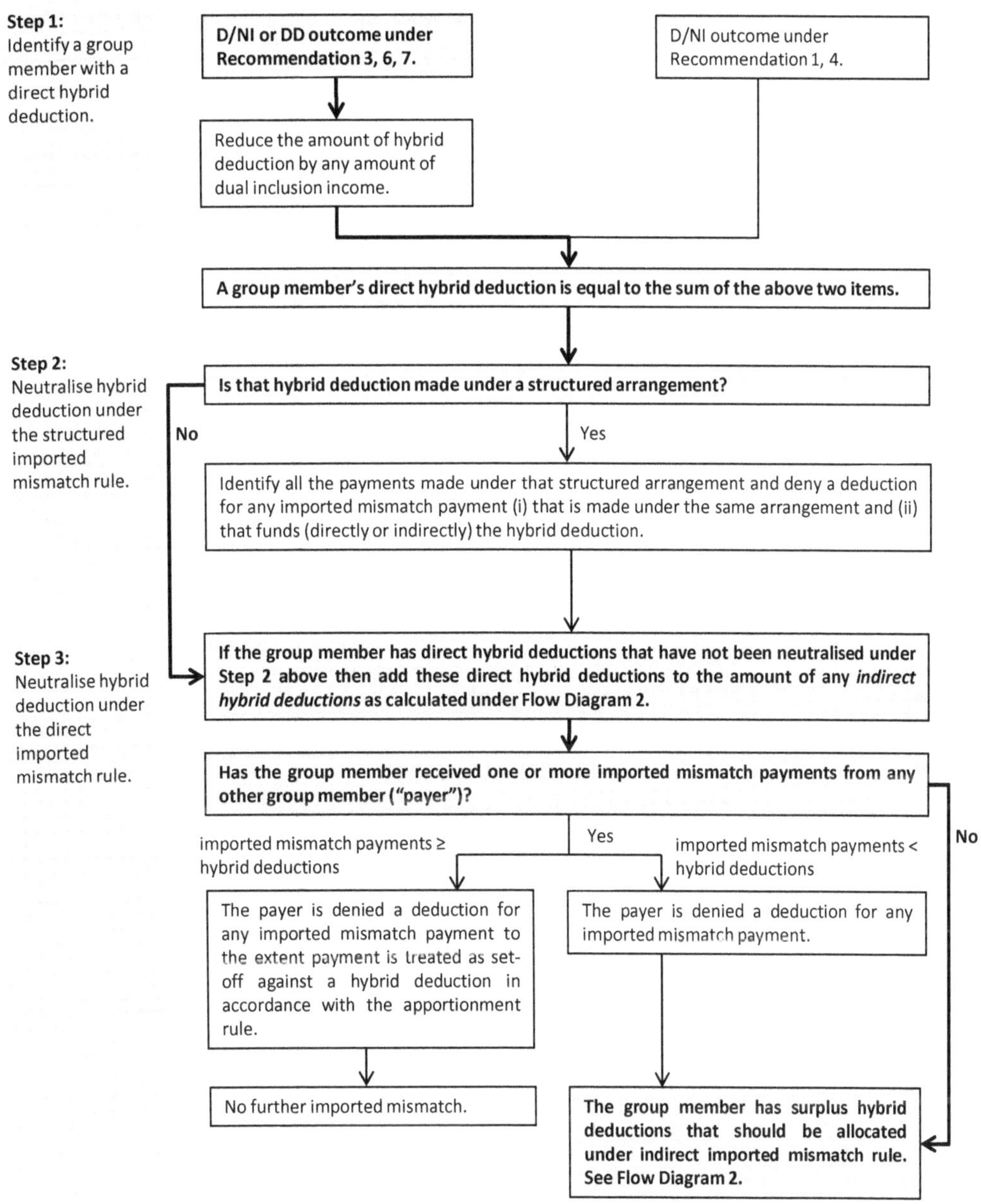

Flow Diagram 2 (Example 8.10)

Allocating surplus hybrid deduction under the indirect imported mismatch rule

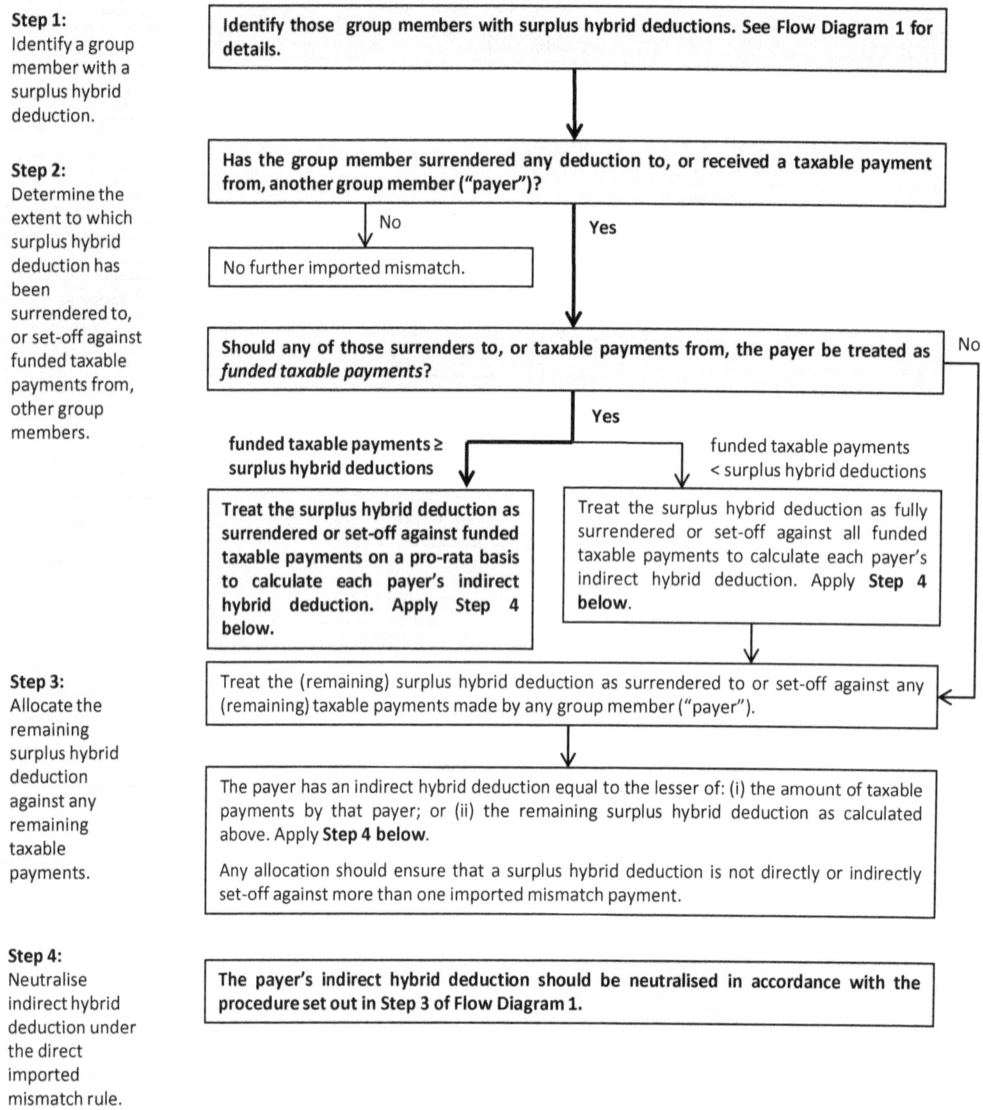

Example 8.11

Payment of dual inclusion income not subject to adjustment under imported mismatch rule

Facts

1. The figure below sets out the financing arrangements for companies that are members of the ABCD group. A Co is resident in Country A and is the parent company of the group. B Co 1, C Co and D Co are all direct subsidiaries of A Co and are resident in Country B, Country C and Country D respectively. B Co 2 is a wholly-owned subsidiary of B Co 1 and is also resident in Country B.

2. All companies are treated as separate tax entities in all jurisdictions, except that B Co 1 is a hybrid entity (i.e. an entity that is treated as a separate entity for tax purposes in Country B but as a disregarded entity under Country A law).

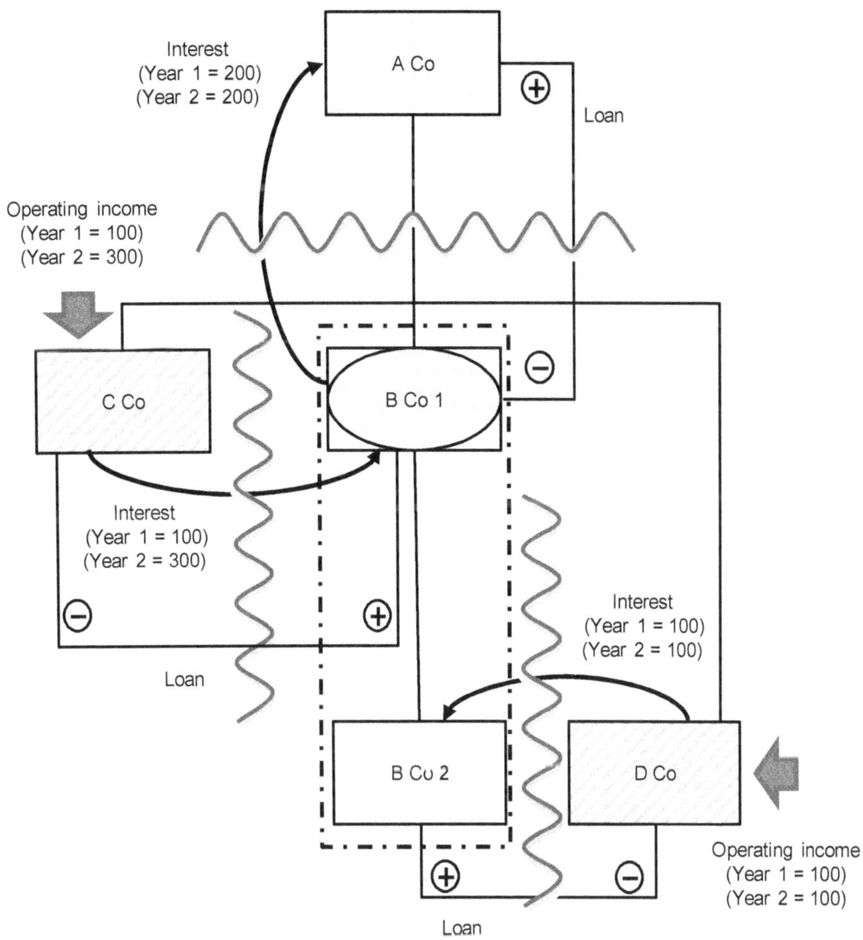

3. A Co has lent money to B Co 1. B Co 1 has lent money to C Co and B Co 2 has lent money to D Co. Each of these financing arrangements are entered into independently and do not form part of single scheme, plan or understanding.

4. Because B Co 1 is a hybrid entity, the interest payments it makes to A Co are deductible under Country B law, but not recognised as income by A Co under Country A law. For the same reason, interest payments by C Co to B Co 1 are included in the income of both A Co and B Co 1 under the laws of Country A and Country B respectively (i.e. the interest payment gives rise to dual inclusion income). B Co 1 and B Co 2 are members of the same tax group for tax purposes under Country B law, which means that the net loss of B Co 1 can be set-off against any net income of B Co 2. All jurisdictions impose corporate tax at the rule of 30%.

Tax position before applying the imported mismatch rule

5. The tables below set out the tax position in respect of the ABCD group under this structure as at the end of the first year.

	Country A A Co			Country B B Co 1		
		Tax	**Book**		**Tax**	**Book**
Year 1	Income			Income		
	Interest paid by B Co 1	-	200	Interest paid by C Co	100	100
	Interest paid by C Co to B Co 1	100	-			
				Expenditure		
				Interest paid to A Co	(200)	(200)
				Net return		**(100)**
				Taxable income	(100)	
				Loss surrender to B Co 2	100	
				Loss carry-forward	**0**	
				B Co 2		
				Income		
				Interest paid by D Co	100	100
				Expenditure		
				Loss surrender	(100)	-
	Net return		**200**	**Net return**		**100**
	Taxable income	**100**		**Taxable income**	**0**	

Year 1	Country C Law C Co	Tax	Book	Country D Law D Co	Tax	Book
	Income			Income		
	Operating income	100	100	Operating income	100	100
	Expenditure			Expenditure		
	Interest paid to B Co 1	(100)	(100)	Interest paid to B Co 2	(100)	(100)
	Net return		**0**	**Net return**		**0**
	Taxable income	**0**		**Taxable income**	**0**	

6. The tables below set out the tax position in respect of the ABCD Group under this structure as at the end of the second year.

Year 2	Country A A Co	Tax	Book	Country B B Co 1	Tax	Book
	Income			Income		
	Interest paid by B Co 1	-	200	Interest paid by C Co	300	300
	Interest paid by C Co to B Co 1	300	-			
				Expenditure		
				Interest paid to A Co	(200)	(200)
	Net return		**200**	**Net return**		**100**
	Taxable income	**300**		**Taxable income**	**100**	
	Tax on income (30%)	(90)		Tax on income (30%)	(30)	
	Credit for tax paid in Country B	30				
	Tax to pay		(60)	Tax to pay		(30)
	After-tax return		**140**	**After-tax return**		**70**
				B Co 2		
				Income		
				Interest paid by D Co	100	100
				Net return		**100**
				Taxable income	**100**	

Year 2	Country C Law C Co	Tax	Book	Country D Law D Co	Tax	Book
	Income			Income		
	Operating income	300	300	Operating income	100	100
	Expenditure			Expenditure		
	Interest paid to B Co 1	(300)	(300)	Interest paid to B Co 2	(100)	(100)
	Net return		**0**	**Net return**		**0**
	Taxable income	**0**		**Taxable income**	**0**	

Result under Country A law

7. A Co has taxable income of 100 and 300 in Years 1 and 2 respectively. Under Country A law, A Co is entitled to a foreign tax credit in Year 2 for taxes paid by B Co 1 in Country B so that the amount of ordinary income derived by A Co is 200.

Result under Country B law

8. In Year 1, B Co 1 has a net loss of 100 while B Co 2 has net income of 100. B Co 1's net loss is surrendered through Country B's tax grouping regime and applied against B Co 2's net income so that the group is treated, under Country B law, as having net income of zero for that year. In Year 2, B Co 1 has net income of 100 (interest income of 300 and a deduction of 200) and B Co 2 has net income of 100.

Result under Country C and D law

9. Country C and D have income that is equal to their expenses and therefore have no net income in either of the two years.

Mismatch in tax outcomes

10. In aggregate the ABCD Group generates a net return of 600 over the two years. The total amounts of taxable income recognised in each jurisdiction is also 600, but 100 of this is income that is sheltered by foreign tax credits. Accordingly, the total amount of ordinary income recognised under the structure is 500.

Question

11. Whether the interest payments made by C Co and D Co are subject to adjustment under the imported mismatch rule and, if so, the amount of the adjustment required under the rule.

Answer

12. As the interest payments made by C Co to B Co 1 are dual inclusion income, they are not treated as set-off against a hybrid deduction and therefore no adjustment is required for the payments made by C Co under the imported mismatch rule.

13. Indirect imported mismatch rule applies to interest payments from D Co to B Co 2. Country D should therefore deny D Co a deduction for all (100) of the interest paid to B Co 2 in Year 1 but no adjustment is required in Year 2. See the flow diagrams at the end of this example which outline the steps to be taken in applying the imported mismatch rule.

Analysis

Interest payments made by B Co 1 are not made under a structured arrangement

14. The loan between A Co and B Co 1 is independent of the other intra-group financing arrangements. Unless such loan was entered into as part of wider scheme, plan or understanding that was intended to import the effect of a mismatch in tax outcomes into Country C or D, then the interest payment made by B Co 1 to A Co should not be treated as made under a structured imported mismatch arrangement.

The interest payments by C Co to B Co 1 are not offset against a hybrid deduction

15. As explained in the facts above, the interest payments made by B Co 1 to A Co give rise to a D/NI outcome under the disregarded payments rule. However, a hybrid mismatch does not arise under the disregarded hybrid payments rule to the extent the deductions attributable to such payment are set-off against dual inclusion income. In this case, C Co's interest payments to B Co 1 are dual inclusion income and therefore cannot be treated as giving rise to an imported mismatch. Hence, no adjustment is required for the payments made by C Co in either year under the imported mismatch rule.

B Co 1's hybrid deduction is not set-off against an imported mismatch payment under the structured or direct imported mismatch rule

Step 1 – B Co 1's disregarded hybrid payment gives rise to a direct hybrid deduction

16. The interest payment B Co 1 makes to A Co is a disregarded hybrid payment. Any deduction claimed for that payment will be a direct hybrid deduction to the extent it exceeds the payer's dual inclusion income. In this case, the disregarded interest payment made by B Co 1 in Year 1 (200) exceeds Co 1's dual inclusion for that year (100) and accordingly B Co 1 has a hybrid deduction in Year 1 of 100.

Step 2 – the structured imported mismatch rule does not apply

17. The facts of this example assume that the disregarded hybrid payment is not made under a wider structured imported mismatch arrangement. Therefore the structured imported mismatch rule does not apply.

Step 3 – the direct imported mismatch rule does not apply

18. In this case the direct imported mismatch rule does not apply as B Co 1 does not directly receive any imported mismatch payments from another group member.

The interest payment made by D Co in Year 1 should be subject to adjustment under the indirect imported mismatch rule

19. As B Co 1's hybrid deduction has not been neutralised under the structured or direct imported mismatch rule, the indirect imported mismatch rule applies to determine the extent to which B Co 1's surplus hybrid deduction should be treated as giving rise to an indirect hybrid deduction for another group member.

Step 1 –B Co 1 has surplus hybrid deductions of 100

20. In this case B Co 1's surplus hybrid deduction will be the amount of hybrid deduction that arises under the hybrid mismatch arrangement (100) minus any amount that has been neutralised under either the structured or direct hybrid mismatch rules (0).

Step 2 –B Co 1's surplus hybrid deduction are treated as fully set-off against funded taxable payments

21. B Co 1 has surrendered a loss of 100 to B Co 2. This loss surrender is treated in the same way as a funded taxable payment because the surrendered hybrid deduction is set-off against an imported mismatch payment. In this case the amount of the loss surrender is equal to the imported mismatch payment and so 100% of the amount surrendered should be treated as set-off against a funded taxable payment under the indirect imported mismatch rule.

Step 3 – B Co 1 has no remaining surplus hybrid deduction

22. B Co 1's surplus hybrid deduction is fully set-off against funded taxable payments and B Co 1 therefore has no remaining surplus hybrid deduction to be set-off against other taxable payments.

Step 4 – B Co 2's indirect hybrid deduction is neutralised in accordance with the direct imported mismatch rule

23. B Co 2 treats the indirect hybrid deduction as being set-off against imported mismatch payments made by C Co. The amount of deduction that is treated as set-off against C Co's imported mismatch payment is calculated on the same basis as under the direct imported mismatch rule:

$$\text{Imported mismatch payments made by D Co} \times \frac{\text{B Co 2's hybrid deduction}}{\text{Imported mismatch payments received by B Co 2}} = 100 \times \frac{100}{100} = 100$$

C Co should therefore be denied a deduction of 100.

Tax position after applying the imported mismatch rule

24. The effect of the adjustment under the imported mismatch rule is to deny D Co a deduction for the entire amount of the interest payment in Year 1. This brings the total ordinary income under the structure into line with the aggregate income under the

arrangement. The tables below sets out the tax position of the ABCD Group, as at the end of the first year, after applying the imported mismatch rule.

Year 1

Country A – A Co	Tax	Book	Country B – B Co 1	Tax	Book
Income			Income		
Interest paid by B Co 1	-	200	Interest paid by C Co	100	100
Interest paid by C Co to B Co 1	100	-			
			Expenditure		
			Interest paid to A Co	(200)	(200)
			Net return		**(100)**
			Taxable income	(100)	
			Loss surrender to B Co 2	100	
			Loss carry-forward	**0**	
			B Co 2		
			Income		
			Interest paid by D Co	100	100
			Expenditure		
			Loss surrender	(100)	-
Net return		**200**	**Net return**		**100**
Taxable income	**100**		**Taxable income**	**0**	

Year 1

Country C Law – C Co	Tax	Book	Country D Law – D Co	Tax	Book
Income			Income		
Operating income	100	100	Operating income	100	100
Expenditure			Expenditure		
Interest paid to B Co 1	(100)	(100)	Interest paid to B Co 2	-	(100)
Net return		**0**	**Net return**		**0**
Taxable income	**0**		**Taxable income**	**100**	

Flow Diagram 1 (Example 8.11)

Neutralising hybrid deduction under the structured and direct imported mismatch rule

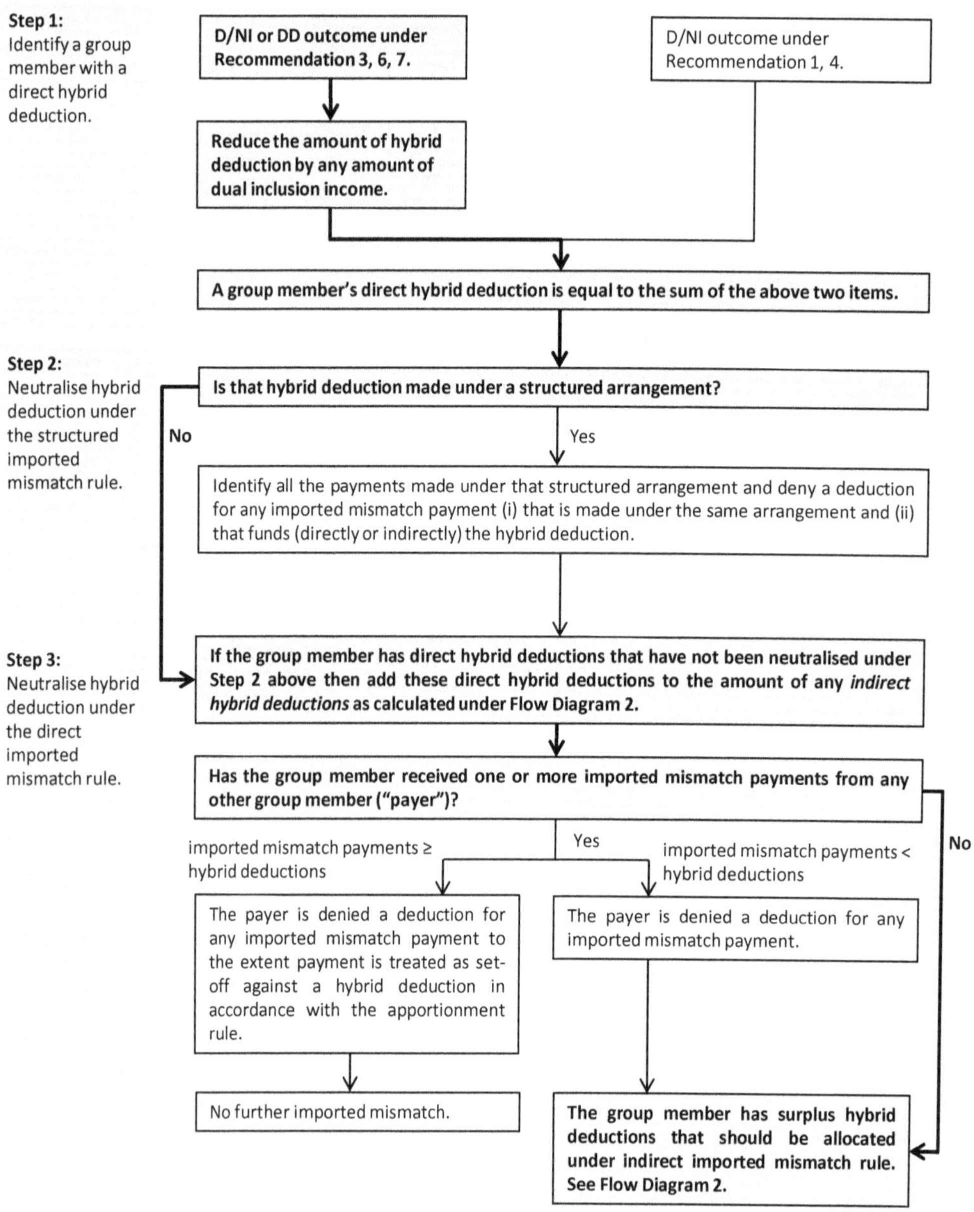

Flow Diagram 2 (Example 8.11)

Allocating surplus hybrid deduction under the indirect imported mismatch rule

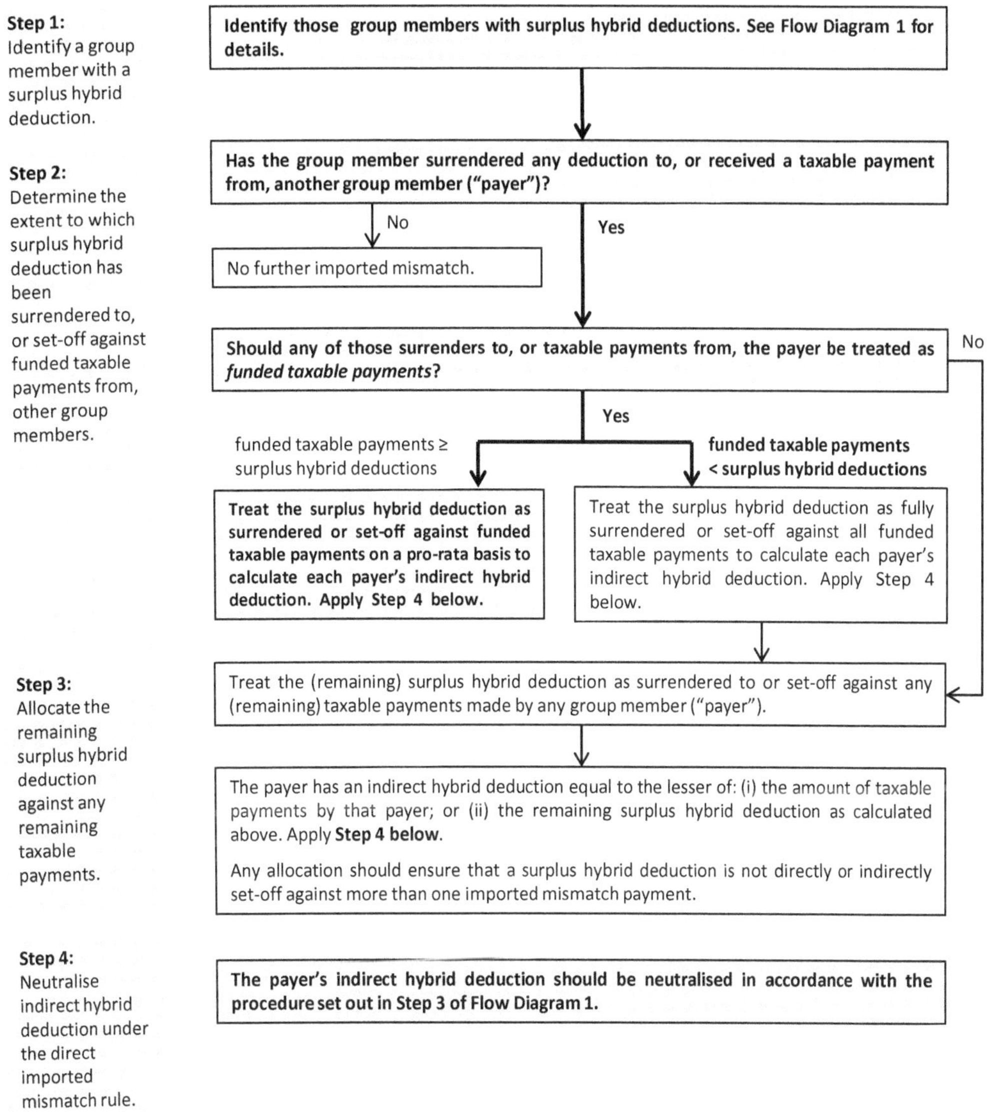

Example 8.12

Imported mismatch rule and carry-forward losses

Facts

1. The facts are the same as in **Example 8.11** except that B Co 1's net loss is not surrendered to B Co 2 in the first year. The tables below set out the tax position in respect of each member of the ABCD Group under this structure as at the end of the first year.

	Country A A Co			Country B B Co 1		
		Tax	Book		Tax	Book
Year 1	Income			Income		
	Interest paid by B Co 1	-	200	Interest paid by C Co	100	100
	Interest paid by C Co to B Co 1	100	-			
				Expenditure		
				Interest paid to A Co	(200)	(200)
				Net return		**(100)**
				Taxable income (loss)	**(100)**	
				B Co 2		
				Income		
				Interest paid by D Co	100	100
	Net return		**200**	**Net return**		**100**
	Taxable income	**100**		**Taxable income**	**100**	

Year 1

Country C Law – C Co	Tax	Book	Country D Law – D Co	Tax	Book
Income			Income		
Operating income	100	100	Operating income	100	100
Expenditure			Expenditure		
Interest paid to B Co 1	(100)	(100)	Interest paid to B Co 2	(100)	(100)
Net return		**0**	**Net return**		**0**
Taxable income	**0**		**Taxable income**	**0**	

2. The tables below set out the tax position in respect of each member of the ABCD Group under this structure as at the end of the second year.

Year 2

Country A – A Co	Tax	Book	Country B – B Co 1	Tax	Book
Income			Income		
Interest paid by B Co 1	-	200	Interest paid by C Co	300	300
Interest paid by C Co to B Co 1	300	-			
			Expenditure		
			Interest paid to A Co	(200)	(200)
Net return		**200**	**Net return**		**100**
Taxable income	**300**		Taxable income	100	
Tax on income (30%)	(90)		Loss carry forward	(100)	
			Adjusted income	0	
Tax to pay		(90)	Tax to pay		0
After-tax return		**110**	**After-tax return**		**100**
			B Co 2		
			Income		
			Interest paid by D Co	100	100
			Net return		**100**
			Taxable income	**100**	

Year 2	Country C Law C Co			Country D Law D Co		
		Tax	Book		Tax	Book
	Income			Income		
	Operating income	300	300	Operating income	100	100
	Expenditure			Expenditure		
	Interest paid to B Co 1	(300)	(300)	Interest paid to B Co 2	(100)	(100)
	Net return		0	**Net return**		0
	Taxable income	0		**Taxable income**	0	

Result under Country A law

3. A Co has net income of 100 and 300 in Years 1 and 2 respectively. A treats these amounts as ordinary income.

Result under Country B law

4. In Year 1, B Co 1 has a net loss of 100 (interest income of 100 and a deduction of 200), while B Co 2 has net income of 100. B Co 1's net loss is carried-forward to the subsequent year and set-off against dual inclusion income in Year 2. Accordingly in Year 2, B Co 1 has an adjusted taxable income of 0 (interest income of 300, a deduction of 200 and a carry-forward loss of 100) and B Co 2 has net income of 100.

Result under Country C and D law

5. Country C and D have income that is equal to their expenses and therefore have no net income in either of the two years.

Question

6. Whether the interest payments made by D Co are subject to adjustment under the imported mismatch rule and, if so, the amount of the adjustment required under the rule.

Answer

7. Because B Co 1 does not surrender its Year 1 loss to B Co 2 under the tax grouping regime, B Co 2's income from the imported mismatch payment is not set-off against any hybrid deduction. Accordingly, no adjustment is required for the payments made by C Co or D Co under the indirect imported mismatch rule. See the flow diagrams at the end of this example which outline the steps to be taken in applying the imported mismatch rule.

Analysis

Interest payments made by B Co 1 are not made under a structured arrangement

8. The loan between A Co and B Co 1 is independent of the other intra-group financing arrangements. Unless such loan was entered into as part of wider scheme, plan or understanding that was intended to import the effect of a mismatch in tax outcomes into Country C or D, then the interest payment made by B Co 1 to A Co should not be treated as made under a structured imported mismatch arrangement.

B Co 1's hybrid deduction is not set-off against an imported mismatch payment under the structured or direct imported mismatch rule

Step 1 – B Co 1's disregarded hybrid payment gives rise to a direct hybrid deduction

9. The interest payment B Co 1 makes to A Co is a disregarded hybrid payment. Any deduction claimed for that payment will be a direct hybrid deduction to the extent it exceeds the payer's dual inclusion income. In this case, the disregarded interest payments made by B Co 1 in Year 1 (200) exceed B Co 1's dual inclusion for that year (100) and accordingly B Co 1 has a hybrid deduction in Year 1 of 100.

Step 2 – the structured imported mismatch rule does not apply

10. The facts of this example assume that the disregarded hybrid payment is not made under a wider structured imported mismatch arrangement. Therefore the structured imported mismatch rule does not apply.

Step 3 – the direct imported mismatch rules does not apply

11. In this case the *direct imported mismatch rule* does not apply as B Co 1 does not directly receive any imported mismatch payments from another group member.

The interest payment made by D Co in Year 1 should be subject to adjustment under the indirect imported mismatch rule

12. As B Co 1's hybrid deduction has not been neutralised under the structured or direct imported mismatch rule, the indirect imported mismatch rule applies to determine the extent to which B Co 1's surplus hybrid deduction should be treated as giving rise to an indirect hybrid deduction for another group member.

Step 1 –B Co 1 has surplus hybrid deductions of 100

13. In this case B Co 1's surplus hybrid deduction will be the amount of hybrid deduction that arises under the hybrid mismatch arrangement (100) minus any amount of hybrid deduction that has been neutralised under either the structured or direct imported mismatch rules (0).

Step 2 –B Co 1's surplus hybrid deduction is not surrendered or set-off against a taxable payment from any group member

14. B Co 1's surplus hybrid deduction is not surrendered under the tax grouping regime or set-off against the taxable payment of any group member. Therefore the hybrid deduction is not treated as giving rise to any indirect hybrid deduction for any other group member. B Co 1, however, has a surplus hybrid deduction that is converted into a net loss that is carried-forward into the subsequent period. The carried-forward loss should be treated as giving rise to a hybrid deduction in that period (see the analysis in **Example 8.15**). In this case, however, because the hybrid deduction has arisen in respect of a disregarded payment and is offset against dual inclusion income in the following year the net effect of the hybrid deduction is neutralised and no imported mismatch arises in Year 2. The carry-forward of the net loss eliminates the foreign tax credit that would otherwise be available to A Co in Year 2, bringing the aggregate amount of ordinary income under the structure into line with the overall group profit.

Flow Diagram 1 (Example 8.12)

Neutralising hybrid deduction under the structured and direct imported mismatch rule

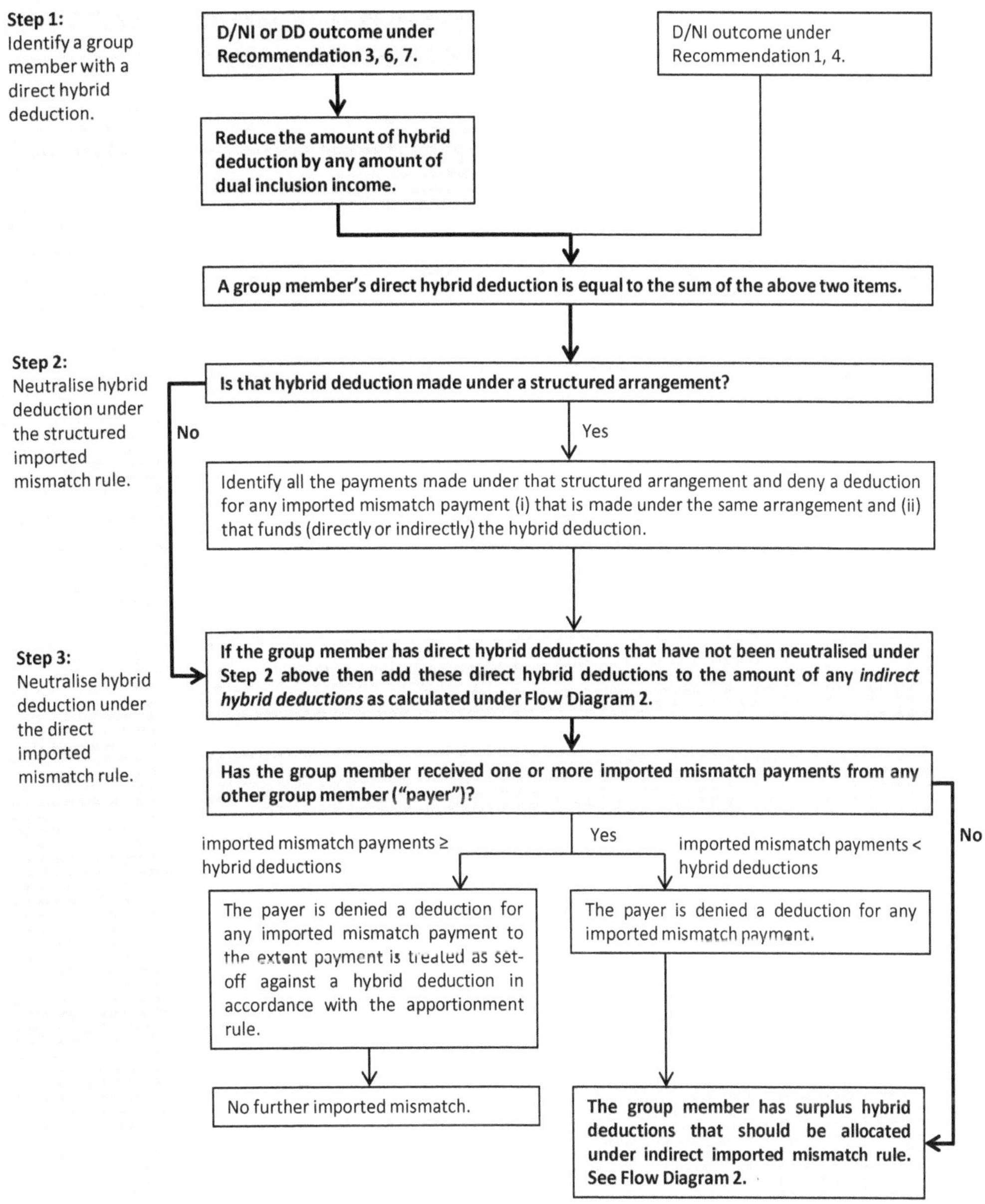

Flow Diagram 2 (Example 8.12)

Allocating surplus hybrid deduction under the indirect imported mismatch rule

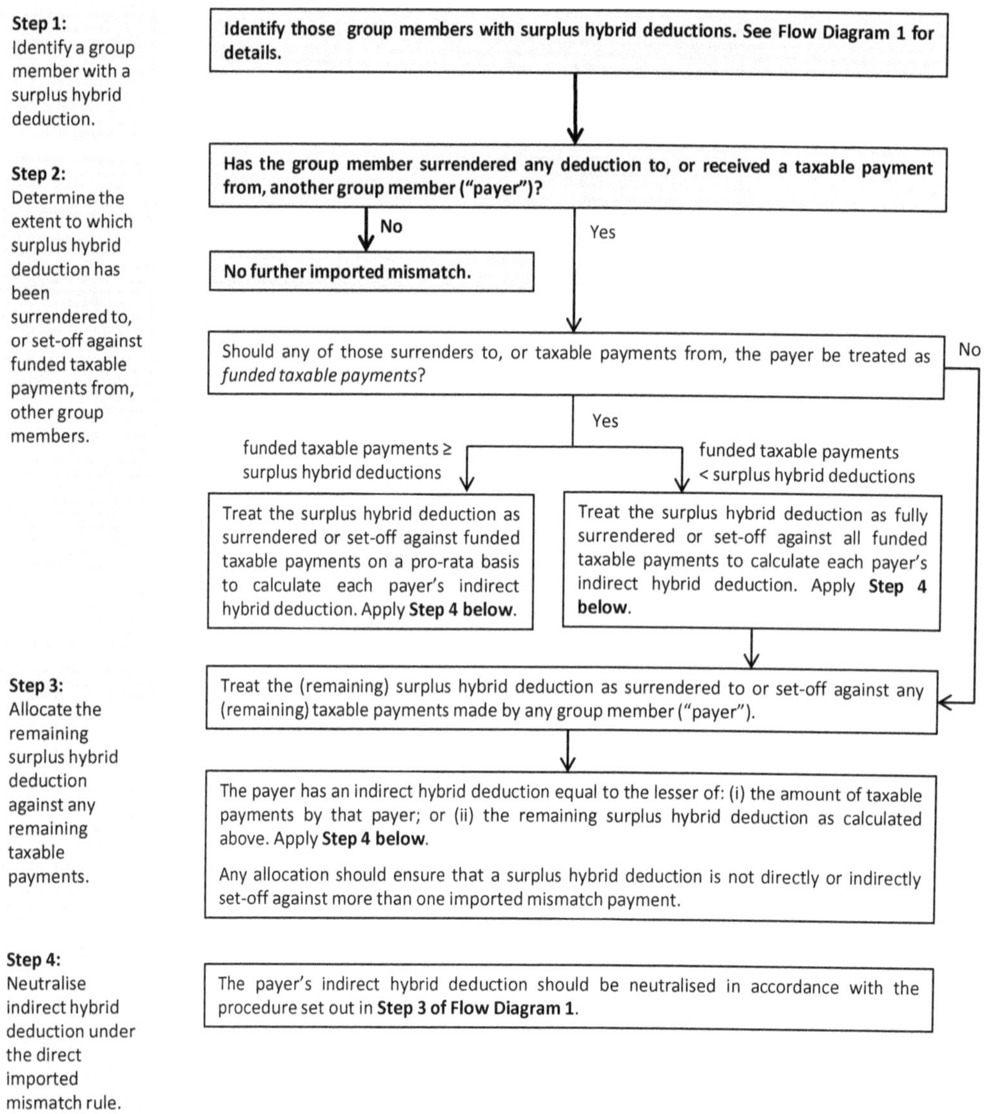

Example 8.13

Deductible hybrid payments, reverse hybrids and the imported hybrid mismatch rule

Facts

1. The figure below sets out the intra-group financing arrangements for companies that are members of the ABCD group. A Co is the parent of the group and is resident in Country A. B Co 1 and C Co are both direct subsidiaries of A Co and are resident in Country B and C respectively. B Co 2, a company resident in Country B, is a wholly-owned subsidiary of B Co 1 and D Co, a company resident in Country D, is a subsidiary of C Co.

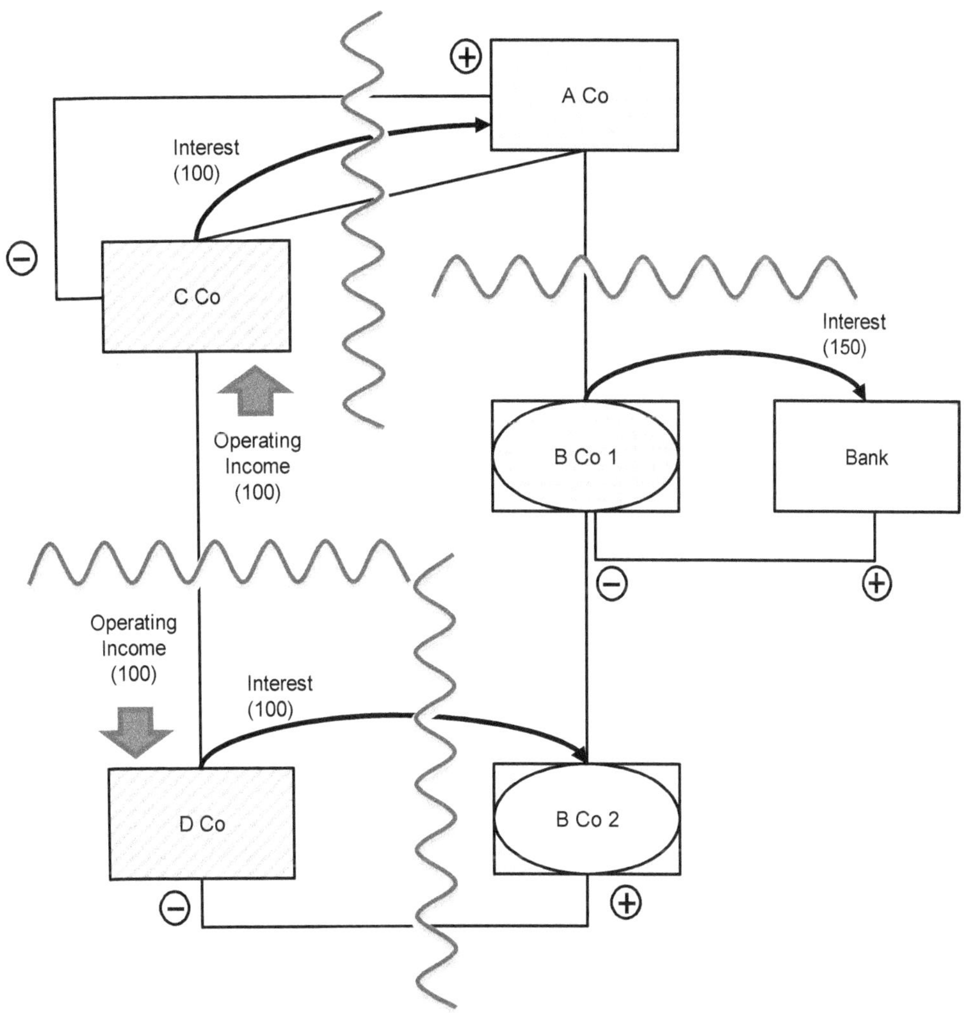

2. B Co 1 is a hybrid entity, i.e. an entity that is treated as a separate entity for tax purposes in Country B and as a disregarded entity in Country A. B Co 2 is a reverse hybrid entity, which means that it is treated as a separate entity under the tax laws of both Country A and D but as a disregarded entity for the purposes of Country B law.

3. The funding arrangements for the group are illustrated in the figure above. Each of these financing arrangements are entered into independently and do not form part of single scheme, plan or understanding. C Co pays interest of 100 on the loan from A Co and D Co pays interest of 100 on the loan from B Co 2. B Co 1 pays interest of 150 on the loan funding it receives from Bank. The table below illustrates the net income and expenditure of the entities in the group.

Country A A Co			Country B B Co 1 and B Co 2 Combined		
	Tax	**Book**		**Tax**	**Book**
Income			Income		
Interest paid by C Co	100	100	Interest paid by D Co	100	100
Expenditure			Expenditure		
Interest paid by B Co 1	(150)	-	Interest paid by B Co 1	(150)	(150)
Net return		**100**	**Net return**		**(50)**
Taxable income (loss)	**(50)**		**Taxable income**	**(50)**	

Country C Law C Co			Country D Law D Co		
	Tax	**Book**		**Tax**	**Book**
Income			Income		
Operating income	100	100	Operating income	100	100
Expenditure			Expenditure		
Interest paid to A Co	(100)	(100)	Interest paid to B Co 2	(100)	(100)
Net return		**0**	**Net return**		**0**
Taxable income	**0**		**Taxable income**	**0**	

4. Because B Co 1 is treated as a transparent entity for the purposes of Country A law, the tax positions of A Co and B Co 1 are combined. The combination of A Co and B Co 1 accounts mean that the payment of 150 made by B Co 1 to Bank is deductible in both Country A and Country B (a DD outcome). For the purposes of Country B law, the positions of B Co 1 and B Co 2 are combined, because B Co 2 is a reverse hybrid and thus the payment of 100 that B Co 2 receives from C Co is treated as if it was received directly by B Co 1. This payment is not, however, dual inclusion income.

5. Country C and Country D have implemented the full set of recommendations set out in the report. For the purposes of this example it is assumed that the structured imported mismatch rule does not apply.

Question

6. Whether the interest payments made by C Co and D Co are subject to adjustment under the imported mismatch rule, and, if so, the amount of the adjustment required under the rule.

Answer

7. Country C and Country D should apply the direct imported mismatch rule to deny a deduction for half the interest payments made by C Co and D Co respectively. See the flow diagram at the end of this example which outlines the steps to be taken in applying the imported mismatch rule.

Analysis

Interest payments made by B Co 1 are not made under a structured arrangement

8. B Co 1's loan from the Bank is independent of the intra-group financing arrangements. Unless such loan was entered into as part of wider scheme, plan or understanding that was intended to import the effect of a mismatch in tax outcomes into Country C or D, then the interest payment made by B Co 1 to the Bank should not be treated as made under a structured imported mismatch arrangement.

Payment of interest by C Co and D Co are offset against the same hybrid deduction

9. B Co 1 makes a deductible hybrid payment of 150 that gives rise to a DD outcome. The resulting hybrid deduction is automatically set-off against income on interest paid by C Co to A Co and on the interest paid by D Co to B Co 2. Because, however, this is a double deduction structure, the payments made by C Co and D Co are effectively set-off against the same hybrid deduction and both these payments should be taken into account when applying the apportionment approach under the direct imported mismatch rule.

The interest payments made by C Co and D Co should be subject to adjustment under the imported mismatch rule

Step 1 – B Co 1's deductible hybrid payment gives rise to a direct hybrid deduction under both Country A law and Country B law

10. The interest payment B Co 1 makes to the Bank is a deductible hybrid payment. Any deduction claimed for that payment will be a direct hybrid deduction to the extent it exceeds the payer's dual inclusion income. In this case the deductible payment is not reduced by any dual inclusion income so that B Co 1's interest payment gives rise to a direct hybrid deduction of 150 under both Country A and Country B law.

Step 2 – the structured imported mismatch rule does not apply

11. The facts of this example assume that the deductible hybrid payment is not made under a structured imported mismatch arrangement. Therefore the structured imported mismatch rule does not apply.

Step 3 – the imported mismatch payments made by C Co and D Co D Co should be treated as set-off against the same hybrid deduction under the direct imported mismatch rule

12. The direct imported mismatch rule should be applied in both Country C and Country D to deny C Co and D Co (respectively) deductions for the interest payments made to A Co and B Co 2 (respectively). Because Country C and Country D are applying the direct imported mismatch rule to the same hybrid deduction, those countries should apply an apportionment approach to determine the extent to which the imported mismatch payment has been set-off against the same hybrid deduction.

13. The guidance to the imported mismatch rule sets out an apportionment formula which can be used to determine the extent to which an imported mismatch payment has been directly set-off against a counterparty's hybrid deductions. The formula is as follows:

$$\text{Imported mismatch payment made by payer} \quad \times \quad \frac{\text{Total amount of remaining hybrid deductions incurred}}{\text{Total amount of imported mismatch payments received}}$$

14. As observed above, in this case the same hybrid deduction is set-off against two imported mismatch payments (from C Co and D Co) and the amount of those payments that should be treated as set-off against the hybrid deduction is calculated as follows:

$$\frac{\text{B Co 1's hybrid deduction}}{\text{Imported mismatch payments received by A Co and B Co 2}} = \frac{150}{100 + 100} = \frac{150}{200} = \frac{3}{4}$$

15. Applying this ratio under the imported mismatch rules of Country C and Country D, the amount of interest deduction denied under Country C law will be 75 (i. e. 3/4 x 100)and the amount of interest deduction denied under Country D law will be 75 (i. e. 3/4 x 100).

The net income of the companies in the group after application of the imported mismatch rule is presented in the table below.

Country A A Co	Tax	Book
Income		
Interest paid by C Co	100	100
Expenditure		
Interest paid by B Co 1	(150)	-
Net return		**100**
Taxable income (loss)	**(50)**	

Country B B Co 1 and B Co 2 Combined	Tax	Book
Income		
Interest paid by D Co	100	100
Expenditure		
Interest paid by B Co 1	(150)	(150)-
Net return		**(50)**
Taxable income	**(50)**	

Country C Law C Co	Tax	Book
Income		
Operating income	100	100
Expenditure		
Interest paid to A Co	(25)	(100)
Net return		**0**
Taxable income	**75**	

Country D Law D Co	Tax	Book
Income		
Operating income	100	100
Expenditure		
Interest paid to B Co 2	(25)	(100)
Net return		**0**
Taxable income	**75**	

Flow Diagram 1 (Example 8.13)

Neutralising hybrid deduction under the structured and direct imported mismatch rule

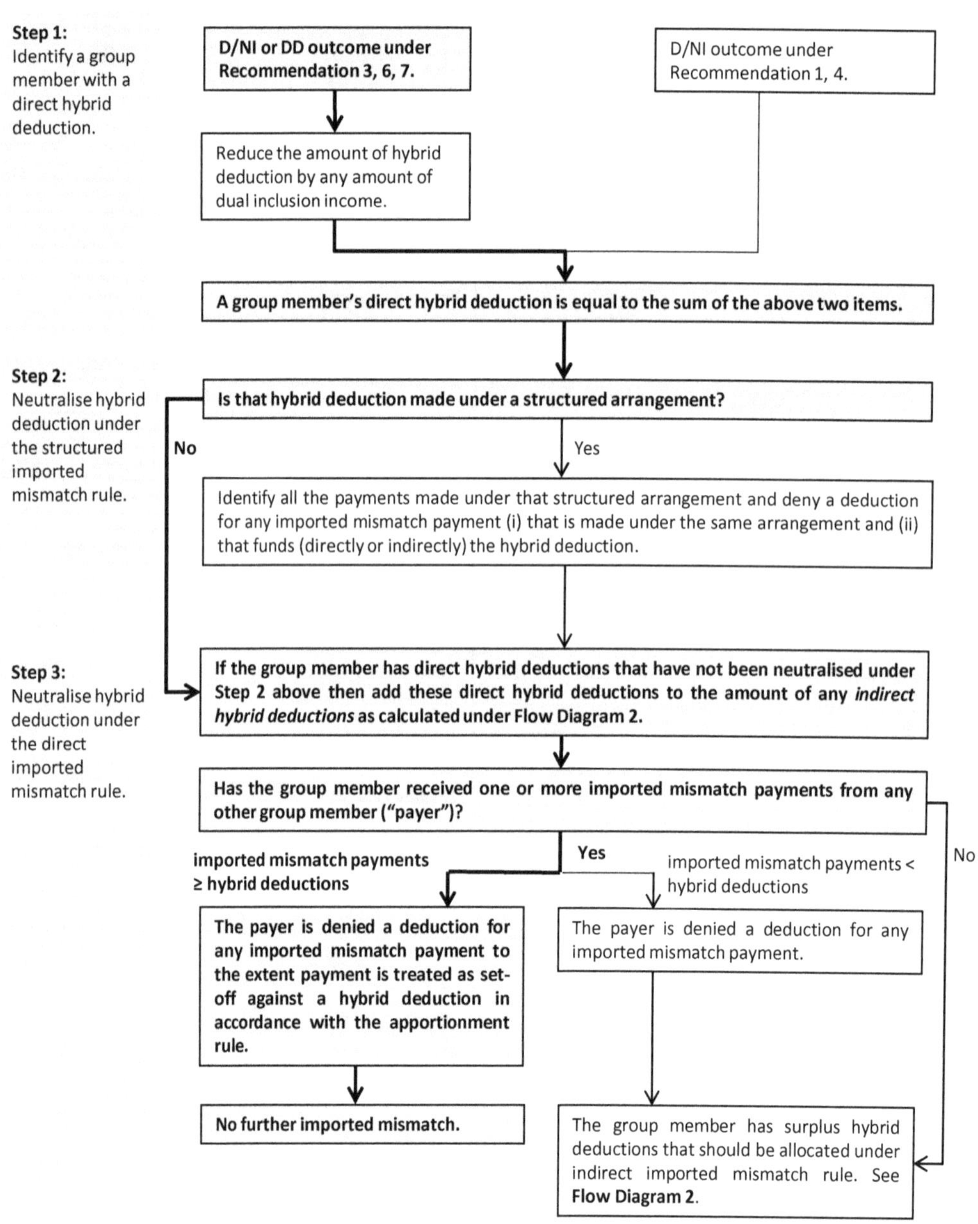

Example 8.14

Deductible hybrid payments, tax grouping and imported hybrid mismatch rules

Facts

1. The facts illustrated in the figure below are the same as **Example 8.13** except that B Co 2 is not a reverse hybrid but a member of the same tax group for the purposes of Country B tax law. Members of a tax group calculate their income (or loss) on a separate entity basis but are able to surrender any net loss to another group member and set it off against that group member's income arising in the same accounting period. The group structure and financing arrangements are illustrated in the figure below.

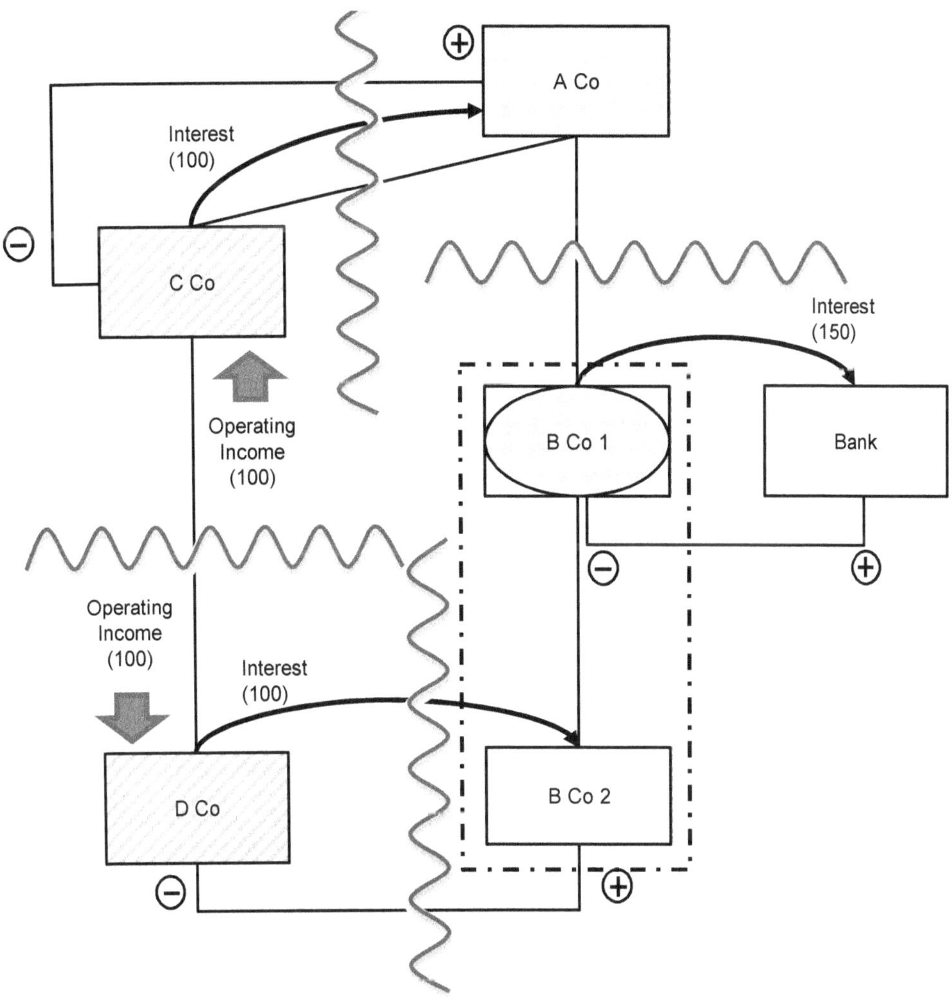

2. The net income accounts of the entities in the ABCD group are the same as in **Example 8.13** and are set out in the table below. Unlike in the example above, B Co 1 and B Co 2 accounts are not combined.

Country A A Co	Tax	Book	Country B B Co 1	Tax	Book
Income					
Interest paid by C Co	100	100			
Expenditure			Expenditure		
Interest paid by B Co 1	(150)	-	Interest paid by B Co 1	(150)	(150)-
Net return		**100**	**Net return**		**(150)**
Taxable income (loss)	**(50)**		Taxable income (loss)	(150)	
			Loss surrender to B Co 2	100	
			Loss carry forward	**(50)**	
			B Co 2		
			Income		
			Interest paid by D Co	100	100
			Expenditure		
			Loss surrender	(100)	
			Net return		**100**
			Taxable income	**0**	

Country C Law C Co	Tax	Book	Country D Law D Co	Tax	Book
Income			Income		
Operating income	100	100	Operating income	100	100
Expenditure			Expenditure		
Interest paid to A Co	(100)	(100)	Interest paid to B Co 2	(100)	(100)
Net return		**0**	**Net return**		**0**
Taxable income	**0**		**Taxable income**	**0**	

Question

3. Whether the interest payments made by C Co and D Co are subject to adjustment under the imported mismatch rule, and, if so, the amount of the adjustment required under the rule.

Answer

4. Country C should apply the direct imported mismatch rule to deny a deduction for all of the interest payments made by C Co. Country D should apply the indirect imported mismatch rule to deny a deduction for half the interest payment made by D Co. See the flow diagram at the end of this example which outlines the steps to be taken in applying the imported mismatch rule.

Analysis

5. B Co 1's loan from the Bank is independent of the other group financing arrangements. Unless such loan was entered into as part of wider scheme, plan or understanding that was intended to import the effect of a mismatch in tax outcomes into Country C or D, then the interest payment made by B Co 1 to the Bank should not be treated as made under a structured imported mismatch arrangement.

Payments of interest by C Co and D Co are offset against the same hybrid deduction.

6. B Co 1 makes a deductible hybrid payment of 150 that gives rise to a DD outcome. The resulting hybrid deduction is set-off against income on interest paid by C Co to A Co and on the interest paid by D Co to B Co 2 (after having been surrendered under the tax grouping regime in Country B). Because, however, this is a double deduction structure, the payments made by C Co and D Co are effectively set-off against the same hybrid deduction. Accordingly, the tax consequences attaching to the imported mismatch payment in Country C should be taken into account when applying the indirect imported mismatch rule in Country D.

The interest payment made by C Co should be subject to adjustment under the direct imported mismatch rule

Step 1 – B Co 1's deductible hybrid payment gives rise to a direct hybrid deduction under both Country A law and Country B law

7. The interest payment B Co 1 makes to the Bank is a deductible hybrid payment. Any deduction claimed for that payment will be a direct hybrid deduction to the extent it exceeds the payer's dual inclusion income. In this case the deductible payment is not reduced by any dual inclusion income so that B Co 1's interest payment gives rise to a direct hybrid deduction of 150 under both Country A and Country B law.

Step 2 – the structured imported mismatch rule does not apply

8. The facts of this example assume that the deductible hybrid payment is not made under a structured imported mismatch arrangement. Therefore the structured imported mismatch rule does not apply.

Step 3 – B Co 1's hybrid deductions should be treated as set-off against the imported mismatch payment made by C Co

9. This hybrid deduction is automatically set-off against income on the interest C Co pays to A Co (see the analysis in Example 8.13). In this case the amount of A Co's hybrid deduction (150) is greater than the imported mismatch payment made by C Co (100). Therefore, the whole of the deduction claimed by C Co should be denied under the direct imported mismatch rule leaving a surplus hybrid deduction of 50.

The interest payment made by D Co should be subject to adjustment under the indirect imported mismatch rule

Step 1 –B Co 1 has surplus hybrid deductions of 50

10. In this case B Co 1's surplus hybrid deduction will be the amount of hybrid deduction that is attributable to the deductible hybrid payment (150) minus any amount of hybrid deduction that has been neutralised under either the structured or direct imported mismatch rules (100).

Step 2 –B Co 1's surplus hybrid deduction are set-off against funded taxable payments

11. B Co 1 has surrendered a loss of 100 to B Co 2. This loss surrender is treated in the same way as a funded taxable payment because B Co 2 is a direct recipient of an imported mismatch payment. In this case B Co 1 does not receive any other taxable payments so the remaining surplus hybrid deduction should therefore be treated as fully surrendered to B Co 2.

Step 3 – B Co 1 has no remaining surplus hybrid deduction

12. As B Co 1's surplus hybrid deduction is set-off against an imported mismatch payment, B Co 1 has no remaining surplus hybrid deductions

Step 4 – B Co 2's indirect hybrid deduction is neutralised in accordance with the direct imported mismatch rule

13. B Co 2 should treat the resulting indirect hybrid deduction as being set-off against imported mismatch payments made by D Co. The calculation is the same as under the direct imported mismatch rule and the proportion of the deduction for the interest payment that should be denied is calculated as follows:

$$\frac{\text{B Co 2's hybrid deduction}}{\text{Imported mismatch payments received by B Co 2}} = \frac{50}{100} = \frac{1}{2}$$

Therefore half the interest payment made by D Co should be subject to adjustment under the imported mismatch rule. The tables below illustrate the net income accounts of the group entities after application of the imported mismatch rules.

Country A A Co	Tax	Book	Country B B Co 1	Tax	Book
Income					
Interest paid by C Co	100	100			
Expenditure			Expenditure		
Interest paid by B Co 1	(150)	-	Interest paid by B Co 1	(150)	(150)
Net return		**100**	**Net return**		**(150)**
Taxable income (loss)	**(50)**		Taxable income (loss)	(150)	
			Loss surrender to B Co 2	100	
			Loss carry forward	**(50)**	
			B Co 2		
			Income		
			Interest paid by D Co	100	100
			Expenditure		
			Loss surrender	(100)	
			Net return		**100**
			Taxable income	**0**	

Country C Law C Co	Tax	Book	Country D Law D Co	Tax	Book
Income			Income		
Operating income	100	100	Operating income	100	100
Expenditure			Expenditure		
Interest paid to A Co	0	(100)	Interest paid to B Co 2	(50)	(100)
Net return		**0**	**Net return**		**0**
Taxable income	**100**		**Taxable income**	**50**	

Flow Diagram 1 (Example 8.14)

Neutralising hybrid deduction under the structured and direct imported mismatch rule

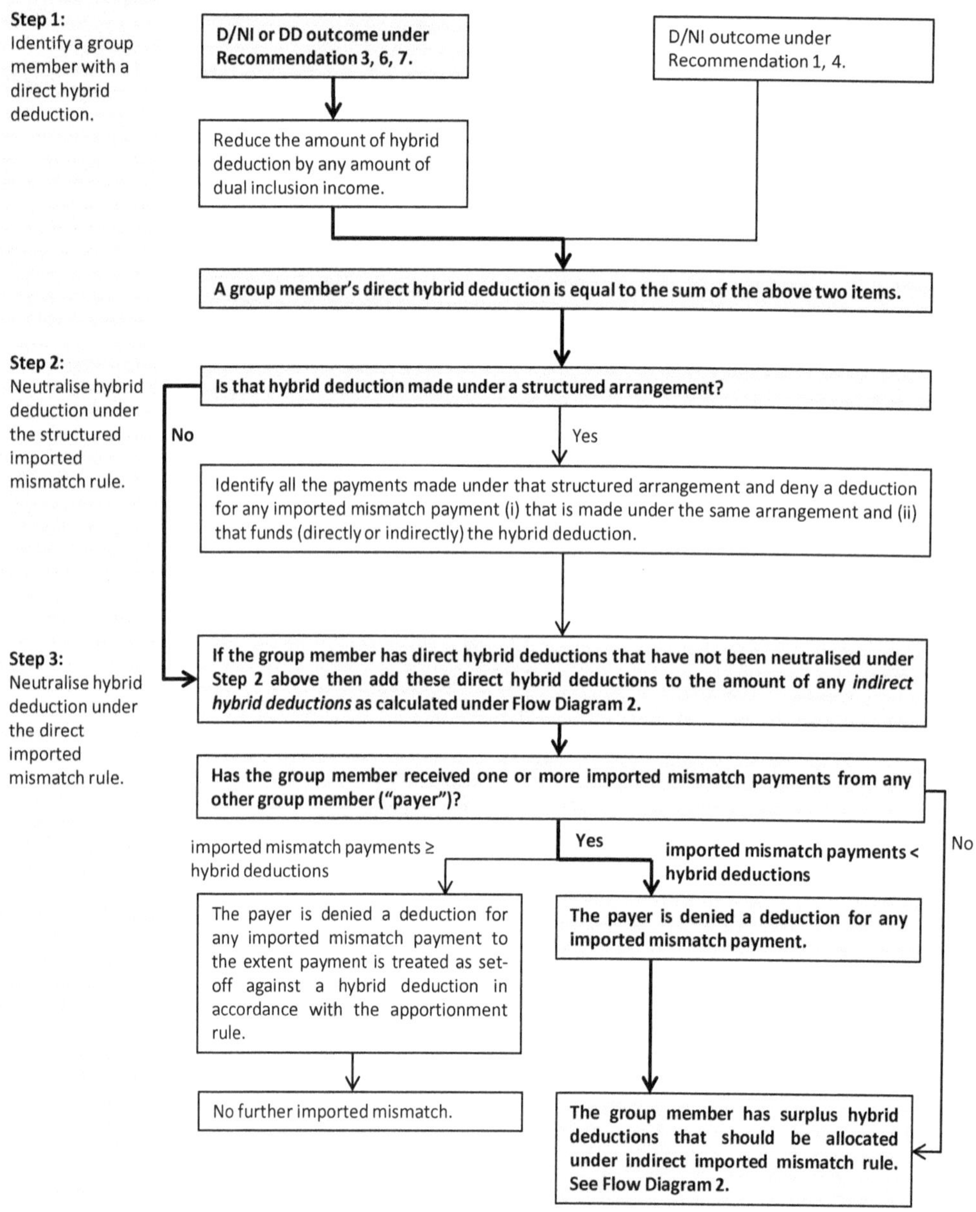

Flow Diagram 2 (Example 8.14)

Allocating surplus hybrid deduction under the indirect imported mismatch rule

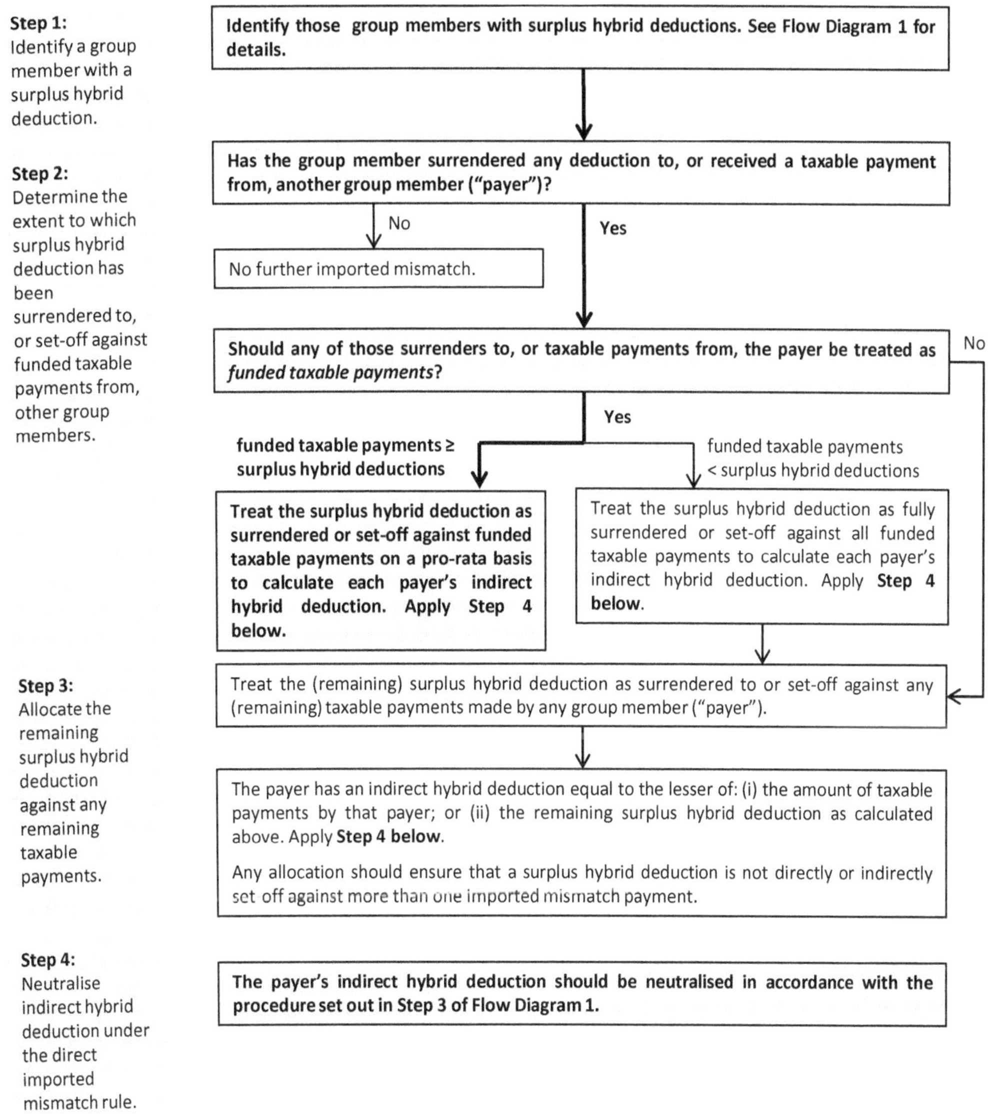

Example 8.15

Interaction between double deduction and imported mismatch rule

Facts

1. The figure below sets out the intra-group financing arrangements for companies that are members of the ABCDE Group. A Co is the parent of the group and is resident in Country A. B Co 1 and C Co are direct subsidiaries of A Co and are resident in Country B and Country C respectively. D Co (a company resident in Country D) is a direct subsidiary of C Co and E Co (a company resident in Country E) is a direct subsidiary of E Co. B Co 2 is a wholly-owned subsidiary of B Co 1 and is also resident in Country B.

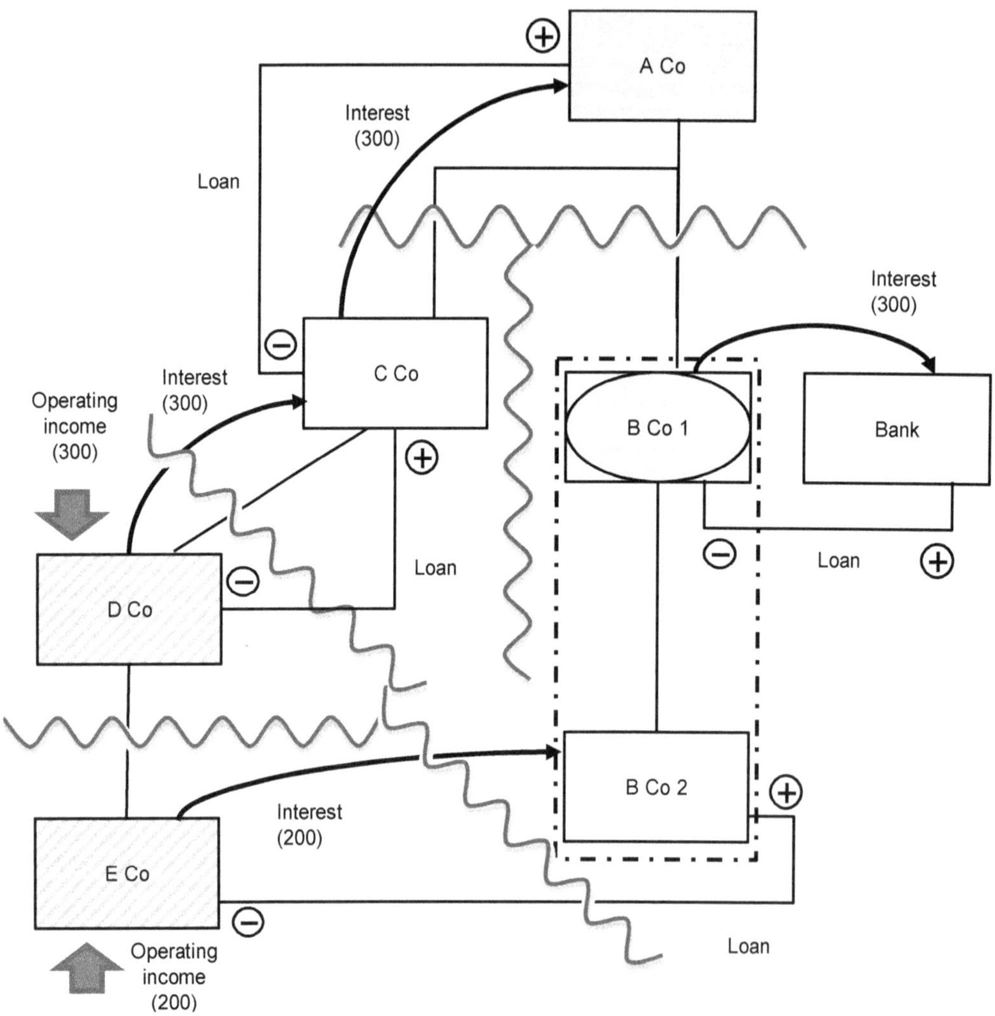

2. All companies are treated as separate tax entities in all jurisdictions, except that B Co 1 is a hybrid entity (i.e. an entity that is treated as a separate entity for tax purposes in Country B but as a disregarded entity under Country A law).

3. A Co has lent money to C Co, and C Co has on-lent that money to D Co. B Co 1 borrowed money from a local bank. B Co 2 lent money to E Co. Each of D Co and E Co receives operating income. Each of these financing arrangements are entered into independently and do not form part of single scheme, plan or understanding. The figure above illustrates the operating income and the total gross interest payments for each group entity.

4. Because B Co 1 is a hybrid entity, the interest payments made to the local bank are deductible by both A Co and B Co 1 under the laws of Country A and Country B respectively. B Co 1 and B Co 2 are members of the same tax group for tax purposes under Country B law, which means that the net loss of B Co 1 can be surrendered to set-off against any net income of B Co 2.

Tax position before applying the imported mismatch rule

5. Below is a table setting out the tax position in respect of the ABCDE group (before the application of any imported mismatch rule).

Country A A Co			Country B B Co 1		
	Tax	Book		Tax	Book
Income					
Interest paid by C Co	300	300			
Expenditure			Expenditure		
Interest paid by B Co 1	(300)	-	Interest paid by B Co 1	(300)	(300)
Net return		**300**	**Net return**		**(300)**
Taxable income	**0**		Taxable income (loss)	(300)	
			Loss surrender to B Co 2	200	
			Loss carry forward	**(100)**	
			B Co 2		
			Income		
			Interest paid by D Co	200	200
			Expenditure		
			Loss surrender	(200)	
			Net return		**200**
			Taxable income	**0**	

Country C Law C Co	Tax	Book
Income		
Interest paid by D Co	300	300
Expenditure		
Interest paid to A Co	(300)	(300)
Net return		0
Taxable income	0	

Country D Law D Co	Tax	Book
Income		
Operating income	300	300
Expenditure		
Interest paid to B Co 2	(300)	(300)
Net return		0
Taxable income	0	

Country E Law E Co	Tax	Cash
Income		
Operating income	200	200
Expenditure		
Interest paid to B Co 1	(200)	(200)
Net return		0
Taxable income	0	

Result under Country A law

6. A Co has net taxable income of zero (interest income of 300 and a deduction of 300).

Result under Country B law

7. B Co 1 has a net loss for tax purposes of 300 (a deduction of 300), while B Co 2 has net income of 200. B Co 1's net loss is surrendered through the tax grouping regime and applied against, and to the extent of, B Co 2's net income.

Result under Country C, D and E law

8. C Co, D Co and E Co have income that is equal to their expenses and therefore have no net income in either of the two years.

Mismatch in tax outcomes

9. In aggregate the arrangement generates a net return for the ABCDE Group of 200, however the total net taxable income recognised under this structure is nil. Country D and Country E have implemented the recommendations set out in this report.

Question

10. Whether the interest payments made by D Co and E Co are subject to adjustment under the imported mismatch rule and, if so, the amount of the adjustment required under the rule.

Answer

11. Indirect imported mismatch rule applies to the interest payment of 200 from E Co to B Co 2, and the interest payment of 300 from D Co to C Co. As a result of apportionment of surplus hybrid deduction of 300 between those payments, Country D should deny D Co a deduction for 180 of the interest paid to C Co, and Country E should deny E Co a deduction for 120 of the interest paid to B Co 2. See the flow diagrams at the end of this example which outline the steps to be taken in applying the imported mismatch rule.

Analysis

Interest payments made by B Co 1 are not made under a structured arrangement

12. B Co 1's loan from the Bank is independent of the intra-group financing arrangements. Unless such loan was entered into as part of wider scheme, plan or understanding that was intended to import the effect of a mismatch in tax outcomes into Country C or D, then the interest payment made by B Co 1 to the Bank should not be treated as made under a structured imported mismatch arrangement.

The hybrid deduction is not set-off against an imported mismatch payment under the structured or direct imported mismatch rule

Step 1 – B Co 1's deductible hybrid payment gives rise to a direct hybrid deduction under both Country A law and Country B law

13. The interest payment B Co 1 makes to the Bank is a deductible hybrid payment. Any deduction claimed for that payment will be a direct hybrid deduction to the extent it exceeds the payer's dual inclusion income. In this case the deductible payment is not reduced by any dual inclusion income so that B Co 1's interest payment gives rise to a direct hybrid deduction of 300 under both Country A and Country B laws.

Step 2 – the structured imported mismatch rule does not apply

14. The facts of this example assume that the deductible hybrid payment is not made under a structured imported mismatch arrangement. Therefore the structured imported mismatch rule does not apply.

Step 3 – the direct imported mismatch rules does not apply

15. In this case the direct imported mismatch rule does not apply as the group entities that are recipients of the loss surrender or that are directly funding the hybrid deduction (i.e. B Co 2 and C Co) are resident in jurisdictions that have not implemented the imported mismatch rules.

The interest payments made by D Co and E Co should be subject to adjustment under the indirect imported mismatch rule

16. As B Co 1's hybrid deduction has not been neutralised under the structured or direct imported mismatch rule, the indirect imported mismatch rule applies to determine the extent to which B Co 1's surplus hybrid deduction should be treated as giving rise to an indirect hybrid deduction for another group member.

Step 1 –B Co 1 and A Co have surplus hybrid deductions of 300

17. A group member's surplus hybrid deduction will be the amount of hybrid deduction that is attributable to deductible hybrid payment (300) minus any amount of hybrid deduction that has been neutralised under either the structured or direct imported mismatch rules (0).

Step 2 –Surplus hybrid deduction is set-off against funded taxable payments

18. Both B Co 1 and A Co must first treat the surplus hybrid deduction as being surrendered or offset against funded taxable payments received from group entities calculated as follows:

(a) A taxable payment will be treated as a funded taxable payment to the extent the payment is directly funded out of imported mismatch payments made by other group entities. In this case the interest payments of 300 that A Co receives from C Co constitute funded taxable payments.

(b) B Co 1 has surrendered a loss of 200 to B Co 2. This loss surrender is treated in the same way as a funded taxable payment because B Co 2 is a direct recipient of an imported mismatch payment.

Accordingly the total amount of funded taxable payments is equal to 500.

19. In this case the amount of funded taxable payments (500) exceeds the amount of the surplus hybrid deduction (300). Both A Co and B Co 1 should therefore treat the surplus hybrid deduction as set-off pro rata against the funded taxable payments and the loss surrendered to B Co 2 under the tax grouping regime. Therefore:

(a) B Co 2 has indirect hybrid deduction of 120 (i.e. 300/500 x 200).

(b) C Co has indirect hybrid deduction of 180 (i.e. 300/500 x 300).

Step 3 – C Co has no remaining surplus hybrid deduction

20. C Co's surplus hybrid deduction has been surrendered or fully set-off against funded taxable payments and C Co therefore has no remaining surplus hybrid deduction to be set-off against other taxable payments.

Step 4 – B Co 2 and C Co's indirect hybrid deductions are neutralised in accordance with the direct imported mismatch rule

21. B Co 2 should treat the resulting indirect hybrid deduction as being set-off against imported mismatch payments made by D Co. The calculation is the same as under the direct imported mismatch rule and the proportion of the deduction for the interest payment that should be denied is calculated as follows:

$$\frac{\text{B Co 2's hybrid deduction}}{\text{Imported mismatch payments received by B Co 2}} = \frac{120}{200} = \frac{3}{5}$$

Therefore D Co should be denied a deduction for (3/5 x 200) = 120 under the imported mismatch rule.

22. The calculation with respect to E Co is the same. C Co treats indirect hybrid deduction as being set-off against imported mismatch payments made by E Co. Calculation is the same as under the direct imported mismatch rule and the proportion of deduction that G Co should be denied on its IM payments is calculated as follows:

$$\frac{\text{C Co's hybrid deduction}}{\text{Imported mismatch payments received by C Co}} = \frac{180}{300} = \frac{3}{5}$$

Therefore D Co should be denied a deduction for (3/5 x 300) = 180 under the imported mismatch rule.

23. The table below sets out tax position in respect of the ABCDE group (after the application of any imported mismatch rule).

Country A A Co			**Country B B Co 1**		
	Tax	**Book**		**Tax**	**Book**
Income					
Interest paid by C Co	300	300			
Expenditure			Expenditure		
Interest paid by B Co 1	(300)	-	Interest paid by B Co 1	(300)	(300)-
Net return		**300**	**Net return**		**(300)**
Taxable income	**0**		Taxable income (loss)	(300)	
			Loss surrender to B Co 2	200	
			Loss carry forward	**(100)**	
			B Co 2		
			Income		
			Interest paid by D Co	200	200
			Expenditure		
			Loss surrender	(200)	
			Net return		**100**
			Taxable income	**0**	

Country C Law C Co		
	Tax	Book
Income		
Interest paid by D Co	300	300
Expenditure		
Interest paid to A Co	(300)	(300)
Net return		**0**
Taxable income	**0**	

Country D Law D Co		
	Tax	Book
Income		
Operating income	300	300
Expenditure		
Interest paid to B Co 2	(120)	(300)
Net return		**300**
Taxable income	**180**	

Country E Law E Co		
	Tax	Cash
Income		
Operating income	200	200
Expenditure		
Interest paid to B Co 1	(80)	(200)
Net return		**0**
Taxable income	**120**	

Flow Diagram 1 (Example 8.15)

Neutralising hybrid deduction under the structured and direct imported mismatch rule

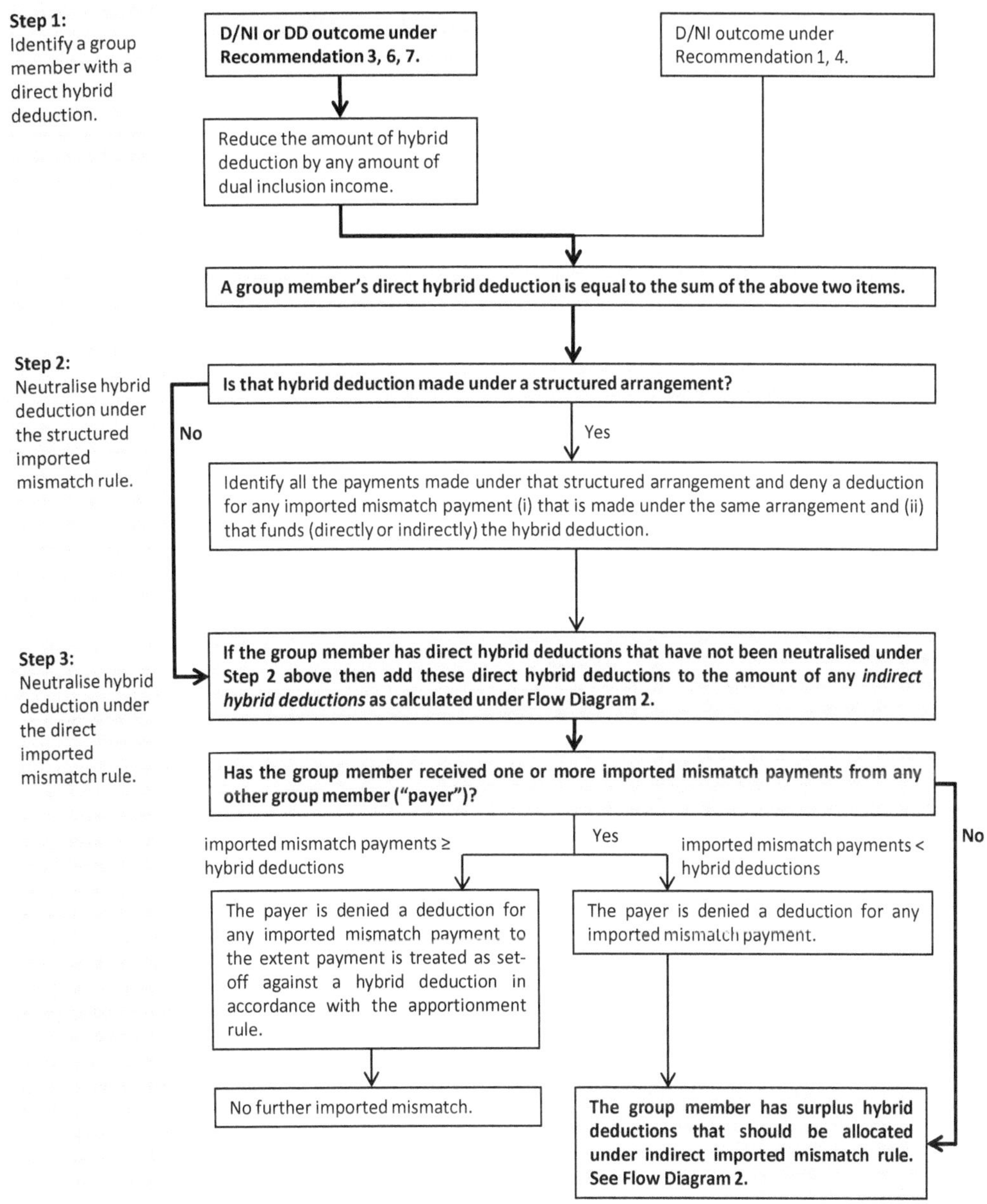

Flow Diagram 2 (Example 8.15)

Allocating surplus hybrid deduction under the indirect imported mismatch rule

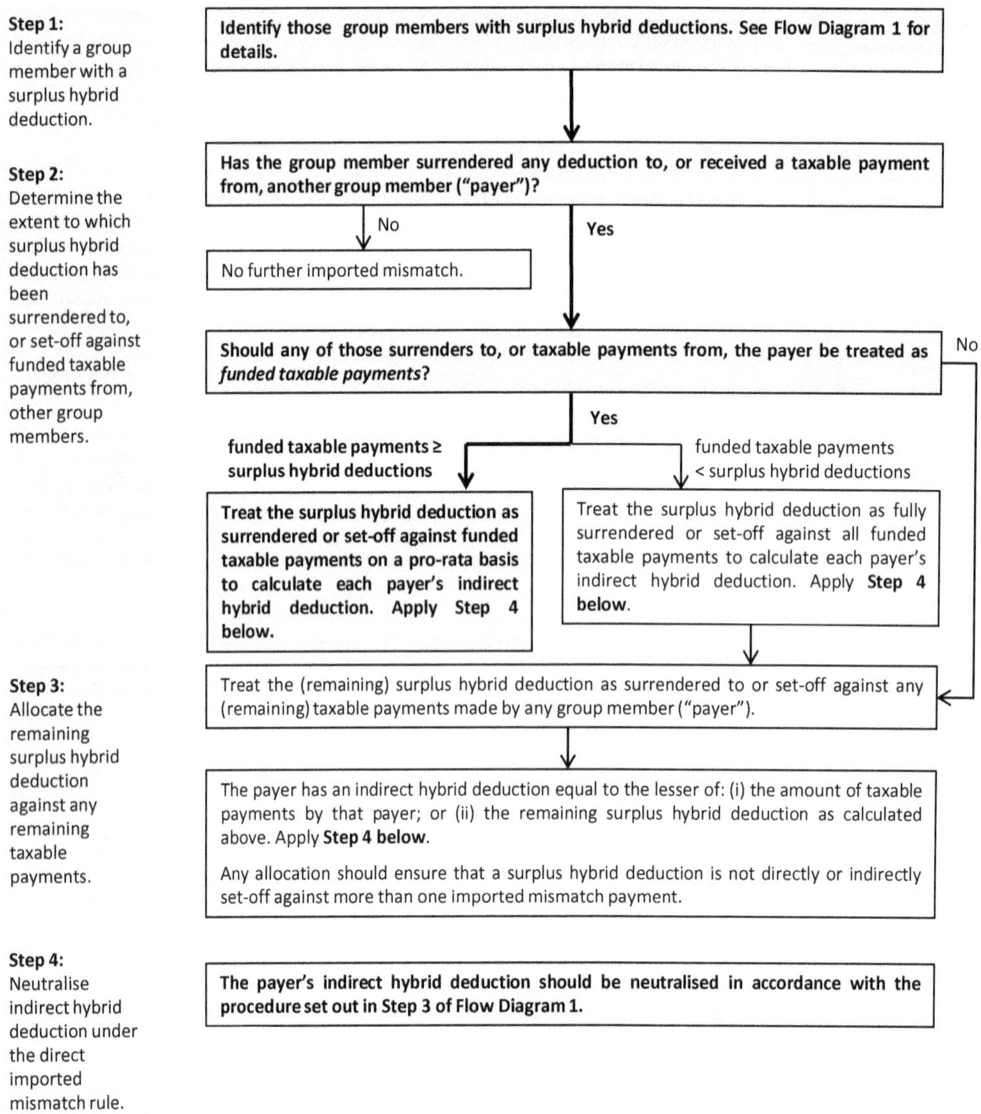

Example 8.16

Carry-forward of hybrid deductions under imported mismatch rules

Facts

1. In the example illustrated in the figure below, A Co wholly owns B Co, which, in turn, wholly owns C Co. A Co, B Co and C Co are resident in Country A, Country B and Country C respectively.

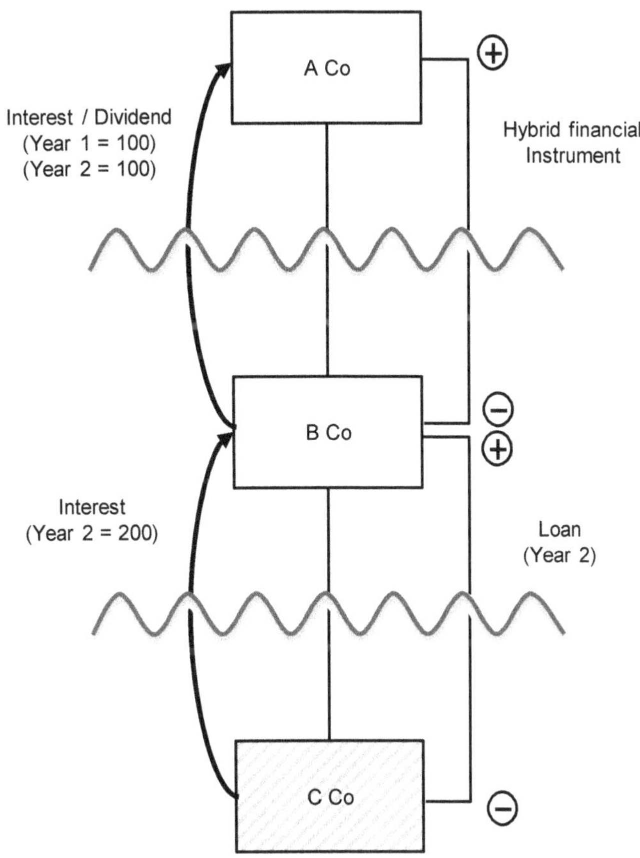

2. In Year 1, A Co lends money to B Co under a hybrid financial instrument. Interest payments under the hybrid financial instrument are treated as deductible interest expenses under Country B law but treated as exempt dividends under Country A law. The payments are equal to 100 each year. At the end of the first year B Co has a net-loss carry-forward of 100.

3. In Year 2, B Co lends money to C Co under an ordinary loan. The interest payable under the loan in Year 2 is 200.

4. Only Country C has implemented the recommendations set out in the report.

Question

5. Whether the interest payments made by C Co are subject to adjustment under the imported mismatch rule and, if so, the amount of the adjustment required under the rule.

Answer

6. B Co carries over a hybrid deduction of 100 from Year 1. The direct imported mismatch rule applies to the interest payment of 200 from C Co to B Co and Country C should deny C Co a deduction for all the interest paid to B Co.

Analysis

Application of direct imported mismatch rule to interest payments from C Co to B Co

7. As explained in the facts above, the interest payments by B Co to A Co in Year 1 give rise to a D/NI outcome under a hybrid financial instrument. B Co's hybrid deduction is carried-forward to Year 2 and set-off against interest income paid by C Co in the following year. The direct imported mismatch rule applies to the full interest payment from C Co to B Co since this payment (of 200) is directly set-off against a deduction for the interest paid under the hybrid financial instrument in both Year 1 (100) and Year 2 (100).

Example 9.1

Co-ordination of primary/secondary rules

Facts

1. In the example illustrated in the figure below, A Co holds all the shares of a foreign subsidiary (B Co). B Co is a hybrid entity that is disregarded for Country A tax purposes. B Co borrows from A Co and pays interest on the 5 year loan. Interest is payable in arrears every 12 months on 1 October each year.

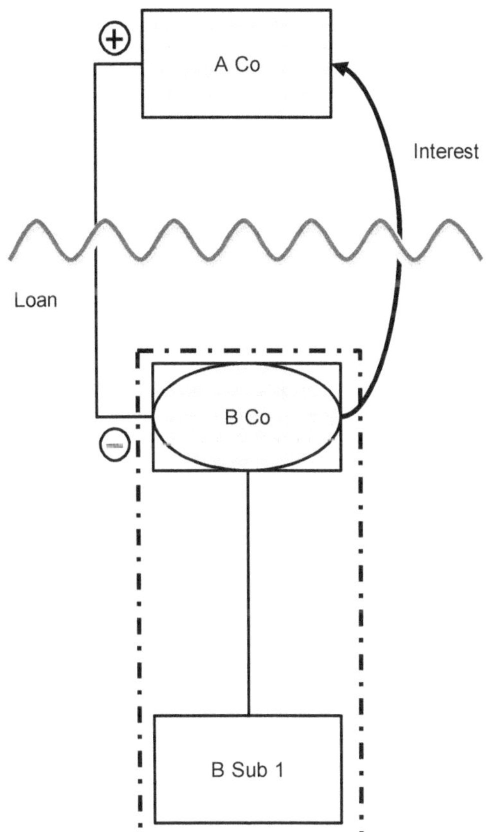

2. B Co is treated as transparent under the laws of Country A and (because A Co is the only shareholder in B Co) Country A simply disregards the separate existence of B Co. Disregarding B Co means that the loan (and by extension the interest on the loan) between A Co and B Co is ignored under the laws of Country A. Under the laws of Country B, B Co and B Sub 1 form part of the same tax group which allows B Co to

surrender the tax benefit of the interest deduction to B Sub 1 where it can be set-off against non-dual inclusion income.

3. In Year 2 of the arrangement, Country A implements the hybrid mismatch rules so that the interest payment is included in the income of A Co through the operation of the disregarded hybrid payments rule set out in Recommendation 3. This income in Country A is recognised on an accrual basis. In Year 3 of the arrangement, Country B also implements the hybrid mismatch rules to take effect from the beginning of Country B's tax year commencing in Year 4. The tax year for Country A is the calendar year (1 January to 31 December) while B Co's tax year runs from on 1 July to 30 June of the following year.

Question

4. What proportion of the payment is required to be brought into account under the hybrid mismatch rule by A Co and B Co in Years 3 to 5 of the arrangement?

Answer

5. A jurisdiction applying the secondary or defensive rule in a period when the counterparty jurisdiction introduces hybrid mismatch rules (the switch-over period), should cease to apply the defensive rule to the extent the mismatch is neutralised by the introduction of the primary rule in the counterparty jurisdiction. This should not affect the adjustments made under the secondary rule in periods prior to the switch-over period. Accordingly:

(a) Country A should:

- require A Co to include a payment in ordinary income to the extent it gives rise mismatch in an accounting period that begins on or after the introduction of the hybrid mismatch rules in Country A; and
- grant A Co relief for any payment made during the switch-over period to the extent the mismatch is neutralised due to the operation of the primary rule in Country B.

(b) Country B should apply the primary rule to the amount that is treated as paid, under its laws, after the commencement of hybrid mismatch rules in Country B while taking into account any payment that has previously been included in income under the laws of Country A in a prior accounting period.

Analysis

Defensive rule applies only where the mismatch is not neutralised in payer jurisdiction

6. Recommendation 3.1(b) provides that a disregarded payment made by a hybrid payer must be included in ordinary income to the extent it gives rise to a D/NI outcome. This rule only applies, however, to the extent the mismatch in tax outcomes has not been neutralised in the payer jurisdiction. Accordingly, if and when Country B introduces hybrid mismatch rules to deny a deduction for the disregarded hybrid payment, Country A should cease to apply the defensive rule.

Co-ordination of the primary and secondary rules

7. Complications in the application of the rule and a risk of double taxation could arise, however, in situations where the counterparty jurisdiction introduces hybrid mismatch rules from a date that is part way through the taxpayer's accounting period (the switch-over period). In order to ensure the primary and secondary rules are properly co-ordinated without causing undue disruption to the domestic rules of the counterparty, the payer and payee jurisdictions should apply the co-ordination rules as follows:

(a) The secondary or defensive rule will apply to any amount that is treated as paid, under the laws of the payee jurisdiction (Country A), in a period prior to the commencement of the switch-over period.

(b) The primary rule will apply to any amount that is treated as paid, under the laws of the payer jurisdiction (Country B), during the switch-over period (after taking into account any amounts caught by the secondary rule in accordance with paragraph (a) above).

(c) Any other payments that give rise to a hybrid mismatch and that are not captured by paragraph (b) above will be caught by the application of the secondary rule.

8. A table setting out the effect of these adjustments in Years 3 to 5 is set out below. The table shows the payments of accrued interest income or expense under the loan in each calendar year and the income tax consequences applying to payments made under the loan. In this table it is assumed that the interest payment is 100 each year. and that B Co and A Co have no other income or expenditure other than the disregarded hybrid payment. Both countries tax income and expenditure under a debt instrument on an accrual basis.

	Country A A Co			Country B B Co 1			Total
Year 2		**Tax**	**Book**		**Tax**	**Book**	
	Income			Income			
	Interest paid by B Co 1	100	100				
				Expenditure			
				Interest paid to A Co	(100)	(100)	
	Net return		**100**	**Net return**		**(100)**	**0**
	Taxable income	**100**		**Taxable income**	**(100)**		**0**

Year 3	Country A A Co	Tax	Book	Country B B Co 1	Tax	Book	Total
	Income			Income			
	Interest paid by B Co 1	50	100				
				Expenditure			
				Interest paid to A Co	(50)	(100)	
	Net return		**100**	**Net return**		**(100)**	**0**
	Taxable income	**50**		**Taxable income (loss)**	**(50)**		**0**

Year 4	Country A A Co	Tax	Book	Country B B Co	Tax	Book	Total
	Income			Income			
	Interest paid by B Co 1		75				
				Expenditure			
				Interest paid to A Co		(75)	
	Net return		**75**	**Net return**		**(75)**	**0**
	Taxable income	**0**		**Taxable income**	**0**		**0**

9. In Year 3, 100 of interest accrues on the loan. The primary rule has not yet been introduced into Country B law so the entire amount of accrued interest is included in income under Country A law (see para 7(a) above).

10. In Year 4, the primary rule is introduced in Country B and takes effect from the beginning of Country B's tax year (which commences on 1 July).

(a) In this case, Country B will apply the primary response under its own law with no adjustment (see para 7(b) above). Because Country B recognises expenditure under a financial instrument on an accrual basis for tax purposes:

- the interest that accrues after the commencement of the rules will be subject to the adjustment under the primary rule; and
- the portion of the interest payment that has accrued prior to the commencement of the hybrid mismatch rules (50) will be outside the application of the primary rule as it will be treated as derived in a prior tax year.

(b) Country A should apply the secondary rule to the extent the mismatch has not been eliminated by the primary rule in Country B (see para 7(c) above). This means that Country A should continue to apply the secondary rule for the switch-over period to the extent the deduction for the payment has not been denied under Country B law.

If, in practice, it would be unduly burdensome to require A Co to determine the actual amount of the payment that has been subject to adjustment under the primary rule, the amount of the payment falling within the scope of the secondary rule can be calculated based on the amount accrued under Country A law for the switch-over period where the primary rule will not apply (in this case 1 January to 30 June). This will result in only half the accrued interest payment being recognised as income in Country A under the hybrid mismatch rule.

11. In Year 5, the loan matures and the final payment of accrued interest on the loan is paid. The secondary rule does not apply in Country A as all the payments made under the instrument are caught by the primary rule in Country B.

Differences in the timing in the recognition of payments

12. The above table was calculated on the assumption that both Country A and B apply the same rules regarding the recognition of income and expenditure under a financial instrument. However differences between jurisdiction in the timing of the recognition of income and expenditure will impact on the amounts caught by the primary and secondary rules. The effect of these differences can be illustrated by changing the facts of this example so that, rather than granting deductions on an accrual basis, Country B only grants deductions for interest when such amounts are actually paid. A table setting out the effect of these adjustments in Years 3 to 5 based on this modified assumption is set out below.

	Country A A Co			Country B B Co 1			Total
		Tax	Book		Tax	Book	
Year 2	Income			Income			
	Interest paid by B Co 1	100	100				
				Expenditure			
				Interest paid to A Co	(100)	(100)	
	Net return		**100**	**Net return**		**(100)**	**0**
	Taxable income	**100**		**Taxable income**	**(100)**		**0**

	Country A A Co	Tax	Book	Country B B Co 1	Tax	Book	Total
Year 3	Income			Income			
	Interest paid by B Co 1	0	100				
				Expenditure			
				Interest paid to A Co	(25)	(100)	
	Net return		**100**	**Net return**		**(100)**	**0**
	Taxable income	**0**		**Taxable income (loss)**	**(25)**		**(25)**

	Country A A Co	Tax	Book	Country B B Co	Tax	Book	Total
Year 4	Income			Income			
	Interest paid by B Co 1		75				
				Expenditure			
				Interest paid to A Co	25	(75)	
	Net return		**75**	**Net return**		**(75)**	**0**
	Taxable income	**0**		**Taxable income**	**25**		**25**

13. As above, the table shows the payments of accrued interest under the loan in each calendar year and the income tax consequences applying to those payments for the same period. It is assumed that the interest payment is 100 each year (paid on 1 October of each year) and that B Co and A Co have no other income or expenditure other than the disregarded hybrid payment.

14. In Year 3 the primary rule has not yet been introduced into Country B law so that the entire amount of the payment is included in income under Country A law (see para 7(a) above).

15. In Year 4 the primary rule is introduced in Country B and takes effect from the beginning of Country B's tax year (which commences on 1 July).

(a) In this case, the amount of the deduction denied under the primary rule should not include a payment to the extent it has been already subject to adjustment under the secondary rule in a prior period. Because Country A recognises income under a financial instrument on an accrual basis, 25% of the interest payment has already been included in income in Year 3 (see para 7(b) above).

(b) Country A does not apply the secondary rule for the switch-over period as the entire amount of the payment for that period is caught by the primary rule under Country B law (see para 7(c) above).

16. In Year 5 the loan matures and the final payment of accrued interest on the loan is paid. The secondary rule does not apply in Country A as all the payments made under the instrument are caught by the primary rule in Country B. The primary rule in country B denies a deduction for the full amount of the interest payment (100) effectively triggering an additional 25 of taxable income in the hands of B Co and reversing out the timing advantage that arose in the previous year due to the differences in the timing of the recognition of payments.

Example 9.2

Deduction for interest payment subject to a general limitation

Facts

1. In the example illustrated in the figure below, A Co (a company resident in Country A) owns all the shares in B Co (a company resident in Country B). A Co has invested 2.5 million by way of equity and 7.5 million by way of debt. The debt is in the form of two interest bearing loans that pay regular arm's length interest at an annual rate of 10% per year. The senior loan is for a principal amount of 5 million and the subordinated loan is for a principal amount of 2.5 million.

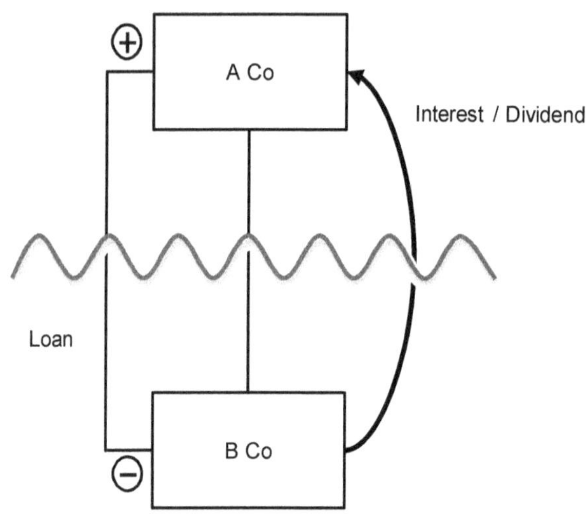

2. The subordinated loan is treated as an equity instrument (i.e. a share) under the laws of Country A and payments of interest are treated as dividends. Country A exempts foreign dividends under its domestic law and has not introduced a specific restriction on this exemption in accordance with Recommendation 2.1. The subordinated loan is treated as a debt instrument under the laws of Country B and interest payments on the loan are generally treated as deductible.

3. Country B has introduced a thin capitalisation rule which disallows interest deductions on debt to the extent the debt to equity ratio of the debtor exceeds 2:1. B Co has a debt to equity ratio of 3:1 accordingly one-third of the interest expenses incurred by B Co will be subject to limitation under the Country B thin capitalisation rule.

Question

4. Whether the interest payments under the subordinated loan fall within the scope of the hybrid financial instrument rule and, if so, what adjustments are required under the rule?

Answer

5. Payments of interest under the loan will give rise to a D/NI outcome that is a hybrid mismatch. This will be the case even if, as a technical matter, the deductibility of the interest is limited under the thin capitalisation rule.

6. The primary recommendation under the hybrid financial instrument rule is that Country B should deny a deduction for the payment to the extent it gives rise to a D/NI outcome. Accordingly B Co should be denied a deduction for the interest paid on the subordinated loan. The interaction between the interest limitation rule and the hybrid financial instrument rule is a matter for domestic law implementation however the interaction between these rules should not result in the hybrid financing instrument rule being used to deny a deduction for interest under a non-hybrid loan.

7. If Country B does not apply the recommended response, then Country A should treat the entire interest payment on the subordinated loan as ordinary income in order to neutralise the D/NI outcome.

Analysis

The arrangement is a financial instrument between related parties

8. Recommendation 1 only applies to payments made under a *financial instrument*. The loan meets the definition of a *financial instrument* because it is treated as an equity instrument in Country A and a debt instrument in Country B. B Co is a wholly-owned subsidiary of A Co and therefore A Co and B Co are related parties.

A payment made under the financial instrument will give rise to a hybrid mismatch

9. As with Example 1.1, the D/NI outcome that arises in this case is the result of B Co's entitlement to a deduction for the interest paid to A Co and the fact that the interest payment is treated as an exempt dividend in the hands of A Co. The hybrid financial instrument rule looks to the terms of the arrangement and its expected tax treatment and not to the detail of how the payments under a financial instrument have actually been taken into account by the parties to the arrangement. The fact that a taxpayer is subject to a general interest limitation, based on overall leverage or interest expense, will not, generally be relevant to a tax analysis based on the terms of the instrument. This will be the case even if it is the subordinated loan that triggered the interest limitation rule.

Primary recommendation – deny the deduction in the payer jurisdiction

10. In this case the interest payments made by B Co to A Co are treated as exempt dividends under the tax laws of Country A. A full denial of the deduction will therefore be required in order to neutralise the D/NI outcome.

11. The adjustment is limited to neutralising the mismatch in tax outcomes. In order to avoid double taxation under the hybrid financial instrument rule the interaction between the interest limitation rule and the hybrid financial instrument rule should be co-ordinated to achieve an overall outcome that is proportionate on an after-tax basis. The mechanism for co-ordinating the interaction between the two rules is a matter for domestic law however the interaction between these rules should not result in the hybrid financing instrument rule being used to deny a deduction for interest under a non-hybrid loan.

Defensive rule – require income to be included in the payee jurisdiction

12. If Country B does not apply the recommended response, then A Co should treat the deductible payment as ordinary income under Country A law. Country A should not restrict the application of the rule to reflect the fact that a portion of the interest paid under the subordinated loan may be subject to the interest limitation rule unless it is Country B's general policy to permit taxpayers to re-characterise interest receipts that are treated as non-deductible under an interest limitation rule.

Example 10.1

Hybrid mismatch priced into the terms of the arrangement

Facts

1. In the example illustrated in the figure below, A Co (a company resident in Country A) and B Co (a company resident in Country B) are unrelated parties. A Co lends 0.3 million to B Co under a loan that pays annual interest. The bond is treated as a debt instrument under the laws of Country B but as an equity instrument (i.e. shares) under the laws of Country A. Under its domestic law Country A generally exempts foreign dividends. Hence, the payment results a D/NI outcome that is a hybrid mismatch.

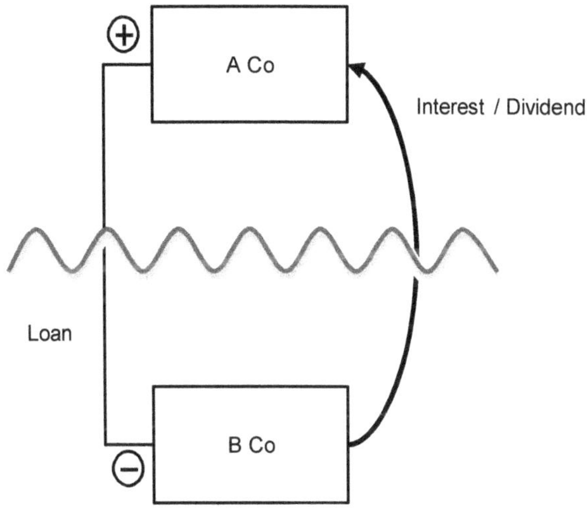

2. Formula for calculating interest payment on the debt instrument provides for a discount to the market rate of interest which is calculated by reference to the corporation tax rate in Country A (i.e. the interest formula is equal to *market rate x (1 – tax rate)*). This means that while an expected market rate of interest on the loan might be 6% (i.e. 18 000 each year) the rate of interest on the hybrid financial instrument (assuming a corporate tax rate of 30% in Country A) would be 12 600 each year.

Question

3. Whether the parties have entered into a structured arrangement within the meaning of Recommendations 1 and 10?

Answer

4. The tax benefit is priced into the terms of the hybrid financial instrument and therefore the instrument is a structured arrangement.

Analysis

Tax outcome is priced into the terms of the instrument

5. Recommendation 10.1 explains that an arrangement will be treated as structured where the tax benefit arising from a hybrid mismatch is priced into the terms of the instrument. In this case, the terms of the instrument explicitly provide for a formula that discounts what would otherwise have been a market interest rate by the amount of the tax benefit under the loan.

Taxpayer is a party to the structured arrangement

6. A Co and B Co are parties to the arrangement because they are direct parties to the financial instrument. The fact that the tax benefit is priced into the calculation of the interest rate means that they can reasonably be expected to be aware of its tax consequences.

Example 10.2

Back-to-back loans structured through an unrelated intermediary

Facts

1. In the example illustrated in the figure below, B Co (a company resident in Country B) is a wholly-owned subsidiary of A Co (a company resident in Country A). A Co intends to provide subordinated debt financing to B Co, but is advised that this arrangement would be caught by the hybrid mismatch rules in Country B as A Co and B Co are related parties.

2. A Co is advised to organise the financing through C Co, an independent third party which is also resident in Country A. C Co's loan to B Co will be funded by a back-to-back loan arrangement. By structuring the financing in this way, the hybrid financial instrument is between unrelated parties. The domestic law of Country C treats the loan between C Co and B Co as equity, whereas the domestic law of Country B treats that loan as an ordinary debt instrument.

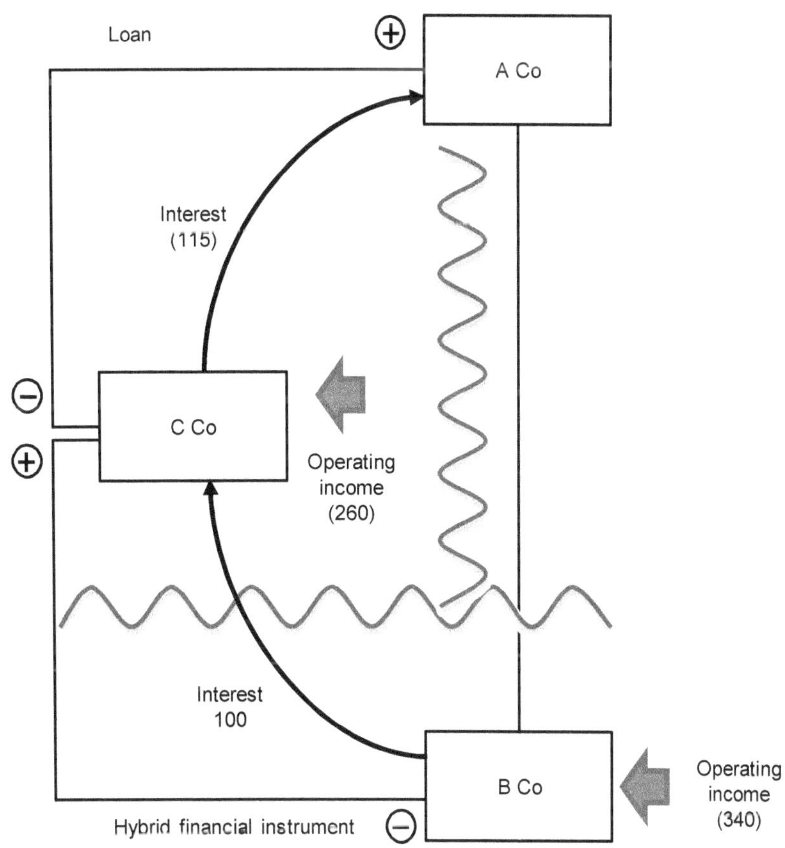

3. The table below illustrates the tax consequences to the parties of entering into the above arrangement.

Country A Law A Co	Tax	Book
Income		
Interest paid by C Co	115	115
Net return		115
Taxable income	115	
Tax to pay (at 20%)		(23)
After-tax return		92

Country B Law B Co	Tax	Book
Income		
Operating income	340	340
Expenditure		
Payment to C Co under hybrid financial instrument	(100)	(100)
Net return		240
Taxable income	240	
Tax to pay (at 20%)		(48)
After-tax return		192

Country C Law C Co	Tax	Book
Income		
Operating income	260	260
Payment from B Co under hybrid financial instrument	-	100
Expenditure		
Interest paid to A Co1	(115)	(115)
Net return		245
Taxable income	145	
Tax to pay (at 20%)		(29)
After-tax return		216

4. Under the arrangement B Co claims a deduction of 100 for a payment of interest under the hybrid financial instrument. This payment is treated as an exempt dividend under Country C law and is not brought into account as income by C Co. C Co pays a deductible amount of 115 of interest to A Co which is recognised as income under Country A law. The net effect of the payment under the hybrid financial instrument is to decrease the overall taxable income under the arrangement by the amount of the payment (100) with the value of the resulting tax benefit (20) being shared between C Co and A Co under the interest payable on the loan.

Question

5. Whether the payments under the hybrid financial instrument should be treated as entered into under a structured arrangement within the meaning of Recommendations 1 and 10.

Answer

6. The interest payments under the hybrid financial instrument should be treated as being made under a structured arrangement as:

(a) the tax benefit arising from the mismatch has been priced into the terms of the arrangement;

(b) the facts and circumstances indicate that the arrangement was designed to create a hybrid mismatch; and

(c) the parties have introduced an unnecessary step into the structure to create the mismatch.

7. Further, in cases such as this, it is likely that the terms of the arrangement will contain provisions that allow the arrangement to be unwound, at no cost to the terminating party, in the event the tax benefit under the structure is no longer available.

Analysis

The mismatch is priced into the terms of the instrument

8. The test of whether the mismatch is priced into the arrangement looks to the terms of the arrangement. This includes both the hybrid financial instrument and the loan from A Co to C Co.

9. In this case C Co appears to be paying an above-market rate of interest on the loan. This interest rate is intended to provide A Co with the benefit of the mismatch in tax outcomes. The pricing of the tax benefit arising from the mismatch into the arrangement would further be indicated by the fact that C Co's return on the arrangement is pre-tax negative and if there are terms that permit the structure to be unwound if the tax benefit is no longer available.

The facts and circumstances indicate that there is a structured arrangement

10. As stated in Recommendation 10.1, the determination of whether the hybrid mismatch was priced into the arrangement can be made on the basis of the terms of the underlying instrument or the facts and circumstances of the arrangement. This case contains a number of factors listed in Recommendation 10.2 that point to the existence of a structured arrangement.

The arrangement was designed to create a hybrid mismatch

11. In this scenario A Co was advised before the arrangement was entered into, to lend the money to its subsidiary through an unrelated intermediary in order to avoid the effect of the related party test under the hybrid financial instrument rule in Country B. Therefore, it can be said that the arrangement was designed in such a way as to allow

A Co to take advantage of the hybrid mismatch without implicating the hybrid mismatch rules.

The arrangement uses a step to create a hybrid mismatch

12. The arrangement contains an additional step or steps (i.e. the back-to-back loan arrangement) that have the effect of avoiding the related party rules and where there is no obvious business, commercial or other reason that could explain why the financing is routed through a third party.

Pre-tax negative return

13. C Co receives 100 of interest from B Co under the hybrid financial instrument but is required to pay an 115 of interest to A Co under the back to back loan entered into as part of the same arrangement. This structure only makes economic sense for C Co if the 20 of tax benefit from the hybrid mismatch is factored in to the overall return.

Change to the terms under the arrangement in the event the hybrid mismatch is no longer available

14. If the terms of the arrangement allow one or both parties to terminate the arrangement in the event the tax benefits of the transaction are no longer available, that will also be a strong indicator of the arrangement having structured to produce a D/NI outcome.

Example 10.3

Arrangement marketed as a tax-advantaged product

Facts

1. In the example illustrated in the figure below, C Co (a company resident in Country C) subscribes for bonds issued by B Co (an unrelated company resident in Country B). Due to the differences in treatment of the underlying instrument under the respective laws of Country A and Country B, the interest payments give rise to a hybrid mismatch resulting in a D/NI outcome.

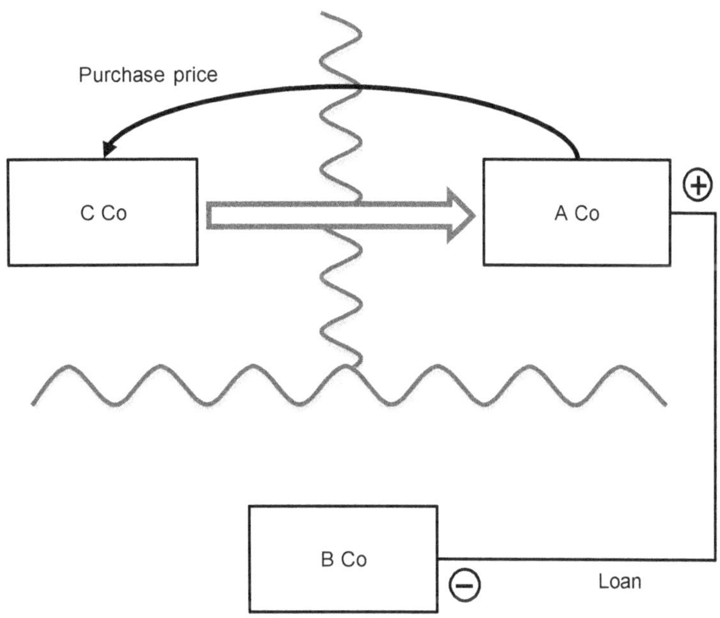

2. C Co subscribed for these bonds after receiving an investment memorandum that included a summary of the expected tax treatment of the instrument (including the fact that payments on the instrument will be eligible for tax relief in Country A). A similar investment memorandum was sent to a number of other potential investors in Country A. Subsequently, C Co sells the bond to A Co, an unrelated company resident in Country A.

Question

3. Whether the payments under the hybrid financial instrument should be treated as made under a structured arrangement within the meaning of Recommendations 1 and 10, and whether A Co is a party to that structured arrangement.

Answer

4. The original issue of the bonds will give rise to a structured arrangement because the facts indicate that bond has been marketed as a tax-advantaged product and has been primarily marketed to persons who can benefit from the mismatch. C Co is a party to that arrangement because it acquires the bond on initial issuance. On the other hand, A Co may not be a party to the structured arrangement if it pays market value for the bond and could not reasonably have been expected to be aware of the mismatch in tax treatment.

Analysis

Marketed as a tax advantaged product

5. The investment memorandum includes a description of the expected tax consequences for the holder including a reference to the fact that payments on the instrument will be eligible for tax relief in Country A. This is evidence that the instrument has been marketed to investors as a tax advantaged product.

Marketed to a class of investors

6. In this case, in order to avoid the definition of a structured arrangement the issuer would further need to show that the instrument had not been primarily marketed to investors in jurisdictions that could benefit from the mismatch in tax outcomes. If the majority of the investors by both number and value are located in jurisdictions where the tax benefit does not arise, then this will be evidence that the arrangement has been widely-marketed to a diverse group of investors.

C Co is a party to the structured arrangement

7. C Co is a party to the structured arrangement because it can be reasonably expected to have been aware of the mismatch at the time it subscribed for the bonds.

A Co may not be a party to the structured arrangement

8. A Co may not be aware of the mismatch in tax outcomes if it acquires the bond from C Co on arms-length terms and at a market price.

Example 10.4

Beneficiary of a trust party to a structured arrangement

Facts

1. In the example illustrated in the figure below, a trust established in Country A subscribes for an investment that gives rise to a hybrid mismatch and has been marketed by the issuer as a tax advantaged product (see **Example 10.3**). The trust is transparent for tax purposes and allocates the payment to a beneficiary who is a resident of Country A. The beneficiary has no knowledge of the investment made by the trustee.

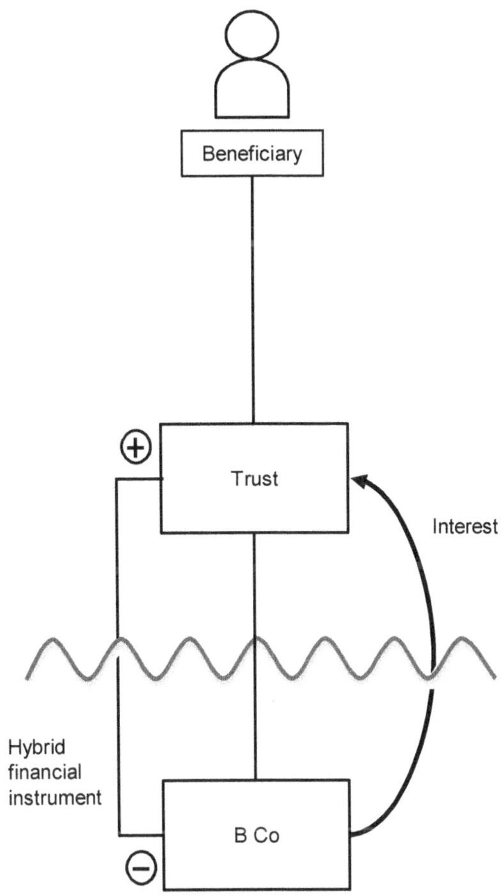

Question

2. Whether the beneficiary is a party to the structured arrangement within the meaning of Recommendation 10.3?

Answer

3. The beneficiary is a party to the arrangement because the tax consequences arising to the trust are attributed to its beneficiaries.

Analysis

4. Although the beneficiary is not a direct party to the arrangement tax consequences of the investment are imputed to the beneficiary under the laws of Country A. These tax consequences should include the fact that the trust subscribed for the investment under conditions that gave rise to a hybrid mismatch.

Example 10.5

Imported mismatch arrangement

Facts

1. In the example illustrated in the figure below, a fund resident in Country A, which is in the business of lending money to medium-sized enterprises (Fund), enters into negotiations to provide an unsecured loan to Borrower Co, a company resident in Country C, to fund Borrower Co's working capital requirements.

2. Once negotiations for the loan have commenced, C Co and the Fund receive tax advice that the subordinated terms of the loan mean that it will be treated as an equity instrument (i.e. a share) under Country A law, but as debt under Country C law. In order to avoid the negative effects of the hybrid mismatch rules in Country C, the Fund structures the loan through a back-to-back arrangement with a wholly-owned subsidiary in Country B. Country B also treats these types of subordinated loan as debt but it has not implemented the hybrid mismatch rules. The loan between the Fund and B Co therefore produces a mismatch in tax outcomes and the whole lending arrangement gives rise to an imported mismatch under Country C law.

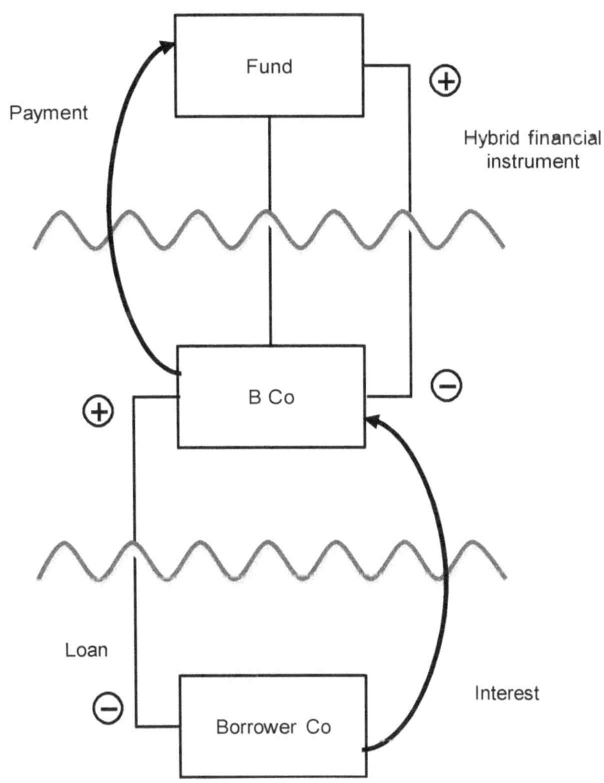

Question

3. Whether Borrower Co is a party to the structured arrangement within the meaning of Recommendation 10.3?

Answer

4. Borrower Co should be treated as a party to the structured arrangement.

Analysis

5. Borrower Co should be treated as party to the structured financing arrangement if it has sufficient involvement in the design of the arrangement to understand its mechanics and anticipate its tax effects.

6. In contrast to the facts described in **Example 4.1**, Borrower Co is already engaged in financing discussion with A Co at the time the potential for hybrid tax treatment is identified by the parties. The potential impact of the hybrid financial instrument rule is then mitigated by introducing another entity (B Co) into the lending structure. While Borrower Co may not know the precise details of the financing arrangements between A Co and B Co, Borrower Co (or a member of Borrower Co's control group) can reasonably be expected to be aware of the fact that B Co and A Co are affiliates and that funding for the loan has come indirectly from A Co. Borrower Co is also aware that B Co has been inserted into the structure for tax reasons, notably to avoid Borrower Co losing its interest deduction under the hybrid financial instrument rule. Therefore, although Borrower Co has no direct involvement or knowledge of the hybrid financial instrument between A Co and B Co, it has sufficient involvement in the overall design of the arrangement to understand how the arrangement has been structured (as a back-to-back financing arrangement through an intermediary); and to anticipate what the tax outcomes will be for the parties to the arrangement (avoiding denial of the deduction in Country C while preserving the tax outcomes under Country A law).

Example 11.1

Application of related party rules to assets held in trust

Facts

1. In the example that is illustrated in the figure below, Individual A is the settlor of a trust that is established for the benefit of A's immediate family. Under the trust deed, the settlor has no vested or contingent beneficial entitlement to the income or assets of the trust or the power to amend the trust deed but the settlor is entitled to appoint trustees to the trust. A appoints an independent bank to act as a trustee of the trust. The trust owns all of the ordinary shares in A Co. A enters into a hybrid financial instrument with A Co.

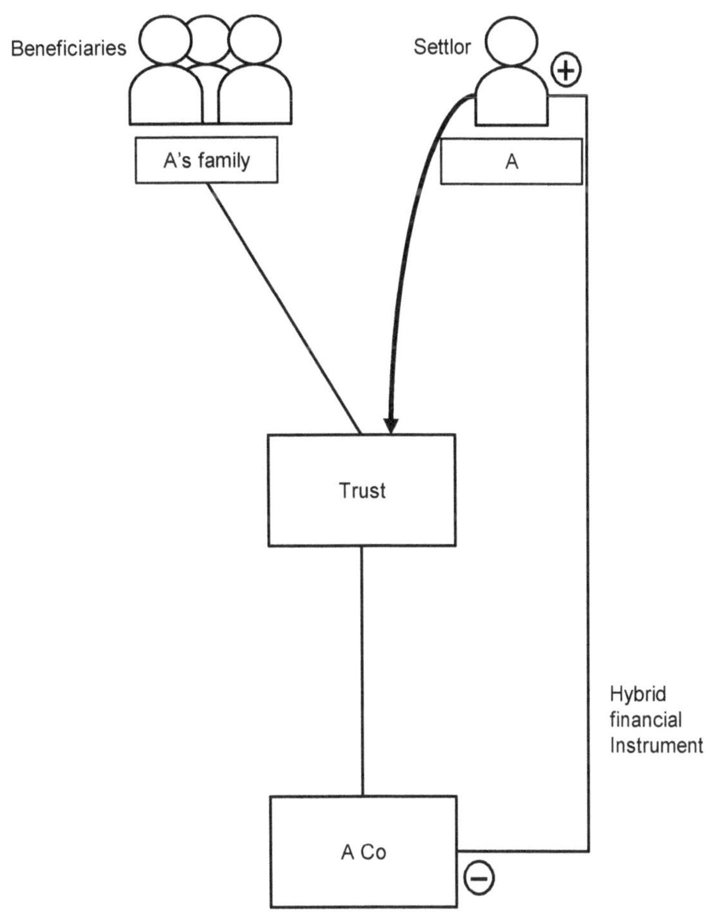

Question

2. Is A related to A Co for the purposes of Recommendation 11?

Answer

3. The trust holds all the voting and equity interests in A Co and A is either treated as having an *indirect voting interest in A Co* (through A's right to appoint trustees to the trust) or is deemed to hold *an indirect equity interest in A Co* (because the beneficiaries of the trust are A Co's immediate family). Further A may be considered related to A Co if the facts of the case indicate that trust is under the effective control of A.

Analysis

The trust owns all the voting and equity interests in A Co.

4. Although the trust may be transparent for tax purposes, it is treated as a person under the related party rules in Recommendation 11. The trust holds all the ordinary shares in A Co which will give the trust 100% of the voting and equity interests in the company.

A is treated as having 100% of the voting interests in the trust

5. As settlor of the trust, A has the sole right, under the terms of the trust deed, to appoint trustees, which is one of the enumerated voting rights described in the related party rules. The fact that the constitutional documents (in this case the trust deed) do not give A the power to authorise distributions or alter the terms of the trust, does not affect the conclusion that A holds 100% of the voting interests in the trust.

A's family are treated as holding 100% of the equity interests in the trust

6. As the named beneficiaries of the trust, A's family are treated as the holders of the equity interests in the trust. Under the "acting together" test in Recommendation 11.3. A is deemed to hold any equity interests that are held by his family.

A is the indirect holder of the voting and equity interests in A Co

7. The measurement of a person's voting and value interests in another person includes interests that are held indirectly through others. As the holder (or deemed holder) of the voting and equity interests in the trust A is deemed to hold, indirectly, all of the voting and equity interests in A Co.

A could be treated as holding a direct voting or equity interest if A and the trustee can be shown to be acting together.

8. Subject to more precise facts, A can also be considered to be directly related to A Co if it can be shown that the trustee effectively acts in accordance to A's instructions.

Example 11.2

Related parties and control groups - partners in a partnership

Facts

1. In the example illustrated in the figure below A, B, C and D are four partners in a partnership resident in Country B. All the decision in the partnership require unanimous vote. All the partners have the same voting rights and equal share in the profits of the partnership. The partnership is treated as tax transparent under the laws of Country B.

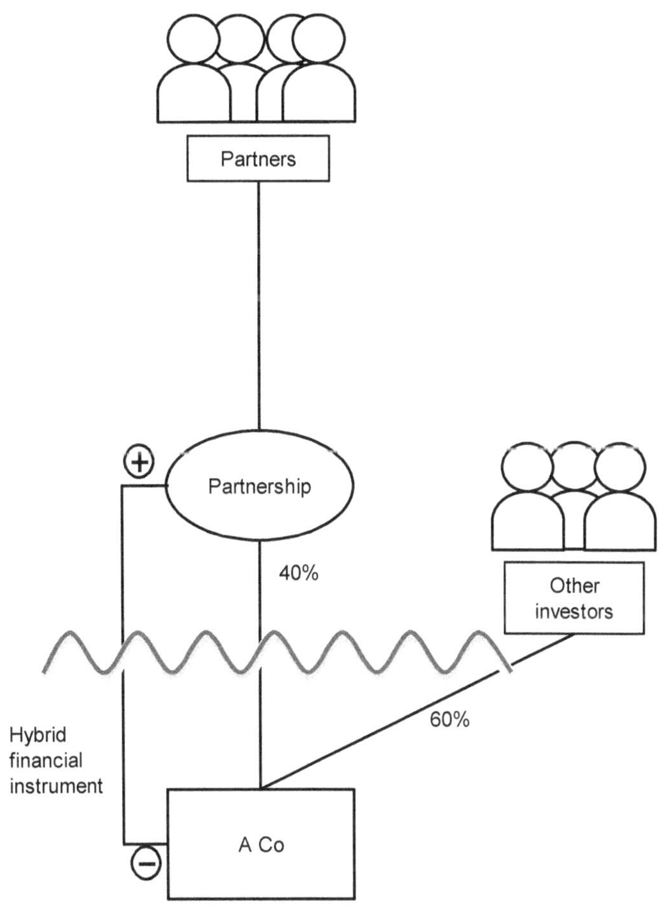

2. The partnership has a substantial shareholding in a company resident in Country A (A Co). The partnership lends money to A Co. The way this loan is taxed under Country A and B laws gives rise to a mismatch in tax outcomes.

Question

3. Whether the partners are related to A Co for the purposes of Recommendation 11?

Answer

4. The partners are treated as directly related to A Co because, in this case, each partner is treated as acting together with the other partners in respect of the partnership's substantial shareholding in A Co.

Analysis

The partner's indirect holding in A Co is insufficient to bring that partner within the related party rule

5. Although the partnership is transparent for tax purposes, it is treated as a person under the related party rules in Recommendation 11. The partnership holds 40% of the ordinary shares in A Co which will give the partnership 40% of the voting and equity interests in the company. This holding will be attributed equally to the partners in the partnership in proportion to their voting and value interest in the partnership. In this case, however, this leaves each partner with only a 10% indirect holding in A Co which is insufficient to bring that partner within the related party rules.

Each partner is treated as having a direct holding in A Co under the acting together test

6. In this case, the shares in A Co are held by a person that is treated as transparent under Country B law so that the shares in A Co, and the payments made under the financial instrument, are treated as made directly to the partners in accordance with their interest in the partnership. In this case where the ownership or control of the shares in A Co are managed by the partnership and where that management or control has a connection with the arrangement that has given rise to the mismatch (because both the equity interest and the financial instrument are held by the same person) each partner will be treated as holding the shares of the other partners under the acting together test in Recommendation 11.3(d) and accordingly will be treated as holding sufficient shares in A Co to bring that partner within the scope of the related party rule.

The partners are not related to each other

7. Although the partners are related to the partnership and to A Co they are not related to each other. There is no third person who holds at least a 25% investment in two or more partners nor can they be said to be in the same control group within the meaning of Recommendation 11.1(b).

Example 11.3

Related parties and control groups - calculating vote and value interests

Facts

1. In this example illustrated in the figure below, A Co is the ultimate parent of a group. It has two wholly-owned subsidiaries B Co and C Co and has a holding of 20% of the ordinary shares in D Co. B Co has a holding of 25% of the ordinary shares in E Co. C Co and D Co have a 20% and 40% holding in F Co (respectively).

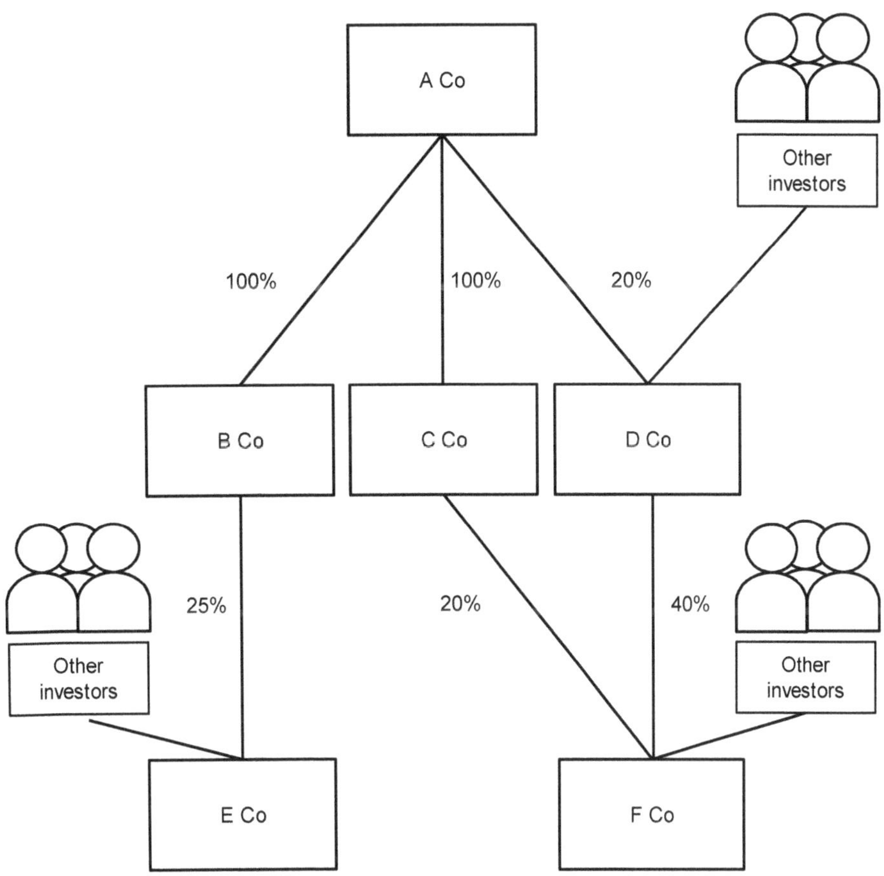

Question

2. Which entities in this group structure are related within the meaning of Recommendation 11?

Answer

3. A Co, B Co, C Co, E Co and F Co are related parties. D Co is related to F Co but not to any other group member (unless, for example, D Co's other ordinary shares are widely-held).

Analysis

Related parties through direct shareholding

4. A Co is related to B Co and C Co through its 100% direct holding of shares. On the same basis D Co is related to F Co.

Related parties through indirect holding

5. A Co is related to E Co through an indirect holding of 25% of E Co's voting and value interests. A Co is also related to F Co as it holds an indirect 28% investment in F Co.

Related parties due to membership in the same control group

6. A Co does not hold, directly or indirectly, more than 25% of the voting or value interests in D Co. But A Co may be related to D Co if they are both found to be in the same control group. This particular case could fall within the second test in Recommendation 11.1(b) if A Co holds an investment that gives it an effective control over D Co. If, for example, the shareholding of D Co is otherwise widely-held, except for the 20% holding by A Co, then A Co may have effective control of D Co even with a minority stake.

Example 11.4

Acting together - aggregation of interests under a shareholders' agreement

Facts

1. In the example illustrated in the figure below A Co and a number of other investors, including C, hold together 100% of equity and voting rights in B Co. A Co is a majority shareholder with 40% holding and the other investors each own 5% of shares in B Co. The shareholders entered into a shareholders' agreement that provides the majority shareholder with a first right of refusal on any disposal of the shares and drag-along and tag-along provisions in the event that an offer is made for a majority of the shares in the company.

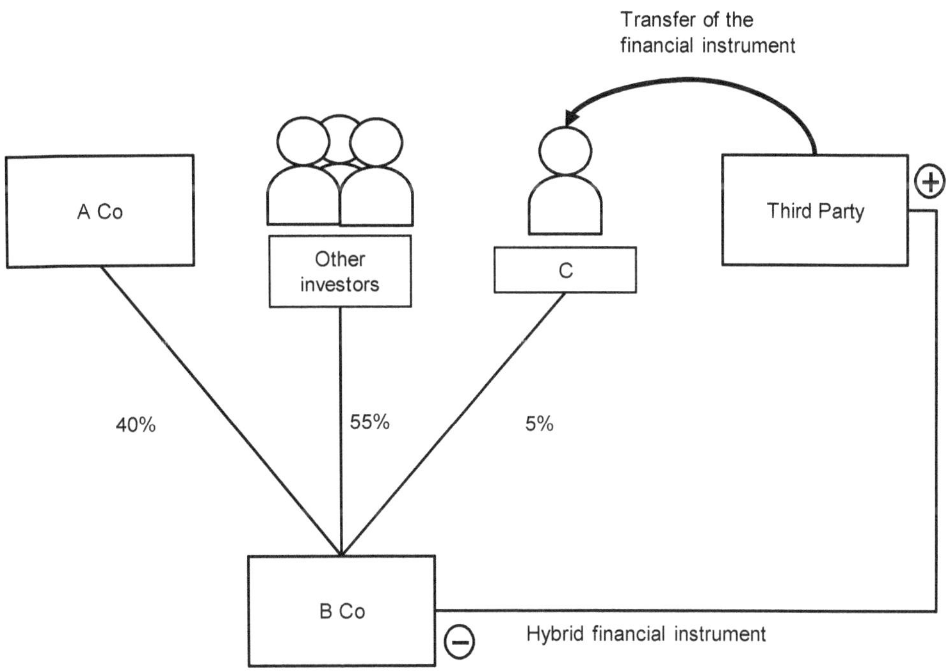

2. B Co issues a financial instrument that is purchased from an unrelated third party by C (one of the minority shareholders). This instrument results in a hybrid mismatch giving rise to a D/NI outcome.

Question

3. Whether the investors in B Co are acting together, within the sense of Recommendation 11.3(c) such that C should be treated as related to B Co.

Answer

4. Provisions that are commonly found in a shareholders agreement and that do not have a material impact on the value or control of the interests held by a shareholder will not be treated as common control agreements within the meaning of Recommendation 11.3(c).

5. If the shareholder's agreement does have a material impact on the value of C's shareholding, C will be treated as a related party under the acting together test in respect of the acquisition of the financial instrument even if there is no link or connection between the shareholders' agreement and the transaction that gave rise to the hybrid mismatch.

Analysis

Shareholders' agreement is on standard terms

6. The right to buy C Co's shares at market value, as well as the drag along and tag along rights are relatively standard terms in a shareholders' agreement for a closely-held company. These types of provisions will not generally have a material impact on the value of the holder's equity interest and therefore should not be taken into account for the purposes of the acting together requirement.

No nexus required between transactions giving rise to the mismatch and the common control arrangement

7. The acting together test does not impose any definitional limits on the content of the common control arrangement and the acting together test can capture transactions between otherwise unrelated taxpayers even if the common control arrangement has not played any role in the transaction that has given rise to the mismatch. Thus, if the shareholders' agreement does have a material impact on the value of C's shareholding, C will be treated as a related party under the acting together test in respect of the acquisition of the financial instrument even if there is no link or connection between the shareholders' agreement and the transaction that gave rise to the hybrid mismatch.

Example 11.5

Acting together - rights or interests managed together by the same person/s

Facts

1. In the example illustrated in the figure below, a widely-held investment partnership provides additional financing to A Co, a company in which it already has an 80% holding. The terms of this loan agreement result in a mismatch in tax outcomes for one investor in that partnership.

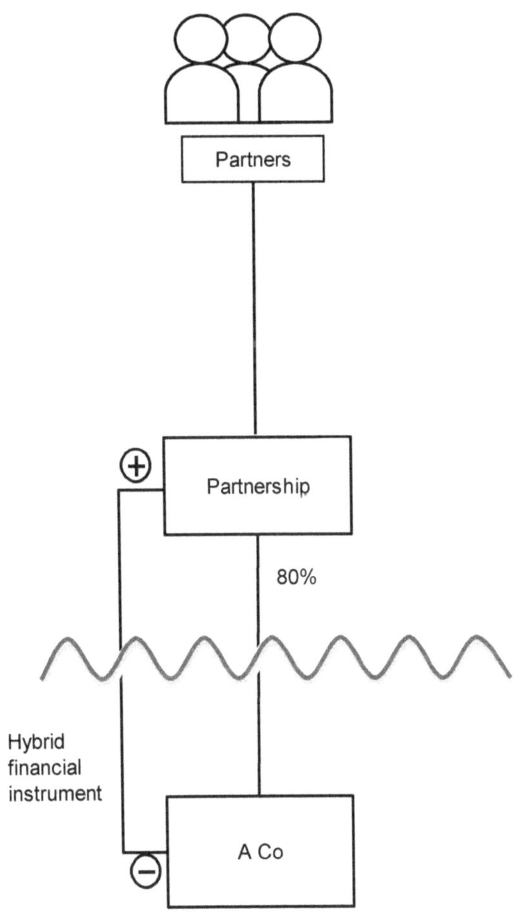

2. The terms of the partnership agreement give the general partner the primary right to decide on the investments of the partnership. The general partner when making its decisions must act in good faith and in the best interest of all the partners.

Question

3. Whether the partner is related to A Co through the aggregation of interests rule under Recommendation 11.3?

Answer

4. In this instance the partner that is a party to a hybrid financial instrument will be treated as related to A Co through the aggregation of interest rule in Recommendation 11.3(d). This will be the case even where it cannot be said that the partnership is acting together with all the other partners in respect of the mismatch in tax outcomes.

Analysis

5. Consistent with the analysis in **Example 11.2**, where the shares and debt are held by the same investment partnership the joint management or control of the equity interest will result in each partner being treated as holding the shares of the other partners under the acting together test in Recommendation 11.3(d).

6. The fact that the partnership is widely-held and otherwise meets the test for a CIV does not permit the partnership to rely on the exclusion to Recommendation 11.3(d) because that exception only applies to investors that are CIVs and not investors in a CIV.

ORGANISATION FOR ECONOMIC CO-OPERATION AND DEVELOPMENT

The OECD is a unique forum where governments work together to address the economic, social and environmental challenges of globalisation. The OECD is also at the forefront of efforts to understand and to help governments respond to new developments and concerns, such as corporate governance, the information economy and the challenges of an ageing population. The Organisation provides a setting where governments can compare policy experiences, seek answers to common problems, identify good practice and work to co-ordinate domestic and international policies.

The OECD member countries are: Australia, Austria, Belgium, Canada, Chile, the Czech Republic, Denmark, Estonia, Finland, France, Germany, Greece, Hungary, Iceland, Ireland, Israel, Italy, Japan, Korea, Luxembourg, Mexico, the Netherlands, New Zealand, Norway, Poland, Portugal, the Slovak Republic, Slovenia, Spain, Sweden, Switzerland, Turkey, the United Kingdom and the United States. The European Union takes part in the work of the OECD.

OECD Publishing disseminates widely the results of the Organisation's statistics gathering and research on economic, social and environmental issues, as well as the conventions, guidelines and standards agreed by its members.

OECD PUBLISHING, 2, rue André-Pascal, 75775 PARIS CEDEX 16
(23 2015 29 1 P) ISBN 978-92-64-24108-4 – 2015

www.ingramcontent.com/pod-product-compliance
Lightning Source LLC
Chambersburg PA
CBHW061153240926
51846CB00006B/1004